GARDENING IN THE DESERTS OF
ARIZONA

Catalog in Publication data is available.

ISBN: 1-59186-345-7
EAN: 978-1-59186-345-8

Published by Cool Springs Press
P.O. Box 2828
Brentwood, Tennessee 37024

First printing 2007

Printed in the United States of America
10 9 8 7 6 5 4 3 2

Managing Editor: Melany Klinck
Designer: James Duncan, James Duncan Creative
Horticulture Contributor: Diana Maranhao
Illustrator: Bill Kersey, Kersey Graphics
Production Artist: S.E. Anderson

On the cover: *A. marlothii*, photographed by Thomas Eltzroth
Cover Design: Marc Pewitt

Visit the Cool Springs Press website at **www.coolspringspress.com**

PHOTOGRAPHY AND ILLUSTRATION CREDITS

All illustrations by Bill Kersey, Kersey Graphics
Tom Eltzroth: Pages 21 (top), 22, 24, 27, 28, 37, 42 (bottom), 48, 52, 57, 58,
72, 74, 87, 96-100 (top), 96, 102, 112, 122-127 (top), 122 (bottom), 125,
132, 135, 146, 150-155 (top), 150 (bottom), 168, 173, 178-181 (top),
186, 189, 192, 197, 198, 210, 212, 222, 262-265 (top), 262 (bottom),
276 (top), 238, 242, 253, 256, 258, 271, 275, 276, 278, 254
Lorenzo Gunn: Pages 118, 233
Mary and Gary Irish: Pages 156, 217, 220
Charles Mann: Pages 2-14 (top), 7 (bottom), 31, 71, 80, 126, 159, 174,
204-209 (top), 218, 260
Judy Mielke: Pages 204, 246, 250
Jerry Pavia: Pages 15 (bottom), 42-47 (top), 71-75 (top), 73, 76, 78, 89,
110, 164, 167, 178 (bottom)
Neil Soderstrom: Pages 66, 128, 165

Month-By-Month™
WHAT TO DO EACH MONTH TO HAVE A BEAUTIFUL GARDEN ALL YEAR

GARDENING IN THE DESERTS OF ARIZONA

MARY IRISH

COOL SPRINGS PRESS

Brentwood, Tennessee

DEDICATION

This book belongs to those two fine hombres, John White and Wynn Anderson, who carry on a dedication to desert gardens and the special plants that fill them—and do so with humor, hard work, and verve. Thanks for all your help.

ACKNOWLEDGEMENTS

This book is an attempt to collect the accumulated knowledge of a wide range of gardeners throughout the region. My thanks go out to them all, whether I spoke to them personally or read their books, bulletins, newsletters, or pamphlets. They all told me their tales correctly, and it is my doing if anything got lost in the translation.

A special thanks goes to Dennis Swartzell for his help with those tricky lawns and Cheryl Garing, who clarified so many things in El Paso.

Martha and Rex were of more help than they could possibly imagine, keeping me on target and fit to work. And Gary did it all in the house and the garden with a smile that forever keeps me going.

CONTENTS

INTRODUCTION

GARDENING IN THE DESERTS OF ARIZONA

The Desert Southwest is that part of the western United States that stretches from the El Paso, Texas area westward through Arizona's Tucson, Phoenix, and Yuma; continues north up the Colorado River to include the river cities and Las Vegas; and ends in the Coachella Valley of California with the cities of Palm Springs and Palm Desert and up north to Palmdale and Lancaster.

Although the region is interrupted many times by high mountain ranges, broad plateaus, and expansive areas of arid grasslands, this book is for the gardeners who live in the lower elevations of Arizona where the summers are long and warm, often extremely hot, and the winters are mild and in some parts frost-free. Rainfall is scarce, intermittent, and unreliable.

Despite the seeming severity of the climate, Arizona's desert is an outstanding gardening climate. Even though freezing temperatures occur, winters are mild and of short duration, and the growing season is long. Winter vegetable gardens abound, and fruit of many kinds is easily grown in home gardens. Citrus is the most widely grown fruit in the state, but deciduous fruit varieties suited to the climate are also available. Gardeners will find a huge range of ornamental plants that grow well here, and plants from deserts and other arid regions of the world are increasingly available.

The Phoenix metropolitan area is a complicated mix of temperature patterns. In the older areas, urbanization has increased temperatures to the point that it is almost frost-free and easily falls within USDA Zone 10. But many of the surrounding cities are better designated as Zone 9b, the warmer part of zone 9. The far northern suburbs are almost identical to Tucson, a cooler Zone 9a.

Phoenix has an average January minimum of 43 degrees Fahrenheit, and freezes, when they occur, are infrequent and of short duration. July highs average 104 degrees, but days over 110 degrees are common and sometimes stretch for a week or more at a time. Rainfall averages $7^1/2$ inches a year, split between slow winter rains and hard-driving summer monsoon rains. Winter rain accounts for about 40% of the rainfall.

Citrus and other cold-tender shrubs are widely grown in the Phoenix area. Heat-tolerant shrubs and perennials like dalea, globe mallow, tecoma, and justicias are excellent in this zone. Most succulents do well if given sufficient shade.

Tucson has a higher elevation, so that despite its location farther south it has colder winters and more moderate summers. January lows average 39 degrees Fahrenheit, and short, light freezing spells occur regularly. Average summer highs are 100 degrees, but days

over 110 degrees are far fewer than elsewhere in the desert parts of the state. Rainfall is the greatest difference; Tucson averages 12 inches of rain a year, split between winter and summer, in a similar pattern to that of Phoenix.

Tucson gardeners enjoy the same mix of plants that the warmer zones can grow, with the exception of the most tender varieties. Here lime trees are difficult, but all other citrus grows well. Deciduous fruit can be grown with attention to appropriate varieties. Many perennials and shrubs perform a little better, owing to the somewhat milder temperatures and higher rainfall. Winter vegetable gardens are highly productive.

Soils in Phoenix and Tucson are highly variable. Old agricultural areas and the plains between the low hills are tight clays. As you climb up the slopes that are so common in both cities, the soil is thinner because of erosion, revealing large expanses of rock and caliche.

Sierra Vista, Benson and Wilcox are cities within USDA Zone 8, but they are so arid and their summers are so warm that they easily fall within the parameters of the Desert Southwest. Winters are colder than those of the rest of the region, with lows in the mid-20s routine. Nearly half the days in December and January have overnight lows below freezing, although daytime temperatures are mild. Summers are warm,

milder than most of the rest of the region, with highs in the 90s on the hottest days. Summer temperatures sometimes rise to 105 degrees, but it is rare for them to be higher. Rainfall averages 9 inches a year, mainly in the summer. Soils are similar to soils in the rest of the region, with tight clays in the lower parts and rocky soils higher on the slopes. There are significant pockets of open, sandy soils around these cities.

These are areas where deciduous fruit is easier to grow and more varieties are available to the home gardener. Winter gardens are limited to the most cold-hardy varieties, and citrus and other subtropicals are not recommended. Many of the blooming perennials used by gardeners in the rest of the state as winter annuals are spring- and summer-flowering perennials here.

Because of this great diversity of temperature, gardening schedules can be quite different from one part of the state to the other. As a rough guide, any gardening activity that takes place in the westernmost part of the state will occur three or four weeks later in the cooler parts of Zone 9 and up to two months later in Zone 8. While this book offers timing recommendations and guidelines for the entire region, use the lists of references and sources at the back of the book to find information and further refine your skills for your particular area.

BASIC HORTICULTURAL PRACTICES

It all sounds so simple and straightforward. Take a seed or a plant, put it in the soil with just the right amount of sunlight, add water as needed, and presto: a garden is born. Of course it rarely seems to work out like that, and many of us find stumbling blocks along the way. What kind of plant works best? How do you adjust the soil you have to suit the plant you want? How much light? How much water and when to add it? The questions go on and on.

But gardening is like anything else that is good—it takes a little practice and an understanding of a few of the basics to get it right. As anyone can attest who has moved here from cooler and wetter climates, even experienced gardeners find that some of the basics are a little different in the desert from what they are accustomed to. And where you start is where all plant life starts: with the soil.

BASIC HORTICULTURAL PRACTICES

MAINTAINING HEALTHY SOIL

Soil is so crucial to the health and success of any garden that it is shocking how little attention is given to maintaining and nurturing a healthy soil. When first faced with the soils of this region, many gardeners are stunned to find that they grow anything at all. They look so forbidding and unusable. But these soils, with few exceptions, are excellent for plants, and with only minimal attention can grow almost anything. It is wise, however, to understand a bit about them.

Desert soils are alkaline, with a pH well over 7 and usually between 8 and 8.5. Plants that demand acidic growing conditions will do very poorly indeed, while plants that are well suited to growing in alkaline conditions—as are most plants native to arid or desert regions—will do splendidly in these soils.

But many of the gardening plants with which we are all familiar, and almost all vegetables, rely on growing in soils that are closer to neutral (7 to 7.5). Changing the fundamental chemistry of the soil is difficult, usually temporary, and best done in a closed system like a raised bed.

The most reliable and effective way to lower the pH and improve many other aspects of garden soil is the generous and continuous addition of compost. Compost is formed during the breakdown and decay that all plants undergo when they die. Through the action of a small army of insects, fungi, and associated bacteria, all the organic matter is converted slowly and steadily into a rich, crumbly, black product that is the pot of gold at the end of any soil's rainbow.

Compost provides nutrients and minerals to the soil and makes them easier for plants to absorb. But its greatest contribution to the soil is to change its texture. Soil texture is a reflection of how big the soil particles are—small particles are clay, and the largest ones are sand. Clay soils hold moisture tightly between the particles, allowing both nutrients and minerals to attach firmly to the particles. Sandy soils have such large grains that they allow water, and its dissolved nutrients, to zoom right through the soil.

Compost opens up clay soils, enlarging the grain size, and provides more space for water. This creates a soil that drains better and makes nutrients more efficiently available to the plants. Compost helps wrap organic matter around large sand particles, making them better buffers for the action of nutrients without sacrificing their excellent drainage.

Compost is not a permanent solution but must be added continuously to maintain and nurture a healthy soil. The regular addition of compost improves soil each time, and the cumulative effect of years of good compost is a vastly improved gardening soil.

In some parts of the region the soil is underlaid with a mineral called caliche. Caliche is common in the Phoenix and Tucson areas. It is calcium carbonate that has precipitated over the years and formed a dense rock layer. It may be a deep, invisible layer or a solid mass of stone at or near the surface and can be fractured or solid.

Although there are chemical treatments that purport to dissolve or crack this layer, caliche cannot be dissolved. If you find yourself with caliche within the root zone of a proposed planting, use an iron bar or heavy pick to break it up. Once the hole is mined out, fill it with water. If it will drain, it will grow a plant, even a tree. If it does not drain, do not plant anything that will have a root system larger than the hole. If water can't find a way out, neither can roots.

HOW TO MAKE COMPOST

There are as many styles of compost piles as there are gardeners, and one way or another they all work. Compost can be a simple pile that is placed anywhere that is convenient, and leaves, twigs, and other organic matter will be thrown onto the

BASIC HORTICULTURAL PRACTICES

pile. In urban gardens it is usually more convenient to enclose a compost pile with wire, boards, or concrete block. Enclosed piles should be no more than 3 feet tall and 4 feet square to allow for good airflow and water penetration. The following tips will help you make the best use of a compost pile and have plenty of compost for your garden.

• Add only vegetation to a compost pile. Any kind will do, even leftover cooked vegetables as long they weren't cooked in oil. Do not add meat products, including bones or fat of any kind, as they do not decay properly in the pile and can attract unwanted pests like rats.

• Unless your pile generates a great deal of heat in the center, do not add diseased plants. It takes more heat than most home compost piles generate to kill pathogens. The same holds true for the seed of weedy species. If they do not break down completely, spreading compost will just spread the weeds around.

• Add some soil from time to time. As you dig beds, repot plants, or do other work around the garden, you may notice that you have extra soil. Put it on the pile and the microorganisms in the soil will help move the composting along, acting like a yeast starter to maintain the process.

• In the dry air of the deserts, compost piles need to be watered weekly when it is hot. Dry compost piles will eventually form humus, but it could be years before there is enough to use, and it can disappear quickly. Keeping the pile evenly moist speeds up the process enough that you will get to use all the compost that is made.

• In the hottest areas, put your compost pile in the shade. This will cut down on evaporation and help keep the pile moist.

• Cut or shred material that goes into the pile into small pieces. Although a piece of any size will eventually break down, the process is speeded up considerably when all the pieces are small and close to the same size.

• Turn the pile from time to time. Turning can be just as it sounds, using a pitchfork to put the top materials on the bottom. This rearrangement offers fresh vegetation to the center, where the real action is, and keeps the process moving ahead quickly. Turning can also be accomplished by having a multiple bin method of composting. In this method, two or three bins are placed side by side. Material is put into one of the bins first and then moved to each successive bin as more new vegetation is brought into the first bin. By the time the material leaves the third bin, it is finished compost.

No matter how complicated or how simple your compost pile is, making your own compost is the most direct method of improving your gardening conditions. But even if you have good healthy garden soil, there are times when a bit of fertilizer is just the ticket.

TOOLS

Using the proper tools is very important. The most common ones recommended include:

• Hoe: for breaking up the soil surface, removing weeds, and leveling the surface of soil or mulch

• Rake: used to collect debris into piles for removal, and to smooth soil surface

• Shovel: used to dig up plants for transplanting or removal; to dig holes for planting; to distribute materials such as soil, mulch, and soil conditioner; and to mix amendments into soil

• Cultivator: to loosen soil in preparation for sowing seeds or planting small plants, and to mix materials such as fertilizer into the soil surface

• Spade: for digging deep holes, particularly for planting trees, or to dig up very deep-rooted plants

• Turning Fork or Pitchfork: for turning compost piles, or distributing compost and other coarse materials in the garden

BASIC HORTICULTURAL PRACTICES

FERTILIZERS

Fertilizers are products that provide nutrients to plants in quick, often readily available form, on a temporary basis. The fertilizers with which we are most familiar are made from inorganic sources in a wide array of processes and are formulated to offer the three so-called macronutrients, N—nitrogen, P—phosphorus, and K—potassium. These are the nutrients that are required by all plants.

Some fertilizers are made to provide only one of these nutrients, while others are blended products. Balanced or complete fertilizers provide all three in roughly even proportion. Blended formulas that are in multiples of 3:2:1 generally provide a nutrient balance that is particularly useful in our region. Plants also need a wide range of minerals and nutrients in smaller quantities, and these are called micronutrients. Many complete fertilizer blends contain these nutrients as well.

Organic fertilizers provide the same nutrients as all other fertilizers, but they are derived from organic sources like ground grains (cottonseed and alfalfa meal), animal waste (bloodmeal, bonemeal, and manure), or sea plants (seaweed and kelp), just to name a few. Like inorganic products, they can be formulated to provide one nutrient abundantly or blended into a balanced formula.

The difference between these two types of fertilizer is not only in the source of their nutrients, but in how they work. All nutrients must be dissolved in water to be available to a plant's roots. Inorganic fertilizers are in compounds that dissolve quickly and are almost immediately available to roots. By the same token, they do not last long. Because they are quickly depleted, they must be reapplied often to maintain the benefit. To delay this fast release, many formulations are coated or otherwise treated to permit the gradual dissolution of the fertilizer; these are known as slow-release formulas.

Organic fertilizers work more slowly, making nutrients available over a longer period of time.

In addition, organic products continue to break down, and with the addition of compost they maintain the long chain of activities that keeps soil thriving and healthy.

Water-soluble formulations of either type are the fastest-working of all fertilizers because the nutrients are already in the form the plant needs. But they, too, are removed from the soil quickly.

While fertilizers have their place, they should be understood and used much more sparingly than they generally are. In the salty, alkaline soils of the deserts, the salt buildup resulting from the steady use of inorganic fertilizers can turn healthy soil lethal over the years.

Manure is an outstanding fertilizer, and anyone who has farm animals adds manure to the compost piles. But manure must be well composted before it is used around plants. The urine of many animals is salty at the outset, and if manure is used fresh it will create an unhealthy salt buildup in the soil. If you have access to fresh manure, compost it first. If you purchase manure, be sure it is well composted before you apply it. Composted manure is a fertilizer, or soil additive, and it is best used periodically rather than continuously applied.

WATERING

Knowing how much water to use and how often to provide it is the single most important skill any gardener can acquire in the desert. Rainfall is unreliable, bountiful in some years but often followed by many years of sub-par rains. Rain does not fall regularly even in a good year, and all parts of the area experience months without any rainfall at all. In addition, irrigation water supplies are low and dwindling and were never abundant in the first place. It is important to learn how to manage and control watering of your garden to get the greatest benefit from the least amount of water possible.

Water quality is an increasing problem in all the cities of Arizona's low desert. Most treated water

is becoming saltier over the years, and in years of serious drought this problem becomes acute. Watering with recycled or reclaimed water adds to the problem of salt buildup, and it is clear that managing the salt load of municipal water supplies will be the water story of the coming decades.

Drip irrigation is popular throughout the region and is a wonderful way to water many plants. This is a system of flexible hoses with decreasing diameters that thread through the garden from a valve or faucet and end at an emitter. There are many styles of emitters, but all are designed to deliver water at a prescribed rate, from $1/2$ gallon/hour to 10 gallons/hour. This slow-release (drip) of water directly to the root zone of the plant is the principal advantage of drip irrigation and what makes it so efficient. All the water is directed to where plants need it, and none is lost to runoff or evaporation.

Drip irrigation may not be advantageous for large plants, woody shrubs, and trees, however. After a time these plants can become so large or their root systems so wide that it is virtually impossible, and certainly unwieldy, to install enough emitters to provide sufficient water.

There are other forms of efficient watering besides drip irrigation. Building a basin around a tree or other large plant allows for adding large amounts of water with no runoff and only minimal evaporation. Basins can be built around an entire bed or even an area of the garden and can be camouflaged or gently sloped to make them invisible. In some yards it is possible to connect basins beginning at a water source (often a roofline) and have them overflow or be connected to each other down a slope.

Soaker hoses are flexible hoses that are perforated to allow water to weep gently out of the wall of the pipe. They are most effective in areas that are densely planted (like vegetable gardens) where all plants need the same irrigation levels. They can also be used underground, which

cuts down on evaporation and hose breakdown by the sun.

Sprinkler systems are common irrigation systems, especially for a lawn. While these can be effective ways to deliver water, they have one serious drawback, and that is their high evaporation rates. Water is released in fine sprays, and the small droplets evaporate quickly in the heat of the region. Watering when evaporation rates are lower helps, but these are inherently wasteful systems for delivering water.

Whatever type of irrigation is used, its convenience and reliability is enhanced by attaching it to an automated timer. There is a wide array of timers on the market that run on either electricity or batteries. Battery-operated timers attach directly to a faucet and are handy for areas where electrical power is unavailable or for temporary irrigation needs.

There are numerous guidelines for calculating water needs of plants. Much depends on the soils where you live and what style of watering you use.

In this book, I have used a watering system based on watering depth. With this system, trees are generally watered to a depth of 3 feet but must be watered in such a way that the entire root zone (defined by the drip line plus a foot or two for mature trees) is covered. Shrubs are watered to a depth of 2 feet, and perennials to a depth of 1 foot. Watering depths for plants with special needs, like roses, lawns, and vegetables, are found in the text.

While these guidelines work for most plants, watch your plants, and water to suit their needs. The hardest part of watering is finding just the right combination of frequency and duration so that the plants get what they need without wilting, but aren't overwatered. It takes some practice to figure out the watering needs of your yard, but once done, it will enable you to water your plants reliably and efficiently.

BASIC HORTICULTURAL PRACTICES

To find out how much and how often to water to achieve the recommended depth, start by watering for a known amount of time—15 minutes is handy. Then stick a probe, a thin metal stake, or even a long screwdriver in the ground. It will easily penetrate moist soil and stop or become difficult to continue when it reaches dry soil. Measure the depth and continue to water, increasing at set intervals until the ground is moist to the recommended depth. This will give you the time it takes to water to a specified depth.

After you water to the recommended depth, check the soil the same way every two days. For most plants, once the soil moisture depth is 6 inches it is time to water again. This will tell you how frequently you should water.

GROWING VEGETABLES

One of the greatest of all gardening delights is going out into the yard and picking something to eat for dinner. Nothing beats homegrown vegetables for flavor and nutrition. Vegetables grow well throughout the region, and the long, mild winters of most of the Southwest enable us to have year-round vegetable gardens.

It is important to choose vegetable varieties that are well suited to your area. Look for booklets and recommendations from the County Extension Service—these are the most comprehensive and reliable lists of vegetable varieties wherever you live. But do not be afraid to experiment. Trying at least one new variety each year should be a requirement for any vegetable gardener.

Whoever said timing is everything had growing vegetables in mind. The planting time for all vegetables is important, as they are short-lived crops that need to grow up quickly and provide edible leaves, roots, or fruit without interruption. Look for recommended planting times throughout the text, and consult County Extension bulletins for more details on timing.

Vegetables grow best in rich, healthy, loose soil. For most gardeners this is most easily attained by growing vegetables in raised beds. Not only can you create the perfect vegetable soil in a raised bed, but such a bed is also easy and efficient to water.

COLD PROTECTION

Although generally warm, Arizona winters can have cold spells regularly enough to warrant taking some precautions for your plants. Here, freezing nights are the result of radiant cooling. Cold nights are clear nights, and because the relative humidity is low during a cold night, the heat that builds up during the day is quickly released as the air cools after sundown. This fast cooling means that freezing temperatures happen quickly during the night but rarely occur for many hours a time. This type of cooling also means that any kind of overhead protection will help slow down the heat loss and prevent serious cold damage.

To take advantage of this process, plant susceptible plants under an eave or a tree (evergreens are particularly effective), or cover them on cold nights. Coverings can be anything that won't harm the plant: old blankets or sheets, burlap, a cardboard box, or in the special case of cactus tips, styrofoam cups. Coverings are most effective when they are put up in the afternoon so that some of the heat of the day is trapped beneath them. With few exceptions, they should be removed in the morning after the temperature is above freezing.

Frost cloth is a spun material that is translucent and will maintain a temperature about 5 degrees Fahrenheit greater than the air temperature. In the warmest regions it provides all the cold protection most plants need. Frost cloth is particularly effective for plants that are small or delicate, or where you need to leave the covering on for more than a day or two at a time. Because it allows in over 80% of available light, it can be left on for a week or more during the winter.

BASIC HORTICULTURAL PRACTICES

You can also build a structure or frame covered with plastic or frost cloth to protect cold-sensitive plants. The frame can be constructed of wood, plastic pipe, or any other available material. It should be large enough to fit completely over the plant. A frame that is covered with plastic can be left on the plant throughout the winter, but be sure the plant's leaves do not touch the plastic, as it will burn them on a cold night. This miniature greenhouse traps a lot of heat during the day and releases it slowly overnight, and it prevents frost from forming on the plants. Frames can also be covered only when freezes threaten with any of the coverings mentioned above, which are then removed when temperatures rise.

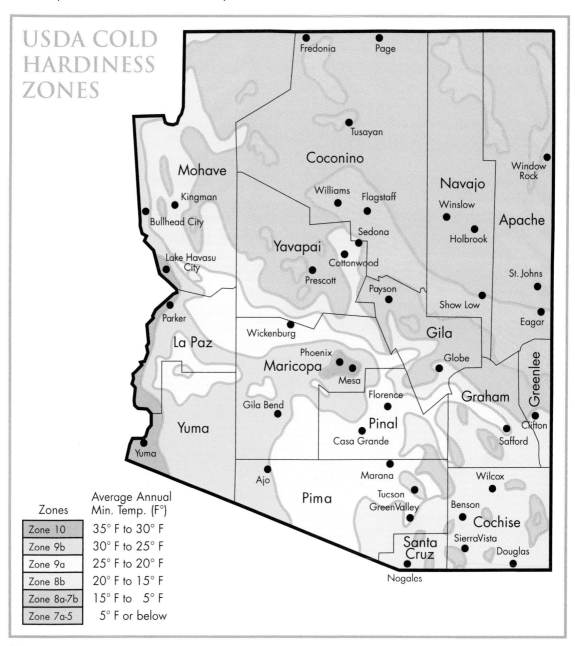

USDA COLD HARDINESS ZONES

Zones	Average Annual Min. Temp. (F°)
Zone 10	35° F to 30° F
Zone 9b	30° F to 25° F
Zone 9a	25° F to 20° F
Zone 8b	20° F to 15° F
Zone 8a-7b	15° F to 5° F
Zone 7a-5	5° F or below

ANNUALS

Annuals are like spices in a good stew. Just the right amount of annual plantings transforms the garden from mundane to spectacular, adding new dimensions and unexpected delights.

By their nature fleeting, annuals are beloved for their fast growth, showy flower displays, and ease of culture. After all, they have a lot to accomplish in a very short time.

In the desert parts of Arizona, there are two kinds of annuals used in gardens. One type is what we call true annuals, meaning species that naturally grow up, bloom, set seed, and finally die out in one growing season. Lots of these true annuals make up that indefinite class we

gardeners call wildflowers. Deserts encourage annuals; it is a successful strategy for evading the long, dry summers by living out an entire life in the mild—often wet—winter. Some of the most renowned native annuals used in and out of the region include bladder pod, California poppy, clarkia, desert bluebells, Mexican gold poppy, and tidy tips. Favorites like cosmos, scarlet flax, Shirley poppy, sunflower, and zinnia, while not native, thrive in Arizona gardens.

The second type of annuals are those that are usually described as "grown as annuals." These are plants that by their nature are either perennial (plants that live out their life over

more than two growing seasons) or biennial (plants that live out their life in two growing seasons). These plants are some of the most familiar annuals in mild-winter areas of Arizona: larkspur, lobelia, pansy, petunia, snapdragon, stock, and sweet William. Vinca, also known as Madagascar periwinkle, is a mainstay of summer annual plantings in the desert areas and falls into this category as well. Even natives like desert marigold are so closely associated with annual plantings that we forget they are truly perennial.

Annuals have a wide range of uses in the garden. They are superb at filling in blank spaces or holding the ground while other, more permanent, plantings take hold. Because they grow so quickly—most are up and blooming in a matter of weeks—they are especially helpful in a new yard. In yards with steep slopes or embankments, annuals add splashes of color while they stabilize the soil.

Annuals are also excellent at masking the bare stems and tired leaves of summer-flowering perennials in the winter. Tall species like canyon lupine, coreopsis, scarlet flax, Shirley poppy, and sunflowers hide barren lantana, fading bulbs, and frost-nipped salvias with their bold forms and showy flowers.

Smaller annuals can be planted in tight groups or lines to form borders in front of larger plants, or to exaggerate the effect of their flowers. Plants like creeping zinnia, dwarf marigolds, or tidy tips sparkle in this role.

GROWING ANNUALS FROM SEED

Annuals as a rule are easy to grow. Some of the native species will grow in almost any soil conditions, but all annuals have more prolific growth and bloom when they are grown in soils that are lightly amended with organic matter.

To prepare a bed or an area within a larger bed specifically for annuals, begin by raking the soil to remove any large rocks, debris, or other material. Add compost or mulch. The addition of a well-balanced, slow-release fertilizer or organic fertilizer blend is optional but is recommended for annuals that are not native. Mix it all together by raking back and forth or turning gently with a turning fork.

Water well, letting water soak down at least a foot. Then let the bed rest for a few days before planting.

Growing annuals from seed is an economical way to get a lot of plants into the garden. Almost all annuals grow readily from seed. Check the chart on pages 18–21 or the seed packages for the best time to plant annuals from seed for your area.

Sow seed by broadcasting it evenly over the surface of the soil. Using the back side of a rake, smooth over the bed to lightly cover the seed. Water well after planting.

BUYING ANNUALS AS TRANSPLANTS

Small packs of four or six annual plants in a container are commonly available, in all seasons, throughout the region. While these plants are a bit more expensive than those grown from seed, they are well on their way to flowering when you buy them. Set out transplants as early as they are available; the longer they grow in the ground, the better the bloom and longevity of the plants. Buying plants at the end of the season, often on sale, is rarely successful. These plants do not have time to set a good root system before the drying heat of the summer kills them off.

WATERING AND FERTILIZING ANNUALS

To encourage seed to germinate quickly, keep beds evenly moist until the seeds have germi-

nated and grown four or five true leaves. A light application of mulch will help keep the soil moist; do not apply too much, or it can smother your seedlings. Once there is a set of true leaves, water only to prevent the soil from completely drying out. It is much better to water annuals to a depth of 4 to 6 inches with each watering and spread out the waterings than to water them shallowly and often.

Healthy soil, rich with organic matter, does not need supplemental fertilizer to grow annuals. If you want to fertilize, however, it is much better to use a slow-release fertilizer early in the growing season than to shock annuals with a big dose. Some gardeners like to use a water-soluble fertilizer, which is very fast-acting, just as plants begin to bloom. This "pop" is effective for a quick bloom.

SELF-SEEDING ANNUALS

Many of the plants we call weeds are annuals. These plants earn their title from their ability to aggressively self-seed, often to the detriment of other plants in the area.

But some self-seeding is fortunate, assuring that certain well-loved annuals will return year after year. Plants that are particularly good at self-seeding include the following.

• African daisy is almost too good at self-seeding. If you live adjacent to or near parks, preserves, or wild areas, do not use this plant. But once planted in an urban yard, you will never lose it.

• Scarlet flax is a well-behaved, reliable self-seeder. Yet, it never seems to produce quite enough. Use additional seed every year for fuller displays.

• Desert bluebells, a charming plant, finds the most interesting places to self-seed—but like scarlet flax, it never seems to offer as much as you want. Add more seed.

• Sunflower self-seeds well in parts of the garden that are well irrigated, like vegetable beds.

• Wild poinsettia can be so successful that you will be pulling them out everywhere. But these plants are beautiful, and they never seem to leave the boundaries of a well-watered bed.

GROWING ANNUALS IN CONTAINERS

Annuals make outstanding container plants. Planted singly, they form a mass of color in the pot. Species like the multicolored cosmos, toadflax, and zinnia, or dramatic bloomers like California poppy and Cape daisy lend themselves well to this style. Annuals can be mixed with other annuals or perennials in containers to create a miniature garden. Use a wide array of colors, textures, and styles to make the planting more interesting. In addition, annuals can provide seasonal color to pots of succulents, including agaves and yucca. Let Arizona poppy, desert bluebells, or tidy tips fall over the edges of pots of succulents to soften their hard texture and add a dash of color.

USING ANNUALS AS CUT FLOWERS

It is one of the great joys of gardening to be able to go outside and bring parts of the garden into the house as cut flowers. Many annuals are good cut flowers. Some enterprising gardeners set aside specific beds just to grow flowers for cutting. To keep a steady supply of flowers for the house, plant annuals in two- or three-week successions. Here are some good cut flower choices.

• Calendula	• Safflower
• Coreopsis	• Snapdragon
• Cosmos	• Stock
• Farewell-to-spring	• Sunflower
• Globe amaranth	• Sweet pea
• Marigold	• Zinnia

CHAPTER ONE

ANNUALS AND WILDLIFE

Every healthy garden is a haven for a considerable array of living things in addition to the plants we put into it. Insects of a startling variety live happily in our gardens, generally outside our notice.

Native bees and other pollen-feeding insects are drawn to many of our annuals. These tiny marauders fill up on the pollen and nectar of almost all kinds of plants, taking a bit of their bounty from flower to flower as they forage. The pollen finds it way onto the pistils. The cycle of pollination/fertilization/seed formation would never happen without the bees.

Birds, too, find many annuals irresistible for food. Seed from members of the sunflower family, and sunflowers themselves, are ravaged by house finches, sparrows, cardinals, and many birds as they ripen. Leaving large sunflower heads to dry and ripen naturally after flowering creates a living bird feeder that will draw birds from all over the neighborhood.

During their short adult lives, butterflies feed deliriously on the nectar of chinchweed, golden fleece, and verbena, among others. Watch your plants carefully and see which of these garden visitors are attracted to your annuals.

Annuals

Name	Botanical Name	Blooming Period		Type
African daisy	Dimorphotheca sinuata	Cool		Annual
Arizona lupine	Lupinus arizonicus	Cool	Native	Annual
Arizona poppy	Kallstroemia grandiflora	Hot	Native	Annual
Aster	Aster spp.	Cool		Annual
Baby blue eyes	Nemophila menziesii	Cool	Native	Annual
Bachelor's buttons	Centaurea cyanus	Cool		Annual
Bladder pod	Lesquerella gordonii	Cool	Native	Annual
Beebalm	Monarda austromontana	Cool		Annual
Bells-of-Ireland	Moluccella laevis	Cool		Annual
Bishop's weed	Ammi majus	Cool		Annual
Black-eyed Susan	Rudbeckia hirta	Cool/Warm		Perennial/annual
Blazing star	Mentzelia involucrata	Cool		Annual
Blue thimble flower/ starflower	Gilia capitata	Cool	Native	Annual
Bread poppy	Papaver somniferum	Cool		Annual
Calendula	Calendula officinalis	Cool		Annual
California poppy	Eschscholzia californica	Cool/Warm	Native	Annual
Candytuft	Iberis amara/umbellata	Cool		Annual
Canyon lupine	Lupinus succulentus	Cool		Annual
Cape daisy	Arctotis spp.	Cool		Annual
Chia	Salvia columbariae	Cool	Native	Annual
Chinchweed	Pectis papposa	Warm/Hot	Native	Annual
China aster	Callistephus chinensis	Cool		Annual

CHAPTER ONE

Name	Botanical Name	Blooming Period		Type
Chinese houses	Collinsia heterophylla	Cool	Native	Annual
Clarkia	Clarkia amoena	Cool/Warm	Native	Annual
Cockscomb	Celosia hybrids	Cool		Annual
Common heliotrope	Heliotropium arborescens	Cool		Perennial/annual
Coneflower/ Mexican hat	Ratibida columnifera	Cool/Warm	Native	Perennial
Coreopsis	Coreopsis tinctoria	Cool/Warm		Annual
Cosmos	Cosmos bipinnatus/ sulphureus	Cool/Warm		Annual
Coyote gourd	Cucurbita digitata	Hot	Native	Annual
Creeping zinnia	Sanvitalia procumbens	Warm/Hot		Annual
Cypress vine	Ipomoea quamoclit	Warm/Hot	Native	Annual
Delphinium	Delphinium × cultorum	Cool		Annual
Desert bluebells	Phacelia campanularia	Cool	Native	Annual
Desert chicory	Rafinesquia neomexicana	Cool	Native	Annual
Desert coreopsis	Coreopsis bigelovii	Warm	Native	Annual
Desert lupine	Lupinus sparsiflorus	Cool	Native	Annual
Desert sunflower	Geraea canescens	Warm	Native	Annual
Devil's claw	Proboscidea parviflora	Hot	Native	Annual
English daisy	Bellis perennis	Cool		Perennial/annual
Firewheel/ blanket flower	Gaillardia pulchella	Warm/Hot	Native	Annual
Five spot	Nemophila maculata	Cool	Native	Annual
Floss flower	Ageratum houstonianum	Cool		Annual
Forget-me-not	Myosotis sylvatica	Cool		Annual
Gazania	Gazania hybrids	Warm/Hot		Perennial/annual
Gerbera daisy/ Transvaal daisy	Gerbera jamesonii	Cool/Warm/Hot		Annual
Globe amaranth	Gomphrena globosa	Warm/Hot		Annual
Gypsophila	Gypsophila elegans	Cool		Annual
Hollyhock	Alcea rosea	Cool Season		Biennial/annual
Hyacinth bean	Dolichos lablab	Warm		Annual
Iceland poppy	Papaver nudicaule	Cool/Warm		Perennial/annual
Impatiens	Impatiens balsamina	Warm/Hot		Annual
Indian paintbrush	Castilleja chromosa	Cool Season	Native	Annual
Johnny-jump-up	Viola tricolor	Cool		Perennial/annual
Joseph's coat	Amaranthus tricolor	Warm/Hot		Annual
Larkspur	Consolida ajacis	Cool Season		Annual
Lisianthus	Eustoma grandiflorum	Cool/Warm		Annual
Lobelia	Lobelia erinus	Cool		Annual

CHAPTER ONE

Name	Botanical Name	Blooming Period		Type
Love-lies-bleeding/ tassel flower	Amaranthus caudatus	Warm/Hot		Annual
Lupine	Lupinus spp.	Cool		Annual
Madagascar periwinkle/vinca	Catharanthus roseus	Cool/Warm/Hot		Perennial/annual
Marigold	Tagetes erecta/patula	Warm/Hot		Annual
Mexican gold poppy	Eschscholzia mexicana	Cool	Native	Annual
Mexican hat	Rudbeckia columnifera	Cool/Warm	Native	Annual
Mexican sunflower	Tithonia rotundifolia	Warm/Hot		Perennial/annual
Mignonette	Reseda odorata	Cool		Annual
Morning glory	Ipomoea tricolor	Cool/Warm		Annual
Moss rose	Portulaca grandiflora and spp.	Warm/Hot		Annual
Nasturtium	Tropaeolum majus	Cool/Warm		Annual
Nemesia	Nemesia strumosa hybrids	Cool		Annual
Nicotiana	Nicotiana alata/sylvestris	CoolWarm		Perennial/annual
Ornamental cabbage	Brassica spp.	Cool		Annual
Owl's clover	Orthocarpus purpurascens	Cool	Native	Annual
Painted tongue	Salpiglossis sinuata	Cool		Annual
Paludosum daisy	Chrysanthemum paludosum	Cool		Annual
Pansy	Viola × wittrockiana	Cool		Perennial/annual
Pentas	Pentas lanceolata	Warm/Hot		Annual
Petunia	Petunia hybrids	Cool/Warm		Perennial/annual
Phlox	Phlox spp./drummondii	Cool/Warm		Annual
Pincushion flower	Scabiosa atropurpurea/ stellata	Cool/Warm		Annual
Primrose	Primula veris	Cool		Annual
Purple aster	Machaeranthera bigelovii	Cool	Native	Annual
Purple coneflower	Echinacea purpurea	Cool		Perennial/annual
Purple thistle	Cirsium neomexicanum	Cool	Native	Annual
Red morning glory	Ipomoea cristulata (I. coccinea)	Warm/Hot	Native	Annual
Safflower	Carthamnus tinctorius	Cool		Annual
Sand verbena	Abronia villosa	Cool	Native	Annual
Scarlet flax	Linum grandiflorum 'Rubrum'	Cool/Warm		Annual
Scorpionweed	Phacelia crenulata	Cool	Native	Annual
Shirley poppy	Papaver rhoeas	Warm		Annual
Snapdragon	Antirrhum majus	Cool		Annual

CHAPTER ONE

Name	Botanical Name	Blooming Period		Type
Spider flower	Cleome hasslerana	Cool		Annual
Starflower	Gilia latifolia	Cool	Native	Annual
Statice	Limonium sinuatum	Cool/Warm		Annual
Stock	Matthiola incana	Cool		Annual
Strawflower	Helichrysum bracteatum	Cool/Warm		Annual
Sturt's desert pea	Clianthus formosus	Cool/Warm		Perennial/annual
Sunflower	Helianthus annuus	Warm/Hot	Native	Annual
Sweet alyssum	Lobularia maritima	Cool		Annual
Sweet pea	Lathyrus odoratus	Cool		Annual
Sweet sultan	Centaurea moschata	Cool		Annual
Sweet William	Dianthus barbatus	Cool/Warm		Biennial/annual
Tahoka daisy	Machaeranthera tanacetifolia	Cool	Native	Annual
Tidy tips	Layia glandulosa	Cool	Native	Annual
Toadflax	Linaria maroccana	Cool	Native	Annual
Viola	Viola cornuta	Cool		Annual
Wallflower	Erysimum spp.	Cool/Warm		Perennial/annual
Wild delphinium	Delphinium scaposum	Cool	Native	Annual
Wild poinsettia	Euphorbia heterophylla	Year-round	Native	Annual
Zinnia	Zinnia angustifolia/ elegans	Warm/Hot		Annual

Cool—plant in September to December in warmest zones for bloom January to March; plant in April elsewhere for bloom in late spring and early summer

Warm—plant in September to December in warmest zones for bloom in February to April; plant in May elsewhere for bloom through the summer

Hot—plant from September to March in warmest zones for bloom from May to August or September; plant in April to July for summer bloom

Annual—lives out its entire life cycle in one season

Perennial/annual—technically a perennial but used as an annual in the region usually because it cannot tolerate the summers

Biennial/annual—technically a plant that takes two season to complete its life cycle but used as an annual usually because it cannot tolerate the summers

Native—Native to the Desert Southwest from southern California to western Texas

JANUARY
ANNUALS

 PLANNING

Wildflowers along the Colorado River will begin to bloom late in the month if winter rains have been sufficient.

As nursery catalogs flood the mailbox, take time during the long winter nights to look for new or interesting annuals to grow next year. Throughout the region, look for plants that are rated for Zone 8 or higher, have a tropical or subtropical origin, or are considered by the catalog to be particularly heat- or drought-tolerant. Most mail-order nurseries are well outside desert regions, and the use of the terms heat- or drought-tolerant, or "grows in full sun," is often misleading for this region. Most spring-flowering annuals do well in the long, cool winter growing season of Zones 9 and 10, but it can take some experimentation to find those that work well through the warm spring and summer in these zones.

Many annuals (and a lot of perennials) that are sold as summer-flowering do their best growth and flowering in this region, especially in Zones 9 and 10, in the cooler winter/spring season; they will die out when the weather turns hot. The best strategy for finding good

Pansy

new annuals is to watch what is grown around the area, experiment with something new each year, and keep good records of what has worked for you. You may find that wonderfully unexpected plants perform well in your yard.

 PLANTING

In Zones 9b and 10, set out transplants of spring-flowering annuals throughout the month. Prepare a planting bed, or portion of a bed, by raking the soil gently in one direction to break up the surface. Add a thin layer (1 inch or less) of compost or mulch mixed with well-composted manure, and continue to rake in opposite directions to work it into the soil. Water the area well, checking to be

sure that it drains well and that there are no low spots where water could pond. Add organic matter carefully—a soil that is too rich encourages tremendous leaf growth, often at the sacrifice of flowering. This is especially true of native desert annuals and both **bread poppy** and **Shirley poppy.**

Sow seed of **California poppy, clarkia, nasturtium,** and **scarlet flax** this month in the warmest zones. Cast seed of native annuals in pots of succulents to add some spring color to your containers.

In Zone 8, set out transplants of cold-hardy **calendula, candytuft, English daisy**, **pansy,** and **snapdragon.** Be prepared to protect them from a hard freeze while they are establishing their roots.

Set transplants in the soil with the crown of the plant well above the soil line. **Pansies** in particular are susceptible to rot in the center when planted too deeply. Firm the soil around the plants, apply a light layer of mulch, and water well.

CARE

Seed-grown annuals often come up too thickly. Keeping them regularly thinned encourages rapid, steady growth and better flowering. Thin to space plants so that the edges just touch.

Annual weeds can crowd out your cultivated flowering annuals, especially those grown from seed. The best strategy is to remove weed seedlings as soon as they emerge. In wet winters, this is a weekly chore; in drier years, weeding every two weeks will keep the numbers to manageable levels. Some of the worst culprits in the region are dandelion, London rocket, red brome, sow thistle, and yellow clover. Remove any flowering heads you find before they are able to set seed.

The coldest nights of the year are expected this month. Most annuals are tough enough to tolerate the moderate freezes

---

HELPFUL HINTS

• Use portable spike sprayers or oscillating sprinklers for uniform coverage of annuals planted in beds or large areas. It is best to water during the day at this time of the year.

• Pulling out crowded seedlings can damage or destroy those you wish to keep. Use scissors or sharp floral shears to cut unwanted seedlings at ground level.

---

typical of western Arizona and Phoenix, the western edge of the region, but in other areas, cover tender plants like **sweet peas** and **petunias** on frosty nights. Use lightweight frost blankets. Newspaper works well to protect young seedlings or fragile plants. Secure it with rocks or bricks if the weather is windy, and be sure it won't get wet; the added weight will break tender plants.

WATERING

Water established annuals to a depth of 4 to 6 inches, about once a week. Take note of rainfall, and if it is frequent and abundant, skip watering altogether. Water seedlings every other day until they have five true leaves, then reduce the frequency gradually until they are being watered once a week.

FERTILIZING

Native annuals do not need fertilization, but to speed up blooming and increase the number of flowers, fertilize annuals late in the month. Use a balanced formula that has high phosphorus but relatively low nitrogen content. Too much nitrogen and the plants will grow leaves lushly at the expense of flowers.

PESTS

Handpick aphids that may show up toward the end of the month in the warmest zones. If they are numerous, spray with a soapy water solution or strong jet of water.

FEBRUARY

ANNUALS

PLANNING

Begin thinking of where to interplant warm-season annuals. These annual species germinate as the temperatures begin to warm in the spring and will be ready to bloom about the time that the cool-season varieties finish and go to seed. Use them to mask cool-season annuals as they go to seed by planting taller species of warm-season plants among shorter cool-season annuals.

In Zones 9 and 10, it is not too late to put in a few last-minute transplants of cool-season annuals. It is too far into the season, however, to expect seed-grown plants to perform well. Take a tour around nurseries and gardens in the area and find out what is available and what is still looking good.

In the cooler parts of the state, there is still ample time to set out colorful, spring-flowering transplants through the end of the month. Late-season cold spells and cold winds can be devastating to small transplants, so be prepared to lightly cover newly planted annuals with mulch, row cover, or even newspaper.

If you haven't been in the habit of keeping notes or a journal, this is a good time to consider it. Keep a list of annuals that appeal to you that you have seen growing in friends' and neighbors' yards, public gardens, and nurseries. Take note of how your own annuals did this year. Make a list now of what you would like to try next year, and be sure to add at least a few that you haven't grown before. Seed catalogs have been arriving over the winter—go ahead and make your order for next fall's planting while the list is fresh in your mind.

Some annuals are good cut flowers, and using them generously in the house brings the spring indoors. **Snapdragon, stock,** and **sweet pea** are especially good cut flowers.

PLANTING

In Zones 9 and 10, sow seed of warm-season annuals like **aster, calendula, coreopsis, cosmos, gaillardia, marigolds, Mexican sunflower, sunflower,** and **zinnia.** Many of these annuals are also available as transplants, which can be planted this month.

Cosmos

Plant annual vines like **hyacinth bean** and **morning glory** where they will receive at least six hours of strong sunlight a day. Provide a trellis or arbor for support. Both of these annual vines do well in the region in plenty of sun, but in the hottest parts of the region, plant where the roots are shaded, but the top is in the sun.

In Zone 8, wait until the end of the month to set out transplants of **bells of Ireland, calendula, pansy,** and **snapdragon.** Sow seed of **African daisy, candytuft, gaillardia, nasturtium,** and **sweet alyssum** late in the month in these areas as well.

CARE

Continue to weed regularly to keep beds tidy and the plants properly spaced. Unless you are saving seed, remove spent plants as soon as they begin to decline. Deadhead annuals regularly, especially those in the **sunflower** family, and they will continue to bloom for a longer time.

WATERING

As temperatures begin to rise, especially in the westernmost cities, increase frequency of watering to maintain soil moisture to a depth of 4 to 6 inches. Even highs in the 80s greatly affect winter and spring-flowering annuals, so be prepared to water them, especially those in containers, more often to prevent wilting.

FERTILIZING

Fertilize plants in containers every other week with a balanced water-soluble fertilizer, using the recommended strength for houseplants.

Plants in the ground in a well-prepared bed usually do not need fertilizing. The slow release of organic fertilizers, like composted manure or seaweed formulations, benefits the plants over a long period of time and are all that most annuals ever need. Some gardeners provide a monthly fertilization of annual beds to help maximize the bloom. This regimen of fertilization is particularly helpful if it has been a dry winter or the soil is not abundant in nutrients.

PESTS

Aphids show up in the cool spring months. They are attracted to the lush new growth and flowerbuds that are abundant during this time. Control aphids by spraying with strong jets of water, or remove them by hand. In small numbers they are only a nuisance, but in large numbers these tiny sucking insects can be detrimental to small plants. Early detection and removal is the best way to keep the population in check.

MARCH

ANNUALS

 PLANNING

This is one of the most beautiful times of the year in the deserts of Zones 9 and 10. In years with plenty of winter rain, the natural wildflower displays are breathtaking. It is always worthwhile to plan several hikes or leisurely drives during this time to appreciate the wildflower gardens that naturally occur.

This is also the peak month in these zones for garden tours. Watch for local tours, as these are some of the finest ways to find new ideas for your own garden and see plants that you might not have tried before. Take your journal with you and make notes about what might be useful in your beds next year.

In the gardens of Zones 9 and 10, everything seems to be in bloom at once this month. This is the month to take some time and enjoy the effect of all the annuals you have planted.

Nurseries will be crammed this month; get there early for the best selection and quality of warm-season transplants. Many cool-season annuals will still be for sale, but think carefully before you buy them this late. Most cool-season annuals are at the end of their allotted life span and won't grow much more than what you see in the

pot. Unless you need a quick lift right away or a few last-minute plants to fill in gaps for a special event, it is better to buy only warm-season annuals now.

 PLANTING

Set out warm-season annuals either from seed or transplants. Fast-growing species like **cosmos, firewheel, Mexican sunflower, sunflower,** and **zinnia** are reliable and economical to grow from seed. Prepare the bed as described on page 22, and sow seed evenly. In Zones 9 and 10, plant seed of **hollyhock** from now through May.

Although vegetable gardens may be bursting at this time, use any available space for flowering annuals that are also edible. **Nasturtium** is not only an effortless plant for vivid color, but its spicy new leaves (and flowers) are delicious in salads. **Hyacinth beans,** including the pod, are excellent when lightly steamed, and **sunflower** seeds are tasty both raw and roasted.

In Zone 8, continue to plant cold-hardy annuals. At the end of the month begin early plantings of **clarkia, cosmos, globe amaranth, marigold, mignonette, morning glory, nasturtium, portulaca,** and **zinnia.** In some years, late freezes or cold weather may inhibit germination,

but seedlings will come up later as the weather moderates. In other years, it is warm enough in March to allow seed to germinate for a head start on spring annual displays.

 CARE

As winter-growing annuals begin to decline at the end of the month, remove them. It is hard to be ruthless when there are still a few flowers or a bit of green, and to fill the gap, replace them immediately with a warm-season annual. Unless you are saving seed, keep replacing spent annuals weekly to keep the garden looking sharp and tidy.

Seed of warm-season annuals that were planted last month should be germinated, and the small seedlings will be growing quickly. Thin regularly to keep the plants from crowding each other out.

 WATERING

Maintain deep, regular watering on established cool-season annuals as they finish out their life span. This is particularly important if you are saving seed from the plants. Water all annuals deeply and more frequently as the weather heats up. Newly planted transplants need to be watered to a depth of 4 to 6 inches, which is usually every three to four days—but it is best to use a soil probe or rod to be certain.

FERTILIZING

In Zones 9 and 10, cease fertilizing cool-season annuals this month. They are almost finished, and fertilizing will not help them. Fertilize newly planted annuals after they have been in the ground two weeks or when they begin to set out new growth. When using an inorganic fertilizer, use a low-nitrogen, high-phosphorus formula every two weeks while

the plants are actively growing. Apply a 2- to 3-inch layer of compost or mulch to the entire bed every other month throughout the summer.

PESTS

Small, round holes in the leaves of annuals indicate the presence of flea beetles or their relatives. Like cutter bees, these little black insects use the harvested leaves in their nest holes, and their damage is cosmetic and short-term. Try a general insecticide if the numbers are enormous, but they are usually gone by the time it gets hot.

Marigold

APRIL

ANNUALS

PLANNING

As the deserts heat up and the weather dries out, cool-season annuals—both in your garden and in the natural desert—begin to dry out and fade quickly. These standing dried-out plants, including grasses, become ready fuel for the wildfires that plague the region in the early summer. To minimize fire danger, cut down all dried grasses, weeds, and annuals that are growing within 10 feet of your house and in nearby alleys or vacant areas. This removal is especially critical if you live near the edge of town, in a remote area, or in proximity to a park, preserve, or other natural area. If you are saving seed, leave only a few plants rather than the entire bed; they will provide more than enough seed for your use.

PLANTING

In Zones 9 and 10, continue to sow seed of warm-season annuals like **coreopsis** and **sunflower** until mid-month In Zone 8, plant all the annuals listed in March plus warm-season annuals like **coreopsis, gaillardia,** and **sunflower** throughout the month.

Sow seed of **hollyhock** from now until June.

In all zones, continue to set out transplants of warm-season annuals like **aster, coneflower, creeping zinnia, gaillardia, lisianthus, pentas, portulaca, vinca,** and **zinnia.** Follow planting recommendations on page 22.

In Zones 9 and 10, most cool-season annuals in containers will have died out by this time. But a few, like **gerbera daisy,** can last all summer if you move the container into the shade and continue to feed and water plants regularly.

Replant containers for the summer with heat-tolerant annuals that can survive the high soil temperatures of a pot. **Cosmos, gaillardia,** and **Madagascar periwinkle (vinca)** are among the toughest annuals for these conditions. Interplant these annuals with equally heat-toler-

Gerbera daisy

ant perennials like **angelonia**, **bougainvillea,** and **lantana** for continued summer color.

CARE

Harvest seed of cool-season annuals as soon as the seed-pod turns brown or begins to dry out. Put the seed in a paper bag or container without a lid, and let it dry out for a week or two in a dry, shady spot. Remove all the chaff, pods, and other debris before you store the seed. Store seed in containers with tight lids—film canisters and glass jars are ideal— away from light and moisture, and be sure you include a paper label both inside and outside the container. Most annual seed keeps for at least one year at room temperature in the house and will keep for many years if refrigerated. Seed in the refrigerator should be kept in moisture-proof containers.

HELPFUL HINTS

When you plant annuals from seed, anything can happen. Sometimes you get a plant with a remarkable flower size or shape, or a particularly pleasing color, or a form that is taller or shorter than average. To save the seed of these special flowers, mark the flowering stalk with an adhesive-backed mailing label on which you have noted the name of the plant and whatever special feature (color, size of bloom, odd form) made you pick this flower's seed to save. Wrap the label around the stem, folding the label in half so it adheres to itself.

Continue to deadhead blooming plants, particularly those in the **sunflower** family, to encourage repeat flowering.

WATERING

Increase watering of annual vines and larger plants like **sunflowers** so that water penetrates to a depth of 1 foot. Smaller annuals should be watered to a depth of 6 to 8 inches for the remainder of the summer. Water plants in containers every other day, but be prepared to increase it to daily if they wilt or if the weather remains above 100 degrees Fahrenheit. If the plants are wilting continuously, or drying out too fast, move the container to a shadier location

FERTILIZING

Fertilize summer-flowering annuals every two to four weeks with a balanced slow-release formula or a dry organic fertilizer. Be sure to water the area well both before and after application.

Use a water-soluble fertilizer for annuals in pots. Follow label directions for the concentration and apply it every other week.

PESTS

Water all annuals from below, rather than spraying the foliage. This helps prevent leaf diseases from infecting your plants.

MAY

ANNUALS

 PLANNING

This is a good time to take out your garden journal and record the performance of your cool-season annuals. Take note of what worked well, what failed, and what you want to plant next fall. Look over your warm-season annuals that have been in bloom for about a month; they should be looking their best by this time. Consider how well they are doing and how they are placed. If you are growing some for the first time, record how tall they are growing. If some varieties got taller than expected or wanted, make a note to plant them in the back of the bed next time.

 PLANTING

In Zones 9 and 10, set out transplants of **coreopsis, cosmos, gaillardia, globe amaranth, lisianthus, Madagascar periwinkle (vinca), marigold, portulaca,** and **zinnia** early in the month.

In these hot areas, there is still time to sow seed of **coreopsis, cosmos, gaillardia, gazania, globe amaranth, marigold, Mexican sunflower, portulaca, sunflower,** and **zinnia.** Sow seed into a prepared bed and keep evenly moist until the plants

have germinated and begun growing. Keep thinning small seedlings to prevent crowding and get the best growth and bloom from your plants.

Plant native summer-flowering annuals like **Arizona poppy, coyote gourd,** and **wild poinsettia** throughout the region. **Arizona poppy,** which is in the same family as **creosote,** can be difficult to germinate in some soils. Hot water soaking helps in some circumstances, but this beautiful trailing plant grows best in well-drained, sandy soils with intermittent but not consistent water.

Coyote gourd germinates easily with ample moisture during the late spring and early summer. This is an easy plant to start in a small pot and then put out as transplants, or it can be planted by direct-seeding. The spreading vines make a useful groundcover in barren areas or for newly planted areas, easily covering 20 to 30 feet. The huge bright-yellow flowers occur throughout the summer, and the resulting gourds make a welcome addition to dried arrangements and holiday decorations later in the year.

Wild poinsettia is extremely easy to grow, and the explosive seed capsules mean that once this species is established in your garden you will have ample plants forever. This smaller

version of the holiday **poinsettia** thrives in desert gardens with minimal care. Plants germinate and grow throughout the year, so there are some in bloom all the time.

In Zone 8, continue to plant **sweet alyssum, impatiens, cosmos, marigold, portulaca,** and **zinnia.** Plant **four o'clock** now in these areas. While **four o'clock** is perennial in Zones 9 and 10, it grows as an annual where freezing temperatures are common.

 CARE

Recently planted annuals need afternoon shade until they are well established. Cover with a light-colored cloth, shade cloth, or other material (not plastic) that is draped over a frame. Small plants are delicate, and the weight of the cloth can break them. Use natural shade in the garden effectively by planting annuals on the east side of large shrubs or walls so they receive afternoon shade. Planting beneath trees with high, filtered shade is ideal for warm-season annuals—it will keep them in bloom throughout the summer in Zones 9 and 10. Continue to remove late-flowering cool-season plants like **clarkia** and **poppies** as they fade and begin to die out.

HELPFUL HINTS

• Sometimes it is hard to tell when seed is ripe—a capsule or pod looks green one day and pops open the next to shoot seed far away, making it almost impossible to find the seed. To harvest seed reliably, put a small paper or fine cloth mesh bag over the spent flowers long before the seed is ready. Harvest any time after the seed has been released.

• As **sunflowers** go to seed, allow the seed of one or two plants to ripen naturally on the plant. Although this will cause the plant to quit flowering and decline, birds will flock to the nutritious seed. These natural bird feeders are a wonderful way to attract birds to the garden.

Sunflowers are a great way to attract birds to the garden.

Maintain a regular schedule of deadheading **coreopsis, cosmos, gaillardia,** and **marigolds** to extend their bloom.

 WATERING

Water large annuals like vines and gourds to a depth of 1 foot. With increasing temperatures, this may be as often as every three days. Water all other annuals to a depth of 6 to 8 inches. To conserve soil moisture, provide a thick layer of organic mulch to all annuals in the ground, even native ones.

 FERTILIZING

Every two weeks, fertilize annuals in pots with a water-soluble fertilizer at the recommended strength for houseplants. If plants grow well but are not blooming satisfactorily, switch to a formula with a lower nitrogen content.

 PESTS

Hollyhock weevils spend the winter inside the seedheads of the **hollyhock,** and as the weather warms in the spring they lay eggs in the emerging flower buds. To prevent damage next year, discard all spent seedheads as they arise.

 NOTES

_____
_____
_____
_____
_____
_____
_____
_____
_____
_____
_____
_____

31

JUNE
ANNUALS

PLANNING

Just as you did in winter, consider acquiring plants that are technically perennial and using them as if they were annual for summer color. Look for the wide variety of **ornamental peppers** now available. Most of these short, compact plants have multicolored fruit on one plant. They can be used either in the ground or in containers.

- **Basil** varieties with dark leaves like 'Dark Opal' or showy flowers like the **African basil** fill in spaces in the annual beds during the hottest days of summer. If you are growing **basil** for its bloom, prune back hard after each blooming cycle and water well, and it will come into bloom again. Fertilize once a month with a balanced fertilizer.
- **Pentas** (also known as **Egyptian star-cluster**) is a perennial that is generally grown as an annual throughout the region. The open, star-shaped flowers are found in bright red, white, lilac, and pink. This perennial masquerading as an annual is excellent in well-amended beds with high, light shade and will bloom throughout the summer. **Pentas** make fine cut flowers.
- **Gerbera daisy** blooms continuously through the late spring and summer if provided with a rich soil, ample water, and lots of shade. These low-growing plants have a huge range of flower color from deep pink and red to yellow, orange, and white.

PLANTING

Sow seed of **Arizona poppy, Mexican sunflower, sunflowers,** and **zinnia** this month. You can still set out transplants of the most heat-tolerant annuals like **cosmos, lisianthus, Madagascar periwinkle,** and **portulaca.** But even these plants do best if planted with afternoon shade. In cooler areas, continue to plant **cosmos, marigold,** and **zinnia.**

CARE

Deadhead warm-season annuals regularly, as soon as the flowers are spent. This will encourage repeat blooming. Cut back flowering stalks to the first junction with a leaf-forming bud.

WATERING

Water plants in containers daily. Be sure that the water flows out the bottom of the pot with each watering. Water as early in the morning as possible, spraying the leaves to increase humidity for the plant. On extremely hot days (over 110 degrees Fahrenheit), spraying the foliage in the evening can cool the plant and mitigate the heat stress. Water annuals in the ground to a depth of 6 to 12 inches, depending on their size. This can be as often as every two to three days, depending on temperatures and soil conditions. Water daily when temperatures are extreme.

FERTILIZING

It is best not to fertilize or to do so only very lightly during high temperatures. The tender new growth that results from regular fertilization may burn quickly in the heat of early summer. If you choose to fertilize, do so only once using much less fertilizer than normal. Fertilizers, especially inorganic ones, are high in salts that can accumulate quickly in the dry, hot conditions of early summer.

PESTS

While it is tempting to water a lot as the weather turns hot, take care that the soil is draining well and drying out slightly between waterings. Soggy or waterlogged soils promote root rots that weaken or destroy your annuals. These fungal infestations are almost impossible to treat, so prevention is best.

JULY
ANNUALS

PLANNING

Do not be surprised if many of the annuals that have been so lovely through the summer simply give up this month. The intense summer heat and dry air finally wears some of them out.

Time to take out the journal and take note of how your annuals fared. Which ones lasted the longest? Were they growing in full sun or shade or a little of both? Notice what kind of culture you had for them, and make plans to adjust it for next year.

If the annuals you are growing in containers are looking sun-weary but are still in overall good shape, move the entire container to more shade. A week or two in the shade is often all the help they need to continue to look their best through the remainder of the summer.

PLANTING

You can still sow seed of **cosmos, globe amaranth, lisianthus, marigold,** and **sunflowers** in Zones 9 and 10. They will grow up quickly if kept well watered, and they will bloom again in the late summer. Set out transplants of these same annuals, as well as vigorous **Madagascar periwinkle** and **portulaca.**

Continue to plant summer-flowering native annuals like **Arizona poppy, chinchweed,** or **coyote gourd.** These plants may germinate in the summer rainy season and grow quickly in the late summer.

CARE

Continue to deadhead regularly to prolong bloom. Cut back long-lived annuals like **coreopsis, cosmos, gaillardia,** and **vinca** to encourage new flowering.

WATERING

Water plants in containers daily. Be sure that water drains completely through the holes. On cloudy days, or if it rains, adjust watering to every other day.

Water annuals in the ground to a depth of 6 to 12 inches, depending on their size. In most areas this will be every two to three days. Skip a watering if it rains more than 1/2 inch.

FERTILIZING

Fertilize annuals in pots with a water-soluble formula once this month. Do not overfertilize if it is very hot or the resulting flush of tender growth will easily burn. Do not fertilize plants in the ground.

PESTS

Mildews erupt this time of the year with the high heat and increasing humidity. They are especially a problem on **sunflower** and **zinnia**. Prevention is the best approach. Water plants from below to prevent spreading the spores from the ground onto the leaves. Provide plenty of mulch to reduce water loss and help prevent splashing. Remove infected leaves quickly, and pick up leaves that fall around the plants, as they are full of spores. Annuals with their short life spans are rarely worth an aggressive spraying campaign—if they become too infested, pull them out.

HELPFUL HINTS

This is a good time to buy annuals for next year from the catalogs that pile up in any gardener's home. Look for varieties that are called summer-flowering in northern gardens, as they often make excellent winter annuals in the desert. Because winters are so mild in Zones 9 and 10, plants labeled as "hothouse or greenhouse only" are often good choices for the cool-season garden.

AUGUST

ANNUALS

 PLANNING

Fall planting is just around the corner. If you want to have a wildflower garden, start planning for it now. Natives of the region that are especially well suited to home gardens are the following.

• **Mexican gold** and **California poppy**—both of these **poppies** bloom gold to yellow, although white ones may show up from time to time. **Mexican gold poppies** are a little smaller and lower to the ground, while **California poppies** have big, bouquet-like forms when well grown. There are many color forms and selections of **California poppy** that are excellent in the garden.

• **Desert bluebells** are one of the easiest of all natives to grow and are reliable reseeders. Grow them in rocky, unamended soil or in richer beds mixed with other annuals or perennials. They are low and short with intense dark-blue flowers, and are particularly striking in pots with **agaves** or other succulents.

• **Clarkia,** also known as **farewell-to-spring** or **godetia,** blooms later than most of the other spring-flowering natives in a wide range of colors from red and pink to mauve and lavender. Plants can be loose and benefit from being grown in mass groups to maximize the effect.

• **Chinchweed** and **golden fleece** are similar yellow-flowered annuals that bloom throughout the year. They have small, needlelike leaves and bright golden or yellow flowers. They reseed well in yards with gravel mulch and good drainage.

• **Tidy tips** are short, slightly spreading plants with daisy-like yellow flowers that are rimmed with white. There is a native Arizona species (*Layia glandulosa*) that has all-white ray flowers, but it is much less common. **Tidy tips** make good borders at the edge of a flower bed. When mixed with other wildflowers, they show up best grown in large numbers.

 PLANTING

Continue to plant heat-loving annuals like **Madagascar periwinkle, portulaca,** and **sunflowers** either from seed or transplants.

If you are creating new beds, begin to lay them out this month. Cultivate the soil lightly by turning it to a depth of only 2 inches, or by using a hard-tined rake over the area in a crisscross pattern. Spread the area with a thin layer of well composed or finely ground bark, compost, mulch, or other organic material. Work it into the soil and water the area well. Do this at least two weeks before you intend to plant to let the area settle, allowing the nutrients from the organic matter work into the soil.

 CARE

Continue to deadhead any annuals that are still blooming. This will prolong the bloom. In cooler areas, cut back **coreopsis, cosmos, gaillardia,** and **vinca** to encourage a flush of new flowering. Continue with regular watering in the hottest zones, but do not cut back plants severely.

WATERING

Continue to water potted annuals daily, and be sure each watering is thorough. Water annuals in the ground deeply, and avoid overhead spraying to cut down on mildew problems.

FERTILIZING

Fertilize container plants once this month with a water-soluble fertilizer. If you have newly planted annuals that have been in the ground over two weeks, fertilize once with a low-nitrogen, high-phosphorus fertilizer.

PESTS

Whiteflies begin to show up this month. These tiny flying insects appear as clouds arising from the underside of the leaves when a plant is watered or disturbed. Thin-leaved plants like **sunflowers** are especially susceptible. Use a soapy water solution (1 tablespoon dishwashing liquid—the brand Dawn™ is especially good—to 1 gallon water) on the underside of the leaves daily to keep them under control. Large infestations are almost impossible to control.

HELPFUL HINTS

Build a cold frame to germinate your own seeds. This will allow you to have more variety in the garden and to get things going sooner so that you have a longer season of bloom.

1. Begin by selecting a spot that receives morning sun or that can be shaded in the afternoon. Using any kind of wood or other building material, make an open box that has two identical sides, each of which has one end higher than the other. The back side is slightly taller than these two identical sides and is level along the top edge; the front side is half the size of the back and is also level along the top edge. This makes a box that slopes from back to front, which helps water drain off quickly.

2. Cover with an old window, a wooden frame covered with plastic, or anything similar. A lid can be hinged or not but should fit completely over the box.

3. If it will be set on the ground, put a layer of plastic under the box to serve as the floor. This will help prevent soilborne insects and diseases from getting into the frame.

4. Use a rod or stick to hold up the lid when the weather is hot to prevent the frame from overheating.

A cold frame not only serves as an excellent germination chamber but can be a good place to keep cold-tender plants on a freezing night.

An example of a cold frame. Putting a layer of plastic underneath will keep out soilborne insects and diseases.

SEPTEMBER

ANNUALS

PLANNING

In a small garden like an entry courtyard or small patio, planting annuals close enough to fill in all the spaces will give the area a lush array of color. Do not be afraid to plant generously and let all the colors blend together on their own. Use annual vines like **canary creeper, morning glory,** or **sweet pea** to give height and dimension to the space. **Sweet pea** will also add their lovely fragrance to the area. Mix annuals of varying sizes to add interest. Tall species like **coreopsis** and **poppies** can form a backdrop for the smaller species like **alyssum, California poppies,** or **clarkia.** A wide range of color and size will give the small space dimension, making it appear larger. The diversity keeps your eye moving around and adds to the illusion of spaciousness.

PLANTING

You can begin to plant cool-season annuals in the warmer areas as temperatures ease downward. It is best to wait until temperatures are below 100 degrees Fahrenheit to assure fast germination and quick growth. Most annuals will tolerate some heat once they are germinated and are actively growing.

Traditional cool-season annuals include **lobelia, pansy, petunia, snapdragon, stock,** and **sweet alyssum.** These species are most often set out as transplants and are available in nurseries throughout the area. Because they are generally sold in bloom, mix and match the colors to suit your garden's style and your color preferences.

There are some excellent cool-season annuals that are not as commonly used. These include **bachelor's buttons, bells of Ireland, forget-me-not, nemesia,** and **sweet sultan.** While some of these are available as small transplants, all are sold in seed packets.

Gardeners in Zone 8 can plant cold-hardy annuals like **bachelor's buttons, candytuft, cape daisy, clarkia, English daisy, larkspur, pansy, snapdragon, statice, stock,** and **wallflower.** Plant frost-tender plants like **aster, lobelia, nicotiana, petunia, phlox, strawflower, sweet pea,** and **toadflax** before October 1.

CARE

Clear out all the old summer annuals to make room for the cool-season annuals. If you are making a new bed, follow the guidelines on page 22. Harvest **gourds** once they have stopped growing and are beginning to show yellow on the underside. They should feel firm and heavy for their size. Once you have harvested all the **gourds** you want, including some to use for seed next year, remove the vines.

WATERING

While the weather is still warm, water newly planted annuals daily until they begin to show new growth. Then water to a depth of 6 to 8 inches, every three to four days, depending on the soil and the temperature.

Continue to water container-grown plants often while temperatures are high. Check to be sure that the pot is dry an inch below the surface before you water. This is approximately the length of your finger to the first knuckle.

HELPFUL HINTS

Vines need a way to get to the sun. Trellises, arbors, and other supports are widely available in nurseries and garden centers. But you might want to try to make your own.

• Drive wooden stakes or posts into the ground the length of the area you want the vine to grow. String monofilament, twine (sisal lasts the longest), or fine wire at 6- to 12-inch intervals between the posts. Set the first row 2 to 4 inches from the ground to give the vine's tendrils a head start.

• Another type of trellis, and one that can be portable, is made from masonry ladders (also called masonry wire). These wire ladders come in 6-, 8-, or 10-foot lengths. Set each end in the ground, bending the wire to form a U-shaped arbor. Set them end to end to create an undulating arbor for vines.

• For small gardens or where space is tight, grow vines in large containers. Use masonry ladders either straight up or bent into a tight U-shape in the pot to provide a trellis for the vines.

• The easiest trellis of all is to plant your vines at the base of a tall tree and let it climb through the branches.

Gourds growing on an arbor.

FERTILIZING

Lay down a good layer of compost or mulch and let it work into the bed over the next few months.

Wait to fertilize newly planted annuals until they have been in the ground at least two weeks and they begin to show signs of growth. Fertilize once a month with a balanced complete fertilizer. Water plants well and scratch the fertilizer into the soil gently, taking care not to disturb the roots. Water well after fertilizing.

PESTS

Whiteflies may still be active, but as temperatures fall their numbers decline. Spray with water or a soapy water solution to keep populations under control. Light floating row covers can help prevent large infestations on plants.

OCTOBER

ANNUALS

PLANNING

Many gardeners in Arizona have become fascinated with growing wildflowers. Although the term is loosely applied to a wide range of plants, most gardeners think of a wildflower planting as an exuberant mix of native plants, both annual and perennial. These glorious displays begin by preparing a bed as described on page 22. Be cautious about how much organic matter is added—too much, and the plants will grow leaves at the expense of flowers.

Once the bed is prepared, rake it smooth. Most wildflower plantings are done from seed, but if you have transplants of some of the species you want, set them in first. Part of the glory of wildflower beds is their randomness, so scatter the transplants around the bed at irregular intervals.

One of the ways to achieve a really wild look is to take all the seed of the various species you are interested in growing and mix it together. Put it in a container and add a small amount of sand. Mix it all up well. Broadcast the seed mix as evenly as you can over the entire bed.

Rake over the bed to cover the seeds. Annual seeds do not need to be planted deeply, and just running the rake gently back and forth provides sufficient covering. Use the back of the rake rather than the tines for more even spreading. Water well after planting, taking care that water does not run off the bed carrying precious seed with it.

Some of the best natives for spring-flowering wildflower beds are annuals like **bladder pod, California poppy, desert bluebells, desert sunflower, gaillardia, Mexican gold poppy,** **owl's clover,** and **tidy tips.** Native perennials like **penstemon, globe mallow, Gooding's verbena,** and **desert marigold** are usually considered part of a wildflower garden as well. Add later-flowering species like **clarkia, coreopsis,** and **coneflower** to prolong the wildflower blooming season.

There are equally outstanding non-native annuals that blend well with natives in wildflower displays. Some non-native annuals to consider adding to a wildflower garden are **scarlet flax, Shirley poppy,** and **toadflax.**

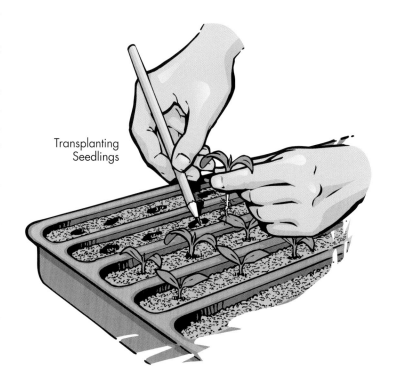

Transplanting Seedlings

PLANTING

This is prime planting season for all cool-season annuals in Zones 9 and 10. Continue to plant annuals from either transplants or seed through the end of the month.

Tender annuals may need protection on frosty nights.

CARE

All native annuals, as well as many non-natives, grow particularly well in rocky soils or with a fine gravel mulch. The small rocks hold the tiny seedlings in place, protecting them both from harsh winds and being uprooted by fast- moving water. Rocky mulch holds in moisture so that the seedlings and young plants are prevented from completely drying out. After planting, spread fine gravel mulch over the bed to a depth of $^1/_2$ to 1 inch.

HELPFUL HINTS

Lupine seeds have a very hard outer covering and are often slow to germinate. To speed germination and to make it more uniform, soak seeds overnight in hot water. Heat water to a boil and turn it off, or run water through a coffee maker, then pour it over the seeds. Let them stand overnight, and plant them the next day.

WATERING

Water beds that are newly planted with seed every day until the seeds germinate. Once the seedlings have three to five true leaves, begin to reduce the watering frequency until you are watering once a week. Never let the seedlings dry out completely.

Water transplanted annuals to a depth of 4 to 6 inches. Depending on the temperatures, this may be two to three times a week, but it is best to use a probe or rod to check because temperatures fluctuate a lot during this time of the year.

FERTILIZING

Do not fertilize native wildflowers or other annuals this month. You can apply fertilizer to plants growing in containers beginning two weeks after they were planted. This should be plenty of time for the root systems to get established and be able to take up the nutrients. Another indication that container-grown plants are ready to accept fertilizer is when they begin to show signs of active growth. Container-grown plants can be fertilized every two weeks until December to maintain the strongest bloom.

PESTS

It is always important to correctly identify any insects that you suspect have caused damage to your plants. If you do not know what the insect is, collect one in a jar and take it to your local County Extension Service office or a reputable nursery for identification. Sometimes the insects you see are not the ones that are causing the damage.

NOVEMBER

ANNUALS

PLANNING

Cut flowers are one of the nicest ways to accent the house, and many annuals make excellent cut flowers. If you have the room, create a bed or area of the garden devoted to cut flowers. When growing for cut flowers, replant every two to three weeks. The resulting succession provides a longer bloom period and a consistent amount of flowers.

Species that are especially good as cut flowers include **calendula, clarkia, coneflower, delphinium, Mexican sunflower, purple coneflower, snapdragon, stock, sunflower,** and **sweet pea.** Look for varieties that have tall flowering stalks, large or especially showy flowers, and a long season of bloom.

One of the most interesting annuals for desert gardens is the succulent *Dorotheanthus bellidiformis*. This low-growing relative of **ice plants** grows quickly from seed planted in the fall or late winter. It thrives in rocky unamended soil, but is tolerant of almost any soil type as long as it drains well and is not too rich. These diminutive plants make an excellent display in a shallow container. The flowers are open, multipetaled blooms 2 or more inches across in an astounding array of brilliant purple, red, lavender, pink, and white. Use this charmer anywhere you want a potent color display in the early spring.

PLANTING

In Zones 9 and 10, continue to plant native wildflowers from seed through mid-month. Many gardeners plant all their annuals, regardless of the season of their bloom, during the fall. Most seed germinates in response to soil temperature, and it will rest in the ground until conditions are suitable for germination. Continue to set out transplants of cold-hardy annuals like **cockscomb, Iceland poppy, larkspur, lobelia, pansy, snapdragon, statice,** and **strawflower.**

CARE

An early freeze is possible in Zones 8 and 9a. Be prepared to cover tender annuals if a freeze is forecast. Use frost blankets or other light cover for these small, tender plants. Lay the covering gently over the bed and secure it with bricks or rocks to keep it from blowing away.

WATERING

Monitor the water needs of growing annuals carefully Water to keep soil moist to a depth of 4 to 6 inches. Depending on the temperatures, this may be every three to four days, or every week. Once plants are over 2 inches tall, extend the time between waterings so that the soil is dry to the touch before you water.

Water container-grown annuals when the soil in the pot is dry to the touch.

FERTILIZING

Fertilize container-grown annuals once this month with a water-soluble fertilizer at the strength recommended for houseplants. Alternately, add a slow-release fertilizer to the top of the soil and scratch it in lightly. This fertilizer will be released over a time with each watering. Fertilize established annuals in the ground once this month.

PESTS

Watch the watering of seedlings carefully. Soil fungus, particularly damping off disease, is stimulated by cool moist soils. The best prevention is to be sure the soil is slightly dry between waterings and the plants are not too crowded.

December

ANNUALS

PLANNING

Pressing flowers is an old craft for saving the beauty of flowers throughout the year. Begin by selecting a flower that is newly opened before it has had time to get wilted, marred, or faded. Dry it between two sheets of absorbant paper or newsprint, or within the pages of a discarded telephone book. Do not crowd the flowers, and be sure there are one or two pieces of paper between the sheets of flowers. Place a heavy weight like a book, teakettle full of water, or heavy cooking pans on the top layers of drying flowers.

Drying can take a few days or a couple of weeks, depending on the size and condition of the flowers and the humidity at the time. Once they are dried, gently remove them from the paper. They are now ready to be used.

One easy method of using pressed flowers is to use clear contact paper to attach the flowers to a card, note, or rigid paper cut the size of a bookmark. For added interest, include a packet of seed of the same type flower.

Plant a small garden of colorful annuals in a container and give it to a gardening friend who is housebound or who has an apartment or yard that is too small for growing his or her own. Mix the large flowers of **Gerbera** daisy with the delicate flowers of **petunia, primrose,** or **sweet alyssum.** Such tiny gardens will light up the dullest room.

PLANTING

In Zones 9 and 10, continue to set out transplants of hardy annuals like **calendula, candytuft, dianthus, Iceland poppy, larkspur, pansy, petunia, primrose, snapdragon, stock, sweet alyssum,** and **viola.**

Although technically a perennial, bedding **begonias** are used throughout the region for their long season of color. These plants are widely enjoyed for their colorful, crisp foliage and pastel blooms. Plant out transplants from now through mid-January for best results.

Delay planting seed until mid-January. Most annuals do not germinate in cool winter soils.

CARE

Take precautions against freeze damage on tender annuals or newly planted ones. Plants that have been in the ground less than two weeks are much more susceptible to freeze damage than those with well-established root systems. Protect with any lightweight covering on a frosty night, and remove it in the morning. Tents of newspaper work well as temporary frost protection. Secure with rocks, bricks, or other heavy objects. Do not use newspaper if you expect rain with the cold, as the weight of the water makes it heavy and it can break the tender plants beneath.

WATERING

The short days and cool temperatures of this month make it important to monitor watering needs carefully. Most annuals are not actively growing and will not need excessive watering. Water established annuals to a depth of 4 to 6 inches and allow the soil surface to dry between waterings.

Plants in containers may not need watering as frequently as they did a month or two ago. Again, check before watering to be sure the top inch of soil is dry.

FERTILIZING

Do not fertilize this month.

PESTS

Be sure to walk through the garden regularly, looking for early signs of pests or disease. Any infestation or infection is much easier to control if it is found early.

BULBS, CORMS, RHIZOMES, & TUBERS

Bulbs are cheerful plants, and they come up big, boisterous, and ready to go. Every year they spring from their subterranean hideaways full of life, throwing out a full set of leaves and fairly shouting their way into bloom. No wonder they have become the darlings of gardeners around the globe.

Arizona gardeners are fortunate to have a huge array of bulbs from which to choose. Bulbs flower in such a range of styles, colors, and seasons that it is entirely possible to have them in bloom every day of the year. The winter is alight with the soft blue of butterfly lilies, the racy yellows of daffodils, and lovely whites of paper whites.

As spring warms up the soil, a gaudy array of bloom unfolds with orange chasmanthe, multicolored freesia, deep purple grape hyacinth, and variously colored Persian ranunculus and tulips. As spring moves into summer, gardens are adrift in the large trumpets of red, pink, and white amaryllis, iris, and gladiolus. Even in the hottest parts of the state, summer-flowering bulbs such as the pastel rain lily and the crisp white spider lily (*Hymenocallis*) flower over and over again despite the heat. Finally, as the year wears down, the scarlet of oxblood lily and spider lily (*Lycoris*) and the deep violet of crocus find their way to the sun.

CHAPTER TWO

TYPES OF BULBS

The term bulb is handy—gardeners use it to gather up a wildly disparate group of plants. What these plants have in common is the ability to gather and store nutrients in a specialized underground storage organ.

True bulbs are made up of a short, flat stem called the basal plate. Above that is swollen modified leaf tissue, called scales, that creates the storage vessel for the plant. In the center are leaves and flower buds protected by the blanket of scales. Covering the entire bulb is a dry, papery layer called a **tunic** that protects the delicate scales from drying out. Onions are true bulbs, and if you cut one open end to end, you can see these layers clearly. Other true bulbs include amaryllis, daffodil, rain lily, spider lily (*Hymenocallis* and *Lycoris*), and tulip.

A corm is a short, flattened fleshy stem growing underground. Like true bulbs, most corms have a papery covering called a tunic. But if you cut a corm end to end, it would be solid, not layered like a bulb. Plants that grow from corms include butterfly iris, chasmanthe, crocus, freesia, gladiolus, and iris.

Both bulbs and corms make smaller bulbs (bulblets) or corms (cormlets) at the base of the bulb as they mature. They can therefore multiply very rapidly. A mature corm blooms once and is replaced every year by newly formed cormlets. Individual bulbs, on the other hand, can live for many years, sometimes decades.

A rhizome is a swollen underground stem that is elongated rather than flattened like a corm. Rhizomes have growing buds along their length and can form numerous individual plants as they grow. If they are broken apart or divided, each section must have some of these buds to continue to grow. If you cut open a rhizome, it will be solid just like a corm. Some plants that grow from rhizomes are calla, canna, iris, manfreda, and Queen of the Nile.

A tuber is a swollen root, many of which grow to astounding size over the years. Tubers, like rhizomes, have many growing buds (called eyes) from which new stems arise. And like rhizomes, if you cut up a tuber and replant it, there must be at least one of these eyes in the segment. Some of the plants that grow from tubers are caladium, dahlia, Persian ranunculus, and windflower.

HOW BULBS GROW

Many bulbs (and I use the term to include all the plants described above) have a strong dormancy after bloom is finished and the leaves have died off. The most successful bulbs for the Desert Southwest are those that have a strong summer dormancy and an active growing season in the cool, mild winter.

Many bulbs, especially those from subtropical or tropical locales, are evergreen, with active leaf growth throughout the year. But even these types of bulbs have a period of time when they are not actively growing. Gardeners call this a rest. It is important to continue to care for your bulbs appropriately whether they are truly dormant or just at rest.

The most critical time for all bulbs is when they have shot up their leaves and are actively growing. During that time, it is vital to provide conditions that maintain uninterrupted growth, providing regular watering and fertilization, if necessary, and leaving them undisturbed in the ground. It is during this time that all the energy and nutrients for next year's growth and flowering is marshaled into the leaves, stem, or roots. It is always best to move bulbs when they are dormant, or at least resting, and to never remove leaves from a growing plant until they die off naturally.

FLOWERING

Some bulbs, such as oxblood lily, saffron, and spider lily (*Lycoris*), bloom before the leaves emerge. Flowering stalks seem to erupt from bare dirt and can be a splendid surprise if you aren't looking for them.

CHAPTER TWO

Many bulbs, such as butterfly lily, freesia, gladiolus, iris, Naples garlic, and tulip, grow leaves for some time before flowering begins. Others grow leaves all the time and bloom seasonally. Plants like crinum, some rain lilies, and spider lily (*Hymenocallis*) bloom in this way.

USING BULBS

Bulbs blend beautifully into mixed plantings of annuals, perennials, and even succulents. Bulbs that bloom later than the extravagant displays of spring annuals or the displays in a wildflower garden will carry a bed through a longer season with ease. Many bulbs enjoy the same rich, well-drained soils and moderate watering that produces a long perennial display. Tall bulbs such as bugle flower, crinum, and iris offer splendid contrast to the rounded leafy form of most perennials.

Many bulbs, such as arilbred iris, chasmanthe, freesia, and saffron, demand a long, dry summer dormancy. This makes these outstanding partners for succulents such as cactus, agaves, or aloes, either planted among them in the ground or as colorful additions to these plants in containers.

Shade-loving bulbs like caladium, calla, crinum, and spider lily (*Hymenocallis*) brighten up dark corners in the garden, and many have such modest watering needs that they are excellent in areas of deep shade that are not routinely irrigated.

GROWING BULBS IN CONTAINERS

Most of the traits that make bulbs so useful in the garden also make them excellent plants for containers and planters. A single species or variety can be planted in a close spacing in a pot to make a powerful color display. Bulbs that are difficult to culture in the ground can have all their cultural requirements taken care of in a pot. They can be brought out to the patio or porch in their pots while they are in full bloom and parked away out of sight while they are finishing their growth or during dormancy.

CARING FOR BULBS

One of the reasons that bulbs are so popular is that they are so easy to care for. Once you have found bulb species or varieties that are suited to your area, the bulbs generally take care of themselves.

While actively growing, bulbs of all kinds prefer regular, deep watering. Like almost all plants, it is better to water deeply less often than to water lightly and frequently. With very few exceptions, bulbs do not want to dry out entirely when they are growing, nor do they want to be swamped with water.

Mulch bulbs well to keep the soil cool, cut down on evaporation, and maintain an even soil moisture. Mulch is especially crucial for plants that are actively growing through the summer or are grown in areas with hot, drying winds.

If bulbs are given well-amended healthy soil, they usually have all the nutrients they need to grow. But to encourage vigorous flowering, many bulb growers use a steady fertilization regimen for their bulbs. Bulbs grown in containers where nutrients are regularly leached out by steady watering need to be fertilized frequently while they are growing. I find that putting down a rich mix of compost and mulch, often with a small amount of well-composted manure or other organic amendments, twice a year (spring and early fall) is all that well-adapted bulbs need to grow and flower well.

Bulbs are not plagued by many insects and diseases. But birds and ground-dwelling rodents can cause havoc by digging up and eating the bulbs they like. Caging and wire mesh coverings are the only remedies for these relentless predators.

Bulbs

Common/Botanical name	Type	Time of Bloom	Height*	Planting Depth
		Spring	2–3 ft.	1–2 in.
		Spring	3–4 ft.	4–6 in.
		Spring	2–4 ft.	half above soil
		Spring	8–12 in.	1–2 in.
		Spring	10–24 in.	1–2 in.
		Spring	2–4 ft.	4 in.
		Winter/spring	1–2$\frac{1}{2}$ ft.	1–2 in.
		Summer	1–2 ft.	6 in.
		Spring	2–4 ft.	2 in.
		Spring	6–12 in.	2–4 in.
		Summer	1–6 ft.	5 in.
		Spring	2–3 ft.	1–2 in.
		Spring	2–3$\frac{1}{2}$ ft.	1–2 in.
Chives / *Allium schoenoprasum*	Bulb	Spring	8–12 in.	2–3 in.
Common hyacinth / *Hyacinthus orientalis*	Bulb	Spring	8–12 in.	4–6 in.
Crape flower / *Nerine* spp.	Bulb	Summer/fall	1–2 ft.	3–4 in.
Crinum / *Crinum* hybrids	Bulb	Summer	2–5 ft.	neck above soil
Daffodil / *Narcissus* hybrids	Bulb	Winter/spring	6–16 in.	3 × bulb
Dahlia / *Dahlia* hybrids	Tuber	Spring/summer	1–7 ft.	12 in.
Drimiopsis / *Drimiopsis maculata*	Bulb	Summer	8–12 in.	1–2 in.
Fortnight lily / *Dietes bicolor*	Rhizome	Spring/summer	2–3$\frac{1}{3}$ ft.	2–3 in.

CHAPTER TWO

Common Name Botanical Name	Type	Time of Bloom	Height*	Planting Depth
Freesia *Freesia alba/hybrids*	Corm	Spring	4–6 in.	1–2 in.
Garlic chives *Allium tuberosum*	Bulb	Spring	1–1¹/₂ ft.	2–3 in.
Gladiolus *Gladiolus hybrids*	Corm	Spring	2–4 ft.	2–4 in.
Golden crocus *Sternbergia lutea*	Bulb	Fall	6–9 in.	1–2 in.
Grape hyacinth *Muscari armeniacum*	Bulb	Spring	6–8 in.	1–2 in.
Habranthus *Habranthus robustus*	Bulb	Summer	8–10 in.	1–2 in.
Harlequin flower *Sparaxis tricolor*	Corm	Spring	8–12 in.	1–2 in.
Iris *Iris hybrids*	Rhizome	Spring	2–4 ft.	1 in.
Jersey lily *Amaryllis belladonna*	Bulb	Summer	2–4 ft.	neck above soil
Lady tulip *Tulipa clusiana*	Bulb	Spring	6–9 in.	1–2 in.
Louisiana iris *Iris fulva hybrids*	Rhizome	Spring/summer	2–4 ft.	1 in.
Manfreda *Manfreda maculosa/others*	Rhizomes	Spring/summer	4–6 ft.	3–4 in.
Montbretia *Crocosmia hybrids*	Corm	Spring/summer	2–4 ft.	2 in.
Naples garlic *Allium neopolitanum*	Bulb	Spring	10–24 in.	2–3 in.
Natal lily *Clivia miniata*	Bulb	Spring	1¹/₂–2 ft.	half above soil
Ornamental onion *Allium christophii*	Bulb	Spring	1–2 ft.	3–5 × bulb
Oxblood lily *Rhodophiala bifida*	Bulb	Fall	1–1¹/₂ ft.	3–4 in.
Paper white/Jonquil *Narcissus tazetta* and hybrids	Bulb	Spring	8–12 in.	3 × bulb
Persian ranunculus *Ranunculus asiaticus*	Tuber	Spring	1¹/₂–2 ft.	2 in.
Pink sorrel *Oxalis bowiei*	Bulb	Spring/summer	4–6 in.	1 in.
Pregnant onion *Ornithogalum longibracteatum*	Bulb	Summer	1–3 ft.	half above soil
Queen of the Nile *Agapanthus orientalis*	Rhizome	Spring/summer	2–5 ft.	1 in.

CHAPTER TWO

Common Name Botanical Name	Type	Time of Bloom	Height*	Planting Depth
Rain lily *Zephyranthes citrina/grandiflora*	Bulb	Summer	6–9 in.	1–2 in.
Rain lily *Zephyranthes reginae/rosea*	Bulb	Summer	6–9 in.	1–2 in.
Red squill/sea onion *Urginea maritima*	Bulb	Winter/spring	1–3 ft.	half above soil
Saffron *Crocus sativus*	Corm	Fall/winter	3–6 in.	2–3 in.
Snowdrop *Galanthus elwesii*	Bulb	Winter/spring	10–12 in.	3–4 in.
Society garlic *Tulbaghia violacea*	Rhizome	Spring	1–2 ft.	2–4 in.
Soldier-in-the-box/ Sentry box *Albuca canadensis/nelsoni*	Bulb	Spring	8–12in.	1–2 in.
Spider lily *Hymenocallis* hybrids	Bulb	Summer	2–4 ft.	half above soil
Spider lily *Lycoris radiata*	Bulb	Summer/fall	1–1^1/2 ft.	3–4 in.
Spring star flower *Ipheion uniflorum*	Bulb	Spring	4–6 in.	1–2 in.
Squill *Scilla peruviana*	Bulb	Spring/summer	6–12 in.	3–4 in.
Star of Bethlehem *Ornithogalum arabicum*	Bulb	Spring	1–2 ft.	2–4 in.
Sweet potato *Ipomoea batatas*	Tuber	Summer	10 ft.	4–6 in.
Texas star flower *Zephyranthes drummondii*	Bulb	Summer	6–9 in.	1–2 in.
Tiger flower *Tigridia pavonia*	Bulb	Summer	1–2^1/2 ft.	2–4 in.
Tuberose *Polianthes tuberosa*	Rhizome	Spring	1–2 ft.	2 in.
Tulip *Tulipa* hybrids	Bulb	Spring	1–3 ft.	4–10 in.
Windflower *Anemone coronaria*/hybrids	Tuber	Spring	6–18 in.	1–2 in.
Zephyr lily *Zephyranthes candida*	Bulb	Summer	4–6 in.	1–2 in.

*Height includes bloom

JANUARY
BULBS, CORMS, RHIZOMES, & TUBERS

Daffodil

PLANNING

To make sure markers are not lost, it is a good idea to take time to check for those that were set out in the fall when new bulbs or **iris** were planted. **Saffron crocus** blooms this month in Zones 9 and 10. If you like **saffron,** try drying the red pistils to make your own supply of this delectable spice.

Daffodils and **jonquils** begin to emerge late in the month, and early varieties may begin to bloom in all zones. Take note of how thick they are and whether they cover as much area as you intended. While many varieties multiply readily in the desert regions, others remain almost solitary. Taking notes now will help you plan for better effects next fall.

PLANNING

In Zones 9 and 10, set out **hybrid tulips** and **hyacinth** bulbs that have been prechilled. Bulbs that require prechilling are essentially annuals in this region and rarely hold over and rebloom. Be sure they have been in the refrigerator for a minimum of six to eight weeks before you set them out.

Plant these bulbs in well-amended soil, 4 inches deep, and toss a handful of balanced fertilizer in the bottom of the hole. Water well after planting.

Prechilled bulbs may also be planted in containers. Use a well-drained mix incorporating slow-release fertilizer. Set the bulbs 4 inches deep in the pot, and water well after planting. Keep in full sun while they continue to grow and bloom.

If you have the room and enough bulbs, stagger the planting every two weeks to extend the blooming season.

In Zone 8, plant **amaryllis** bulbs late in the month.

CARE

Most **iris** can tolerate light frost, but if it is going to be especially cold, cover with straw mulch for the night and remove the mulch in the morning.

WATERING

Cool soils hold moisture for a long time, and it is important not to overwater bulbs and **iris** this month. Water only when the soil is dry 1 to 2 inches below the surface. Depending on the temperatures, this could be every other week.

While plants in pots will need to be watered more frequently, water only when the soil surface is dry.

FERTILIZING

Fertilize **iris** in Zones 9b and 10 late in the month. In areas of Zone 9a that may still have freezing nights, wait a month before fertilizing **iris**, whch respond well to balanced complete formulas like 15-15-15. Apply fertilizer by carefully scratching the soil around the rhizomes, taking care not to nick or cut them. Spread the fertilizer around the plant, following label directions for the correct amount. Scratch it in gently and water it in well.

Organic gardeners may apply a 1- to 2-inch layer of compost or mulch, or an organic blended fertilizer this month. Organic amendments work more slowly than inorganic sources and continue to provide nutrients over a long period of time. Use a cultivator or a trowel to scratch the amendments into the soil, and water thoroughly.

Bulbs growing in containers are fertilized one of two ways. One way is to add slow-release granular fertilize to the soil mix when planting the bulbs; these formulas typically last one to two months. Alternately, fertilize bulbs by using a water-soluble fertilizer at two-week intervals while the bulbs are actively growing. Mix the fertilizer with water at the rates recommended on the package in a bucket or watering can, and pour into the pot.

GROOMING

Do not prune this month.

PESTS

Birds are fond of many bulbs, especially **crocus, harlequin flower,** and **moraea.** If you find that your bulbs are being ravaged by birds, protect them with a covering of wire mesh, or plant in a wire cage. One-inch-diameter wire keeps out the birds but allow the stems to grow up through the holes. After planting bulbs, cut a piece of wire large enough to fit over the entire area where the bulbs are planted, laying it on top of the soil. Secure the wire with metal hairpin stakes or stones. Cover lightly with soil to hide the wire.

If you have moles, voles, squirrels, or other animals that regularly eat bulbs, protect the bulbs by growing them inside a wire mesh cage that is plunged into the ground. These cages also are built from 1-inch-diameter wire that is bent to look like a bucket. Put the bulbs in the bottom of the cage and bend the top to close it. Plunge the entire cage in the ground.

HELPFUL HINTS

Many bulb books and catalogs recommend applying wood ash as a fertilizer or supplement to bulbs or bulb beds. This is not recommended in the Desert Southwest because wood ash is very alkaline, and so are our soils. Continuous additions of wood ash can quickly raise the alkalinity in a bed to levels toxic to plants. Organic matter like mulch and compost are much better soil additives for our soils.

FEBRUARY
BULBS, CORMS, RHIZOMES, & TUBERS

 PLANNING

Begin to look for bulbs of summer-flowering species like **crinum, canna, spider lily** (*Hymenocallis*), and **tiger flower.** Buy bulbs that are large and firm and have no visible spots or deformities.

Gladiolus last longer and are more reliable in the cooler parts of Zone 9 and throughout Zone 8. In areas where they do not hold up to the heat, consider them annuals and replant each year.

There are hundreds of **gladiolus** cultivars in a bewildering array of colors and styles. Plant a selection of **gladiolus** that vary in height and color for added effect. **Gladiolus** also do well planted at two-week intervals through the late spring, regardless of your zone, to provide a succession of bloom.

Gardeners in the hottest areas find that **acidanthera** and the so-called 'nana' or 'trista' varieties of **gladiolus** are especially successful as spring-flowering bulbs. But even these varieties do not usually live through the summer.

 PLANTING

Late in the month, begin planting summer-flowering bulbs like **calla, crinum, spider lily,** and **tiger flower** in Zone 10 and the warmest parts of Zone 9. **Amaryllis, crape flower, crinum,** and **spider lily** (*Lycoris radiata*) can be planted this month in Zone 8.

Plant in soil that has been enriched with organic matter and has excellent drainage. In Zone 10 and the hottest parts of Zone 9, plant these bulbs in either high, filtered shade or deep shade, although **crinum** will tolerate full sun if well watered. For best results, pick a spot that has full protection from afternoon sun in the summer. In Zone 8, plant these bulbs in full sun or light, filtered shade.

Consult the bulb chart on pages 45-47 for recommended planting depths for other bulbs. **Crinum** and **spider lily** (both genera) resent being lifted or moved, so plant them where they can grow undisturbed for many years.

Continue to set out prechilled bulbs like **hybrid tulips** and **hyacinth** through the middle of the month in Zone 10 and the warmest parts of Zone 9.

In Zone 8, begin to plant **gladiolus.** To extend the blooming season, plant some bulbs weekly through the end of the month.

 CARE

In Zones 9 and 10, cut back the foliage of established clumps of **canna** almost to the ground, and apply a well-balanced, slow-release fertilizer around the rhizomes. Apply a 4- to 6-inch layer of compost or mulch around the roots, or apply a slow-release balanced fertilizer. Water deeply and continue to water regularly as the rhizomes begin to send up new shoots.

Canna grows quickly and multiplies each year. Every three or four years, dig up the entire clump to decrease its size and increase its vigor. Look over the rhizomes carefully; discard the largest and oldest rhizomes or any with signs of damage or disease, then replant the rest. Fertilize after replanting, and water regularly.

Lady tulip and many **gladiolus** are the last bulbs to begin growth in the spring.

 WATERING

Water blooming or actively growing bulbs when the surface of the soil is dry. Water to a depth of 4 to 6 inches each time.

Bulbs in pots should be watched closely, as the weather can warm quickly this month in Zones 9 and 10. Water container-grown bulbs when the soil is dry to the touch. This may be once or twice a week this month.

Begin to increase the watering frequency of iris to once a month.

 FERTILIZING

Apply another round of fertilizer to **iris. Tall bearded iris,** in particular, are sensitive to the amount of nitrogen they receive, and they need a low-nitrogen fertilizer. Continue to regularly fertilize container-grown bulbs if you are using a water-soluble fertilizer. Be sure to water the pot thoroughly as you apply it.

Some fertilizer formulas are available as spikes or small pellets that can be plunged into the pot. These convenient applications work well for plants growing in containers.

There are numerous organic formulations that are water-soluble. Check that the formula is well balanced and contains all three of the major nutrients (NPK) before using it on bulbs.

 GROOMING

Do not prune this month.

HELPFUL HINTS

• Most bulbs need a reliable source of phosphorus to bloom best, but phosphorus does not move through the soil as readily as nitrogen and other nutrients. This is why it is important to put whatever phosphorus source you are providing to the bulbs in the bottom of the hole when planting. As they grow, the roots will encounter the area where the phosphorus is located, making it readily available to the plant.

• Many bulbs make outstanding cut flowers. Spring-flowering bulbs that are especially good cut flowers are **daffodil, hyacinth, iris,** and **tulip.** To keep cut flowers fresh and extend their life, cut them just before they open in the early morning. Make a diagonal cut, and plunge the blooms in tepid water immediately. Change the water in the vase daily to prevent bacterial growth. Freshly cut **daffodils** and **iris** last four to seven days, **tulips** last three to four days, and **hyacinth** flowers last over a week.

 PESTS

In Zones 9 and 10, aphids may begin to show up as the weather warms. Strong jets of water remove these tiny sucking insects, or they can be removed by hand if the infestation is small. If you choose to use an insecticide, be sure it is rated to work on aphids, follow directions carefully, and use it only when the number of aphids is significant enough to warrant treatment.

If you were not able to cage bulbs and you still have problems with rodents or other animals, try the red pepper treatment. Mix dried red peppers—the hotter the better—with water and a tiny amount of detergent to create a pepper spray. A good rule-of-thumb formula is eight to ten dried peppers, a quart of water, and a scant teaspoon of detergent (Dawn® is particularly effective). Put the mixture in a marked spray bottle and keep it on hand for use throughout the season. Spray the pepper mixture on the plant, and be sure to get it on the underside of the leaves as well as on the soil. It needs to be applied frequently and reapplied after a rain or overhead watering.

Another variation is to take very hot dried peppers, crush them in a blender or spice grinder to make a fine powder, and shake it over the soil. This volatile dust helps deter four-footed pests and has long been used and recommended to prevent dogs from digging.

51

MARCH
BULBS, CORMS, RHIZOMES, & TUBERS

PLANNING

Shop for **amaryllis, caladium, canna, manfreda,** and **rain lily** (both *Habranthus* and *Zephyranthes*). All of these summer-growing, summer-blooming bulbs want to be planted in soils that are at least 65 degrees Fahrenheit. Look for bulbs that are large for the group offered, firm to the touch, have no soft, brown, or discolored spots, and feel heavy for their size. Bulbs that are sprouting are fine if you are planning to plant them immediately; otherwise, be sure there is no sign of green on the bulb. If you store purchased bulbs, keep them in brown paper bags in a cool, dry location until ready to plant.

Cannas are often tall, over 6 feet, and this can be difficult for many gardens. Look for shorter varieties if you have a small garden. Try 'Grand Opera', 'Pfitzer's Dwarf', and 'Seven Dwarfs'. These plants grow only to about 2 feet tall.

If you were not able to plant **calla, crinum, spider lily,** or **tiger flower** because it was too cold, begin to plant this month as the danger of frost recedes.

Dry shade is one of the most difficult locations for many desert gardens. Good shade choices include:
• **Caladium**

• **Calla** (especially good in dense shade)
• **Drimiopsis** (commonly available in succulent nurseries)
• **Manfreda**
• **Natal lily**
• **Spider lily** (including the native *Hymenocallis sonorensis*)

PLANTING

Plant **amaryllis, caladium, calla, crinum, manfreda,** and **spider lily** as soon as the soil temperature is above 65 degrees Fahrenheit and the air temperature is well over 70 degrees. In Zones 9b and 10 these temperatures occur by the end of the month, but they will come one or two months later in Zone 9a and Zone 8, respectively.

An **amaryllis** bulb is planted with at least half the bulb above the soil line. Many growers recommend that the entire bulb be above the soil line, with only the roots in the soil.

Iris

Small bulbs like **rain lily** and **manfreda** are planted so that the top of the bulb is just below the surface of the soil.

Plant **canna** deep, about 5 inches below the surface, but leave the neck of the bulb exposed. Because **canna** grows and spreads quickly, space the bulbs about 10 inches apart to avoid having to divide them too frequently.

Provide a 3- to 4-inch layer of mulch, more if you are using something light like pine straw, for all summer-growing bulbs. This helps keep moisture levels even, roots cool, and prevents the soil from drying out too quickly.

In Zone 8, plant **canna, crape flower, crinum, gladiolus,** and **spider lily** (*Lycoris*) once the soils have begun to warm late in the month. Continue planting through April.

CARE

Clean out **canna** beds to remove winter-damaged leaves and other debris. Keeping these old leaves and stems cleaned out is the best way to prevent insect infestations. If you have not cut back **canna** already, do so this month. After cutting back, fertilize and resume regular watering.

HELPFUL HINTS

There are many ways to mark the bulbs you have in the ground. Aluminum tags provide one of the most permanent ways to mark bulbs. When you write directly on the tag with a pencil or ballpoint pen, you make a permanent impression. The tag is then attached to a stake, wrapped around a piece of coat hanger or threaded through a metal hairpin stake. If you cannot find aluminum tags, tin roof flashing cut to the desired size works just as well. Aluminum tags last a long time without disintegrating and can be covered with mulch or soil to hide them without losing the information.

WATERING

The weather warms quickly this month in Zones 9 and 10, so keep a sharp eye on watering schedules for blooming and growing bulbs. Increase the watering frequency in these areas for **iris**. Once temperatures are routinely over 90 degrees Fahrenheit, water **iris** once a week. Water actively growing or blooming bulbs when the surface of the soil is dry. Water to a depth of 6 inches.

FERTILIZING

Fertilize actively growing and blooming container plants with a soluble fertilizer every other week.

GROOMING

Cut off spent flowers as they finish. Maturing seeds take a lot of energy from a bulb, so it is best to remove any seedpods that set unless you are saving the seeds. Do not cut off yellowing or dying leaves from early-flowering bulbs. Let them die off naturally before removing them.

PESTS

Most bulbs have few pests, but watch for aphids, and control quickly. In wet winters, weeds can be overwhelming in all zones. Remove weeds continuously from around bulbs to reduce competition, keep the beds tidy, and reduce the number of weeds that go to seed.

APRIL
BULBS, CORMS, RHIZOMES, & TUBERS

 PLANNING

Continue to shop for **amaryllis, caladium, canna, crinum,** and **spider lily** bulbs in Zone 8.

As bulb varieties, especially **iris,** come into bloom, be sure that you have marked them. If you plan to divide **iris** this year, write the name of the variety with a permanent marker pen on one of the leaves.

Look for bulbs of the **oxblood lily.** This South American relative of **amaryllis** sends up its scarlet flowers in September before the leaves emerge. This plant is well known in the Deep South and is often found growing among abandoned farmhouses and settlements. It grows best in at least a half-day of sun but will grow, spread, and bloom in any kind of soil, including unamended native soils.

Many of the most well-known summer-flowering bulbs have a difficult time in the warmest parts of the region. **Montbretia** and **Queen of the Nile** in particular can be difficult in the hottest areas. These bulbs thrive in Zone 8, however, and in the cooler parts of Zone 9 with afternoon shade. Put both in beds with well-amended, rich soils, and provide generous mulch to maintain even moisture through the summer.

In most areas, **society garlic** declines in the summer, but if kept well watered and shaded from the afternoon sun, it will come back in the fall. It is a good late-spring bloomer in the warmest parts of the region.

 PLANTING

Continue planting summer-flowering bulbs such as **crinum, habranthus, rain lily,** and **spider lily** in Zones 9 and 10.

Begin planting summer-flowering bulbs such as **callas, canna, crinum, dahlia,** and **spider lily** once all danger of frost is past in Zone 8.

 CARE

It is sometimes hard to know whether to lift and store bulbs, leave them in the ground, or just start all over again every year.

Generally, any bulb that had to be artificially prechilled must be lifted, stored, and prechilled again to get them to rebloom the following year. Many of the varieties of **hybrid tulip** and **hyacinth** are not reliable rebloomers, however, and it may be best to just consider them as annuals.

Amaryllis, daffodil, and **lady tulip** may be left in the ground through the summer even when they are dormant. These bulbs do not like to be entirely dry during that time, however, and should receive intermittent watering then. Mixing them with perennials and other summer-flowering plants makes this easy.

Candia tulip, chasmanthe, freesia, homeria, soldier-in-the-box, and **star of Bethlehem** may be left in the ground through the summer but need to be kept as dry as possible. This makes them excellent choices to mix with succulents or other sturdy desert plants that will receive only intermittent or occasional watering during the summer.

Arilbred irises need to be kept entirely dry during the summer and thus make a good choice for beds that are watered only occasionally.

Gladiolus in all parts of the region survive best if they are lifted when the leaves die off, dried out in a shady spot, and then stored before fall replanting.

 WATERING

Keep a sharp eye on the water needs of **iris** and **amaryllis** this month. The weather can warm quickly in the warmest areas, and they will need regular deep soaks to continue growing and blooming. Apply a 3- to 4-inch layer of mulch to help maintain even soil moisture.

FERTILIZING

Continue to fertilize **iris** monthly while they are growing and blooming. If you did not fertilize summer-flowering bulbs growing in the ground in March, do so this month.

If you are using water-soluble fertilizer for container bulbs, continue to apply it every other week while they are blooming and the leaves are still green.

GROOMING

This month it can be hard to keep the pruners off the plants, and most spring-flowering bulbs are losing their leaves steadily in the increasing heat in Zone 10 and the warmest parts of Zone 9. But hold off on cutting the leaves off bulbs; wait until they will pull off in your hand. Never cut green leaves from a bulb, as this can compromise the bloom and vigor for next year.

PESTS

Iris can be invaded by the iris borer. Symptoms include a sudden decline of a flowering stalk or failure of buds to open, coupled with dark, watery masses on the leaves. Cut off and destroy the infected part and the insect inside. It is possible to use systemic insecticides to prevent infestations, but they must be applied according to package directions. It is usually only worth the effort in large beds that are devoted to **iris** to prevent a quick population explosion of the insect.

HELPFUL HINTS

• The leaves of many bulbs remain for one or two months after the end of flowering. This growth is critical to the health of the bulb and the bloom next year, but sometimes they are unsightly as they turn yellow and decline. Hide them by bundling the leaves. To do this, gather all the leaves in your hand and gently twist the entire mass from the base upward to hold them tightly together. Secure with twine or twist-ties. Fold over once or twice, depending on the length, toward the ground, and secure the bundle again with twine or rubber bands. Once they are entirely dormant, pull off the entire bundle and throw it on the compost pile.

• Hybridizing **iris** is fun, not difficult, and does not require any special equipment. To begin, select two plants that bloom at roughly the same time and that you want to cross. Decide which one you will use for its pollen (pollen parent) and which one you want to set the seed (seed parent). As soon as the blooms open, remove an anther from the pollen parent and rub the pollen on all three of the stigmas on the seed parent. Noting the names of both parents and the date, put a tag on the blooming stalk. If your pollination was successful, a pod will form in seven to ten days. It will then take about six weeks for the seed to be mature. Seed should be harvested when it is dark and the pod begins to open. Dry it out, store in a dry, cool spot, then plant in the fall in well-drained potting soil. The seedlings should grow 5 to 6 inches by the following spring, at which time they can either be planted out or put in larger containers. It can take from one to three years for your new variety to bloom, and then you will find out what you have.

NOTES

MAY

BULBS, CORMS, RHIZOMES, & TUBERS

 PLANNING

The late-blooming varieties of **bearded iris** like 'Dusky Challenger', 'Gypsy Romance,' 'Tequila Sunrise', and 'Thrillseeker' continue to bloom. In the cooler areas of Zone 9 and in Zone 8, this is the prime blooming month for **bearded iris.** Excellent varieties include 'Gladys Austin', 'Masked Bandit', 'Memo', 'Navy Blue', 'Pale Cloud', 'Perfume Shop', and 'Space Age'.

Iris are such familiar garden plants that it is easy to get lost in the welter of names, cultivars, and types that are available. The most reliable forms of **iris** for this region include:

• **Bearded iris,** which is also known as **German iris, germanica,** or **flags.** It has three erect petals that close together like a cup called **standards,** and three that hang down toward the stem called **falls.** At the base of each of the falls is a set of fine hairs known as the beard. **Bearded iris** come in many colors and color combinations, are generally very cold hardy, and arise from rhizomes. There are over 1100 named cultivars, but most gardeners are wise to choose from ones that are well-known, or well-tested for their particular area. Growers have developed newer cultivars that may bloom again in fall, and

they are known as rebloomer or remontant varieties.

• **Arilbred** refers to a complicated **iris** hybrid group that combines the bizarre, often spectacular, blooming style of a group of hybrids known as **arils** and **tall bearded iris.** The colors of most of these varieties are a heady mixture of chartreuse, purple, and brown intermingled with yellow and blue. The resulting **arilbreds** are vigorous plants with tall blooming stalks, extreme heat tolerance, and a demand for a long, hot, dry summer dormancy. These rhizomatous plants are among the most drought- and heat-tolerant of all **iris.**

• **Louisiana iris** are cultivars of *Iris fulva,* a Southeastern United States native. The plants are tall, with thin leaves and slim form. **Louisiana iris** spread rapidly when grown with abundant moisture and high heat. They grow from a rhizome and can also be grown in or around ponds. They bloom much later than **bearded iris** or **arilbred.**

• **Spuria iris** is a group of cultivars that are tall, erect plants with flowers that are smaller than those of most **bearded iris.** They grow well in full sun in most areas of the region, but afternoon shade is advised in the hottest areas. Some **spuria** are evergreen, while others require a dry late-summer dormancy. **Spurias** are not as cold

hardy as the previous groups and need to be protected with a thick layer of mulch on freezing nights.

• **Dutch iris** have true bulbs and are not reliably hardy where temperatures can be expected to fall below 10 degrees Fahrenheit. Even in milder areas it is best to protect them during extended cold spells, or plant them in the spring. So-called **Spanish iris** are quite similar.

 PLANTING

Continue to plant **caladium, crinum, dahlia** (Zone 8), **rain lily** (both *Habranthus* and *Zephyranthes*), and **spider lily** (both *Hymenocallis* and *Lycoris*).

To plant **dahlias,** dig a hole that is up to 12 inches or more deep, depending on the size of the tuber. Place the tuber in the hole and cover it with up to 3 inches of soil. As the shoot grows, continue to fill the hole until the tuber is completely covered. Keep well watered during this time and all during active growth. **Dahlias** are tricky in the hottest parts of the region—it often gets too hot just as they are ready to bloom. In these areas, plant early in the year, mulch plants heavily, and hope for a cool spring.

Rain lily bulbs do not like to dry out and are therefore often sold while actively growing. To plant container-grown **rain lilies,** dig a hole that will accommodate the entire root mass of the plant and work a balanced fertilizer into the bottom of the hole. Set the entire mass of plants in the hole just deep enough to cover the top of the bulb. There are often countless individual bulbs in the pot. Take the time to separate the bulbs into three or four groups, and spread the clumps around the bed to enhance their impact. Apply a 2-inch layer of mulch to plants after planting, and water in well.

Crinum

CARE

Continue to allow the foliage of spring-blooming bulbs to die back naturally. Once the leaves of bulbs in pots begin to turn yellow and die, stop fertilizing, reduce watering by half, and let the foliage die down completely. If the pot has nothing but bulbs in it and you want to try to rebloom the plants next year, set it aside in the shade for summer. Water sparingly according to the dormancy needs of the bulb.

WATERING

After **iris** have completed their bloom, reduce the frequency of watering to every ten days. This will slow down growth and provide a moderately dry summer rest. Be careful not to water **iris** from overhead; this will encourage rotting of the rhizomes.

FERTILIZING

In the warmest areas, fertilize **iris** one more time this month, then do not fertilize at all over the remainder of the summer. For all **iris,** lay down a 2- to 4-inch layer of mulch, but be careful that the mulch does not cover the rhizomes or mound up around the leaves. If the leaves seem especially yellow, add an iron supplement or iron chelate to the soil.

Continue to fertilize container-grown bulbs until the leaves start to die back.

GROOMING

Do not prune dead leaves from bulbs; wait until they come away easily in your hand. Clip out spent flowers at any time to keep plants tidy. Remove any seedpods that you are not saving as soon as they form.

PESTS

Watch for signs of iris borer. Treat quickly by removing the affected stem and killing the insect. Some growers recommend using systemic insecticides to control this pest where it is prevalent. Follow package directions carefully for best results.

JUNE
BULBS, CORMS, RHIZOMES, & TUBERS

PLANNING

Rain lily (*Habranthus*) and **crinum** begin to bloom this month in Zones 9 and 10. Both of these bulbs do best with light, filtered shade, or in a location with morning sun. Although tolerant of very alkaline soils, both of these types of bulbs prefer soils with good drainage and lots of organic matter. If your plants seem smaller than you expected, or bloom weakly, it is usually a sign that the soil is not rich enough or the plants are drying out too quickly. To ameliorate these problems, add plenty of mulch to all summer-growing bulbs, and replenish it frequently through the growing season.

Ornamental sweet potato is a fast-growing tropical vine that arises from a tuberous root. **Sweet potatoes** thrive in high heat and humidity. Although more commonly grown as annuals for the edible roots, these frost-tender plants have had a number of ornamental selections made in recent years. **Ornamental sweet potatoes** are especially effective when grown in containers where the long, colorful vines can hang down. If the vines freeze back, lift and store the root to replant next year. Selections include:

• 'Blackie', a vigorous vine with large, dark purple, nearly black, leaves

• 'Margarita', which has pale chartreuse foliage

• 'Tricolor', also known as 'Pink Frost', which has light-green leaves marked with pink or white

PLANTING

Rain lily (*Zephyranthes*) can still be planted in Zones 9 and 10. The small size and repeat bloom through the summer make **rain lily** a good choice for containers. Mix equal parts compost, sand, perlite or pumice, and high-quality potting soil. Add a slow-release fertilizer to the pot, incorporating it into the soil mix. Place the bulbs in the soil so

Canna

that the bulb is barely covered. Spread the bulbs evenly around the pot; they multiply quickly and within two or three years will completely fill the pot.

CARE

Protect **canna** from high winds and fierce afternoon sun. **Canna** appreciates increased humidity, so when there are dry, scalding winds, spray the plants every morning.

Provide plenty of room for **crinum;** both the original bulb and subsequent bulbs can grow very large. **Crinum** may cease to bloom for a year or two after being moved, so try to find a place where the plants can grow undisturbed for many years. If it is necessary to lift or divide **crinum,** begin by taking bulbs from the outer edge of the clump rather than digging out the entire mass of bulbs. When you do it this way, you leave the oldest bulbs in place, where they will continue to thrive and bloom for many years to come.

Continue to keep **iris** beds clean by removing spent flowering stalks and weeds that might crowd around the rhizomes. Do not cut any leaves at this time.

Mulch all summer-growing bulbs with a 3- to 4-inch layer of bark, pine straw, clean hay, or other organic matter. Do not use fresh grass clippings as mulch—they begin to decompose quickly and can rob the soil of available nitrogen.

WATERING

Watch plants carefully, and water deeply when the temperatures are very high. All bulbs prefer infrequent deep soaks that wet the soil to a depth of 6 inches over light frequent waterings. Be especially careful not to overhead-water **iris**—it encourages rotting.

Bulbs in pots need water when the surface of the soil is dry, and this could be every day when temperatures are very high. The best strategy is to check pots every day, plunging your finger in the soil to the depth of your first knuckle. If the soil feels dry, water thoroughly. You can also use handheld water meters or a long screwdriver to check the moisture level.

FERTILIZING

Do not fertilize this month.

GROOMING

Do not prune except to remove spent flowering stalks or seed-pods.

PESTS

Iris soft rot is a bacterial disease that can infect the rhizome of an **iris.** Symptoms are soft, dark to black areas at the base of the leaves and a putrid smell. To treat an infestation, pull or cut out all portions of the infected rhizome and discard it. Mix a solution of one part bleach and nine parts water, and drench the rhizomes with this solution. Follow with a dusting of powdered sulphur or the cleaning powder Comet™ (it, too, contains bleach).

Decide if root nematodes or other soilborne pests are severe enough to warrant solarizing the soil. See Helpful Hint on page 63 for details.

JULY
BULBS, CORMS, RHIZOMES, & TUBERS

PLANNING

This is a good time to look through catalogs and place your final orders for **iris.** Most vendors ship iris in the late summer or early fall.

As moisture from the monsoon wind shift flows into the region, **spider lily** (*Hymenocallis*) and **rain lily** (*Zephyranthes*) begin to bloom in most areas. **Rain lilies** are a large group of bulbs, many of which are new to desert gardeners, from southern Texas and Mexico. They are some of the most reliable summer bloomers for the region and will live many years with minimal care, coming back year after year to bloom in the hottest part of the summer. Most send up flowers repeatedly in late summer after it rains. Varieties include:

* *Zephyranthes grandiflora* has the familiar 3-inch pink flowers that pop up in lawns after a rain.
* *Z. rosea* is similar but smaller, with deep-pink flowers that have pale pink-and-green centers that look like eyes.
* *Z. citrina* (often mistakenly called *Z. sulphurea*) has a deep golden-yellow flower.
* *Z. reginae* has bright pure-yellow flowers and is nearly evergreen.

* *Z. candida* is entirely evergreen and grows as a thick clump of deep-green rounded leaves with white flowers late in the summer through fall.
* *Z. drummondii* (also sold as *Cooperia drummondii*) has 8-inch tubular white flowers in the late summer and early fall.
* 'Ajax' is a hybrid between *Z. candida* and *Z. citrina* whose blooms begin yellow and age to pale gold.
* 'Prairie Sunset' blooms pale apricot to pink.

Look for these and other varieties of **rain lily** through Telos Rare Bulbs of Arcata, California, and Yucca Do Nursery in Hempstead, Texas. Some of these species are available as potted plants in the region.

PLANTING

Plant **iris** rhizomes this month in Zone 8. Provide a location with full sun, rich well-amended soil, and excellent drainage. In this same area, begin to divide **iris** that have been undisturbed for over three years, or if they are declining. In hotter zones (Zones 9 and 10), wait until late August or September to divide **iris.**

CARE

Iris may begin to look yellowed and dry in the hottest areas. Maintain watering every ten days, and resist the urge to cut off or remove the dead leaves. Add a layer of mulch to any bulbs that are growing and still blooming if the soil appears to be drying out too quickly between waterings. Be careful that mulch is not smothering the rhizome or holding too much water close to it.

Iris rhizome

True bulb

BOOKS FOR BULB FANCIERS IN THE DESERT SOUTHWEST

Here are some special books you can give as gifts or collect for your library.

• Bryan, John E. *Bulbs*. Portland, Oregon: Timber Press, 2002. This revised edition of the author's two-volume set published in 1989 is the bible for all serious bulb growers.

• Howard, Thad. *Bulbs for Warm Climates*. Austin, Texas: University of Austin Press, 2001.

Howard is particularly knowledgeable about Mexican bulbs.

• Ogden, Scott. *Garden Bulbs for the South*. Second Edition. Portland, Oregon: Timber Press, 2007. This is a delightful study of bulbs that do well in the Deep South, but most are equally suitable for Arizona.

 WATERING

Continue to water summer-growing bulbs to a depth of 6 inches through the long days of summer. In the hottest areas, this usually means watering weekly.

 FERTILIZING

For summer-growing bulbs in containers, apply a water-soluble fertilizer once a month during the summer. Follow label recommendations, and dissolve fertilizer in water in a jar or watering can before applying to the plants.

If you have lots of pots to water and fertilize, siphons are a quick, handy way to get it done. A siphon is a brass fitting that is attached to a faucet on one end and the hose on the other. There is a rubber tube on the side that is placed into a container of dissolved fertilizer. The solution is drawn up through the hose and applied as you water. Look for siphons in any garden center or full-service nursery.

 GROOMING

When dividing **iris**, cut back the leaves to 6 or 8 inches when you remove them from the ground. Otherwise, do not prune any bulbs this month except to remove spent flowers and seedpods.

 PESTS

Watch for grasshoppers or other chewing insects that arrive in high numbers in some years. Handpick these chewing insects if there are only a few, or apply products specifically formulated for grasshoppers for larger infestations.

 NOTES

_____

_____

_____

_____

_____

_____

_____

_____

_____

AUGUST
BULBS, CORMS, RHIZOMES, & TUBERS

PLANNING

If you are planning a new bed for bulbs or **iris,** prepare the bed two or three weeks before you intend to plant. Turn the soil; remove any weeds, rocks, or other litter from the soil. Add a 4- to 6-inch layer of compost or mulch. Mix in a slow-release balanced fertilizer or a mixture of organic amendments like well-composted manure, bloodmeal, alfalfa meal, and bonemeal. If the drainage needs to be improved, add sharp sand. Mix it all well by turning it to a depth of 6 to 8 inches. Water the bed slowly and deeply, and let it sit for a few days. Check to be sure that the drainage is excellent and there are no low spots in the bed. Keep moderately watered until you are ready to plant.

This is a fine time to look through the catalogs and make decisions on which varieties you wish to grow for spring blooming next year. Consult the journal notes you made in the spring about which plants did well, and decide how many you want.

While botanists disagree on whether there are fifty or seventy species of **daffodil** in the genus *Narcissus,* gardeners and bulb enthusiasts recognize hundreds of varieties and hybrids divided into thirteen divisions, based on

their flowering form. In Zones 9 and 10, **daffodils** in Division 7, **Jonquilla** and Division 8 **Tazetta** groups perform the best. These types of **daffodils** need little or no chill and therefore can accommodate the mild winters of most of the region. **Paper whites** fall into the tazetta group. Almost any type of **daffodil** can be grown in containers or prechilled if necessary. Many, like **paper whites,** can be forced to bloom earlier than normal to provide indoor bloom through the winter.

Tulips are one of the most stunning additions to a spring garden but are unreliable rebloomers in the desert. The hybrid forms that crowd bulb catalogs need to be prechilled before planting. Some of the **species tulips,** however, especially **lady tulip** and **candia tulip,** do extremely well in the ground, blooming for many years.

PLANTING

In Zone 8, continue to plant newly purchased **iris,** or divide plants that have been in the ground for more than three years. Planting **iris** this early gives them plenty of time to establish a root system and gain size before it gets cold.

Growing bulbs from seed is an easy and rewarding way to

increase the number of types of bulbs that you have. Now is the time to put down seed of spring-flowering species in the warm parts of the region. Plant seeds in a good all-purpose soilless mix or a 50:50 mixture of perlite and vermiculite. Water the mix well before you plant the seeds. Spread seed evenly over the top of mix and cover lightly. Water well, and keep evenly moist until the seeds germinate. If you provide strong but indirect light and keep evenly moist, plants should grow quickly to 5 or 6 inches tall by next spring. Bulbs grown from seed vary greatly in the amount of time it takes them to reach blooming size, but two to four years is common.

CARE

In Zones 9 and 10, **Dutch** and **Spanish iris** grow and bloom best if they are lifted this month and given a dry rest for six to eight weeks before they are replanted. Inspect the bulbs carefully for insect damage or rot, and discard damaged bulbs. Store in a cool, dry place until you are ready to replant in late September or October. In colder areas, these bulbs should be planted in the spring.

In Zones 9 and 10, begin to divide **iris** that have been in the ground for three years or more. Carefully lift and inspect the rhizome and discard all old, leafless rhizomes from the center. Break or cut the thick, vigorous rhizomes into pieces 3 to 4 inches long. Trim the leaves to 6 to 8 inches long and clip the roots back to 6 inches. If you do not plan to replant immediately, store the rhizomes in a dry, shady spot until time to replant.

While **iris** are out of the ground, no matter how briefly, renew the fertility of the bed by adding a generous amount of compost or mulch mixed with either a slow-release fertilizer or a blend of alfalfa meal or well-composted manure. Mix it thoroughly into the soil.

Replant rhizomes 1 to 2 feet apart, leaving at least half the rhizome above the soil. Firm the soil around the base of the rhizome and water well after planting.

WATERING

Maintain a regular watering schedule for bulbs that are actively growing and blooming. Be sure to water to a depth of 6 inches each time you water. If you have created new beds but not planted yet, continue to water them to help work nutrients into the soil. Keeping a new bed watered also encourages the growth of beneficial soil organisms.

HELPFUL HINTS

If there have been severe problems with root nematodes or other soilborne pests or disease in a bed, it may be advisable to solarize the soil. This should never be done annually, but it can be beneficial every three to five years. It is especially advisable in beds that grow only one type of plant (monoculture), because once an infestation begins in a monoculture, whether it is wheat or cotton or iris, it can become devastating.

To solarize soil, begin by lifting all the bulbs from the bed, marking them carefully, and storing in a cool, dry spot. Inspect the rhizomes or bulbs for insects, rot, or other damage. Keep only firm, healthy bulbs or rhizomes. Amend the soil with compost, fine screened mulch, or a blend that is mixed with organic amendments like alfalfa meal, well-composted manure, or bloodmeal. Add iron or sulphur if necessary. Cover the entire bed with either clear or black plastic sheets. Secure the plastic sheets with stones or boards so that the plastic is touching the soil and will not blow away. Leave the plastic sheets in place for two weeks. Remove the plastic sheets and water the bed thoroughly. Wait at least another two weeks before planting.

FERTILIZING

Do not fertilize any bulbs other than those in containers this month.

GROOMING

Remove spent blooming stalks or unwanted seedpods from summer- flowering bulbs. Otherwise, do not prune any bulbs.

PESTS

Handpick grasshoppers or other chewing insects as soon as they appear. Look for products specifically formulated for grasshoppers if infestations are severe.

September
BULBS, CORMS, RHIZOMES, & TUBERS

PLANNING

In most of the region, a shopping spree of bulb buying begins late in the month. If you want to have **hybrid tulips, hyacinth,** or other bulbs that require prechilling for spring bloom, buy them at the end of the month so there is plenty of time to chill them. And if you plan to try to force **paper whites** or **amaryllis** for winter blooming, look for good bulbs now. There is a greater selection and better bulb quality early in the season.

Many South African bulbs that are winter-growing and spring-flowering do especially well in Zones 9 and 10. Some are available in retail outlets, but others are found only in bulb catalogs. These are bulbs that require no chill to bloom and return each year to multiply and rebloom vigorously. Look for the following:

• **Bugle flower** blooms with tall, nodding stalks of long tubular flowers in shades of purple, pink, red, and white. They are common in southern California gardens but do well in good garden soil in our region.

• **Butterfly iris** is the only member of this genus routinely offered. It has purple iris-like flowers that can begin to open as early as September and continue

through March. This species multiplies well in the garden.

• **Cape tulip** has long grass-like leaves and stalks of yellow or light-orange flowers.

• **Chasmanthe** are tall, erect plants whose stalks grow up to 3 feet; they have dark-orange or yellow flowers. They prefer a very dry location in the summer.

• *Freesia alba* and **freesia** hybrids have flat leaves held in a fanlike sheath. *F. alba* flowers are white with a pale yellow center and are exuberantly fragrant. The commonly sold hybrid strain has larger flowers in a wide range of colors that repeat-bloom for many years in the hottest parts of the region.

• **Harlequin flower** has flowers in a stunning array of orange, yellow, deep reds, and chestnut, usually with at least one contrasting color on the petals. **Harlequin flower** is frequently offered in containers.

• **Naples garlic** is a widely available bulb with pure-white flowers arranged in a loose head. In rich soils and mild climates and with ample water, this bulb spreads aggressively, but it is well behaved in Zone 9 and 10. Other **ornamental alliums** also do well in the deserts in richly amended garden soils.

• **Soldier-in-the-box** is a small tubular-leaved bulb with a nodding head of creamy yellow flowers that look like miniature

daffodils. The larger, white-flowered **sentry box** is occasionally offered.

PLANTING

In all parts of the region, begin to plant winter-growing bulbs when temperatures fall below 100 degrees Fahrenheit; below 90 degrees is even better.

Dig the hole to the depth recommended for the type of bulb. Consult the Bulb Chart on pages 45-47 for planting depths. Most growers recommend adding a small amount of bonemeal, phosphorus-rich fertilizer, or slow-release fertilizer to the bottom of the hole and working it into the soil. Place the bulb in the hole and cover with the soil. Water well after planting.

CARE

To prechill bulbs like **tulips** and **hyacinth,** put the bulbs in paper bags or other containers (never plastic bags) that can allow air to reach the bulbs. Put the bags in the refrigerator and keep them well away from apples or other fruit. Leave in the refrigerator for six to eight weeks before planting. Check the bulbs occasionally to be sure they do not begin sprouting or develop any soft spots while chilling.

WATERING

Water newly planted bulbs twice a month until growth begins, then water weekly while temperatures are high. Bulbs planted in containers should be watered every week to ten days until growth begins. After they are actively growing, water when the surface of the soil feels dry.

FERTILIZING

Spread a 4- to 6-inch layer of compost or mulch in established bulb beds or where bulbs are planted. This will renew soil fertility for the winter-growing bulbs as it protects the root zone.

Do not fertilize bulbs in containers until they are actively growing. If you did not provide a slow-release granular fertilizer when you planted the bulbs, you can work it into the pot now while they are just emerging. You can also fertilize container-grown bulbs with water- soluble fertilizer every two to four weeks while they are actively growing.

HELPFUL HINTS

When lifting and dividing **iris**, you may find you have lost track of which varieties you have. Or you may have much more than you can stand to discard. If so, give them to a school, care center, or other public place where they can grow for the sheer beauty of their blooms without regard to their variety.

Shopping Tips for Bulbs

• Always look for bulbs, corms, rhizomes, and tubers that are large for the group offered. Bulbs, corms, rhizomes, and tubers should be firm to the touch with no soft spots or obvious signs of disease. Many inexpensive bulbs, or sets, are inferior bulbs that may bloom poorly or not at all. Check the size and quality of bulbs carefully before ordering.

• Do not be tempted to clean up or pull off the dry material (tunic) that is around bulbs. It is protective and causes no harm. Keep bulbs in paper if they are not being planted immediately, never store in plastic.

• Buying bulbs in bloom is a great way to know what you are getting. Do not transplant a bulb in bloom; instead, let the bulb finish out its bloom in the pot. Transplanting actively growing bulbs can set back their growth and blooming cycle a year or two. If you choose to plant right after bloom, keep this in mind. To be sure it reblooms next year, continue to feed and water the bulb through its entire growing season. Once dormant, label it carefully, and plant the following fall.

GROOMING

Remove any spent blooming stalks from summer-flowering bulbs. Do not cut leaves on summer-growing bulbs, but wait until they dry naturally and can be removed by hand.

PESTS

As you lift rhizomes or bulbs, either to replant them or to store them, inspect them carefully for damage. Discard diseased, damaged, or infected bulbs, and do not add them to the compost pile unless your compost is very hot.

OCTOBER
BULBS, CORMS, RHIZOMES, & TUBERS

PLANNING

Many gardeners only know **oxalis** as a pesky weed or worse. But in the Desert Southwest, many **oxalis** species remain congenial garden plants. There are hundreds of species of this South African genus, many of them from extremely dry regions, and many grow from bulbs. The charming yellow-flowered **Bermuda buttercup** grows in the shade with minimal to no irrigation in Zones 9 and 10. In areas with abundant water, however, this species becomes a garden pest. The lovely **pink sorrel** is a tidy bulb that can also be a terrible pest in mild, wet climates, but is much better behaved in dry desert gardens. Use both of these bulbs in areas that are not routinely irrigated (even in the hottest areas). They prefer rocky soils and abundant shade in the

hottest areas, but full sun is best in Zone 8.

Other excellent choices for deep shade in the region include the following.

• **Caladium** grows from tubers, and it is not its flowers that are colorful, but its wide, heart-shaped leaves. There are countless varieties, with leaves marked with white, pink, or deep burgundy.

• **Calla** needs deep shade in Zones 9 and 10, partial shade in Zone 8. Large white flowers are abundant in late spring.

• **Crinum** grows well in almost all sun conditions if kept well watered. They bloom in shades of white, pink, or deep rose through the summer.

• **Drimiopsis** has long deep-green leaves marked with maroon and spikes of small white flowers in the summer.

• **Manfreda** has low-growing rosettes of brittle green leaves that are often marked with

splotches of brown or maroon.

The tall flowering stalks in late spring have numerous chartreuse or pale cream-colored flowers.

• **Spider lilies** have large, white flowers in the summer.

PLANTING

Continue to plant flowering bulbs such as **alliums, anemone, Bermuda buttercup, butterfly iris, cape tulip, daffodils, Dutch iris, harlequin flower, lady tulip, pink sorrel,** and **ranunculus** in the mild-winter areas. In cooler parts of Zones 9a and 8, plant **crocus, grape hyacinth, snowdrops, squill,** and **tulips** this month.

If you received bulbs in the mail, take them out of the packaging immediately and inspect for any damage or insects. Keep in a paper bag in a cool, dry location until you are ready to plant. Never store bulbs in plastic, and don't refrigerate any bulbs other than those that need a strong prechilling to bloom.

CARE

Many gardeners in the region like to wait this late to divide their **bearded iris.** Follow the recommendations for division

Gardeners often wait until this month to divide their bearded iris.

in August, but if dividing this month, do not store the rhizomes—replant immediately.

Dig **caladium** tubers this month after the tops have entirely died down. Store the tubers in a cool, dry location and replant next spring.

If you are leaving tender bulbs in the ground over the winter in cold areas, apply a deep layer, 6 to 8 inches, of hay or pine straw over the bulbs to protect them from freezing temperatures.

WATERING

As temperatures cool this month, be prepared to reduce watering frequency for all bulbs. Water to a depth of 6 inches for all growing bulbs, including **iris.** This could be as frequent as every ten days or every other week, depending on the temperatures and your soil type.

FERTILIZING

Once spring-flowering bulbs in containers are actively growing, fertilize once a month with a water-soluble fertilizer while the weather is cool.

In Zones 9 and 10, **iris** that have begun to grow can be fertilized beginning this month. Apply a low-nitrogen fertilizer every six weeks through the winter.

FORCING AMARYLLIS BULBS

Soon holiday catalogs will feature exquisite forced **amaryllis** for sale. But you can easily force these bulbs yourself. Follow these steps.

1. Begin with a large, vigorous **amaryllis** bulb in a color that you want. Select a pot that is no more than 1 inch wider than the diameter of the bulb. Mix a growing medium of equal parts sand, peat moss, potting soil, and vermiculite, plus a slow-release fertilizer at half the recommended amount or a cup of good compost. Mix it all thoroughly.

2. Put about half the soil mix in the pot, and position the bulb so that $1/3$ is above the soil line. Water thoroughly, then place the pot where the temperature is 65 degrees Fahrenheit most of the time.

3. Water again in three weeks or when growth starts, whichever is first. Once growth starts, water when the soil feels dry to the touch.

4. After the plant has bloomed, cut off the blooming stalk but continue to water regularly until the leaves wither and yellow (usually in July or August). Apply a water-soluble fertilizer once a month while the leaves are growing.

5. Once the leaves are dead, leave the plant completely dry until late October. At that time, give the plant a deep watering, and when growth resumes, continue care as described above.

Calla are heavy feeders and need a very rich soil, or applications of a balanced fertilizer every two to three weeks during their growing season.

GROOMING

Do not prune this month.

PESTS

If you have been plagued in the past with birds or rodents eating or digging up bulbs, set bulbs in wire cages as you plant them. As an alternative, or for plants already in the ground, fit a layer of wire mesh over the top of the soil; secure it with soil, metal hairpin stakes, or rocks; and cover it lightly to hide it. Mesh that is about 1 inch wide or less is small enough to deter the animals but large enough to allow the stems to grow up through it.

November

BULBS, CORMS, RHIZOMES, & TUBERS

 PLANNING

Holiday bulbs are a wonderful gift for anyone, but especially for friends or relatives who do not have room for a garden, but would enjoy the excitement and beauty of beautiful blooms. **Daffodils, paper whites** in a wide range of colors and blooming styles, **amaryllis, tulips,** and **grape hyacinths** are among the most popular.

Familiar to most gardeners as a houseplant, **cyclamen** is a bulbous plant that grows and flowers through the entire winter. **Cyclamen** have wide, deep-green foliage that is often attractively mottled. The comet-style white or pink flowers are held high above the foliage. After the holidays, keep **cyclamen** on the porch in the deep shade in Zones 9 and 10. Water it when it is dry to the touch and deadhead regularly, and it will bloom until late April and much longer in Zone 8. Many gardeners have had success in letting the foliage die off during the summer, keeping the plants completely dry, and watching them return and bloom the following year.

One easy way to make a long-lasting arrangement of bulbs grown in a pot for a friend, or yourself, is to plant the bulbs in succession every two or three weeks. Or watch for varieties that have early-, mid-, or late-season cultivars, and mix them together. Or plant a mix of bulbs, making sure that you select varieties so that at least two will bloom each month through the spring.

 PLANTING

This is the last chance to put in spring-flowering bulbs like **amaryllis, anemone, bearded iris, crinum, crocus, daffodil, Dutch iris, freesia, montbretia,** and **ranunculus.** In warm-winter areas, plant **gladiolus** from now through January. In Zone 8, plant **daffodils, grape hyacinth, scilla, snowdrops,** and **tulips.**

 CARE

Dutch iris is more cold tender than most bulbs used in the Desert Southwest. Protect bulbs with mulch if freezing temperatures are routine in your area. After the first killing frost, cut back **canna** and **dahlia** and discard the leaves to prevent insects from overwintering in the foliage.

 WATERING

Do not overwater; cut back watering frequency as temperatures drop. If bulbs are actively growing, water when the soil around them feels dry to the touch. Water bulbs in containers only when the soil surface is dry to the touch.

 FERTILIZING

Fertilize **iris, calla,** and container plants only according to a predetermined schedule.

 GROOMING

Prune only to remove spent flowers or seedpods. Hand-remove any remaining dead leaves from summer-flowering bulbs.

 PESTS

Watch for aphids on tender new growth. Blast them off with strong jets of water or remove by hand. Inspect new bulbs carefully to be sure they are not infested with borers or other pests.

FORCING PAPER WHITES

Forcing **paper whites** is easy and a great way for children to create living gifts.

1. Begin with large, healthy bulbs and make a soil mix of one part sand, one part perlite, two parts peat moss, and two parts pine bark. Select a pot that is 2 to 3 inches deeper than the bulb and that will hold at least six bulbs.

2. **Paper whites** can grow as crowded as you wish and are particularly effective when there are as many bulbs as it takes to have them shoulder to shoulder in the pot. Set the bulbs in the pot, leaving $1/3$ of the bulb above the soil. Keep cool—temperatures around 65 degrees Fahrenheit are best. Place the bulbs in indirect light until the bulbs begin to show green tips. Once the leaves are 3 to 4 inches tall, move to a brighter location until the flowering stalks have emerged. Plants can be moved into the house once the first flowers begin to open.

3. Many gardeners place the bulbs completely in the dark to force **paper whites**. To keep the bulbs dark, put them in a closet or shed that is not used, or cover the pot with cardboard or black plastic to keep out light until the bulbs begin to show green growth. Then move the plants out to brighter light gradually until the flowers form and begin to open. At that time they can be moved into the house if you wish. Check weekly, and gradually begin to move the pot into the light when the shoot is 3 inches tall. This takes from four to six weeks. Water whenever the surface of the soil is dry. Fertilize the pot with a water-soluble fertilizer every three weeks while paper whites are actively growing and blooming. I have used both methods and know people who swear by one method or the other so pick the one that is easiest for you to manage.

4. Let the leaves grow and dry out naturally. Once dormant, lift the bulbs and store in a paper bag, or leave in the pot and remove to a cool, dry location. Vigorous **paper whites** often rebloom the following year with the same treatment.

Paper whites and **hyacinths** can also be forced in water. For **paper whites**, choose an attractive container and fill the bottom with pebbles. Place the bulbs on top of the pebbles, nestling them among the rocks so they stay in place. Fill the container with water, but leave the bulb above water. Keep the container where it is cool and in dim light until the shoots are 3 to 4 inches tall. This will take two to three weeks. The container can then be moved to a brighter room or a sunny window. For **hyacinths**, look for special glass pots that have a constricted neck. This allows the bulb to remain dry but the roots to grow in the water.

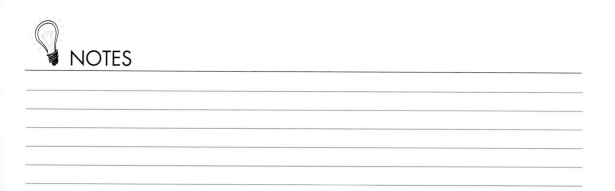

NOTES

DECEMBER
BULBS, CORMS, RHIZOMES, & TUBERS

 PLANNING

Nursery catalogs now begin to fill the mailbox. Look them over carefully for good bulbs to try next year, or for summer-flowering bulbs that may arrive in time to be planted this year. Consult the journal you have kept on your summer-flowering bulbs to see which performed the best for you.

If you are giving gifts to other gardeners, remember that good sturdy tools are always welcome. Tools for planting bulbs would be welcome additions to any gardener's toolshed.

Trowels that are specially designed to plant bulbs are heavy with a thick metal blade that ends in a wedge with a shallow ditch down the middle. Most have markers along the metal so you will know how deep you are digging. They work by plunging into the dirt, and you pull the trowel toward you, setting the bulb in behind it. Another version of this is a wide, metal trowel that has a serrated or notched edge on the blade. It looks like an awkward spoon. This tool scoops out dirt where you intend to plant.

A dibble is an old-fashioned tool for planting bulbs. It is a piece of metal attached to a wooden shaft with a handle set perpendicular to the shaft. The metal piece is tapered to end in a sharp point. It works when you plunge the entire tool into the ground and pull it out, leaving a smooth cone-shaped hole into which you plant the bulb. Such a tool is especially useful for small bulbs.

A **bulb planter** is an open cone of metal that has serrations or notches on the end and a handle on the other. It is used by working or pushing it into the ground to make the hole. Some versions are long enough that you use your foot on a short step to drive it into the ground. They work best in lawns or very soft soil.

 PLANTING

Check on prechilled bulbs, and begin to plant out any that are ready. Follow planting directions on page 48.

 CARE

Check all chilling bulbs once a month and if they are sprouting, plant out immediately. Examine stored summer bulbs and discard any that are showing soft spots or rot. In Zone 8, heavily mulch **dahlia** tubers to prevent freeze damage.

 WATERING

Water carefully, and if there are abundant or frequent winter rains, be sure to skip supplemental irrigation. In Zones 9 and 10, the general rule of thumb is to skip a watering for every $1/2$ inch of rain.

 FERTILIZING

Do not fertilize bulbs this month.

 GROOMING

Prune spent flowers anytime. Remove any seedpods that form unless you are deliberately saving seed. Hand-remove any remaining dead leaves from summer-flowering bulbs.

 PESTS

Aphids can emerge at this time. Use strong jets of water to blast these tiny insects off leaves, or remove by hand. If left alone, the numbers of aphids can increase quickly, and their feeding may cause crooked stems, or deformed leaves and flowers.

CACTI, SUCCULENTS, & OTHER DESERT PERENNIALS

It is easy to take for granted how elegantly designed desert plants are to meet the rigors of relentless heat and sporadic rainfall.

While all of our natives are impressive, cacti, succulents, agaves, yuccas, and similar plants are some of the most extraordinary plants found in deserts.

These plants represent some of the best choices for gardeners in the region. They have outstanding tolerance to heat, aridity, alkaline soils, and erratic rainfall patterns. They are the original low-water-use plants. But more than ease of care recommends them to desert gardens—they are also extremely beautiful.

All gardens look better if there is a mix of plants whose various textures, colors, and forms blend to make an interesting shifting picture. Succulents have rich textures coupled with odd and arresting forms so that using them for contrast and interest is almost effortless.

The same striking forms also make them useful as focal or accent plants. They can be placed against a blank wall or used to fill in a tight corner, or they can be placed so they rise up

Mixed cactuses

as a surprise around a corner. Succulents give a garden bed presence and weight, taking it from a careless mixture to a clear, sharp arrangement.

But in the end, one of the finest contributions these plants bring to our gardens is the remembrance and tone of the deserts that define the state. Using these plants not only makes maintenance and design sense, but it helps mark our yards and planting beds for what they are—desert gardens.

WHAT MAKES DESERT PLANTS SO SPECIAL

Succulence. While cacti, succulents, and desert perennials have many adaptations that allow them to survive the rigorous conditions of the desert, none is more spectacular, or more unusual, than succulence. Succulence is the ability of a plant to store water in specialized cells in a leaf, stem, or roots. This useful trait has crossed over family boundaries, and succulents can be found not only in the cactus family but in the sunflower family, euphorbia family, grape family, and lily family.

1. Plants like agaves, aloes, and gasterias have collected these specialized cells in their leaves. Leaf succulents have thick, hard leaves, usually arranged in a rosette, and compared to woody or herbaceous plants, the leaves are few but long-lived.

2. Stem succulents have the water storage cells in their stem. Cacti are stem succulents, as are the vast number of succulent members of the genus *Euphorbia*. Stem succulents have either abandoned leaves altogether, reduced them to spines, or grow them only in the most favorable season.

3. Root succulents are not as common as the other two styles. The Arizona native Queen of the Night has an immense succulent root that stores water to carry it through long, hot spells in the low-elevation deserts of the region. Many African succulents have a swollen mass that is part root and part stem called a caudex, which holds vital moisture for the plant. Plants like baobab trees, members of the genus *Pachypodium*, and other uncommon species grow in this style.

Roots. All succulents, and most other desert perennials, have widely spreading root systems that grow near the surface of the soil. The web of tiny branches allows even the smallest amount of rainfall to be captured quickly, and the proximity to the surface ensures that even light rain will be available to the plants. In times of drought, many species simply allow most of the root system to die off. But roots can be regenerated in a matter of days, given a good rain.

Leaves or not. Plants have an interesting relationship with their leaves. On the one hand, leaves are the workhorse of the plant—vital for photosynthesis.

CHAPTER THREE

On the other hand, they are quickly shed and easily replaced with a casualness that can be daunting when they are a garden favorite. In cacti, succulents, and desert perennials, leaves have undergone some astounding changes to accommodate their growing conditions. In many of these plants, like cacti, the leaves are changed or reduced to minimize water loss. In others, leaves are present only when times are good, as with ocotillo and euphorbias. Others have reduced their number, covered them with a waxy coat, and shaded them with tiny hairlike projections, as in dasylirion and some yuccas. Most dramatic of all, in order to cut down on the surface area and to reduce the number of stomata that will release vital water vapor, many plants have relocated chlorophyll-bearing cells to their stems, as in cacti and euphorbias.

Skin. Almost all succulents have thin, delicate skin that is easily pierced or injured. Even the spiniest of succulents—like cholla—have delicate skin that should be protected from being poked, stabbed, and cut. In addition, most succulents have a waxy coating on the skin that reduces evaporation.

A different metabolism. In all plants, one of the byproducts of photosynthesis is water vapor, which is released to the air through the minute leaf openings called stoma (plural, stomata). These little faucets are a problem for desert plants, too, and the reduction in the number of leaves and stomata and the use of stem cells for photosynthesis were both developed to reduce this water loss. In succulents, however, a more dramatic adaptation has taken place. Succulents have devised a two-step process for photosynthesis in which a portion of this chemical transformation is performed in the daytime when sunlight is available, and the final steps are completed at night. This allows stomata to open at night, when evaporative loss is lower. Known as CAM Metabolism, this strategy is not only clever, it is effective.

GROWING CACTI, SUCCULENTS, AND DESERT PERENNIALS

So what do all the oddities of adaptation, growth habit, root systems, and metabolism mean when you want to grow these plants in the garden? All the intriguing survival strategies and complicated differences actually work together to make these plants extremely easy to grow.

WATERING

Treat a recently planted succulent, regardless of its size, like any other transplanted plant. Water it generously at first, and give it a chance to set up a new, fully functional root system before you start to treat it like an old hand at desert growing.

Prickly pear cactus

CHAPTER THREE

Most large succulents that have been in the ground two years or more should be watered once a month in the summer, deeply, in the hottest parts of the region. A rainfall of at least $1/2$ inch can replace this watering. Most species grow on natural rainfall in the winter, but if the winter is dry, or it doesn't rain for sixty days, water deeply.

Newly planted succulents or those in the ground less than two years should be watered twice a month in the summer, more often if they look like they need it. Water monthly in the winter.

Agaves, yuccas, and their relatives should be watered every other week in the summer regardless of their age. If they begin to yellow or wither, water more often. Water monthly in the coldest part of the winter, and every three weeks in the warm spring and fall.

FERTILIZING

All succulents should be fertilized with care. Plants in the ground almost never need fertilization.

Agaves and yuccas, especially those from outside desert regions, do respond well to a layer of compost or mulch twice a year around the roots.

Never use high-nitrogen fertilizers or formulas with high NPK numbers on succulents. Plants in pots are different, and most accept a low-strength, low-nitrogen formula when they are actively growing. The active growth of most succulents takes place in spring and the fall—but know your plants, and fertilize only when they are growing.

SHADE

Puzzling as it is to most new gardeners in the region, providing light shade is recommended for all succulents that are not native. Planting all but the most tender succulents in the fall also ensures a long acclimatization period for the skin and helps prevent sunburn the following summer. If you plant in the late spring or summer, provide artificial shade for all newly planted succulents, including agaves, cacti, and yuccas.

Desert spoon

CHAPTER THREE

SO MANY CHOICES

There are hundreds of species of cacti, succulents, and desert perennials. Here are some of the most popular choices.

CACTI
- **Barrel cactus** *Ferocactus wislizeni*
- **Beaver tail prickly pear** *Opuntia basilaris*
- **Cane cholla** *Cylindropuntia spinosior*
- **Golden barrel cactus** *Echinocactus grusonii*
- **Hedgehog** *Echinocereus engelmannii/ triglochidiatus*
- **Jumping cholla** *Cylindropuntia fulgida*
- **Mexican fence post** *Stenocereus marginatus*
- **Night-blooming cereus** *Cereus hildmannianus*
- **Organ pipe cactus** *Stenocereus thurberi*
- **Pincushion** *Mammillaria microcarpa*
- **Purple prickly pear** *Opuntia santa-rita*
- **Saguaro** *Carnegiea gigantea*
- **Senita** *Pachycereus schottii*
- **Staghorn cholla** *Cylindropuntia versicolor*
- **Totem pole cactus** *Pachycereus schottii* v. *monstrosa*

AFRICAN SUCCULENTS
- *Aloe arborescens*
- *Aloe bakeri*
- *Aloe 'Blue Elf'*
- *Aloe chabaudii*
- *Aloe ciliaris*
- *Aloe cryptopoda*
- *Aloe descoingsii*
- *Aloe ferox*
- *Aloe saponaria*
- *Aloe striata*
- *Aloe vaombe*
- *Aloe vera*
- *Carpobrotus* spp.
- **Copper ice plant** *Malephora crocea*
- **Crown of thorns** *Euphorbia milii*
- **Desert rose** *Adenium obesum*
- **Felt plant** *Kalanchoe beharensis*

- *Gasteria acinacifolia*
- **Ice plant** *Drosanthemum floribundum*
- *Kalanchoe blossfeldiana*
- *Lampranthus multiradiatus*
- **Madagascar palm** *Pachypodium lamerei*
- **Maternity plant** *Kalanchoe daigremontiana*
- **Moroccan mound** *Euphorbia resinifera*
- *Pachypodium geayi*
- **Panda plant** *Kalanchoe tomentosa*
- *Ruschia carolii*

AGAVES, YUCCAS, AND OTHER DESERT PERENNIALS
- *Agave americana*
- *Agave angustifolia*
- *Agave havardiana*
- *Agave murpheyi*
- *Agave neomexicana*
- *Agave parryi*
- **Banana yucca** *Yucca baccata*
- **Bear grass** *Nolina microcarpa*
- **Blue yucca** *Yucca rigida*
- **Boojum tree** *Fouquieria columnaris*
- **Desert spoon** *Dasylirion wheeleri*
- *Dudleya saxosa*
- **Foxtail agave** *Agave attenuata*
- **Joshua tree** *Yucca brevifolia*
- **Mexican grass tree** *Dasylirion quadrangulatum*
- **Mohave yucca** *Yucca schidigera*
- **Mountain yucca** *Yucca schottii*
- **Ocotillo** *Fouquieria splendens*
- **Octopus agave** *Agave vilmoriniana*
- **Palo adan** *Fouquieria macdougalii*
- **Red hesperaloe** *Hesperaloe parviflora*
- **Sacahuista** *Nolina texana*
- **Soap tree yucca** *Yucca elata*

JANUARY
CACTI, SUCCULENTS, & OTHER DESERT PERENNIALS

PLANNING

Many **aloes** are hardy, but it pays to check with local growers before planting them, especially in Zone 8. In Zone 10 and the warmest parts of Zone 9, some tender species still need overhead protection on cold nights. Plant under a porch eave, against the house, or beneath an evergreen tree.

Aloes are native to Africa and Madagascar, and most species bloom in the winter in our region. The flowers of **aloes** are held in upright stalks, either branched like a large candelabra or in a spike. Flowers are found in shades of red, pink, apricot, orange, and yellow, and hummingbirds find them irresistible. A generous number of **aloes** in the garden helps provide year-round food for these birds. Here are some **aloes** to consider.

• Small **aloes** like *Aloe bakeri*, 'Blue Elf', and *A. descoingsii* can be used to fill in small spaces among rocks in a dry garden, or on the north face of a rock wall or rocky slope.

• Spreading species like *Aloe arborescens* or *A. saponaria* make vigorous groundcovers for dry shady sites.

• The **vining aloe**, *A. ciliaris*, with its vivid green leaves and bright red blooms in the late win-

ter, climbs tree limbs or makes a good groundcover for a deep-shade location.

• Species like *Aloe cryptopoda*, with its dusky leaves held in a vaselike shape; *A. hereroensis*, with its nearly white leaves; and *A. striata*, with its wide pale-green leaves edged in pink, are excellent as focal points in the garden. They mix well with either leafy perennials or with other succulents.

There are some species that grow a large stem and are tall enough to be an arresting sight in the garden. Some of the most commonly available of the **tree aloes** are *Aloe ferox*, with its huge head of leaves and brilliant red flowers; *A. vaombe*, which has long, thin leaves that turn deep red in cool temperatures; and the white-trunked, multi-headed *Aloe dichotoma*.

PLANTING

Continue to plant winter-growing succulents, either in the ground or in containers. Choose a location with high, filtered shade or one that is shaded from the after-

Aloe

noon sun. While full sun in the winter suits all winter-growing succulents, summer sun, especially in the afternoon, can be too much for them.

CARE

Protect tender succulents or those in bloom when freezing temperatures are predicted. Cover with a blanket, sheet, frost cloth, or cardboard box overnight. Many **aloes** are hardy enough to withstand short-duration freezes, but their flowers are not. To protect flowering **aloes,** use a frame of pipe, wood, or bamboo stakes over the plant, then place the protective covering over that.

WATERING

Water **cactus** and other warm-season succulents every four to five weeks if there has been no rain. Water winter-growing succulents every ten to fourteen days. Water large plants to a depth of 4 to 6 inches and small plants to a depth of 3 to 4 inches. Be sure the surface of the soil is dry before watering again. If there is any doubt about whether to water, do not.

HELPFUL HINTS

The part of a **cactus** that is most vulnerable to freeze damage is the tip. To protect the tip, place a styrofoam cup over the end of the stem. Use a cup that is large enough to fit securely over the tip and can be removed without ripping off any spines. Cups can be left on for two or three days but should be removed once danger of frost is past.

Succulents are built for drought and water storage, and overwatering is much more dangerous than light underwatering. In addition, keeping plants on the dry side in the winter, whether warm- or cool-season plants, helps minimize freeze damage.

FERTILIZING

Do not fertilize succulents this month.

GROOMING

Even if plants experience severe cold damage, do not prune affected stems or leaves until the weather warms next month. The only exception is flowering stalks on **aloes,** which can be removed anytime. When weather is cool, open wounds can cause more problems than cold damage.

PESTS

The tender, juicy leaves of many **ice plants** are irresistible to birds and rabbits. To protect plants from birds, cover them with bird netting or other fine mesh. Only chicken wire cages will deter rabbits completely—most of the rabbit repellants on the market are unreliable or erratically successful.

NOTES

_____
_____
_____
_____
_____
_____
_____
_____
_____

FEBRUARY

CACTI, SUCCULENTS, & OTHER DESERT PERENNIALS

 PLANNING

Among the most colorful cool-season succulents are the **ice plants,** also known as **mesembs**. The members of this vast family of plants are leaf succulents, and in some species the leaves are able to exude salts through their stomata, leaving minute crystals on the leaves. The glimmer of these crystals gives the entire group its name, because to some it appeared that the plants were coated with ice. **Ice plants** may be shrubby or trailing, and while there are hundreds of species, only a few are commonly available for ornamental use. They include the following.

• *Carpobrotus* plants are a plague on the coast of California, but in the desert parts of Arizona they are much better behaved. These large, trailing **ice plants** have large leaves and 3-inch pink or white flowers.

• *Drosanthemum floribundum* (also sold as *D. hispidum*) is a trailing plant with small pellet-shaped leaves and vivid purple-to–rose red flowers. There are other species in this genus that bloom white, pink, and yellow, but they are rarely named correctly.

• *Lampranthus multiradiatus* is a shrubby plant that holds up even in the hottest areas and

Agave

blooms in a range of colors from rosy red to pink or white.

• *Malephora crocea* is one of the most durable of all **ice plants,** thriving in the summer heat of the hottest parts of the region. It flowers for months in a burnished copper color.

• *Ruschia carolii* is a low-trailing plant with pastel pink flowers.

Ice plants make excellent groundcovers for dry gardens or rocky areas, or they can be planted so they fall over a wall or embankment. The shrubby species provide a splendid con-

trast in a succulent or dry garden that is dominated by the rosette forms of **aloes** and **agaves.**

One of the easiest ways to grow **ice plants** is in containers. These succulents enjoy a well-drained soil with only a minimum of organic matter. A mix of 1 part organic matter (potting soil, mulch, or compost) and 5 parts gravel or pumice is ideal. Plants grown in containers can be brought out into the full sun in the winter so you can fully appreciate their spectacular flowering and then move them into a dry, shady spot for their summer rest.

 PLANTING

Continue to plant cool-season succulents. Plants with a summer dormancy or resting period, like **dudleya** and **ice plants,** should be planted before mid-month to give them ample time to establish roots before the summer. Plant succulents in well-drained, even rocky, soil. Make a hole that is three to five times wider than the container but the same depth as the rootball. Do not add mulch, compost, or other amendments to the soil or backfill before planting. Be sure that succulents are not planted more deeply than they were growing previously.

 CARE

Carefully watch succulents like **pachypodium** and **adenium** that are winter- dormant. Be sure they are not getting extra water from unexpected sources like a roof drain or adjacent pots. These plants usually need no watering over the winter, but if the tip begins to shrivel or shrink, water once during the season.

 WATERING

Water winter-growing succulents regularly on the schedule described in January. Water warm-season succulents once deeply during the month unless winter rains are frequent and abundant. If the weather begins to warm dramatically, increase the watering frequency by a day or two for all succulents that are actively growing.

 FERTILIZING

Apply quarter-strength liquid fertilizer every second watering to actively growing succulents in containers. Do not fertilize any plant that is dormant or is a warm-season grower.

 NOTES

 GROOMING

Once all danger of frost is past, prune any frost damage from **cactus** or other succulents. Cut the stem at an angle so that water does not collect in it. Dust the cut with powdered sulphur to both aid in drying out and as a fungicide.

PESTS

Aphids may show up on leafy plants like **crown of thorns.** Remove by hand if there are few, or spray with strong jets of water to remove. Succulents have responses to pesticides that are completely different from those of other plants. Before using any product on a succulent, whether homemade or purchased, test it on a small section of stem or leaf before applying it to the entire plant.

MARCH
CACTI, SUCCULENTS, & OTHER DESERT PERENNIALS

Hedgehog cactus

PLANTING

Begin to plant all warm-season succulents now through May. In Zone 8, wait until all danger of frost is past in early April.

For **agaves,** select a spot that has some shade, particularly in the afternoon, or be certain that the plant can grow in full sun. Dig a wide, shallow hole no deeper than the root system of the plant, and create a small rise in the center of the hole. Place the crown of the plant on the top of the rise and allow the roots to spread out into the hole. Backfill, using no amendments, pressing gently to remove air pockets. Make sure the crown of the plant is well above the soil line. Water in well, checking the crown again after the water has penetrated.

CARE

Watch newly planted succulents like **cactus** and **agave** to be sure they are not sunburning. Protect the south or west sides of the plant (or both) with sunscreen, a shade cloth, or a light-colored cloth. Protection can be draped on the plant or laid over a frame. Pale skin or yellowed patches that appear suddenly are the first sign of sunburn.

PLANNING

It is tempting to look upon succulents like **graptopetalum, sedums,** or **dudleyas**—as collector plants suitable only for growing in containers in greenhouses or a backyard shade house. But many are superb choices for the dry, rocky, alkaline soils of our region. Look for areas where it is shady, especially those that have high, filtered shade and protection from the afternoon sun. Cluster small succulents together in a bed to fill an odd corner or an unused narrow strip, or use as an accent to larger succulents.

WATERING

Increase watering of warm-season succulents to twice a month. As with most plants, it is best to water deeply but infrequently. While most succulents have shallow spreading root systems, watering to a depth of 8 inches to 3 feet, depending on the size of the plant, provides plenty of soil moisture over a long period of time.

Water winter-dormant succulents only when leaves first show. Then begin to water regularly.

Expand the time between waterings for cool-season succulents by a few days.

FERTILIZING

Do not fertilize winter-growing succulents. Wait to fertilize winter-dormant succulents until a full set of leaves has emerged and the plant appears to be growing. Use a low-nitrogen, water-soluble fertilizer for container plants, and add it to every second or third watering. Mix it at half the recommended strength for houseplants. Plants in the ground should be fertilized once as they begin to grow and once again about a month later.

GROOMING

Prune any frost damage from succulents with a clean cut, dusting the cut with sulphur when complete. Cut back **chollas** and **prickly pears** if they have become too large. They will begin to grow quickly by the end of the month.

HELPFUL HINTS

Christmas cactus and its relatives need steady moisture and shade to make it through the long, dry summer. Keep plants in bright, indirect light. A north-facing room or porch or under a dense evergreen tree are ideal spots. Water deeply (water should run out the bottom of the pot) when the surface of the soil feels dry. Fertilize monthly with a water-soluble fertilizer at $^1/_4$ the strength recommended for houseplants.

PESTS

Mealybugs may begin to show up in container-grown plants. Watch for them carefully; they are simple to control in small numbers but can be difficult if their numbers rise. Use a cotton swab drenched in alcohol to kill the bugs as you find them. Cactus bugs and other sucking insects of **cacti** may begin to emerge this month, although they are usually a problem later in the year. Again, watch carefully, especially after you water, and kill the bugs immediately.

NOTES

APRIL
CACTI, SUCCULENTS, & OTHER DESERT PERENNIALS

PLANNING

Ocotillos are regularly sold in the region as bare-root plants. Although most of them have a tiny root system compared to the size of the plant, with careful planting and care they can grow into excellent garden plants.

First be aware of local regulations on the harvesting of wild-growing **ocotillo.** Arizona requires a permit to perform such harvesting, as do other states, and there should be an appropriate tag on the plant if it was collected from the wild.

Purchase a plant with the largest number of roots. Look also to see if there is plenty of green along the stem where the thorns are found. Such plants offer the best chances of success.

PLANTING

Continue to plant warm-season succulents this month. Begin to set out succulents this month in Zone 8, and continue to plant through the summer.

To plant **ocotillos**, dig a hole that is wider than the rootball but just as deep. Soil amendments are not necessary. Backfill, carefully pressing the soil to remove air pockets, and firm the plant into place. It is not necessary to

stake an **ocotillo;** when planted securely it will stand up on its own. Do not plant any deeper than the soil line that you can see at the base of the plant.

Water deeply after planting. Build a shallow basin around a newly planted **ocotillo** to encourage deep watering. Make a basin 2 to 3 feet wider than the plant.

Transplanted **ocotillos** are slow to recover, grow a new root system, and put on leaves. It can take up to two years before the first leaves appear. But the plant is not sitting still, it is actively growing roots. Therefore, it is important to water transplanted **ocotillos** deeply and frequently while they are in this transition period.

Spraying the canes has no effect on root success of **ocotillos.** It may help cut down on some water loss right after transplant, and it may help hold leaves on a transplanted plant for a day or two.

CARE

April can get hot quickly in Zones 9 and 10. Watch newly planted succulents carefully to be sure they are not sunburning. Pale surfaces or yellowed patches that appear suddenly are often a sign of sunburn. Protect the south and west sides of newly planted

succulents, including **cactus,** if they have not been hardened off to the full sun.

Ice plants begin to slow their growth with the heat. Water less frequently, and if they are growing in containers, move them to a dry, shady spot for the summer.

Leaves of winter-growing succulents like **boojum** or *Senecio* spp. may begin to yellow this month. Cut back on watering when this happens, watering half as often as before. Once leaves fall completely, cease watering altogether; if the plants are in containers, move into dry shade for the summer.

WATERING

Water newly planted succulents every seven to ten days. Once new growth appears or the plants have been in the ground a month, expand waterings to every ten to fourteen days for the first summer.

Water established warm-season succulents every two to three weeks unless the temperatures rise over 105 degrees Fahrenheit. Once temperatures are that high, water every other week. Be sure to water deeply and in a wide circle around the base of the plant. While natives can grow on very little water, to keep them healthy and looking fit, water native **agaves, dasylirion, nolina, yucca,** and smaller **cacti,** including all **prickly pears,** every other week. Large natives, like established **saguaro** and **ocotillo,** should be watered monthly during the summer.

FERTILIZING

Apply a soluble low-nitrogen fertilizer to warm-season succulents in containers once during the month. For inorganic formulas, use at half the recommended strength for houseplants.

Cacti, succulents, and most desert perennials do not need regular doses of fertilizer if they are growing in the ground. A 3- to 4-inch layer of compost or mulch spread over the surface of the soil helps keep the soil cooler, cuts down on evaporative loss, and gently nudges up the soil fertility, providing ample nutrients for growing succulents.

GROOMING

Cut back any **cholla** or **prickly pear** that is too large. Cut to a joint with a saw or large clippers. It is not necessary to treat a cut on these type of **cactus** if the cut is made at the joint. For any other cuts, or cuts on other types of **cactus,** dust with sulphur

---

HELPFUL HINTS

• Do not put your succulents on the same line of an automated watering system as trees, shrubs, perennials, or lawns. The long intervals between waterings that are so advantageous for succulents are detrimental to the non-succulents, and the amount and frequency of watering for herbaceous and woody plants is lethal for most succulents. If you want to put succulents on an automated watering system, dedicate one station entirely to these plants.

• It is often puzzling to tell if an **ocotillo** is alive or not when there are no leaves. Here are a couple of ways to know:

1. Take the end of the cane and pull it gently toward the ground. If it bends, it is still alive. If it snaps, it is dead.

2. Look carefully at the stem around the thorn. Surrounding the thorn is a diamond-shaped area that often has tan or whitish bark that peels away. Beneath that bark the stem should be green or yellow-green. If it is dark gray, the cane is dead.

Always prune dead canes as far back as you can to prevent unsightly stumps and spindly branching regrowth.

---

to help dry it out and prevent infection.

Yucca should not be pruned unless it is necessary to remove dead or diseased stems. Cut back to either a joint or as low on the plant as possible if you need to prune. Dust the wound generously with sulphur until it dries completely.

PESTS

Look for signs of dry rot on **prickly pear.** This drying of all or portions of a pad can be the result of a host of agents including cold, sunburn, and tunneling larvae of cactus bugs and wee-

vils. Remove any affected pads and discard them.

Adult agave snout weevils become active this month. They are difficult to locate, but applications of insecticides may kill some of the females who are looking for **agaves** in which to lay their eggs.

Mealybugs are small, white, fuzzy sucking insects. They are a problem especially in greenhouses and around succulents. Look for them in the axil of a leaf or deep in a crevice of the plant. Small numbers are easily controlled with ordinary alcohol, but larger infestations may need chemical controls.

MAY

CACTI, SUCCULENTS, & OTHER DESERT PERENNIALS

PLANNING

Both **agaves** and **yuccas** grow offsets from rhizomes called pups. **Agave** pups are ready made new plants with their own independent root system. **Yucca** offsets usually need to be grown in soil for a time to grow their roots. Early summer is the perfect time to begin propagating these plants for use in other parts of the garden, or to give away to friends.

To remove **agave** pups, begin by making sure the area around the plant is well watered—this will make removal much easier. Slide a shovel, spade, or turning fork under the pup, and gently begin to lift it out of the soil. Some pups come away with almost no effort, others require a lift-and-pull action. Once some of the soil falls away, grab the pup firmly and pull gently away from the main plant. If it doesn't come away in your hand, keep lifting and pulling with the tool until you pull it out. If it is stubborn and you can see the underground stem, cut it cleanly away from the main plant with a shovel or knife.

Leave the pup in a location that is shady and dry for a few days or up to two weeks. This will dry out the roots and heal the tiny cuts that are unavoidable when digging up the pup.

Replant in the ground if it has sufficient roots, or root it by potting it in a mix of half gravel or pumice and sand.

Yucca offsets are attached to the stem or very near it. Look for an offset that is large and vigorous and is increasing in size. Best results occur when offsets are at least 6 inches long and nearly as wide. Cut off the offset as close to the stem as possible. Be careful not to cut into the stem, but flush with it. Dust the cut on the main plant with powdered sulphur; use either powdered sulphur or rooting hormone on the pup. Place it in a pot with a mix of 3/4 pumice or gravel and sand and 1/4 potting soil. Keep the pup evenly moist and in the shade. Roots should form in one to two months. Once roots have formed it can be kept in a container or planted in the ground.

PLANTING

Continue to set out warm-season succulents in Zones 9 and 10, as well as in Zone 8. In Zone 8 gardens, you can continue to plant succulents through the summer. While succulents can be successfully planted in hotter zones throughout the summer as well, it is necessary to pay careful attention to shading the plants and watering them thoroughly.

CARE

Aloes, especially those that form extensive colonies, can become overgrown if not kept divided regularly. Divide **aloes** by cutting out plants along the edge until you have reduced the size of the clump by at least half, although cutting out even more is fine.

Newly planted succulents, regardless of size or type, may need to be shaded during the first summer to prevent sunburn. Drape shade cloth with at least 30% coverage on a frame over the plant if a nearby tree, shrub, or building does not provide enough shade to prevent sunburn.

WATERING

Water large **cactus, ocotillos,** and **yuccas** at least once a month from now through September. Water **agaves,** smaller **cactus, prickly pear,** and smaller **yuccas** every three weeks during the summer. **Barrel cactus** and **beavertail prickly pear** do not need as much water as most other succulents, but watering every five to six weeks in the summer maintains their vigor.

Check newly planted succulents frequently, and be prepared to water as often as once a week through their first summer or if the plants show signs of yellowing or wilting.

Winter-growing succulents will begin to lose their leaves and go dormant. As leaves fade, decrease watering frequency by half. Once all leaves have fallen, discontinue watering.

 FERTILIZING

Succulents in the ground do not need frequent fertilization. If your soil is particularly poor in nutrients or is sandy, spread a 3- to 4-inch layer of compost or mulch over the area where succulents are growing.

Fertilize container-grown succulents with a water-soluble fertilizer once this month. Use it at half the strength that is recommended for houseplants.

 GROOMING

Cactus can be pruned any time it is hot. Remove any damaged or diseased stems as soon as you can to prevent further infection. Always cut with a sharp saw or tool so that you leave a clean cut. Cut at a joint whenever possible. For multi- stemmed **cactus** like **organ pipe** or **senita,** cut the stem as far back to the base as

---

HELPFUL HINTS

When you buy **cactus**, notice which side of the pot is facing south in the nursery. Mark that side. When you replant the **cactus**, be sure it is oriented to the sun the same way. This helps prevent sunburn.

Signs of water stress in cactus are:
• skin that is soft to the touch and offers resistance to gentle pressure;
• shrinking distance between the ribs of columnar **cactus** (if you can't get your finger between the ribs the plant is desperate for water);
• yellowing or paleness of the skin, especially on the south or western side;
• wilting, drooping, or falling pads on **prickly pears;**
• shriveling or shrinking of the skin.

Because **cactus** have large reservoirs of moisture in the stems, these symptoms show up only when the plant is deeply stressed. Water frequently enough to avoid these symptoms, but if they appear, water deeply immediately, and adjust watering schedules.

---

possible. Dust any cut with sulphur to help drying and prevent infection.

 PESTS

Container-grown **agaves** often exhibit a puzzling set of symptoms as the weather warms up. The base of the leaves may turn black or brown, and the area may turn dry and corky. This is thought to be a mite infestation. Control is difficult—miticides are powerful chemicals that are hard to find in some areas, and there is much conflicting information

about the both the nature and control of this problem. Badly infected plants become hosts to a wide range of viruses, bacteria, and fungi and should be destroyed. Most plants are simply scarred on the leaf and do not lose vigor. Many agaves seem to "grow out of it." While controls are not well understood, overwatering and rich or organic potting mixes seem to encourage the infection. At the first sign of trouble, reduce the watering frequency and consider repotting in a faster draining, less organic mix.

JUNE
CACTI, SUCCULENTS, & OTHER DESERT PERENNIALS

PLANNING

Take some time to walk through the garden and see how the succulents are responding to the increased heat. Many **agaves, cactus, yuccas,** and other succulents need light shade in the hottest parts of the region to look their best. Plants in pots are easy to move into a shadier location for the summer, but plants in the ground may need some temporary protection. Plants that are continuously or repeatedly stressed lose vigor, are shorter lived, and often fail to bloom or grow well. Look for locations in the garden to move heat-stressed plants.

PLANTING

Large columnar **cactus,** especially **saguaro,** are popular throughout the region. Native to southern Arizona and a small section of southern California, these mighty **cactus** are spectacular in a desert garden.

When possible, plant **saguaros** when they are small. A 3- to 5-foot plant is not only easier to handle, but is young and vigorous and will grow the wide root system necessary to sustain the plant. Plants over 8 feet

tall usually need to be planted by professionals who have the equipment to move such large plants.

To plant any columnar **cactus,** regardless of size, begin by digging a hole that is 3 to 5 feet wider than the rootball or container and only as deep as the plant root system. Even mature **saguaros** rarely have a root system over 3 feet deep. Soil amendments and additives are not necessary when planting a **cactus.**

Set the plant in the hole, adjusting it to find its center of gravity so that it will stand on its own and making sure that it will be no deeper than it was planted in either the container or its original location. Deeply planted **cactus** fail to survive most of the time, so look for the change of color that marks the soil line, and do not plant deeper.

Backfill the hole, pressing the soil as you go to get rid of air pockets and secure the plant. Water well after planting.

If the plant is large, it may be necessary to stake it at first. Never use boards or carpet-covered stakes to hold up a **cactus;** water collects between the support and the **cactus** and can rot the skin. To stake a large **cactus,** run a ring of tree tape or wire covered with old garden hose around the plant 1/3 to 1/2 up

the stem. From that ring run wire or rope to stakes driven in the ground evenly around the plant. The idea is to prevent the skin from being cut or wounded and to secure the plant evenly but not so tightly it cannot move. Remove it all after three or four months, by which time the plant should have begun to establish its root system.

CARE

Many **agaves,** especially those from tropical areas, begin to show signs of heat stress at this time. Leaves turn yellow or pale green but do not dry out or turn brown, and the skin is softer than normal. If the plants have been well watered through the spring and are kept well watered through the hot summer, these symptoms will disappear when temperatures moderate. Prevention is best. Plant heat-sensitive **agaves** where they receive afternoon shade, and be sure they are well watered long before the high temperatures begin.

WATERING

Water large **cactus, dessert spoon, ocotillo,** and **yucca** at least once during the month. Be

Yucca

GROOMING

Prune only if necessary this month. Old blooming stalks from **agaves, hesperaloe,** or **yuccas** may be pruned any time they are dry and blooming is complete.

PESTS

In dry years, rabbits can be terrible pests for succulents. As vegetation dries out and water supplies disappear, these animals turn to ornamental plantings for food and water. Even well-armed **cactus** and **agaves** are susceptible to rabbit damage if the animals are hungry or thirsty enough. The only certain protections are chicken wire or growing the plants behind a sturdy fence.

sure to water deeply, to a depth of 3 feet and in a large radius around the plant. Water all other warm-season succulents at least every three weeks to a depth of 2 to 3 feet, depending on the size of the plant, and in a wide radius around the plant.

FERTILIZING

Do not fertilize succulents in the ground. Fertilize container-grown plants with a water-soluble fertili-zer once this month. Use low-nitrogen formulas for succulents, especially **agaves** and **cactus.**

HELPFUL HINTS

It takes a lot of water to completely hydrate a **saguaro,** and all of it is taken up by the roots. Newly planted **saguaros** have too small a root system for the plant and they need regular, deep irrigation during their first summer in the ground to stay healthy.

Saguaros are very heavy. A 3-foot plant can weight over 50 pounds, and mature ones weigh hundreds, sometimes thousands of pounds. Use scraps of carpet to make a sling to carry smaller ones—it both protects the skin and you and is sturdy enough to hold the weight.

JULY

CACTI, SUCCULENTS, & OTHER DESERT PERENNIALS

PLANNING

Some of the most familiar succulents to desert gardeners are the stem succulents, **cactus** and **euphorbias.** While they look alike at first glance, there are a few easily recognized differences.

Areoles. Only **cactus** have areoles. Aeroles are collections of tissue on the skin from which the spines, flowers, roots, and new shoots form. They often look like felt pads. **Euphorbias** lack this feature.

Flowers. The flowers of **cactus** are showy, have numerous petals, and are generally in shades of red, orange, yellow, and occasionally purple or white. **Euphorbia** have odd flowers that look like a cup with highly specialized petals that are rigid and waxy. Some are surrounded by colorful, showy bracts, as in **crown of thorns** or the non-succulent **poinsettia.**

Origin. Cactus are entirely from the Americas, and **euphorbias** are from Africa and India.

Thorns. Both **cactus** and **euphorbia** may have substantial thorns. In **cactus** they are usually thin and sharp and occur in a radial array around the areole. In **euphorbias,** they are paired and are generally short, sturdy, and moderately sharp.

PLANTING

Plant warm-season plants, but be careful to provide shade or a covering to prevent sunburn.

CARE

Continue to provide temporary shade for any newly planted succulents through the summer. The south and west sides of plants, even large **cacti**, are especially vulnerable to heat damage.

WATERING

Keep a sharp eye on succulents this time of the year to prevent severe water stress. Summer rains in some areas are helpful, but they are erratic and unpredictable. Be prepared to continue regular watering through the rainy season, but adjust it if there is a good, drenching rain. Water most **cactus** and **agave** to a depth of 1 to 2 feet, depending on the size of the plant. Water large columnar **cactus, ocotillo,** and **yuccas** to a depth of 3 feet.

FERTILIZING

Fertilize container-grown succulents this month following recommendations on page 81.

GROOMING

Prune only if necessary to remove diseased or damaged stems from **cactus** or **euphorbia.** Spent flowering stalks from **agave, dasylirion, hesperaloe,** or **yucca** can be removed anytime.

PESTS

Watch for white cottony masses on **prickly pear** and **cholla** that signal the beginning of infestations of cochineal scale. Wash them off with strong jets of water frequently to keep under control. Chewed-off tips of **cactus** indicate the presence of one of a number of cactus bugs. These large chewing insects are easy to spot on the tips of columnar **cactus** and are generally active at dusk. Destroy them as soon as you see them.

HELPFUL HINTS

Euphorbias exude a white, milky sap that is irritating to most people's skin and is dangerous if it gets in your eyes, nose, or mouth. It can even mar or burn the skin of the plant. Wear gloves or other protective clothing when pruning **euphorbias,** and keep a towel handy to wipe off excess sap from the plant. If you get sap on your skin, wash with soap immediately. If you get sap in your eyes, nose, or mouth, flood with water continuously and get medical help immediately

Cactus plants have three basic styles of growth:

1. **Columnar.** The main stem is much taller than it is wide. Plants can be solitary like **saguaro,** have branches or not, and can be multistemmed like **organ pipe** or **senita.**

2. **Barrel.** The stem is nearly as wide as it is tall, often even round. This is a large group of plants that includes large species like **golden barrel** and **compass barrel**, and small species like the entire genus *Mammillaria*.

3. **Jointed-stem cactus.** The stems are attached to one another at distinct joints and are easily broken off at this juncture. There are two forms within this group: the so-called **prickly pears** which have flattened stems, also called pads, and the **cholla** which have rounded stems. **Christmas cactus** are jointed-stem **cactus.**

In addition, there are some **cacti** that have extremely elongated stems, that vine through forests and thickets using adjacent trees as props for their stems. The familiar **Arizona Queen of the Night** has this form.

Golden barrel cactus

 NOTES

_____

_____

_____

_____

_____

_____

AUGUST
CACTI, SUCCULENTS, & OTHER DESERT PERENNIALS

 PLANNING

Large **cacti,** like **saguaro,** occasionally begin to lean during the summer. This is almost always a symptom of a serious problem with the root system. Check the plant carefully to be sure it is receiving appropriate watering. Too much and the root system rots, too little and there is not enough root to hold up the plant. **Saguaros** are dangerous if they fall on buildings, cars, or places where people can be found.

Check the plant often, and if the leaning progresses, remove it to prevent unwanted damage or injury. Unless the plant is less than 8 feet tall, do not attempt to right a **saguaro** that is leaning without professional equipment and assistance.

 PLANTING

Continue to plant warm-season **cactus** and other succulents, especially in Zone 8. Dig a hole that is wider than the container or root system and just deep enough to hold the root system. Situate the plant so it is at the same depth it was before, and backfill with the dirt from the hole. Do not add compost, mulch, or other soil amendments to the backfill. Water immediately.

 CARE

Inspect **cacti,** especially large plants, regularly to be sure they are receiving adequate water. A plant that needs water may droop, have wrinkled skin, or, in **saguaro** and similar plants, have deep depressions between the ribs. Healthy **cactus** should have skin that is hard to the touch, and the ribs should be far enough apart to put a finger between them.

 WATERING

Maintain regular monthly watering for large **cactus, dessert spoon, ocotillos,** and **yuccas** during the month. Be sure to water large plants to a depth of 3 feet and in a circle around the plant. Water smaller succulents every two to three weeks to a depth of 2 to 3 feet, depending on the size of the plant, and also in a wide radius around the plant.

 FERTILIZING

Do not fertilize succulents in the ground. Fertilize container-grown plants with a water-soluble, low-nitrogen formula.

 GROOMING

Prune to remove spent blooming stalks from **agaves, hesperaloe,** or **yuccas** anytime. Prune out any diseased or damaged stems of **prickly pear** or **cholla,** or to reduce the size of the plant. Allow to air-dry, or apply a light dusting of powdered sulphur on the cut. If a multistemmed plant needs to be pruned, be sure to cut at a joint or as low to the ground as possible and apply sulphur generously to the cut.

 PESTS

Patches of white cottony masses on **prickly pear** and **cholla** indicate cochineal scale. These tiny insects shroud themselves in this waxy, protective covering while they feed on cactus pads. Small infestations do not harm the plants, but these insects multiply rapidly, and left untreated they can become a serious problem. Insecticides are generally ineffective because they cannot penetrate the insect's protective coating. The best control is to regularly remove any cochineal scale by blasting it off with strong jets of water. Remove any visible scale weekly during the late summer when it is most active.

SEPTEMBER
CACTI, SUCCULENTS, & OTHER DESERT PERENNIALS

PLANNING

Leafy succulents may begin to start winter dormancy and slow down growth rates. Do not worry about lower leaf drop. Keep the same water schedule as during the summer until mid-month, then begin to taper off.

PLANTING

Most warm-season succulents grow fastest in the late spring, slow down in the hottest part of the summer, then resume growing as the temperatures become milder in the fall. This makes it an ideal time to plant most succulents, especially **agaves, cactus, and yuccas.**

CARE

Leafy warm-season succulents like **desert rose, Madagascar palm,** and **rock fig** and its relatives may begin to show yellowing leaves. This is the beginning of a return to their winter-dormant cycle. Reduce watering, cease fertilizing, and allow these plants to become dormant over the next month or two.

WATERING

By the end of the month, temperatures usually have moderated enough to shift the watering schedule of succulents. From now until it is cold, water large plants every five to six weeks to a depth of 3 feet. Water smaller plants, including all **agaves,** every three to four weeks to a depth of 1 to 2 feet depending on size. Continue to space out the watering of all warm-season succulents for every reduction of 10 degrees Fahrenheit in the daytime high.

FERTILIZING

Fertilize container-grown warm-season succulents this month. This is the final fertilization of the year for these plants.

For succulents in the ground, spread out a layer of compost or mulch, and scratch it lightly into the soil. This is generally all the enrichment they will need for the remainder of the year.

GROOMING

If cochineal or other diseases ravaged your **prickly pear** or **cholla,** cut them back severely this month to an uninfected portion of the plant. Keep well watered to encourage new growth.

PESTS

Agaves that are infected with agave snout weevil have leaves that suddenly droop, leaving only the tight bud erect on the plant. By the time symptoms appear, the plant is dead and should be removed. Prevention is difficult, and there is no cure. Replant with less susceptible species.

HELPFUL HINTS

It can be hard to tell if succulents are receiving enough water. Signs of water stress in **agaves** include:
- leaves that are soft to the touch;
- leaves that turn pale yellow;
- flattened or falling leaves, especially the oldest leaves;
- death of more than just the oldest leaves on the plant.

OCTOBER
CACTI, SUCCULENTS, & OTHER DESERT PERENNIALS

 PLANNING

Agaves and **yuccas** are outstanding desert ornamentals that fit into almost any gardening style. There are dozens of species available, and the following are some of the best.

• *Agave attenuata* is a delicate plant with a long, whitish stem and wide, pale-green leaves without teeth or spines. This is a cold-tender species that is recommended for the warmest parts of Zone 9 and all of Zone 10.

• *Yucca baccata* and *Y. elata* are native through most of the region and will thrive in gardens anywhere in the area. *Y. baccata* is usually a low- growing, big-headed plant with stiff gray-green leaves, while *Y. elata* has thin grasslike leaves that are smothered in fine white filaments.

• *Agave havardiana* and *A. neomexicana* are native to the Chihuahuan Desert in both the United States and Mexico. Both are moderate-sized plants with dusky-green to pale blue-green leaves and are completely hardy throughout the region.

• *Agave parryi* has tight, regular rosettes whose leaves have a blue-green cast. It is hardy enough for high-elevation gardens as well as Zone 8.

• *Yucca recurvifolia* is native to the eastern United States but has acclimated perfectly to growing in the dry Desert Southwest. The dark-green leaves and short size make it useful in a garden of any size. It is hardy enough to grow throughout the region.

• *Yucca rigida* is one of the prettiest of all yuccas. Tall plants with a big head of stiff blue to blue-gray leaves, it is a gorgeous specimen in any garden. It is hardy enough to grow throughout the region.

• *Agave vilmoriniana* is a large plant with leaves that curve gracefully from the base. Hardy to 17 degrees Fahrenheit, this species can be used in all of Zones 9 and 10 and protected spots of Zone 8.

 PLANTING

In Zones 9 and 10, this is the best month to plant **agaves** and **yuccas.** The warm days and mild nights allow these plants to become well established before the rigors of their first summer. In addition, plants that establish in the fall have the entire winter

to acclimate their leaves to the sun and are much less prone to sunburn. Dig a hole that is just deep enough to accommodate the root system and three to five times wider than the container. Amendments and other additives are not necessary. Be sure the crowns of **agaves** sit well above the soil line after they are planted.

 CARE

At the end of the month, begin the next phase of encouraging **Christmas cactus** to rebloom. Put the plants in a location that is cool at night—55 degrees Fahrenheit to 65 degrees is ideal—and where they will be completely in the dark for twelve to fourteen hours. They can be put in an unused or unheated room, in a garage or shed, or even outdoors if the right conditions apply. Water regularly, but let them dry out somewhat between watering. Flower buds will form in four to six weeks.

WATERING

Continue to water warm-season succulents at long intervals. If summer- dormant succulents like **boojum** begin to show leaves, start watering regularly. **Boojum** grow through the winter, and it is important to water them regularly through the cool months to have them grow well and store enough moisture for the summer. **Boojums** that are getting sufficient water set out regularly spaced, radial sets of branches and leaves. If your plant has wide spaces between the sets of branches, it is probably not getting enough water in the winter.

FERTILIZING

Any container-grown winter-growing succulents can begin to be fertilized monthly, starting this month. Use a soluble fertilizer at $1/4$ to $1/2$ the strength that is recommended for houseplants. Do not fertilize plants in the ground this month.

NOTES

HELPFUL HINTS

Prickly pear and **cholla** grow rapidly from cuttings. If your plant has become too infected with cochineal scale or has seriously declined, consider taking cuttings, removing the original plant, and starting over. Take pads or stems from the newest part of the plant, making sure they are healthy and free of disease or pests. Although one joint or pad will root, take a section of three or four so that the new plant will have a better start. Set the cutting in a shady, dry spot, and let the cut dry out completely. Set the section in a pot with a mix of equal parts pumice or gravel and sand. Place the section deeply enough in the mix so that it stands up on its own. Water well. Keep the cutting in the shade, and water it only enough to keep it barely moist. Too much water and the skin will rot, too little and it won't form roots. Roots should be well established in a month or two.

GROOMING

Do not prune warm-season succulents this month. Remove spent flowers anytime. You can remove pups from **agave** and pot them up this month. Follow the recommendations on page 84. Do not remove **yucca** offsets during cool weather.

PESTS

In the warmest parts of the region, continue to monitor **cactus** for cochineal scale, and treat by spraying with strong jets of water.

NOVEMBER
CACTI, SUCCULENTS, & OTHER DESERT PERENNIALS

 PLANNING

In mild-winter areas, it is often necessary to force dormancy on succulents like **Madagascar palm** and **desert rose.** Gradually dry out the plants, extending the time between watering a day or two at a time, until the leaves begin to fall. Once they are dormant, move the plants to a location that will be protected from winter rains, runoff from the roof, or any accidental watering. Check the top of the plant monthly during the winter while it is dormant. If it begins to shrink or shrivel, water once thoroughly.

 PLANTING

Continue to plant cool-season succulents like **aloes, dudleya,** and **gasteria.** Native succulents can be planted this month, but be careful that they are not overwatered through the winter. Do not plant cold-tender succulents this month.

 CARE

Late in the month, **Christmas cactus** should be showing flower buds. Once buds are set and are about 1/2 inch long, gradually move the plant into more light over a week or two. Plants grow best in a spot with bright, indirect light that is cool and away from drafts and hot spots like a fireplace, heater vent, the top of a television or refrigerator, or in a west-facing window. Sudden changes in temperature or light, or both, will cause the buds to fall off.

 WATERING

Water **Christmas cactus** when the surface of the soil is dry.

Water cool-season succulents every two to three weeks while the weather is cool. Note when it rains, and be sure you account for that water in determining whether the plant needs to be watered. In cool temperatures plants are easily overwatered, so err on the side of dry if you are uncertain.

Reduce watering of all warm-season succulents to every five to six weeks, and skip a watering if it rains more than 1/2 inch.

Water container-grown cool-season succulents when the soil is dry halfway down the pot. Always water potted plants thoroughly, letting the water drain out the holes every time.

 FERTILIZING

Fertilize **Christmas cactus** with a water-soluble fertilizer, mixing a solution at 1/4 strength of what is recommended for houseplants. Apply fertilizer every two weeks while **Christmas cactus** are flowering.

Fertilize any winter-growing succulents growing in a pot once a month with a water-soluble fertilizer at half the strength recommended for houseplants. Use a fertilizer that has a low-nitrogen content.

Do not fertilize any warm-season succulents or any succulents that are dormant.

 GROOMING

Do not prune this month.

 PESTS

Mites can invade **aloes** and cause a distorted, ruined-looking central bud. There is virtually no cure for this infrequent problem other than to destroy the plant before it can infect other **aloes.**

DECEMBER
CACTI, SUCCULENTS, & OTHER DESERT PERENNIALS

PLANNING

In addition to **Christmas cactus,** another succulent has become a holiday favorite. *Kalanchoe* is a large genus of shrubby South African succulents. The most familiar is *Kalanchoe blossfeldiana,* which is sold through the winter as a potted plant and is increasingly used for holiday displays or gifts. This species is cold tender, and in the hottest parts of Zone 9 and 10, it may suffer severe leaf drop in the summer. To prevent this, keep the plants in cool, shaded locations, or in the house for the summer. The mild winters of the area, however, are ideal for growing them outdoors on a porch or patio to add a bright spot of color.

In the mild-winter areas of the region, other members of this group can be grown as groundcovers or shrubby succulents in the shade. Look for the following plants.

• **Felt plant** (*Kalanchoe beharensis*) is a tall, sturdy plant that grows up to 5 feet tall. It is hardy in the warmest parts of Zone 9, and in Zone 10 with only light overhead protection on a cold night. Large, triangular, gray-green leaves occur irregularly on the stem and are curled and crimped along the margins. It is a striking specimen plant, although unlike those of other **kalanchoes,** the blooms are unremarkable.

• **Maternity plant** (*Kalanchoe daigremontiana*) produces numerous tall shoots with long, triangular, deep-green leaves. The edges of the leaves are crammed with small plantlets that fall off easily and root just as well. Like all members of the genus, the flowers are in clusters held high above the foliage in shades of red, pink, and orange.

• **Panda plant** (*Kalanchoe tomentosa*) is a curious plant with dense velvety white hairs on its leaves. Like the previous plant, it can grow to 3 feet tall and makes a good filler for a small dry spot.

PLANTING

Wait until mid-January to plant even cool-season succulents.

CARE

Be prepared to protect tender succulents from sudden or prolonged freezes. Cover with blankets, sheets, frost blankets, or cardboard boxes for temporary protection. Move any tender potted plants under the eaves, on the porch, near the house, or in the house on freezing nights. If you expect freezes regularly, keep succulents dry whether they are growing in pots or in the ground. The water taken up by actively growing plants makes them even more susceptible to freeze damage.

WATERING

Water sparingly this month. Most plants will need no supplemental water if there is any rain this month. If there is none, water cool-season succulents once during the month. Continue to water actively growing container-grown plants when the soil in the pot is entirely dry. Keep soil dry during freezing temperatures.

FERTILIZING

Other than **Christmas cactus,** do not fertilize this month.

GROOMING

Do not prune succulents this month.

PESTS

Inspect houseplants regularly for mealybugs or spider mites, and treat quickly so they do not spread.

FRUITS

Whenever my older relatives get nostalgic about the holidays, they always remind the younger ones that what they remember best about Christmas in their youth was getting oranges in their stocking!

The oranges must have been shipped from a long way to reach those rural Texas hearths, but this gift was common throughout the country at the time. It fixed two things about citrus in the minds of many Americans: it was an exotic, prized fruit, and it grew in places far, far away. Citrus from its earliest cultivation in the West became the poster child for the region's appeal:

sunny skies, warm climes, and oranges right off the tree. How could you beat it?

In fact, in the warmest parts of Arizona (Zones 9 and 10), you can hardly escape citrus. Trees grow in thousands of yards, along rights-of-way, beside commercial developments, and most abundantly of all in the abandoned orchards now full of houses. Commercial groves of citrus are still found around Phoenix and are abundant near Yuma. But anywhere it can be grown, homeowners are thrilled to make citrus a part of their yard. It is so common in the area that it is easy to forget the variety of other fruits that can be grown in home gardens.

CHAPTER FOUR

Apples and peaches have come a long way for desert gardens. These are generally difficult fruit to grow where the winters are mild, but varieties have been developed that perform admirably in even the warmest parts of the region. And in Zone 8, an area still a little warm for apples and cold for peaches, there are many varieties from which to choose. Commercial peach orchards are still found on the eastern end of the Phoenix metropolitan area, and a huge acreage of farmland in southeastern Arizona has been planted with apples.

Grapes grow well in the long sunny days of the region. Varieties and hybrids of the European table grape are recommended for most home gardeners. Table grapes are grown on the farms southeast of Phoenix.

The fruit that has the longest history as a desert fruit is arguably the date. Date palms are native to the deserts of North Africa and were brought to southern Arizona and the Palm Springs area early in the twentieth century. Old groves are still found in Phoenix and surrounding cities.

Not as common, but easy to grow, are jujube or Chinese date, a shrubby tree with fruit that mixes the crisp texture of an apple and the sweetness of a date; persimmon, with its dense golden flesh; and pomegranate, which has beautiful red fruit and luscious juicy seeds.

In the nearly frost-free areas like Phoenix, truly tropical fruits like mango, papaya, cherimoya, and sapote are gaining in popularity. These tropical trees are the delight of gardeners who have them. Bananas are extremely frost-sensitive plants that require a frost-free season of more than year to bear fruit successfully. While bananas are grown occasionally in Phoenix and Yuma, it is not common for them to set fruit.

WHAT FRUIT TO GROW

The fruit you grow is largely a matter of preference, taste, and the number of freezing nights in your area. All deciduous fruit trees need some amount of cool temperatures to set fruit. Varieties that need the least number of chilling hours are best suited to the mild winter areas of the region. Low-chill varieties generally bloom early in the year, which is preferred, because then fruit sets and is ripe before the hottest part of the summer—but it also makes them vulnerable to early or unusual freezes.

In the mildest areas, deciduous fruit with a chill requirement of fewer than 400 hours is recommended. In the colder areas of the state, chill requirements rise to 700 to 900 hours. In these areas, where freezes are common, late-blooming varieties are highly recommended to avoid loss due to a late freeze.

Figs and pomegranate are cold-hardy enough to grow throughout the region, and heat-tolerant enough to grow and set abundant fruit in the hottest areas of the region.

Citrus and tropical fruits are all cold-sensitive to varying degrees. Mature trees take more cold than young or newly planted trees. Citrus bloom in the spring, usually late enough to miss any late cold snaps, and most other tropicals bloom even later.

Fruit trees are an investment in time and maintenance for which you will be rewarded with a great deal of fruit. It only makes sense to grow what you like and what you can use. Give it some thought before you plant an entire orchard. There are older neighborhoods in Phoenix that were once grapefruit and orange orchards. When the houses were built they were simply embedded in the trees, leaving each lot with up to thirty trees. Even with selective removal over the years, this is an immense amount of fruit, and it is now gathered each year for shelters and kitchens for the homeless.

The chart on pages 100–101 lists some of the recommended varieties for each area, using the indicator city as the example. Varieties listed for

CHAPTER FOUR

Phoenix and Yuma have a chill requirement of less than 400 hours. Varieties for Tucson have the same or slightly higher chill requirements. Varieties for Zone 8 have up to 900 hours of chill but not less than 600. In these areas where freezes are common, varieties that flower too early (low-chill) can be devastated by an early freeze.

WATERING FRUIT

Fruit trees are not low-water-use plants, but all fruit varieties can be watered efficiently to maximize production and still not break the bank on water use. To begin, follow the recommendations for depth of soil moisture. To know how deep watering has penetrated, slide a metal rod or probe into the ground right after you water. Dry soil will stop the tool. If it doesn't register the recommended depth, continue to water until it does. Make note of how long you watered. Plunge your tool into the ground two or three days later and note the measurement. Continue until the soil is moist only 6 inches below the surface. This will establish how often you need to water, providing the same amount for the entire season. Because the frequency will change over the seasons, monitor watering depth again when the temperatures change.

In addition to providing the right amount of water over the right interval, your watering style can help conserve water. One way to water fruit efficiently is to build a basin around the plant. Basins should extend to the same diameter as the tree's crown, although for mature trees adding another foot is recommended. If you plant more than one tree very close to each other, build a larger basin to accommodate them all. Basins allow a lot of water to be put in at one time, and because it will penetrate completely, they prevent runoff. They are easy to use and maintain.

If you use either bubblers or drip irrigation to water fruit trees, take care that you have plenty of emitters or bubblers to provide the amount of water the tree needs. It is usually best to dedicate one station to fruit because their watering schedule is different from the schedule of other ornamentals. Bubblers or drip hoses can be automated by using a timer, which is convenient and provides water for only the root system.

Mulch heavily and consistently around the base of the plant. Mulch keeps the soil cool, reduces evaporation, and improves the quality and fertility of the soil.

FERTILIZING FRUIT

Guidelines for fertilizing fruit have been worked out with an eye to keeping the tree producing the largest amount of good fruit possible. But the surest way to ensure good fruit production is to have a healthy tree that is growing in nutrient-rich, healthy soil full of the microorganisms that make soil, nutrients, and water work together. Add generous amounts of compost once or twice a year to the root system of the trees. Keep the entire area mulched heavily. Whenever possible, use products based on organic ingredients, especially those that add microorganisms back into the soil.

All inorganic fertilizer provide a big "pop" to a plant. While this can be beneficial in the short term, it does nothing for the long-term health of the soil or the tree.

PRUNING

Pruning fruit is an art, and forests have been felled for the pulp to print the number and styles of pruning recommendations. My own recommendations are included throughout the text, but it is good to remember why pruning is done at all.

CHAPTER FOUR

Pruning out dead, damaged, or diseased wood discourages insects and disease from entering the healthy parts of the plant. Such limbs are invitations to trouble and should be pruned when appropriate.

Consider the fruiting style of your tree or vine before pruning. Apples set most of their fruit on short spurs that form on branches that are more than two years old. Pruning apples is more like thinning or opening the crown. The more new shoots are removed from the center, the more light enters the branches and the more fruit-bearing spurs are formed. Pears and plums form fruit the same way and are pruned similarly.

Apricots produce fruit on spurs that are more short-lived than those of other fruit. Pruning is done to remove older spurs and encourage newer ones to form. This is accomplished by heading back new growth to encourage more growth and keeping the center thinned to allow in sufficient light for spur development.

Peaches bear fruit on last year's growth and therefore must be pruned hard each year to keep up a steady supply of wood of the right age. Generally about half the growth is removed annually. Grapes also produce on new wood; pruning recommendations for grapes are on page 105.

When pruning any deciduous fruit, watch for the angle of the bud, and cut to direct growth outward from the tree rather than inward. And remember, all deciduous fruit is pruned while it is dormant and before budbreak.

Figs produce the largest crop of fruit on the previous year's wood. Take this into consideration when pruning in early spring while they are dormant so that you leave enough wood for fruit. A large fig tree produces a voluminous amount of fruit, so light pruning for size or shape in the spring will barely affect fruit production. Figs can also be pruned when it is warm to pinch them back and encourage a flush of growth. In many areas, figs set another crop of fruit late in the summer on the shoots of the current year.

Citrus is not pruned for fruit production but to keep it tidy, healthy, and a manageable size. Lemons grow so quickly and to such large size that they can be pinched back early in the spring to control their growth with no effect on fruit production. Other than to remove dead or diseased wood, you do not need to give citrus an annual pruning.

BUYING TIPS

Have the nursery pack roots of bare-root plants in damp peat or sawdust and wrap them in plastic for the trip home. Roots that dry out will damage, and even kill, the tree. Soak the roots in water for twenty-four hours before planting.

When buying bare-root fruit trees, look carefully at the roots. They should be thick and firm and have small branching roots. Roots should not have been pruned back. Reject any plants that have knobby, crusty bumps on the stems or roots—this is a symptom of the deadly and irreversible crown gall.

When purchasing container-grown fruit trees, ask to have the pot removed, or poke around to make sure the tree has a network of healthy roots along the edge of the pot. This indicates that the tree was not planted recently but has spent enough time in the pot to grow a working root system. Reject plants that have girdled roots or roots that are growing out of the drainholes, and plants that are huge for the size of the pot. All of these are signs of a potbound plant.

CHAPTER FOUR

Deciduous Fruit Varieties for the Desert Parts of Arizona

	Phoenix/Yuma	Tucson	Sierra Vista
APPLE			
Anna	X	X	
Arkansas Black			X
Dorsett Golden	X	X	
Einshemer	X	X	
Fuji		X	
Golden Delicious			X
Granny Smith		X	
Jonathan			X
Winesap			X
APRICOT			
Blenheim		X	
Castelbrite		X	
Gold Kist		X	
Katy		X	
Sunglo			X
Tilton			X
CHINESE DATE (JUJUBE)			
Li	X	X	X
Lang	X	X	X
FIG			
Black Mission	X	X	X
Brown turkey	X	X	X
Celeste			X
Conadria	X		
White Kadota		X	
GRAPES			
Black Munukka			X
Cardinal	X	X	X
Exotic	X	X	
Fantasy	X	X	
Flame seedless	X	X	
Perlette	X	X	
Queen			X
Red Malaga			X
Ruby seedless	X	X	
Thomascat			X
Thompson seedless	X	X	X
White Malaga			X
PEACH			
August Pride	X	X	
Babcock	X	X	
Bonanza miniature	X	X	
Desert Gold	X	X	
Desert Red	X	X	
Dixie Red			X
Earligrande	X	X	
Eva's Pride	X	X	
Flordagrande	X	X	

CHAPTER FOUR

	Phoenix/Yuma	Tucson	Sierra Vista
Flordaprince	X	X	
Glohaven			X
Mid-Pride	X	X	
Raritan Rose			X
Redhaven			X
Rio Oso Gem			X
Robin		X	
Sullivan's Elberta			X
Somerset		X	
Tropic Snow	X	X	
Tropic Sweet	X	X	
Vallagrande	X	X	
PEAR			
Bartlett			X
Duchess			X
El Dorado			X
PERSIMMON			
Apple	X	X	
Fuyu	X	X	
Giant Fuyu	X	X	
Izu	X	X	
Jiro	X	X	
PLUM			
Beauty	X	X	
Burbank		X	
Damson			X
Gulf Gold	X	X	
Gulf Ruby	X	X	
Italian		X	
Mariposa		X	
Methley	X	X	X
Santa Rosa	X	X	X
Satsuma		X	
POMEGRANATE			
Wonderful	X	X	X
QUINCE			
Orange		X	
Pineapple		X	
Smyrna		X	
STRAWBERRY			
Camerosa	X	X	
Chandler	X	X	
Fresno		X	
Lassen		X	
Quinault		X	
Sequoia	X	X	
Tioga	X	X	

Phoenix/Yuma (Zone 9b and 10); Tucson (Zone 9a); Sierra Vista (Zone 8)

JANUARY
FRUITS

 PLANNING

Citrus is a specialty of the warmest parts of the state. Many fruits ripen this month, including **blood oranges,** whose red color intensifies with cooler temperatures. Like most citrus, **grapefruit** is best left to ripen on the tree. While it has been edible for a month, it begins to sweeten noticeably this month. To find out if citrus fruit is ready to eat, you have to cut it and taste it.

Bare-root deciduous fruit trees are in nurseries now in the warmest zones. Consult the chart on pages 100-101 for recommended varieties for your area. In Zones 9 and 10, look for varieties that are rated for less than 400 hours of chill. In the cooler areas of Zone 8, look for varieties that have between 700 and 900 hours of chill requirement. Varieties with a chill requirement that is too low will bloom too early in the colder areas, and are vulnerable to late freezes. Many of the most popular varieties of deciduous fruit are able to self-pollinate, but check the tags before you buy a new or unfamiliar variety. Varieties that are not self-pollinating must grow near another variety to set fruit.

 PLANTING

Plant bare-root deciduous fruit trees in Zones 9 and 10. Select a location that receives high, light shade or relief from the afternoon sun. Dig a large hole three or four times the width of the container and at least as deep. Mix the backfill with a generous amount of compost or mulch. Add sand if the drainage is poor. Most fruit trees are grafted, so be sure to plant the tree with the bud union well above the soil surface. Build up a small basin around each tree at least 2 feet from the trunk. Water deeply after planting.

This is the final month for setting out **strawberry** transplants in the warmest parts of the state. **Strawberries** are difficult to grow in most parts of Arizona, but if you have the room and a special interest, they can be successful. Space plants 12 inches apart, and be sure the crown is well above the soil line after they are planted. Mulch heavily, and water well after planting.

 CARE

On nights when freezing temperatures are expected, cover sensitive fruit like **lemons** and **limes.** Most citrus is hardy to 25 degrees Fahrenheit without dam-age, and a bit lower with only tip damage. **Lemons** and **limes** will be damaged at 28 degrees and will be severely damaged at lower temperatures. Citrus fruit is damaged when temperatures are below 25 degrees for more than two hours. Cover plants with blankets, sheets, or frost cloth on a cold night. If fruit is frost-damaged, pick and juice it immediately or within twenty-four hours.

 WATERING

Water established deciduous fruit trees deeply every ten to fourteen days. Water more often if sandy soil or drying winds are prevalent. Water established citrus every three to four weeks

Grapefruit (*Citrus paradisi*)

when temperatures are cold. Be sure to water all fruit trees deeply to a depth of 3 feet.

FERTILIZING

Fertilize dormant deciduous fruit trees beginning in mid-month in the warmest areas of Zones 9 and 10; wait another month in cooler areas of Zone 9. Time this fertilization to occur before leaves emerge. Do not fertilize any tree that has not been in the ground for a year. Use a well-balanced granular fertilizer, and water well before and after applying it. Follow label directions for recommended rates.

Fertilize mature **fig** trees (in the ground more than five years) with a high-nitrogen fertilizer at the rate of 5 to 10 pounds a year, applying half in January, the other half in May. Newly planted **figs** are initially fertilized with small doses of fertilizer (1 or 2 tablespoons) at six-week intervals through the first growing season. Each year add more fertilizer; do it less frequently until you reach the schedule for mature trees.

CHILLING HOURS

Chill hours are calculated as the number of hours between 32 and 60 degrees Fahrenheit during the time a plant is dormant. For most trees, this period begins in November and ends when the tree leafs out in the spring. Research has shown that the number of hours below 45 degrees is the most critical time for the plant. Varieties are considered to have low chill requirements if the number of hours is less than 300; low to moderate when chill hours are between 250 and 400; moderate with a chilling requirement of 500 to 700 hours; and moderate to high with a chill requirement of 700 to 900 hours.

PRUNING

Prune deciduous fruit trees before budbreak. Cut out all dead, diseased, or broken wood, any crossing branches, and watersprouts (upright shoots growing straight up from old limbs). Prune **apple** trees lightly, removing only $1/3$ of the limbs. Prune **apricot, peach,** and **plum** trees to remove $1/3$ to $1/2$ of the previous year's growth. Prune **fig** trees lightly to encourage new shoots and bushy growth. Be careful not to severely prune **fig** trees or fruit production will be set back.

Wait to prune any frost damage on citrus until after the last frost date.

Pruning newly planted deciduous fruit is a daunting chore. It looks much worse that it is. For most fruit trees—other than citrus—it is recommended that you prune a newly planted tree hard, cutting it back to a foot or two from the ground and leaving only three or four main limbs. Get rid of all wispy or stubby growth. Check with area growers and County Extension Services for more detailed pruning directions for each area.

PESTS

Apply horticultural oil to deciduous fruit trees or to citrus to kill overwintering insects, eggs, and larvae. Follow directions carefully; horticultural oils are temperature-sensitive and will harm trees if applied when the weather is too warm.

FEBRUARY

FRUITS

PLANNING

Meyer lemon is a hybrid between **sweet orange** and **lemon** that is much less acidic than most **lemon** varieties. It has been banned in the region for many years because it harbors the lethal disease called citrus tristeza virus. The **Meyer lemon** itself would exhibit no symptoms, but other citrus could become infected. A variety known as 'Improved Meyer' has been developed; it is free of the virus and has been accepted for use in Arizona.

PLANTING

In Zones 9 and 10, plant bare-root **grapes** and container-grown deciduous fruit. In the cooler areas of Zone 9, plant either bare-root or container-grown fruit. Plant **grapes** in the same way described for fruit trees, but be sure to provide a trellis or arbor to support the vines. Consult the chart on pages 100-101 for varieties recommended for your area.

CARE

Do not be alarmed by yellow leaves on citrus. These are just the normal winter loss that all cit-rus trees experience. Cover trees if there is a late freeze.

Peaches are in bloom this month in the warmest areas, and unusual or late freezes can catch you off guard. If a late freeze threatens, protect blooming plants by covering them with a frost cloth or blanket. If the trees lose their flowers they will not rebloom, and you can lose the entire fruit crop for the year.

WATERING

Water established deciduous fruit trees every seven to ten days while the weather is still cool. Water newly planted trees at least that often, but weekly is even better. Be sure to water deeply. Water citrus trees every three weeks.

FERTILIZING

Fertilize established citrus trees this month, but wait until new trees have been in the ground one year before you fertilize them. Water trees deeply the day before you fertilize.

Apply a granular high-nitrogen fertilizer or a fertilizer formulated for citrus, following package directions for application rates. Most large, mature citrus require about 15 pounds of fertilizer for the year, distributed in three applications. Ammonium sulphate is a popular citrus fertilizer and may be applied at the following rates: 2 1/2 pounds per fertilization for **grapefruits;** 4 pounds per fertilization for **oranges** and **tangerines;** and 5 pounds per fertilization for **lemon** trees.

Distribute the fertilizer evenly around the tree, and scratch it lightly into the soil. Be careful not to dig or scratch too deeply so that you do not injure the roots. Water deeply after applying fertilizer.

In Zones 9 and 10, fertilize established deciduous fruit trees with a high-nitrogen fertilizer if it wasn't done last month. Time the second fertilization of the spring for when the trees are in flower, which can be any time in the next two months, depending on area and the variety. That will be the last fertilization for deciduous fruit until next fall.

Fertilize **pomegranates** once a year just as they leaf out. In the warmest parts of the region that will be this month, but it may be April in Zone 8. Use a well-balanced fertilizer rated for either citrus or fruit trees, and follow package directions for the application rates.

If your citrus fruit has symptoms of sheep nose (exceptionally thick skin), skip this month's cit-rus fertilization and resume the regular schedule in May.

PRUNING

Finish pruning deciduous fruit trees by mid-month in the warmest areas.

Prune citrus after all danger of frost is past. Begin by cutting out any dead or winter-damaged wood. Remove crossing branches, watersprouts (long, green branches), and suckers (stems arising below the graft). If you can, walk inside the canopy of the citrus, next to the main trunk, and prune away dead, damaged, and crossing branches from the interior of the plant. Citrus bark is tender and will easily sunburn in the high heat of summer. Prune the tree so branches fall nearly to the ground and it is growing as a large rounded shrub rather than a high-canopy shade tree. The branches will work to protect the tender bark. This type of pruning also makes it easier to harvest the fruit.

Pruning **grapes** is an ancient art that is best learned by practice and by watching someone do it. **Grape** vines should be pruned before they leaf out and before the weather turns warm. There are two general pruning styles.

1. **Cane Method.** Two canes near the top of the plant and two canes near the bottom are selected. Prune each to leave only twelve to fifteen buds. These will be the fruiting canes. Then pick a cane below each of these newly pruned canes and prune it back to leave two buds. These will be the renewal spurs and will grow this year to be the fruiting canes next year.

2. **Spur Method.** Another common method for home gardening is the Spur Method. It is also used to train **grape** vines to a trellis or to grow along a wall or arbor. When the plant is young, select two horizontal canes and prune out all other horizontal canes. As the plants mature, these become the permanent frame or skeleton of the grapevine. These two canes should be pruned only if they become too long, but keep them no less than $2^1/2$ feet long. Buds or spurs are the shoots that grow upright from this cane. Leave six or seven spurs on each of the horizontal canes. Each year, prune each spur back to retain two buds.

PESTS

Aphids are found on the tender tips of deciduous fruit trees, and the deformed or rolled leaves that are characteristic of thrips may become visible on citrus. Aphids can be controlled by hand removal, or with a strong jet of water or soapy water. Thrips cause only minor cosmetic damage and need no control.

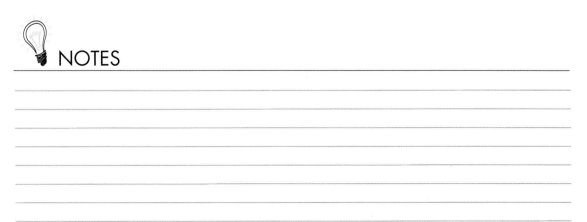

NOTES

MARCH

FRUITS

PLANNING

The range of citrus varieties and types is enormous. Some of the most common for gardens are **oranges, tangelos, grapefruits, lemons,** and **limes.**

Oranges may be eaten out of hand or pressed for juice. Navel varieties like 'Newhall', 'Parent Washington', 'Robertson', and 'Thompson Improved' are often recommended, but in the hottest parts of the area, 'Campbell', 'Hamlin', 'Marrs', 'Olinda', 'Trovita', and 'Valencia' do much better. **Blood orange** and **mandarin orange** (also called **tangerine**) are also recommended for all of Zones 9 and 10.

Grapefruits are the most cold-hardy of all citrus and do well throughout the region. 'Marsh' has white-fleshed sweet fruit and is still the standard for home gardens. Look also for 'Duncan', 'Flame', 'Redblush', and 'Texas Star Ruby', although many red-fleshed **grapefruit** cultivars are not as reliable as the white in the hottest areas.

Mandarin oranges are excellent and perform somewhat better in Zone 9a. Recommended varieties include 'Clementine' (also sold as 'Algerian'), 'Daisy', 'Dancy', 'Fairchild', 'Fortune', 'Fremont', and 'Kinnow'.

Tangelos are popular in home gardens throughout the citrus-growing areas. They have prolific fruit that is excellent fresh or juiced. The **tangelo** is the result of a hybrid between a **grapefruit** and a **mandarin**. 'Minneola' is a cold-hardy variety that is the standard for the group, but 'Orlando' is also recommended.

Lemons are one of those plants you either love or hate. **Lemon** trees are prolific fruit bearers, but like **mandarins,** they have a year with overwhelming fruit set followed by a year with sparse fruit. This boom-and-bust cycle can frustrate home gardeners, but it is just the way of **lemons.** Recommended varieties are 'Eureka', a rough-skinned fruit with mild juice, and 'Lisbon', a smooth-skinned fruit with good flavor. **Limes** are the most cold-tender citrus grown in the region and unlike other citrus, bloom and set fruit throughout the year. **Mexican limes** are small, juicy, and delicious.

PLANTING

Citrus trees are between two and five years old when you buy them, but regardless of their age, it takes three years for fruit production to begin and up to six before they are prolific.

To plant citrus, dig a generous hole three to four times wider than the container and as deep. Mix mulch, compost, or composted manure, or a mix of these additives with the backfill, adding a little to the hole and mixing it with the dirt. Set the tree in the hole, making sure that the bud union is well above the soil line. Backfill, gently pressing the dirt as you go to remove any air pockets. Build a basin around the plant that is at least as wide as the drip line. Water the tree in well after planting.

CARE

Olive trees are common in some parts of southern Arizona and Nevada. If you are allergic to olive pollen, or if you want to greatly reduce the fruit set, spray the trees this month to prevent pollen formation. When using products like Olive-Stop, follow label directions carefully for best results. Most products require three or four applications during the flowering season to be successful.

WATERING

Build a basin around fruit trees that extends at least to the drip line. For older trees, extend the basin a foot beyond the drip line. Fill it once to the top, let the water soak in, then fill it again. Alternately, you can fill the basin and set the hose on a slow enough drip so that it will continue to run into the basin until it will take no more water but will not overtop it.

Fruit trees can be watered by setting the hose on the ground and letting water run at a slow, steady flow. Or you can use a drip system to water fruit trees. Be sure the line is dedicated to fruit trees and that there are sufficient emitters to wet the entire root zone. Whatever method you use, water trees to a depth of at least 16 to 24 inches. Old or large trees should be watered to 3 feet.

Water deciduous fruit trees weekly as the weather begins to warm up. Water newly planted citrus two or three times a week for the first month. After that, water trees every five to seven days through the first summer. In fall, resume a normal citrus-watering schedule.

Too much water is just as much a problem for fruit trees as too little. Check the soil around the trees between waterings. Once it is moist only 6 inches from the surface, it is time to water again.

Strawberries need moist soil to grow well but are sensitive to water ponding or remaining around the crown. Let the surface of the soil dry out between waterings, and provide a heavy mulch to hold down evaporation.

FERTILIZING

Beginning mid-month, fertilize fruit trees in Zone 8, following recommendations on page 104. Be careful not to fertilize fruit while it is blooming; this can shock the plant, causing blossom drop and subsequent loss of fruit.

PRUNING

As soon as fruit has set on deciduous fruit trees (especially **apples, peaches, pears,** and **apricots**) and is about the size of a walnut, begin to thin the fruit. In Zone 8, delay thinning until April because hard spring winds often thin fruit for you.

Remove **plums** until they are 2 inches apart on a branch; **apples, apricots, nectarines,** and **peaches** should be no closer than 4 inches. **Figs** are not as sensitive to thinning, but spacing them 3 to 4 inches apart helps them grow to full size. Keep **pomegranates** 6 inches apart. Thinning helps fruit to size properly and prevents the limb breaking and damage that is caused by a fruit load that is too heavy. Old-time fruit growers always advise that you should have a friend or neighbor perform this thinning, as you will never take off enough yourself.

Continue to clean up dead wood, damaged wood, or crossing branches on citrus after all danger of frost is past. Citrus, unlike deciduous fruit, does not need an annual pruning to keep it healthy and productive. Keep low-growing branches; they will shade the bark and prevent sunburn. Remove all growth below the bud union of grafted citrus.

Grapes begin to grow rapidly at this time of the year. Thin out extra shoots and tendrils to continue to train the vine to the arbor or trellis.

PESTS

If the leaves on **grape** vines are being eaten between the veins, it is probably the work of the grape leaf skeletonizer. Handpick these small black-and-yellow worms daily. Spray daily, especially the undersides of the leaves, with *Bacillus thuringiensis*, also known as Bt solution.

Aphids may erupt this month. Remove by hand if there are just a few, or blast them off the tips of growing plants with a strong jet of water.

Be cautious about spraying around fruit trees and other blooming edible plants. Bees and other insects are working hard to pollinate the flowers so that there will be a good fruit set.

APRIL

FRUITS

 PLANNING

Citrus varieties ripen over a long period of time. Many home gardeners plant more than one variety so there will be fruit for as long as possible. The following are harvest times for Zones 9 and 10.

- **Navel oranges** are ready in December and January.
- **Sweet oranges** ripen in late November through February.
- **Valencia oranges** begin to ripen in February and continue to be delicious through May.
- **Blood oranges** are ready to eat in January and February.
- **Mandarins** peak in December and early January.
- **Tangelos** ripen from late November through February.
- **Grapefruits** will be ready beginning in December and will hold on the tree until May.
- **Lemons** can be harvested from August through February.
- **Limes** ripen throughout the year.

 PLANTING

Continue to plant citrus as described on page 106. Small trees may need protection from the sun for the first year or two until they grow enough branches to shade the bark. Wrap with shade cloth, cardboard, or paper, but never use any type of paint or plastic on the bark. If you do not want to wrap the bark, set up a screen of shade cloth adjacent to the tree on the south and west side of the plant.

Figs can be planted from late spring through the summer. Dig a hole as described for citrus and plant the same way. Many **fig** trees are grafted, so be sure that the bud union is well above the soil line.

 CARE

Citrus trees often drop fruit this month because of high winds and increasing heat. This is a normal response; continue with their regular watering schedule. Clean up the fruit that drops, because leaving it to rot in place encourages insects and disease around the plant.

 WATERING

Water deciduous fruit every seven to ten days. Water citrus every ten to fourteen days. **Strawberries** need to be watered deeply, to 12 inches, but let the top of the soil dry out between waterings; this will help hold down slugs and snails around the plants. Keep well mulched through the summer, both to cut down on evaporation and to hold the fruit off the ground.

 FERTILIZING

Dissolve 1 tablespoon of soluble fertilizer in 1 gallon of water and drench **strawberries** with the solution. Fertilize any newly planted **grapes** that have grown more than 6 inches with $1/2$ ounce of nitrogen fertilizer now and again in June. Next year, fertilize them with twice the amount of fertilizer every month from February to June. The year after that and every subsequent year, feed **grapes** $3/4$ pound of nitrogen fertilizer in February and $1/4$ pound in May. Growers in Zone 8 should adjust the times later by a month to six weeks.

 PRUNING

Lemons can grow too quickly, becoming leggy and overgrown. Prune to remove aggressive watersprouts (green branches that grow quickly from the old branches) and to keep the tree a manageable size. Prune **pomegranates** lightly throughout the year to keep them an appropriate size, or train them against a wall or trellis.

PESTS

If birds are a problem on fruit trees, cover with bird netting just as fruit begins to increase in size. It is important to spread netting before fruit begins to ripen. Birds know when fruit is ripe before we do and will begin to poke holes in fruit to test it, ruining the fruit.

Not all insects harm plants. Some of the so-called "beneficials" in the garden include lacewings, which eat leafhoppers and spider mites voraciously, and the renowned ladybug, which scoops up aphids like candy. A praying mantis may look odd, but it is exceptionally good at eating harmful insects.

Ladybugs are often sold in small bags for release in the garden. Use this method with caution; unless ladybugs are released in exactly the right season, they may leave the bag and just fly away. Check with the local County Extension Service or local nurseries for the proper timing to release these helpful insects.

WATERING BASINS

Fruit trees respond well to basin-style watering. When properly sized, basins provide the deep watering needed by these trees, with minimal loss to evaporation and runoff. Tree roots are not confined to the area at the base of the tree, and in mature trees they extend well beyond the drip line. A basin that is sized to roughly the drip line, however, will deliver plenty of water that will be available to the entire root system.

Basins are not dug out around the tree, they are built up. Draw a circle with a stick around the perimeter of the tree where you want the basin. Build up soil to serve as a dike along that line. The dike should be at least 4 inches tall or up to 6 inches. Firm it gently to keep it in place.

To water using a basin, fill it up, let it all soak in, then fill it again and let it soak in, repeating the cycle as many times as necessary to water to the necessary depth. To determine how many fillings it takes (two or three are generally enough if the basin is properly sized), use a stick or metal rod to measure how far down the water is penetrating after each soak.

It is important to increase the size of the basin every year, as the tree grows until it is fully mature.

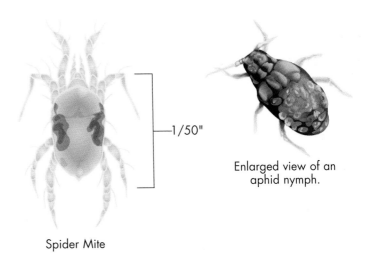

—1/50"

Enlarged view of an aphid nymph.

Spider Mite

MAY

FRUITS

PLANNING

To protect deciduous fruit from the birds, pick it just as it barely ripens. If it has begun to ripen at all, it can finish on the counter in the house.

Figs begin to ripen this month and should be protected from birds as well. **Figs** do not ripen off the tree, so do not pick them before they are ready.

PLANTING

Continue to plant citrus this month in Zones 9 and 10, and deciduous fruit in Zone 8. Many citrus are excellent plants when grown in containers, and in the colder areas like Zone 8, that is the only reliable way to have citrus trees. Containers are also a great way to grow unusual varieties like **limequats,** a delicious variety whose fruit is tiny enough to eat whole, rind and all.

If you want a dwarf fruit tree, choose a variety that is grafted onto dwarf rootstock for best results. Plant the tree in a container that is large enough to hold the entire root system with room for it to expand. Make a rich mix of soil, compost, com-posted manure, and sand. It is usually better to fertilize citrus in containers on the same schedule as those in the ground. Plant the tree so that the graft union is well above the soil line. Leave at least an inch between the top of the soil and the top of the container for watering. Water well after planting.

Plants in containers can be moved into full sun for the long growing season and then put in a garage, shed, or other warm location when freezes threaten. Attaching rollers, or putting the pot on a rolling frame before planting, makes it easy to move around the heavy pot.

CARE

Citrus may continue to shed fruit as the weather heats up. Keep to a steady watering program and the plants will be fine. One of the reasons that **navel oranges** do not perform as well in the hottest regions is their tendency to drop fruit dramatically in hot weather or when subject to hot, dry winds. Continue to clean up fallen fruit to prevent disease spread.

Provide plenty of support for growing **grapevines.** Grapevines become heavy over the years, so be sure to use posts driven in the ground to support the arbor or trellis.

Grapevine in need of support

WATERING

Increase the watering schedule for deciduous fruit trees to every three to five days for the summer. Increase the schedule for mature citrus to every seven to ten days; younger citrus should be watered every five to seven days. **Strawberries** need to be watered daily, similar to vegetables. **Grapes** need watering every five days during the summer. Provide mulch to all fruit plants, but always be careful you do not allow mulch to touch or build up around the bark of the plant.

FERTILIZING

As citrus fruit begins to size, this is the time for the second of its three annual fertilizations. Water the tree well and apply fertilizer at the same rates as the earlier fertilization. Water well again when completed. Do not fertilize any other fruit trees.

PRUNING

Continue to thin deciduous fruit trees as fruit forms.

Fast-growing vertical shoots that grow up from the roots of grafted fruit trees are termed

NATIVE FRUITS

There is a lot of fruit that is native to the region. Much of it is delicious and is feasted on by birds, animals, and tortoises, as well as by people.

• The fruit of **prickly pear cactus,** especially **desert prickly pear** (*Opuntia engelmannii*) and **Indian fig prickly pear** (*O. ficus-indica*), is renowned for its sweet flesh throughout the region. **Saguaro** fruit is outstanding, and if you have a plant and want the fruit, harvest it just as it shows color, but before it splits open.

• The tiny fruit of **wolfberry** (*Lycium brevipes* and others) makes a delicious jam, as do the fruits of native **barberry** (*Berberis* spp.). The sticky red fruit of **lemonade bush** (*Rhus trilobata*) can be made into a refreshing drink that has a slight lemon flavor.

• **Mesquite** pods can be dried and ground into a sweet, earthy-flavored flour. The dried pods need to be pounded or put through a blender repeatedly to separate them from the rock-hard seeds. Mesquite flour is then added to regular flour to make cakes, muffins, and cookies.

• Fresh young pods of **foothills palo verde** are delicious when steamed or stir-fried like **snow peas.**

suckers. They grow from the rootstock and should be removed as soon as you see them. Cut them off flush with the root system. Some growers recommend pulling them off so that the bud of the stem is damaged and it will not resprout.

PESTS

Watch for egg clusters on the undersides of **grape** leaves, and handpick from the plant. These are the eggs of the grape leaf skeletonizer. If you are still finding caterpillars, handpick or spray

with *Bacillus thuringiensis* (Bt). This spray is most effective if used heavily on the undersides of the leaves and applied in the evening.

Yellow dog caterpillars may show up on citrus in Zones 9 and 10. These small black-and-yellow caterpillars are the larvae of the swallowtail butterfly, and citrus is one of the larvae's preferred food plants. They rarely cause more than minimal damage to a large, healthy tree but can be removed by hand if you find they are causing serious damage to a young tree.

JUNE
FRUITS

PLANNING

The fruit of **date palms** ripen in summer. If you want to harvest the fruit, it is wise to put a large bag or covering over the stalk. Birds love this fruit, and as soon as they poke holes it in it, an array of insects joins in the feast. Use a large burlap bag, or create a covering from a sheet and tie it around the entire stalk as soon as the fruit is full-size but hasn't begun to turn color. Taste the fruit every week or two to determine when it is ripe; fresh **dates** can be white, pale golden, or yellowish when ripe, depending on the variety.

PLANTING

Citrus can still be planted in the warmest areas, but be careful to protect the bark from sunburn.

CARE

June is hot and usually dry throughout most of the region. Check soil moisture often, and be sure that plants are being watered sufficiently. Fruit trees suffer from heat stress easily if they are drought-stressed.

Fig

Symptoms of heat stress include splitting fruit, yellowing leaves, and yellow or brownish sunburn patches on both leaves and bark. The best treatment is to maintain a steady, regular, deep watering schedule and wait for the temperatures to calm. If the symptoms seem extreme or prolonged, or the plant is less than two years old, shade the tree and the bark for the summer.

Figs and **pomegranates** are extremely tolerant of high heat and need only a regular, deep watering regimen to withstand summer temperatures.

In the warmest parts of the region, **figs** often make a second crop. The most plentiful and usually better-flavored crop will be ripening in the summer and has risen on last year's branches. The fall crop will be smaller and comes off of this year's growth. Take this into account when you prune **figs**.

WATERING

Water citrus to a depth of 2 to 3 feet (depending on the size of the tree) every seven to ten days. Water deciduous fruit weekly to the same depth. If temperatures become extreme for more than

HELPFUL HINTS

Harvesting rainwater is one of the simplest ways to conserve water in this desert region. Rainwater harvesting can be simple or elaborate—depending on your yard and your interest.

• Begin by looking over the yard and finding out how the runoff water moves when it does rain. If you are not sure and it hasn't rained recently, set up a sprinkler at night and run it long enough to find out how water travels around the yard.

• Once you know where low spots that collect water naturally occur, use them to your advantage by planting large trees, fruit trees, or woody plants that need extra water there.

• Contour the yard to ensure that all rain that falls does not leave the yard. Build berms downhill from low spots so that water slows down behind them. In a yard with lots of changes in elevation, position small check dams at intervals along the path of the water to slow it down, allowing it to slowly percolate into the soil.

• The roof is a superb rain collector. If you are able to use and install gutters, position the drain so that it releases water into a large tree well, a small drainage trench, or a low spot in the yard. Again, the idea is to slow the water down, holding it in place so it percolates rather than races off.

• Connect tree wells and low spots to a source of rainwater like the roofline or the gutter drain. A connection can be as simple as a small depression between tree wells, allowing water to overflow into the connecting path and move to the next well instead of just overflowing the tree well.

• Remember, water travels along the path of least resistance, always going downhill, so the slightest shift in elevation is all it takes to move water from the roof through a string of tree wells or low spots in the yard.

• A French drain is a shallow trench that is filled with rocks or gravel. Water that enters the drain runs out slowly, and much of it penetrates below the surface. French drains are most effective where water is rushing quickly, as off a roofline. They also help prevent erosion under the roofline.

---

a day or two (over 110 degrees Fahrenheit in Zones 9 and 10, and over 100 degrees in Zone 8), water every two or three days until the temperature declines.

If you are using a drip irrigation system on your trees, run it three to four times longer than normal every fourth or fifth time during the summer. This will wash out accumulated salts in the root zone. You can accomplish the same results by flood-irrigating the area around the fruit trees to replace every fifth watering.

FERTILIZING

Do not fertilize this month.

PRUNING

Do not prune fruit trees this month.

PESTS

To keep birds and bugs away from ripening **grapes,** place the fruit in brown paper bags and staple or tie them closed. Paper allows plenty of air circulation while allowing the fruit to ripen.

JULY
FRUITS

PLANNING

Many **apple** varieties do not keep well if left on the tree, so pick **apples** regularly as they become ripe. The variety 'Anna' keeps its flavor for many weeks after being picked, but all the other low-chill varieties recommended for Zone 9 and 10 gardens are not good keepers.

PLANTING

Unless you are planting **palms,** this is not a good time to plant any fruit trees.

CARE

Continue to monitor for heat stress and sunburn, and protect as necessary. Plants respond differently to different soils. If citrus trees begin to look chlorotic, use a soil probe to check that water is being used up between waterings. To check penetration, put in a rod or metal stick that is marked incrementally. It will slide easily through wet soil and stop where it is dry. Note the distance. Check again halfway between waterings and the note the distance. It should be about half. If it is much more, extend the time between waterings. If it is much less, reduce the time between waterings. It is always best to water deeply and less frequently.

WATERING

Water early in the morning to maximize water uptake by plants. Using a timer to water plants not only relieves you of a lot of tedium, but assures that they receive regular waterings. If you do not want to install an electric timer, look for battery-operated timers that attach to hose bibs.

FERTILIZING

Do not fertilize fruit trees in Zones 9 and 10. In Zone 8, apply any fertilizer early in the month. This will be the final fertilization for fruit trees in this zone. Deciduous fruit trees that are overfertilized or are fertilized too late in the growing season put on too many leafy, tender shoots. These tender shoots will crack during an early freeze and can cause early limb dieback.

PRUNING

Do not prune any fruit trees this month.

PESTS

The iridescent color of the green fruit beetle is exquisite, but this small insect forages on ripe fruit, ruining it before it can be harvested. Control is difficult, and prevention is the best remedy. Clean up regularly around any fruit tree that is dropping fruit or that has damaged fruit on the tree. The small white larvae are found wherever there is ample moisture and a feast of organic matter like a compost pile, but they cause little harm.

Leaf-footed bugs—truly well named, their hind legs are large and fattened just like a leaf—also feed by sucking on ripe fruit. They are particularly fond of **peaches, grapes,** and **pomegranates** but can occur on any fruit. They, too, are attracted by fruit that has fallen and is beginning to rot, or fruit that is damaged and remains on the tree.

AUGUST

FRUITS

PLANNING

As **lemons** begin to ripen, harvest them from the tree as needed. Although **lemons** will keep for two or three weeks in the refrigerator, the flavor and juice quality is much better if they are left on the tree until needed. **Lemons** will hold for months on the tree without deterioration.

PLANTING

In Zones 9 and 10, begin to transplant new starts of **strawberries** from now until September. If you are starting your own new plants, begin by pulling out the old plants. Cut off the runners, the long extensions with small plants at the ends, and pot them up in containers with a rich garden soil or a high-quality potting soil. Keep them well watered while they expand their root systems.

CARE

Check the basins around fruit trees to be sure that strong summer rains have not broken the dikes. Modify the size of a basin annually to accommodate the size of the growing tree. Once the tree is mature and as large as it will be, extend the basin about a foot beyond the canopy.

WATERING

Although there can be heavy summer rains in some years, in most of the region you should maintain a regular, deep irrigation schedule for fruit trees. If rains are abundant, watch the watering of fruit trees carefully. If you think the plants are getting plenty of rainwater, skip the irrigation one time.

FERTILIZING

This is the time for the final application of fertilizer to citrus. Water well the day before, and apply fertilizer according to label directions. This fertilization may be applied from now through early September. Water again after application. This late-summer feeding is especially crucial for fall-ripening **navel oranges** and **tangerines**, but is beneficial to all citrus.

PRUNING

Do not prune this month.

PESTS

The disease called gummosis is caused by the soilborne fungus *Phytophthora* and can erupt on citrus during the hot, humid days of late summer. The fungus enters the tree through injuries in the bark. To prevent infestations of this widely occurring fungus, do not let water accumulate around the trunk of trees or stay for a long time around the tree. If drainage is poor in the area and water stands a long time, change watering practices to provide a slow, deep soak that does not create standing water.

Sour fruit beetles may show up on **fig** fruit. This tiny insect burrows into ripening fruit and leaves behind a distinctive sour smell as the fruit decays. The best prevention is to keep the area around the tree clean and free of fallen or rotted fruit.

Sour fruit beetles and other fruit-eating insects can be trapped successfully by taking a one-gallon jar and putting ripe fruit, any type, in the bottom of the jar. Insert a funnel made of window screen in the jar's mouth. The insects will cluster to the fruit but can't get out over the screen. Check it daily and remove and destroy the insects, clean the jar, and add more fruit.

SEPTEMBER

FRUITS

PLANNING

In the hottest parts of the state, it can be difficult to locate appropriate varieties of deciduous fruit trees in mail-order catalogs. Most of the growers are found in the Upper Midwest through New England, and the varieties they offer reflect that. Consult local growers and your County Extension Service for the best varieties in your area, and buy the trees as close to home as you can.

PLANTING

Plant **strawberries** in Zones 9 and 10 early in the month. Use a bed that is dedicated to **strawberries.**

Plant **strawberries** in a rich, well-drained soil that can be regularly watered to at least 12 inches deep. **Strawberry** plants are salt-sensitive—one of the reasons they are tricky to grow in the region—and deep watering to leach out salts in the soil is essential to growing them well. In areas where the water is also salty, **strawberries** can be even more difficult.

Set out plants 10 to 12 inches apart. **Strawberries** grow fast, and although they look small

and tidy when you plant them, they will spread out quickly and cover the entire surface of the bed. Take care that the crown of the plant is well above the surface of the soil.

Spread a 4- to 6-inch layer of organic mulch to conserve moisture and keep stems and fruit off the ground. Some gardeners use a thick layer of newspaper for this mulch with great success.

Set out strawberry plants 10 to 12 inches apart to allow for rapid growth.

For best quality and fruit size, start over each year with new transplants.

CARE

Citrus may look bleak this month after a long hot summer. Yellowed leaves and some leaf loss combine to alarm growers this time of the year. Continue with deep watering and the declining temperatures later in the month will bring them back into good shape quickly.

WATERING

Once temperatures are below 100 degrees Fahrenheit (90 degrees in Zone 8), adjust the watering of citrus to every two weeks. Begin to expand the time between watering on all other fruit by two or three days with each watering until they are being watered twice a month.

Reducing the frequency of watering deciduous fruit and citrus helps to prepare the plants for the winter. Plants slow down their growth so that there are fewer tender, vulnerable shoots on the plants as winter approaches. Reducing watering also begins the shift into dormancy for deciduous fruit.

FERTILIZING

If citrus was not fertilized last month, do so before mid-month. Fertilize **grapevines** for the last time. As new growth begins on **strawberry** plants, fertilize with a water-soluble balanced formula. Use a weak solution (1 tablespoon in 1 gallon of water) to feed **strawberries.** Because they are so salt-sensitive, it is best not to use granular formulas or even well-composted manure.

PRUNING

Do not prune this month.

PESTS

Maintain a rigorous program of cleaning up any fruit that falls from the tree to deter infestations of sour fruit beetles, leaf-footed bugs, and green fruit beetles. As temperatures cool, the population of these insects begins to decline.

HELPFUL HINTS

Oranges and **tangerines** sometimes have split fruit this month. This condition is usually caused by inadequate or irregular watering during the summer. As a result, the rind on the plant thickens, and when the fruit begins to expand in the fall it breaks the skin. Sunburn can also damage the skin and cause it to split, as can excessive water late in the summer when the fruit is nearly full-size. There is nothing to be done now, but resolve to water more carefully next year and provide appropriate shade for the growing fruit.

The first sign of sunburn on citrus is peeling bark that is dry and does not have a gummy or moist substance oozing from the wound. Shade the tree immediately. To prevent fungal infections, be vigilant that moisture does not remain around the open wound.

NOTES

OCTOBER

FRUITS

PLANNING

Pomegranates are ready to eat beginning this month. Not only is the flesh delicious, but the seeds are, too. **Pomegranates** dry well, and because they hold their color for months after drying, they are prized for use in holiday decorations and other dried arrangements.

Although **oranges** and **grapefruit** will begin to change color and become a deep yellow, orange, or gold, that is not a sign the fruit is ripe. Check the harvesting times on page 108, and begin to cut and taste fruit a week or two before the date indicated. Citrus do not ripen or sweeten off the tree, so begin harvesting them when they taste just right to you.

PLANTING

Strawberries may still be planted this month, especially in the cooler parts of the region. Select recommended varieties for your area, and mulch the plants heavily after planting.

Pomegranate

In most of the region, deciduous trees can be planted this month. The warmer soils of the late fall and cooler air temperatures encourage good root growth, which is vital if you want to have a long-lived healthy tree.

CARE

Deciduous fruit trees will begin to lose their leaves in the coldest areas of the region. It is important to maintain a regular watering regimen even while trees are losing leaves, so plan to adjust watering schedules accordingly. In cold areas, apply a 4- to 6-inch layer of mulch around the root zone to protect it from cold and hold in more moisture. Be careful that the mulch does not pile up around the tree.

In the warmer parts of the region it will be a month or more before leaves begin to fall. Maintain a regular care program until the trees are fully deciduous.

WATERING

Cut back on watering deciduous fruit trees to every two weeks until December, then water every three weeks through the rest of the winter. Water more frequently if there is a long warm spell, or if the area is subject to drying winds.

In the warmer areas, water deciduous fruit every two weeks until they begin to drop their leaves, then shift to watering every three weeks for the rest of the winter.

Shift the schedule for citrus to watering deeply every three weeks.

Cut back on watering **grapes** to half the amount and frequency you watered in the summer. In the warmest areas, **grapes** are sometimes slow to shift into dormancy, and reducing the watering gives them a nudge.

FERTILIZING

There is contradictory advice about fertilizing deciduous trees in the fall. The common recommendation has been to not fertilize. It was felt that fertilizing this late might induce plants to grow tender shoots that would not have time to harden-off before the first freeze.

However, there is research to suggest that when fertilizer is applied later in the fall, when the danger of leafing out is minimal, it provides important nutrients to the root system of deciduous trees, nutrients they need for healthy buds and vigorous flowering in the spring. If you decide to try this method, apply the fertilizer just before the tree sheds its leaves. As with all fertilizing, water well before and after application.

PRUNING

Do not prune citrus this month except to take off suckers from below the graft. These shoots grow fast and should be removed whenever they emerge. Many growers recommend pulling them off rather than cutting them. It is thought that the action of pulling them off kills the tissue below the branch collar of the stem and discourages the plant from making a new stem.

Wait until later in the winter to prune deciduous fruit, including **grapes.**

PESTS

Continue to keep the area around fruit trees clear of fallen or decaying fruit. Continue to trap fruit-eating insects like sour fruit beetles, leaf-footed bugs, and green fruit beetles. As temperatures decline, so will the population of these insects.

NOTES

NOVEMBER

FRUITS

PLANNING

Tangelos and **navel oranges** begin ripening by Thanksgiving. **Mandarins** ripen by the end of the month. **Mandarins,** also known as **tangerines,** do not hold long on the tree, usually just about five or six weeks. Use them up as quickly as you can. The dried peel is excellent in cooking and will last for months in a cool, dry place.

To dry the peel, simply remove it from the segments. **Mandarins** peel with ease. Place the peel on a clean, flat surface like a shelf or counter and let it air-dry. Store in a glass jar after it is completely dry.

If you are growing citrus in containers, reduce the frequency of watering to keep the plants somewhat on the dry side. If you have a place with frost protection where they can live for the entire winter, move them in before the first freeze. Be sure the plants have abundant light during the winter.

Pomegranate is one of the few plants that turn color in the fall that actually do well in the warmest areas. The leaves turn an exuberant yellow in late fall. Coupled with the burnished coppery red fruit, **pomegranate** plants offer a brilliant splash of fall color in the desert.

Deciduous fruit that has not already lost its leaves will continue to do so through the month. Continue care for deciduous fruit as recommended on page 118.

PLANTING

In the warmest parts of Zones 9 and in Zone 10, fruit that is not cold-sensitive may be planted this month. Many bare-root varieties begin to show up in nurseries toward the end of the month. Follow guidelines on page 102.

CARE

Citrus or other frost-tender fruit trees will need added frost protection in their first winter. When cold temperatures threaten, wrap the trunk with a blanket, frost cloth, or cardboard. Do not use plastic unless it is attached to a frame. Plastic that touches leaves or stems will burn the plant.

Immediately replace any frost coverings that get wet. The water on them will freeze and damage the plant.

Keep discarded, split, or fallen fruit picked up around the tree. Such fruit provides a perfect harbor for overwintering insects and disease-causing bacteria and fungus.

Provide a 4- to 6-inch layer of mulch around the root zone of all trees. This will help keep the root zone warm in cold areas and maintains steady, even soil moisture. Be sure that any mulch you use does not touch the bark or is piled up around the base of the tree.

WATERING

Water citrus once a month during the coldest part of the year. Continue to water deeply.

Water deciduous fruit every two to three weeks, depending on rainfall. In the eastern part of the region, winter rains are not common, and here you will water deciduous fruit every two weeks. Winter rains are difficult to predict, but regular or abundant rains replace the need for irrigation of deciduous fruit.

FERTILIZING

Do not fertilize this month.

PRUNING

Do not prune this month.

PESTS

You can expect few if any pest problems this month and through the coldest part of the winter.

DECEMBER

FRUITS

PLANNING

Citrus fruit is an excellent gift for relatives and friends who live where it is too cold to grow such fruit. Citrus leaves and fruit make beautiful additions to holiday wreaths, table decorations, and mantle arrangements.

A charming and old-fashioned citrus gift can be made by inserting whole **cloves** in an **orange** so densely that you no longer see the **orange.** Attach a ribbon or decorative rope and hang it in a closet. The smell of the drying citrus and the **cloves** will permeate the closed space, and the **cloves** act as a gentle deterrent to bugs.

Begin to taste-test **grapefruit** around the first of the month. Most will be edible by Christmas.

PLANTING

Nurseries begin to have good selections of deciduous fruit trees and **grapes** this month. Look for varieties that need fewer than 400 hours of chill, and in the hottest parts of the region, the less the better. If plants are bare root, take them home wrapped in wet burlap or other packing material, and be prepared to plant them immediately. If they are in containers, protect them from frost, and plant within a month.

CARE

Citrus fruit generally does not freeze unless temperatures are well below freezing for several hours. If you think fruit was frozen too long, pick it immediately and squeeze it for juice.

If the fruit on your citrus, especially **oranges** or **grapefruit,** seem small, it may be caused by a heavy fruit load, or skipping the final fertilization of the year, or a dry summer. Miraculously, plants know the difference between irrigation and rain, and even with steady, appropriate irrigation, fruit set and growth is better with adequate rain.

WATERING

Water citrus once a month through the coldest months. Water deciduous fruit every three weeks, less often if winter rains are occurring regularly or are abundant.

FERTILIZING

Do not fertilize this month.

PESTS

If you plan to use a dormant oil spray for fruit trees, do so this month or next month in the warmest parts of the region. These oils are temperature-sensitive; be sure to follow label directions carefully.

PRUNING

This month is still too early to prune most fruit trees, even in the warmest areas. To test whether or not to prune a deciduous fruit tree, make a small cut on the end of a branch. If sap runs out, then all the sap has not "fallen" from the tree. Wait to prune until a cut weeps no sap. Do not prune citrus this month.

HOLIDAY GIFT IDEAS FOR FRUIT GROWERS

- Gift certificate to a favorite nursery for a new fruit tree.
- Excellent pruning equipment for those annual pruning chores.
- Long-handled harvester: a splendid tool for all citrus growers. This tool consists of a long pole with a metal basket on the end that is shaped perfectly for pulling out-of-reach citrus off the tree.

GRASSES

I am not a great fan of lawns. I find them monotonous, rigid, and blank compared to the rich textures and abundant forms, colors, and patterns that other plants bring to a garden. Lawns are not for the lazy or the casual gardener—and here I tip my hat to the lawn-lovers of the region.

Lawns require a lot of attention and must be watered, fed, mowed, and dethatched regularly, and like the kids that never grow up, they never achieve any of the independence of well-adapted shrubs, trees, or perennials. And they use a tremendous amount of water.

But lawns are popular garden choices throughout the region, and many gardeners feel they must have at least a little bit of lawn. The first step to having a lawn that works in our region is to pick the right variety of grass for your needs.

In the Desert Southwest, there are five types of lawngrass from which to choose.

1. Bermudagrass is a vigorous grass that has been the standard for lawns in the warm to hot areas for over a century. Regular bermudagrass is a coarse-textured grass that grows 2 or more feet tall if left uncut. Selections and many hybrids are now available that are much finer-textured and a deep-green color but retain the heat-and drought- tolerance of bermudagrass. It can be seeded, but the hybrid varieties must be planted from plugs or sod. It is winter-dormant.

CHAPTER FIVE

2. Zoysia is a fine-bladed grass that does reasonably well in the shade in the warmest zones, but is best in the cooler areas of the region. Zoysia has reasonable heat tolerance, and most varieties are entirely cold-hardy in the region. Zoysia is planted from sod and is winter-dormant.

3. St. Augustine is a wide-bladed grass that is not common in most of the region. In the hottest areas it must be grown in the shade, but it can be grown in sun or shade in cooler regions. St. Augustine is not reliably hardy below 10 degrees Fahrenheit. It is a winter-dormant grass that is planted from either plugs or sod.

4. Fescue, like bermudagrass, is a pasture grass that has been transformed through selection and breeding into a lawngrass. Fescue is generally unsuccessful in the hottest parts of the region but does well in the cool areas. Fescue is evergreen and is grown from seed.

5. Buffalograss is an outstanding grass that is marginal for most of the region. The varieties we can find are recommended only for Zone 8, although there is a great deal of research underway to find varieties tolerant of hot conditions. Buffalograss grows slowly, which limits the amount of necessary mowing, and it is extremely drought-tolerant. It can be planted from seed, but plugs and sod are used for most of the newer varieties.

PLANTING

Details for setting in a new lawn or replenishing an old one are found on page 134. Most home-owners who have never had a lawn are puzzled about whether to plant from seed, plugs, or sod.

Seed-sowing is the most economical way to grow lawngrasses and is the preferred method for overseeding a bermudagrass lawn in the winter. Many newer varieties are hybrids or sterile clones (to help cut down on grass allergy problems), and therefore must be planted from either plugs or sod.

Plugs are small plants that are planted at intervals in a grid pattern where they will grow to fill in the bare spaces as they grow. Fast-growing species like bermudagrass and zoysia cover an area quickly. The slower-growing buffalograss may be frustrating at first, but it will be a better and more long-lasting lawn in the end.

Sod is a strip of dirt with grass growing in it that is in effect peeled from the ground and relaid in the new yard. While sod is expensive, it covers the area immediately. Because the roots are being transplanted entirely, reestablishment is quick.

WATERING

Lawns of any type require a great deal of water. In a region that is dependent on erratic and uncertain supplies of water, most lawns are a generous luxury. To help maintain a healthy balance of low water use and a lawn, remember the following tips.

• Minimize the amount of grass to only what you use.

• Grow the most water-efficient, well-adapted variety for your area.

• Mow less often to keep the grass from growing too quickly.

• Reduce fertilizing to a minimum to keep grass healthy but not growing too fast.

• Do not overseed a dormant lawn.

• Interrupt lawns with pavers or walkways to reduce the amount of grass.

• Water only as needed and as efficiently as possible.

Many lawn-watering guides direct you to provide a given number of gallons of water per week to the lawn. But it is much easier to work out schedules based on how deep you want the water to penetrate. There is an ongoing debate about how to water a lawn, and there are two schools of thought.

CHAPTER FIVE

1. The most common and long-standing recommendation is to water less frequently but deeply. The thought is that deep watering encourages a healthier root system and serves as a reservoir so that the soil does not dry out quickly. The down side is that salts in the soils, which are increasingly supplemented by salty water in the region, build up quickly and are not thoroughly leached out of the root zone.

2. An emerging line of thought, based on research at the University of Nevada at Las Vegas, is that shallow, frequent watering is a better way to control salt buildup. In effect, the salts are never allowed to be out of solution because the moisture level is so consistent. There is much work yet to do on how this translates to overall water use and whether or not there are alternative ways to manage salts.

In this book I have recommended the deep-watering and longer-intervals method. If you notice salt buildup or salt-related problems, I recommend that you periodically flood the area. It also helps to be sure that the soil column never dries out deeper than 6 inches between waterings.

To determine how deeply water is penetrating, turn on the sprinkler (or whatever system you are using) for 15 minutes. Plunge a probe or metal rod into the ground and check how far down the water penetrated. During the warm season, lawns need to have water penetrate 8 to 10 inches. Adjust the timing by 15 minutes until the probe penetrates to the recommended depth.

To decide how frequently to water, keep checking the soil moisture daily; when the lawn has a moisture level of 6 inches, it is time to water again.

Concerns about watering lawns are not restricted to the amount of water it takes to sustain a lawn. It is also important to use a watering method that is appropriate for the size of the lawn and that provides water only to the plants. There are a lot of ways to deliver water to lawns—here are some of the most common.

• Sprinkler systems are a network of underground pipes with risers at prescribed intervals. Risers can be permanently above the soil, or the pop-up style where they are thrust up out of the ground when the water pressure rises. On top of the risers are heads that emit water. Most sprinkler heads are sized to emit a fine, but widely thrown, spray. The fine mist evaporates quickly in the heat, so use sprinklers when evaporation is minimal—at night or in the hours just before dawn.

Sprinkler systems are convenient when used in conjunction with a timer, and once properly set, they deliver exactly the right amount of water to the lawn. Be sure to adjust timers seasonally as the water needs of the plants change.

• Drip irrigation is rarely used for lawns, but a modified version that incorporates soaker or weeping hoses is available. This is an effective watering style for small lawn areas. Made of recycled asphalt or tire rubber or both, these hoses can be joined with standard drip irrigation couplers and attached to a faucet or used in conjunction with a timer. They deliver water slowly underground so there is no evaporation, minimal damage, and, if spaced properly, even coverage.

• In some parts of the region a system that flood-irrigates a lawn has been in place for decades. Even if you do not live in a neighborhood that has this type of watering system available, you can create a version of it by building a berm around the entire lawn. Water is then applied about twice a month in the summer, once a month in the winter, in sufficient quantity to fill up the basin. The walls of the basin are generally 6 to 8 inches tall. Water is delivered slowly so that it penetrates deeply and if flooded at night, loses little to evaporation.

• Oscillating sprinklers and other hand devices are the most inefficient of all watering devices

CHAPTER FIVE

for a lawn. Oscillating, impulse, or other sprinkler types that attach to a hose deliver water in irregular patterns and at erratic levels. Because the potential for evaporation is very high, they should always be used at night or early in the morning.

MOWING

Ask any gardener to name their least favorite chores in the garden, and mowing always makes the list. It is time-consuming, misapplied, misunderstood, and monotonous. But it is the maintenance task that makes the biggest impact on the looks and health of a lawn.

When you mow a lawn you are simultaneously cutting off a good portion of the leaf that provides the power to make the grass grow and inducing the grass to grow more quickly to respond to the trauma. This push-pull for the grass needs to be managed carefully. Here are a few tips to help make things better for you and for the grass.

1. Mow to the appropriate height for the variety you are growing. Mowing heights for grass varieties are listed on page 138. Follow them rigorously, and if there is a range, choose the longest blade length. If you remove more than 40% of the foliage, root growth will stop, with dieback of the entire plant soon to follow.

2. Cut with the right mower. A reel mower gives the smoothest cut. The blades can be kept razor sharp, and this is the style to use if you have a grass that needs to be cut low. A rotary mower has a blade that spins around a central axis and makes a cut that is higher than a reel.

3. Never mow grass that is wet. When grass is wet, mowing bends the grass blade and you do not get a clean, sharp cut. Wet grass also clumps and gums up the mower blades, and the mower can leave ruts in a wet lawn.

4. Leave clippings in place to serve as mulch for the growing grass unless the clippings are exceptionally long.

5. Do not mow any more than you must; the compaction resulting from running the mower over the lawn can prevent water penetration.

FERTILIZING

All lawns benefit from growing in a healthy soil that has a continuously renewed supply of nutrients and minerals. While artificial fertilizers provide nutrients in abundance, they rarely do more than

Deer grass and its relatives are the most commonly used ornamental grasses in desert landscapes.

offer a quick-fix cocktail that needs to be replenished frequently.

The text provides detailed recommendations for fertilizing lawns in the region. But a few general points may be made.

• Use the least amount of fertilizer that will keep the lawn healthy. Most lawns are wildly overfed, and excessive amounts of fertilizer make for weak plants that become more susceptible to disease and insects.

Mexican feather grass

• Look for products that both provide additional nutrients and add soil microorganisms back to the soil. The product Grow Power Plus is one such fertilizer, and there are others. It used to be the practice in Phoenix to spread a heady mix of manure and mulch on a lawn before you overwintered it. The slow release of nutrients nourished the soil, and subsequently the grass, over the course of the long dormant season. A layer of good-quality compost would do the same, and it would be much less offensive to the neighbors.

• Follow the recommendation to water deeply before and after applying fertilizer. Dry granular fertilizers can burn grass quickly if left on the blades. Watering dissolves the fertilizer and removes it to the soil where it belongs.

DETHATCHING

Dethatching is the removal of the accumulated dead stems, roots, and leaf litter (thatch) that builds up at the soil line. A thin layer of thatch is helpful; it serves as mulch, keeping the soil temperature steady and holding in moisture. But as it increases in thickness it becomes detrimental to the lawn, preventing the penetration of water and fertilizer into the soil.

To test the level of thatch, stick a knife or screwdriver into the grass but not into the soil. Measure the distance from the surface of the thatch to the soil. If it is more than $1/2$ inch, it is time to dethatch the lawn.

To remove the thatch, use a dethatching rake (they are widely available in nurseries and garden centers), a rotary mower with dethatching blades, or if the lawn is large or the thatch is especially deep, rent a dethatching machine. Most maintenance contractors perform dethatching as well.

Remove the thatch, leaving the last $1/2$ inch of thatch in place. Move your tool in alternating directions and crisscross the lawn to make an even removal pattern.

CHAPTER FIVE

Time dethatching to coincide with a fertilization, and apply fertilizer once you are finished.

Dethatching is not an annual chore, but it should be done every few years to maintain a healthy lawn.

ORNAMENTAL GRASSES

Ornamental grasses are a refreshing change of form and texture in a garden dominated by shrubs and leafy perennials. Their delicate flowing leaves and lacy, often colorful, flowering stalks provide a pleasant contrast to the deep greens and rounded shapes of many garden ornamentals. Planted among succulents, grasses add a tinge of softness to the otherwise hard-edged symmetry of agaves, cacti, and yuccas.

Like evergreens, ornamental grasses maintain a strong presence in the garden, but like a glorious mirage their form changes through the seasons. In the spring and early summer they are green, full and growing. Late in the summer and continuing through the fall they are transformed as their long flowering stalks shoot out of the clump. These flowering heads, some in brilliant autumnal golds, yellows, and reds, are breathtaking when backlit by the low light of a fall sunset.

Tall ornamental grasses make a good background for summer-flowering perennials, annuals, or bulbs by providing a solid wall that frames the colorful show. Many gardeners interplant ornamental grasses of varying size and color throughout a large perennial bed to carry the whole bed through the fall.

Ornamental grasses are effective when used in mass plantings or large numbers. They can fill a difficult spot at the edge of a garden or a narrow bed along a driveway while adding drama and excitement to the bed. Grasses hold soil tenaciously in their fine, wide network of roots and are useful on a steep slope or other areas where soil erosion is a problem.

There is a wide array of ornamental grasses in horticulture, but few are used with any regularity in the deserts of Arizona. Far and away the most common are deer grass and its relatives, all in the genus *Muhlenbergia*. These grasses are from arid or semiarid parts of the Southwest and adjacent Mexico and are solid performers.

One of the ornamental grasses in longest use is fountain grass (*Pennisetum setaceum*), which has fallen out of favor and is illustrative of a problem with some ornamental grasses. Fountain grass is so well suited to the area and reseeds so aggressively, often without the benefit of extra irrigation, that it has escaped cultivation, has taken over hillsides and natural areas, and is now an invasive pest species.

Mexican feather grass (*Stipa tenuissima*) is a fine-textured grass that grows well in open, rocky ground under dry conditions. The straw-colored inflorescence floats above the foliage for months after blooming is finished. This graceful ornamental grass deserves to be used more widely than it is.

JANUARY
GRASSES

PLANNING

If you find you are having trouble mowing close enough to trees, fountains, or the edge of planted beds, consider adding a mower strip to the lawn. This is an edge of brick or concrete pavers that are set flush to the ground between the lawn and any other planted area or obstruction. It is typically wide enough to accommodate the wheels of the mower and deep enough to allow the appropriate cutting height. When set in correctly, there is little or no need to handprune at the edge. If near ornaments or large trees, the mower strip can be set a distance from the object and a small planting area is created between it and the lawn.

PLANTING

Do not plant grass this month.

CARE

Lawns are made to walk on, but it is best not to walk on them when they are wet or after a heavy rain. Foot traffic and heavy equipment will leave ruts and furrows that can be difficult to correct on wet lawns. If the area is slow to dry out, set out

Cut back your ornamental grasses this month if you did not do it in December.

stones or pavers along frequently used pathways.

WATERING

Water overseeded lawns to a depth of 4 to 6 inches this month, which is usually every other week. Use a long screwdriver or metal rod to test how deeply the water is penetrating.

Water dormant lawns once to the same depth.

Ornamental grasses have significantly slowed growth or are dormant this month. They should be watered once a month to a depth of 4 to 6 inches.

Winter rains are unpredictable—in some years they are abundant, in others sparse. If rains are abundant and regular, be sure that lawns, dormant or growing, need water before turning on the system. Too much water is just as destructive as too little.

FERTILIZING

Perennial rye in overseeded winter lawns may turn yellow this month. This is often the result of overwatering. If you do not think this is what has happened, however, apply a fertilizer specifically formulated for winter lawns or add an iron supplement to the lawn. Lawngrasses of all types are heavy nitrogen feeders, but occasional doses of phosphorus and iron can be beneficial—it is recommended that you don't fertilize with a high-nitrogen content during the winter.

Do not fertilize any dormant lawn that is not overseeded this month.

MOWING

Mow overseeded **rye** lawns regularly. Mow to take off about 1/3 of the length of the blade at each mowing, keeping the overall blade length at 1 to 2 inches. Mowing too low prevents the grass from growing sufficiently to make an even cover and can result in bare patches. If the cut-

HELPFUL HINTS

• If you have a small lawn—and I hope you do—and you have lots of small interruptions in the lawn like stones, walkways, ornaments, or birdbaths, consider using a sheep shearer to clip around them. These tools have been used for centuries by English sheepherders to shear sheep. They are made of hard steel that holds a good, clean edge. They were revived in England for use in the garden and are now available here. The shearers cut cleanly and let you get in-between small places and around tender plants without damage.

• Many gardeners use string cutters to trim around walkways, trees, or other impediments to a lawn mower. While these are effective tools, they are also dangerous to some of your other plants. Take extra care around trees, as string cutters cut the bark of trees with ease. Stay at least 2 feet from a tree when using the cutter.

tings are short, leave them in place, as they provide excellent mulch for the grass. If they are long, gather or rake them away; they can pile up and inhibit water penetration.

If you did not cut back ornamental grasses in December, do it before the end of this month. Cut straight across the top of the bunch, leaving 6 inches of the blade above the ground. Pull out as much dead grass from around the base as will come off in your hand. Remove all the cut stems and debris. Leavings from pruned ornamental grass make great mulch in the vegetable garden.

PESTS

Most lawns are unaffected by pests during the cold months of the year.

NOTES

_____
_____
_____
_____
_____
_____
_____
_____
_____
_____
_____

FEBRUARY

GRASSES

PLANNING

If you have a small garden or a patio, use ornamental grasses in containers either singly or in mixed plantings. Single plants, especially large or vivid-patterned species, make striking specimen plants. Use smaller species as part of a mix of perennials, annuals, or even succulents to create a miniature garden in the pot.

Many of the smaller grasses like the lovely **blue lyme grass** (*Leymus* spp., formerly the genus *Elymus*), **common blue fescue** (*Festuca glauca*), or **tufted hair grass** (*Deschampsia caespitosa*) are unreliable in the high heat of Zones 9 and 10. But they can be useful annuals, potted up in interesting containers during the long spring or fall season in the same way that some flowering perennials are used as winter annuals in the area. Move these containers into the shade when the hot weather strikes, and in some years the grasses may live over the summer. **Indian rice grass** (*Achnatherum speciosum*) is a particularly stunning choice for a potted grass with its graceful heads and large seedheads. This grass dries well and makes a beautiful addition to dried arrangements.

PLANTING

Plant ornamental grasses as they become available this month in the warmest areas. In the cooler area, wait until at least April to plant ornamental grasses.

CARE

In some years winter rains can be heavy and consistent, offering little time for grasses to dry out between rains. Where standing or ponding water is a problem such as beneath a roofline, add pavers or a light covering of gravel. These materials will absorb the energy of the falling water, preventing the formation of a dead zone in the lawn as well as helping to disperse the falling water.

WATERING

Water overseeded lawns every ten days to a depth of 4 to 6 inches. If the weather turns hot at the end of the month, increase watering frequency to weekly.

Water dormant lawns every three weeks in Zones 9 and 10, and once a month in Zone 8 to a depth of 4 to 6 inches.

Established ornamental grasses may begin to sprout late in the month. Water deeply as soon as shoots emerge, then continue deep watering every ten days.

FERTILIZING

There are countless recommendations on how to fertilize lawns from reputable lawn growers. In the desert regions, follow these general guidelines.

• Provide plenty of nitrogen monthly while grass is growing. This will be year-round if you overseed a lawn, but only during the active growing season if you do not.

• Most lawns need an application of iron three or four times during their growing season. Lawns that need iron show a yellowing of the leaves. This can also be a symptom of overwatering, so check the irrigation first before using an iron additive.

• Balanced formulations provide not only sufficient nitrogen, but all other nutrients, including micronutrients that lawns need to grow quickly, recover from mowing well, and stay healthy.

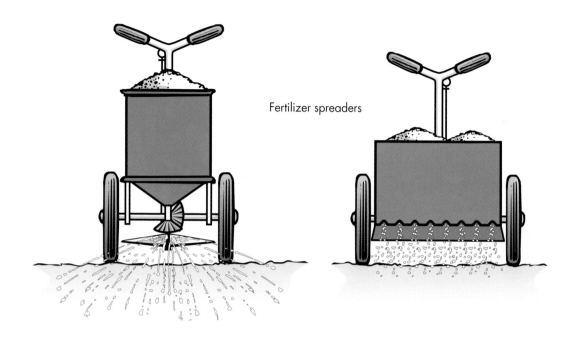

Fertilizer spreaders

• The simplest way to fertilize a lawn is to provide a balanced fertilizer that has a ratio of NPK (nitrogen, phosphorus, potassium) of 3-1-2. This would translate on the package, for example, to 21-7-14. If you prefer to use the nitrogen-only formulas, like ammonium nitrate and ammonium sulfate (usually 21-0-0), add a phosphorus, iron, or balanced fertilizer two or three times a year.

• Organic fertilizer formulations can be used on lawns with no difficulty. They, too, are applied according to package directions. The product Grow Power Plus includes nutrients NPK (5:3:1 ratio), sulphur, a soil penetrant, and microorganisms, all of which work to release nutrients in a readily available form over a long time. It is applied four times a year.

• Regardless of the type of fertilizer you use, water the lawn deeply before applying fertilizer, spread it evenly, and water again after application.

MOWING

Continue to mow overseeded lawns regularly, taking only about 1/3 of the blade with each mowing. Do not cut back ornamental grasses in the hottest areas after mid-month. In other areas, cut back grasses if you haven't already done so.

PESTS

Grasses, both lawn and ornamental, are generally unaffected by pests this time of the year. Prevent any fungal disease problems by watering during the daylight hours and making sure that standing water drains quickly.

MARCH

GRASSES

PLANNING

If you are considering putting in a new lawn, begin to plan and prepare for it this month. The first considerations for any lawn are: How big does it need to be? and, What use will be made of it? In all of the desert regions, lawns should be as small as possible and only grown where they have a definite use. Once you have decided on the area and how big it will be, begin to look around for grasses.

• **Bermudagrass** is the most common type of grass used in desert cities. This pasture grass from Africa has astounding heat tolerance and many varieties and hybrids work well for lawns in the area. **Bermudagrass** is a low-growing grass (although the old pasture forms can be up to 3 feet tall) that grows quickly from stolons. It grows poorly in the shade but takes any amount of heat and sun. It is dormant in the winter and can be overseeded while dormant.

• **Zoysia** is a low-growing grass that spreads by stolons. It makes a dense, carpetlike cover and tolerates some shade. **Zoysia** can be grown throughout the region but does best in the cooler parts of Zone 9 and in Zone 8. **Zoysia** is slower grow-

Close-up view of St. Augustine grass.

ing than most other lawngrasses in the region, so establishment takes longer, but mowing will be less frequent. It is winter-dormant; it should not be overseeded when it is dormant.

• **St. Augustine** has a broader leaf than the other lawngrasses and tolerates shade well. It is a spreading, low-growing grass that can make a thick thatch. It becomes yellow in high heat and requires more water than **bermudagrass.** Like **zoysia,** it is best used outside the hottest parts of the region. **St. Augustine** is winter-dormant and should not be overseeded.

• **Buffalograss** is a bunch grass that spreads to form a lawn. It is extremely drought-tolerant, but varieties currently offered are not heat-tolerant enough for Zones 9 and 10. It is, however, highly recommended for Zone 8, where an established lawn needs minimal irrigation and infrequent mowing.

• **Tall fescue** (*Festuca arundinacea*) is a fine-bladed grass that has some shade tolerance. Over the years, many hybrids have been developed that perform well in the region. **Fescue** is an evergreen grass that should not be overseeded. It grows best in the coolest parts of Zone 9 and in Zone 8.

 PLANTING

St. Augustine breaks dormancy earlier than either **zoysia** or **bermudagrass** and can be planted this month.

Plant ornamental grasses from now through May. Ornamental grasses do not need special amendments or a highly amended soil to grow well. Dig a hole that is three to five times wider than the container and as deep. When you take the grass out of the container, pull soil away from the roots gently but do not remove all the soil. You are trying to free up the roots and help stimulate them to grow out of the potting mix. Set in the hole and backfill, pressing the soil to remove air pockets. Water well after planting.

 CARE

March can be an in-between month for the lawn in the warm areas of the region. It will begin to get hot in much of the region, but it is nearly two months before **bermudagrass** begins to grow. **Perennial rye** lawns usually carry through this time much better than **annual rye,** which will begin to die off as soon as it is warm.

 WATERING

In Zones 9 and 10, increase the watering depth for overseeded lawns to 8 to 10 inches this month. This usually means watering once a week. Water **bermudagrass** lawns every two weeks.

Newly planted lawns should be watered daily for a week, then every other day for another week. In the third week begin deep watering, to a depth of 4 to 6 inches. Check with a stick or metal rod often to determine the interval needed to maintain that soil moisture in the newly planted area.

 FERTILIZING

Feed overseeded lawns again this month with a high-nitrogen or complete balanced fertilizer. Do not feed **bermudagrass** lawns that are not overseeded.

Once you see it is actively growing, fertilize **St. Augustine** with 5 pounds of a 21-7-14 blend per 1,000 square feet.

 MOWING

Mow overseeded lawns regularly. Do not begin to mow a newly planted lawn until it has grown to its full, recommended height.

 PESTS

Take care of emerging weeds quickly. It is both easier and safer to handpull weeds as soon as you see them. Remove weeds before they set seed to minimize future problems.

 NOTES

_____
_____
_____
_____
_____
_____
_____
_____
_____

APRIL

GRASSES

PLANNING

Bermudagrass was originally brought to the United States as pasture grass. It has been a common lawngrass in the Southwest for decades and is still the most heat- and drought-tolerant of all the grasses available.

So-called regular **bermudagrass** is a fairly coarse grass that grows from stolons and can be tall and wispy if left unmowed. **Bermudagrass** grows fast and is relatively pest- and disease-resistant. It is the fast growth and hardiness that permit it to be overseeded in the winter. It can easily withstand the competition of another grass growing more or less on top of it.

There are numerous selections and hybrid forms of **bermudagrass** now on the market. Some of the most commonly planted varieties for home gardens are 'Sahara', 'Santa Ana', 'Tifgreen', 'Tifdwarf', and 'Midiron'. 'Bull's-eye' (Bob sod) and the varieties developed specifically for golf courses are not recommended for home gardens.

PLANTING

Lawngrasses may be planted from seed, from plugs, which are small independent pieces of grass, or from sod, which is a square of growing grass attached to some soil. You can begin to plant **bermudagrass** once night temperatures are above 65 to 70 degrees Fahrenheit for best results.

If you are starting with no lawn at all, begin by removing all debris, rocks, old turf, or weeds, and smooth out the area. Water the entire area to a depth of 10 to 12 inches and leave it for two days. Add at least 2 inches of organic mulch, compost, wood or forest mulch, or gypsum at a rate of 100 pounds per 1,000 square feet, soil sulphur at a rate of 5 pounds per 1,000 square feet, and fairly high nitrogen/phosphorus fertilizer (16-20-0 or similar). Turn it all in and mix well, going down 4 to 6 inches. If you are installing a sprinkler system, do it after this stage. It is helpful to get a lawn roller (they can be rented from most equipment rental agencies) and fill it with water. It both evens out the soil and applies an even watering. You are now ready to plant.

• Sow seed of **bermudagrass** at rate of 1 to 2 pounds of seed for each 1,000 square feet. A thin layer of organic matter like fine compost over the seed will protect it from drying out.

• Grasses like hybrid **bermudagrass, St. Augustine,** and **zoysia** are available only as plugs (or sprigs) and sod.

• Set out plugs or stolons at a rate of about a bushel for each 200 to 250 square feet, or at intervals of 8 to 10 inches.

• Lay sod so that each square touches another one but they do not overlap.

CARE

Established **bermudagrass** may begin to break dormancy late in the month, depending on the temperatures. Once it is growing, begin to water deeply more frequently.

WATERING

Water seed daily, sometimes two or three times a day if it is hot, until the grass germinates. Then water every other day, spreading out the interval until you are watering on a regular schedule after a month.

Water sod or plugs daily, or as often as four times a day, to keep it moist for the first two weeks. For the next two weeks, water once a day to soak it well. By this time roots should be established and you can begin to water on a regular schedule, soaking to a depth of 8 to 10 inches, usually every three to five days.

Water established **bermudagrass** every eight to ten days if it is still dormant, and increase to weekly once the grass is actively growing. Water to a depth of 8 to 10 inches.

Water newly planted ornamental grasses weekly. Established ornamental grasses will need water every ten to fourteen days.

HELPFUL HINTS

To help sow seed evenly, use a fertilizer spreader. Mix the seed with some sand to help move it evenly through the spreader. Walk the area first in one direction then cross it as a right angle for the second pass. This will help spread the seed evenly over the entire area. Handsowing evenly is an art form, but is fun to try. Old-timers used to take a bucket and punch or drill holes evenly in the lower third, walk the area in an even grid, and shake or tap the bucket as they walked, using the bucket like an upside-down salt shaker.

FERTILIZING

Fertilize overseeded lawns with high-nitrogen or balanced fertilizer. Wait until established **bermudagrass** that was not overseeded is growing rapidly before you fertilize it. If actively growing, fertilize **St. Augustine** with five pounds of a 21-7-14 blend per 1,000 square feet.

Fertilize ornamental grasses this month, but this will be the only fertilizer you apply all year. If you are growing ornamental grass in containers, fertilize either with dry organic fertilizer, slow-release fertilizer, or soluble formulations once a month through the entire growing season.

MOWING

Mow overseeded **bermudagrass** lawns regularly. Established **hybrid bermudagrass** lawns are mowed more closely than other lawns, often to $1/2$ inch. Reel-type mowers usually do this type of close mowing best. Many growers recommend dethatching **hybrid bermudagrass** lawns annually to keep them healthy and lush. Dethatch all **bermudagrass** lawns from now through early summer; dethatch all other lawns now through mid-May.

PESTS

If you find insects or their larvae living in your lawn, be sure to have them identified before you attempt to eliminate them. There are numerous insects that are beneficial to growing plants and some that prey on insects that are genuinely a problem. Collect a sample or two, put them in a jar with alcohol, and take it to your County Extension Service or reputable nursery for identification before beginning any treatment.

An established
bermudagrass lawn

MAY

GRASSES

PLANNING

If you have more lawn than you need or want, or you are ready to garden without lawngrasses, this is the month to remove a **bermudagrass** lawn. **Bermudagrass** is a tough, well-adapted grass, and it takes persistence to get rid of it. Begin by watering the grass well, even extravagantly. It will respond quickly to extra water this month. Do not mow after this watering. Once the grass is growing well, apply a herbicide whose active ingredient is glyphosate. There are many on the market; read the label to be sure this is the active ingredient. Choose a day that is calm to prevent unwanted drift of the herbicide to other plants. Protect other plants from the spray with cardboard, plastic sheets, or wood. Glyphosate is a systemic herbicide, which means that once it makes contact with a plant, especially the leaves, it will travel through the vascular system of the plant to kill it. This means that you can't wash it off effectively if it gets on something you do not want to kill, so protect the plants you like.

It takes about a week to notice the first results and up to two weeks to know how much of the lawn is dead. Do not mow or remove any of the grass

yet. When applied uniformly and according to label directions, up to 95% of the lawn is dead after the first application. Make another application two weeks after the first. After a week, remove the dead grass and rake the area to clean it up. Glyphosate is rated to be persistent in the soil for about 72 hours, so there is little danger of it remaining in the soil, and it will not affect any plant that did not receive direct spray.

Begin to water the area to encourage the residual **bermudagrass** to sprout. There will always be a few stragglers left. To eradicate it completely, keep a spray bottle handy with the herbicide and spray as sprouts appear. **Bermudagrass** roots are deep and can arise months later. Seed can drift in from a great distance. It helps to be vigilant during the first summer.

You can begin to plant a month after the final application.

PLANTING

Continue to plant **bermuda-grass, hybrid bermudagrass,** and **St. Augustine** this month. Begin to plant **zoysia** lawns this month through June. **Dichondra,** which is not a grass but is a round-leaved low-growing plant, is often used in lawns where

there is abundant shade and low foot traffic. Plant from late April through mid-July from either seed or plugs, using the same recommendations for bed preparation as grass lawns. For seed planting, spread 12 to 16 ounces per 1,000 square feet; for plugs, set out 6 to 10 inches apart.

CARE

Bermudagrass may begin to break dormancy late in the month throughout the region, if it has not done so already. **Bermudagrass** is dependant on temperature to break dormancy, so it may happen early or late, depending on the temperatures.

WATERING

The way you water your lawn determines how healthy and vigorous it will grow. The current recommendation is to apply a slow, deep delivery—soaking up to 10 inches deep—at somewhat infrequent intervals.

Every three days, water cool-season grasses that are still growing. Water actively growing warm-season grasses every four days, or to a depth of 8 to 10 inches in Zones 9 and 10. Water every eight days in Zone 8.

One effective way to water deeply, particularly for a small lawn area, is to gently slope the edges of the lawn so that it becomes a basin. This helps assure that all the water is soaking into the root zone of the grass and not running off. Lawns in this configuration can even be watered by laying down a hose and filling the basin.

Sprinklers are a popular option for watering lawns. Those that are fitted to a timer are extremely convenient and reliable, once you have determined how long and how often they must run to achieve the amount of water the lawn needs. Check the heads often to be sure they are not clogged and are spraying in an even pattern. If you start to notice yellow or brown spots in the lawn (indicating over- and underwatering, respectively), check that the pattern of spray is adjusted properly.

Oscillating and other types of manual sprinklers that attach to hoses can work to water lawns, but it is difficult to get accurate, even coverage with them. They need to be closely monitored to be sure that areas are not receiving too much or too little water.

For smaller lawns, another option for watering is an underground soaker hose. These hoses are made from reclaimed tires and allow water to weep through the side. They provide extensive uniform coverage when run for a sufficient amount of time, and because they are just below the surface of the soil there is minimal evaporation and runoff. These hoses, too, can be attached to a timer for ease of operation.

FERTILIZING

Fertilize **bermudagrass** lawns this month with balanced complete fertilizer in the 3-1-2 ratio at a rate of 5 pounds per 1,000 square feet. This is a generally accepted rate of application for most balanced fertilizers, but read the recommendations on the label of the product you buy, as some formulations indicate different application rates. Fertilize **St. Augustine** with 5 pounds of a 21-7-14 blend per 1,000 square feet.

MOWING

Dethatch an overseeded **bermudagrass** lawn early in the month. Remove as much of the now-dying **rye** as you can to give the **bermudagrass** space and light to start growing. Machines made for this purpose are available to rent at equipment rental agencies. But you can also use a strong-tined rake to remove the dead stolons and litter from around the emerging **bermudagrass** lawn. **Bermudagrass** or other lawns that were not overseeded need to be dethatched every two or three years.

Although **dichondra** may be used as a groundcover without any mowing to maintain it as lawn, to keep it even and low growing, mow weekly during the growing season.

Mow all established lawns regularly, taking only about 1/3 of the blade with each mowing. Begin mowing newly established lawns carefully, taking short cuts at first until you are sure that the grass is well established and growing rapidly.

PESTS

White grubs and sod webworms may show up in some lawns this month. The adults are beetles that you may see around the lawn. If you find the beetles, wait about 45 days for the larvae to emerge and be vulnerable to treatments. **Bermudagrass** is fairly resistant to these pests. They are difficult to control, but applications of *Bacillus thuringiensis* (Bt) in the late afternoon when the larvae are near the surface feeding may work.

JUNE
GRASSES

PLANNING

If you are setting out a new lawn, consider the traffic patterns of your yard carefully before planting. Lawns grow best when they are subject to moderate or intermittent foot traffic. In parts of the yard like a dog run, a path between the garage and the house, or any route that is used daily, the grass will fail to grow properly and ruts, mud, and weeds will be a constant problem. For those areas it is much better to cover pathways with brick, stone, bark, or gravel.

PLANTING

Plant **bermudagrass, St. Augustine,** or **zoysia** lawns this month. Follow recommendations and guidelines on page 134.

CARE

As the weather heats up, watch for signs of water stress on ornamental grasses. Grasses that lose color or suddenly begin to brown are losing too much water and need to have their irrigation increased.

WATERING

Water every three days in the hottest parts of the region. Check to be sure watering reaches a depth of 8 to 10 inches with each watering. In Zone 8, water every five days to the same depth.

Be prepared to water a newly planted lawn even more often if the weather is especially hot or dry, or if there are drying winds. Water ornamental grasses weekly through the summer.

FERTILIZING

Fertilize lawns once a month while they are actively growing. If you are using Grow Power or a similar formula, fertilize four times a year through the growing season. Many gardeners prefer to follow a schedule of fertilization of every six weeks. For **St. Augustine,** use 5 pounds of a 21-7-14 blend per 1,000 square feet.

MOWING

Mowing correctly not only keeps a lawn looking good, it keeps it healthy. Correct mowing will encourage deep rooting, shade the soil, reduce evaporation, and leave enough grass blades to insulate the growing crown and sustain adequate photosynthesis for the plant. Grass that is properly mowed grows slower (it doesn't have to frantically catch up to stay alive) and requires less-frequent mowing. Mow to the following heights.

- Regular **bermudagrass:** 1 to 1$\frac{1}{2}$ inches
- **Hybrid bermudagrass:** $\frac{1}{2}$ to 1$\frac{1}{2}$ inches
- **St. Augustine, zoysia,** and **dichondra:** 1$\frac{1}{2}$ to 2 inches
- **Fescue:** 2 to 3 inches
- **Buffalograss:** 2 to 3 inches

HELPFUL HINTS

In hot weather, water in the early morning, before dawn if you can. Plants use water most efficiently in the hours right before dawn. This timing cuts down on unnecessary evaporation, helps keep wet leaves from burning, and discourages the growth of fungal diseases. If your irrigation system is on a timer, set it to complete watering by an hour before dawn. If you are watering by hand, do so as early as you can. Watering overnight can encourage conditions favorable to fungal growth in lawns.

Adjust your mower height so that each time you mow you remove no more than $1/3$ of the grass blade to achieve the desired height. Removing more than 40% of the blade has been shown to stop root growth, and it can take days or weeks for the grass to recover.

Summer is a good time to dethatch **bermudagrass,** while it is growing actively and will recover quickly. Dethatch the lawn to $1/2$ inch.

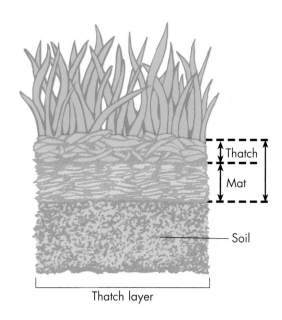

Thatch

Mat

Soil

Thatch layer

PESTS

Brown spots in the lawn may have many causes. The most common is uneven watering. If you have a spray-type sprinkler system, run it for a few minutes during the day to check the wetting pattern. Adjust the sprinkler if you find spots that are not being watered.

Browning can also occur from too much fertilizer. Be sure to following package directions for application rates, pick up any spilled fertilizer, and do not apply it during the hottest part of the day.

Other causes of browning are pesticide drift, mowing too low, poor aeration or dethatching, excessive rain (or a bad water leak), and prolonged high humidity.

If browning is caused by disease, which ironically is the least common cause, it begins as a small round or oval patch that grows in size quickly. Take a soil and grass sample to your local Extension Service and have it analyzed to determine the type of disease so it can be treated appropriately.

NOTES

JULY

GRASSES

PLANNING

If you do not have an automated watering system for your turf area, this is a good time to plan and install one. Manual sprinklers like bubblers, oscillators, or impulse sprinklers can be attached to a battery-operated timer at the faucet to run a prescribed amount of time on a predetermined schedule.

More efficient lawn spray heads, subsurface hoses, or similar systems are usually installed underground, connected to a dedicated valve which is, in turn, connected to an electric or electronic timer. When laying out an irrigation system, the most important consideration is that the water will cover the entire area uniformly. Lay out all the pipe and attachments over the lawn first, then begin to dig. If the lawn is well established, remove the turf in blocks and set it aside. These pieces of sod can then be laid over the backfilled trench to speed recovery of the damaged area. Turf grows quickly in the hot weather, so just give it a little extra water and all the trenching damage will be quickly overgrown once the work of installing an irrigation system is complete.

PLANTING

This is the last month to plant a warm-season grass lawn. Plant according to the recommendations on page 134.

CARE

Even in the cooler areas of the region the summer heat can take a toll on newly planted lawns. Watch watering carefully and increase frequency if the weather is unusually hot. Resist the temptation to water lightly, however. Continue to water deeply, and more often if the grass appears to be water-stressed.

WATERING

In Zones 9 and 10, water deeply every three days, to a depth of 8 to 10 inches. To prevent fungal disease and other problems, check that the surface of the soil is dry, but that the soil is still moist down 6 inches before each watering. Allowing lawns to dry out too frequently allows salts to build up and causes much of the yellowed leaves and brown patches common in the summer. Monsoon summer rains may begin this month in most of the region. Be sure to take heavy rains into account when determining the watering schedule for the lawn.

FERTILIZING

Fertilize **St. Augustine** with five pounds of a 21-7-14 blend per 1,000 square feet.

Maintain a regular fertilization program—monthly, every six weeks, or four times a year is a good fertilization program for **bermudagrass** or **hybrid bermudagrass** lawns.

MOWING

This is still a good month to dethatch **bermudagrass** lawns. Many growers recommend that a lawn be fertilized and heavily watered immediately following dethatching to encourage rapid new growth.

Dethatching is the removal of old stolons, leaf litter, and dead crowns from the lawn. This detritus often builds up faster than it can decay, and removing it helps keep the crown from becoming infected with disease and allows for more water penetration. When the layer is about $1/2$ inch or less, it acts like a mulch and helps out the grass. As it becomes thicker, it becomes a detriment

HOW TO CHECK WATERING DEPTH

1. Take a metal pole, like a ¼- to ½-inch-diameter rebar, or a sharp, sturdy wooden pole of equal diameter, and mark it off in 6-inch increments beginning at the sharp end. The entire rod should be at least 2 feet long, but a 3-foot-long rod is easier to use. Some people use a long screwdriver, which is fine as long as the shaft is at least 10 inches long.

2. Plunge the rod into the soil right after you water. It will easily penetrate the soil. When it stops moving easily or stops altogether, note the measurement. That is how far the watering you just applied percolated into the soil. Wait two days and do it again. Note the measurement. When the moisture level is half the original level, that is the halfway mark between waterings. Keep checking every two days, noting the moisture level. Water when the surface of the soil is dry but the rod will still go into the soil at least 6 inches

Check sprinklers from time to time to be sure they are putting out as much water as you expect and that the water is spread in an even pattern. Set small cans (tunafish cans are ideal) around the lawn, and run the sprinkler for 15 minutes. Pop-up styles should water at least ¼ inch in fifteen minutes, and impact sprinklers usually achieve 2/10 inch in 15 minutes. Adjust as necessary if the sprinklers are under- or overwatering.

to a healthy lawn and should be removed.

Change the direction you mow frequently. This keeps the coverage and look even and helps prevent unnecessary rutting or compaction.

Do not mow when the lawn is wet. This can result in an uneven mow and leave messy clippings that may smother the crown and are difficult to collect.

PESTS

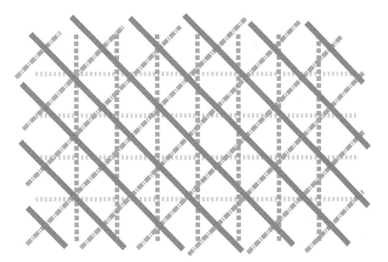

Vary your mowing pattern to lessen the impact on the grass.

During wet periods of the monsoon, summer-season mushrooms may erupt on the lawn. While this is an indication of increased moisture, the mushrooms do no harm to the plants and are not parasitic on the lawn. They are usually gone within a week.

AUGUST

GRASSES

PLANNING

Ornamental grasses are underused in most areas of the region. These are gorgeous perennials, and while they mix well with other perennials and shrubs, they can also be used as pure stands of grass for a highly dramatic effect.

The workhorses of ornamental grasses for the region are those in the genus *Muhlenbergia*. These graceful plants are resistant to the heat, aridity, and alkaline soils of the region. The most widely available are the following.

• **Bamboo muhly** (*M. dumosa*), reminiscent of **bamboo,** is a 5- to 6-foot plant with delicate branching leaves and a tan to cream open-blooming stalk.

• **Bull grass** (*M. emersleyi*) is a smaller plant, up to 3 feet tall, with glossy green foliage.

• **Deer grass** (*Muhlenbergia rigens*) is a 3- to 4-foot grass with thin leaves and a narrow, tan flowering stalk.

• *M. lindheimeri* is about the same size as **bull grass** but has blue-gray foliage.

• **Pink muhly** (*M. filipes,* also sold as *M. capillaris*) is a 3- to 4-foot-thick grass with slender leaves and stunning, openly branched pink to red flowering heads.

PLANTING

This is a slow month for planting turfgrass. It is too far into the summer season to plant warm-season grasses, and it is still too hot to plant cool-season grasses. Even ornamental grasses are best planted much earlier in the spring, or wait until later in the fall to plant.

CARE

Ornamental grasses, especially in the cooler areas, will begin to bloom late this month and into September. To increase the beauty of these plants during their bloom, keep the grasses well groomed by removing any dead culms or ragged growth.

WATERING

Monitor watering carefully during this month, using your probe or rod to determine when the grass needs watering. Summer rains are extremely erratic and can be locally heavy. Because lawns suffer when either under- or overwatered, if you have had a significant rain, be sure to check before watering again.

Water lawns every four days in the hottest zones; weekly in cooler areas.

Symptoms of underwatering include a change in the color of **bermudagrass** from bright green to blue-gray, blades that do not spring back quickly when pressure is applied, and foliage that feels hot to the touch.

Symptoms of overwatering include puddles or standing water in the lawn, a musty odor, soft or mushy soil when pressure is applied, and the eruption of algae or mushrooms.

FERTILIZING

Fertilize all warm-season lawn-grasses according to their regular schedule this month.

Ornamental grasses do not need frequent fertilization, but an application of a balanced fertilizer this month helps ensure good flowering. Apply the same type and amount of fertilizer that you use for perennials, and water it in well after fertilization.

MOWING

Continue to mow regularly, taking off only $1/3$ of the blade with each mowing. If you have dethatched the lawn, the leavings from that effort may not be good for the compost pile right away. This debris will contain live stolons and will begin to grow if it receives moisture. It takes a hot compost pile to kill grass. Instead, take the clippings from dethatching and spread them out on a plastic sheet or a

large surface like a sidewalk or driveway, and let them dry out completely. Once dried, the clippings make good mulch and can be added to the compost pile.

PESTS

Weeds can be a problem in some lawns, particularly newer lawns. To take care of incidental weeds or for spot control, use a solution of equal parts alcohol and water and spray it directly on the weed. You can also use full-strength white vinegar. Another formula that will work to

control invasive weeds, including **bermudagrass** that has run into areas where it is not wanted, is a solution of $12^1/_2$% white vinegar, $12^1/_2$% lemon extract, and 75% water. Saturate the weed with the spray, covering the foliage entirely. For a solution that will work on more firmly established weeds, use 2.5% white vinegar, 2.5% lemon extract, and 95% water. All these solutions kill by making contact with the leaves, and care should be taken not to saturate any plants that you do not want to kill.

To avoid harming adjacent plants, spot treat weeds by enclosing them in a plastic container that has had its bottom removed.

September

GRASSES

PLANNING

To overseed or not to overseed a **bermudagrass** lawn is entirely a matter of personal preference. **Bermudagrass** lawns grow from as early as March to as late as October, although there is some local variation. This means that they are dormant for four to five months of the year. Many gardeners find that the look of a dormant lawn is difficult for them to accept, and given that so much of the best weather in the deserts is in the winter, this feeling is reinforced during the delightful hours of outdoor living at that time.

But consider your own situation before you decide to overseed a lawn. Only **bermudagrass** accepts overseeding. The increased competition of a winter lawn is hard on the slower-growing **zoysia** and **St. Augustine.** **Fescue** is evergreen and is not recommended for overseeding.

Overseeded lawns mean that the cycle continues year-round of mowing, fertilizing, watering, and dethatching. Depending on where in the region you live and the costs and availability of water in your area, this can mean a significant increase in water use compared to allowing the lawn to go dormant.

There are two grasses that are used to overseed lawns in the area, **annual rye grass** and **perennial rye grass. Annual rye grass** is a coarse-bladed grass that does not tolerate heat and generally begins to die out before the **bermudagrass** comes out of dormancy. It requires frequent mowing to keep it vigorous. **Perennial rye** has become the current favorite for overseeding, not only because of its good color and finer texture, but because of its greater heat tolerance.

There are dozens of varieties of **perennial rye,** and most are mixed into seed blends to help maximize the characteristics of each.

If your lawn had a hard summer due to extreme heat, irrigation problems, or a disease or pest outbreak that caused significant damage, do not overseed the following winter. This will allow the grass to grow as long as possible and therefore recover more quickly from the difficulties of the summer.

PLANTING

In cooler areas of Zone 9, begin overseeding late in the month. Otherwise, wait until October to begin overseeding. Plant ornamental grasses from now through November.

CARE

In the hottest parts of the region lawns respond to the warm, moderate temperatures this month by beginning a rapid growth spurt. Continue to water deeply, fertilize according to the recommendations above, and mow regularly to keep the lawn healthy and prevent it from getting away from you.

WATERING

Maintain regular, deep irrigation on the same schedule as the summer until daytime temperatures fall below 90 degrees Fahrenheit. Until then, continue to water every four days in the hottest areas and every week in the cooler ones.

If you are planning to overseed a **bermudagrass** lawn, begin to reduce the frequency of watering. This will slow down growth in the grass. While **bermudagrass** goes dormant in response to temperature, lawns that are growing more slowly will go into dormancy more quickly.

FERTILIZING

If you have not been using a complete balanced fertilizer on **bermudagrass,** use one this month that is high in potassium and phosphorus. Remember to water well before and after applying fertilizer.

If you are planning to overseed your **bermudagrass** lawn, this is the last fertilization you will give the **bermudagrass** until the overseeded grass begins to need fertilization. If you will not

HELPFUL HINTS

Do not plan to overseed a new lawn until it has been established for at least three months, although it is best to allow a new lawn to grow for a full year before it is overseeded.

be overseeding, feed **bermudagrass** with a well-balanced fertilizer once this month and then discontinue any fertilization until it begins to grow next spring.

Withdrawing fertilizer, like decreasing water, helps lawns to slow down growth and prepare for dormancy more quickly when temperatures fall below 65 degrees Fahrenheit.

Fertilize **St. Augustine** and **zoysia** one more time with 5 pounds of a 21-7-14 blend per 1,000 square feet.

Fertilize lawns in Zone 8 in the first week of the month.

MOWING

If you are going to overseed, mow your **bermudagrass** lawn to about 1/2 inch high. Like the watering and fertilizing recommendations, this severe mowing will slow down the growth of the plant and provide room for the emerging **rye** seedlings.

Mow **bermudagrass** lawns that will not be overseeded to 1 inch. Continue to mow other lawns that will not be overseeded regularly.

PESTS

If you have a **dichondra** lawn, you may notice small insects leaping off the grass when you walk over it. These are probably flea beetles, which erupt both this month and in May on these lawns. Small numbers cause minimal damage, but a large infestation can mar the lawn and diminish its vigor. For very large infestations, treat once with an insecticide rated for these chewing beetles.

Compare the relationship between deep watering (plants on right) and root growth.

OCTOBER

GRASSES

PLANNING

Using a finer-textured grass like **perennial rye** is often desirable due to its delicate texture and dense cover, but sometimes there is too much foot traffic to keep it looking good. Mix the grass with open-weave pavers to help relieve the stress of foot traffic and to minimize the amount of grass needed for a given area. These types of pavers, often found in interesting shapes, also act as a mulch for the lawn, further reducing the amount of water needed to sustain it.

PLANTING

If you are overseeding with **perennial rye,** from now until mid-November is the perfect time to plant this cool-season grass. For best results, be sure night-time temperatures are below 65 degrees Fahrenheit when you plant. At those temperatures, the **bermudagrass** will be completely dormant and the **rye** seed will germinate quickly.

The day you plant, mow the grass once at the regular height, again at the next lower setting on your machine, and once again at the next lowest setting. Three mowings are needed to get the dead or dying grass blades removed and off the stems. If **bermudagrass** is very dense (this can be the case with many hybrids), it may need to be dethatched before planting.

Spread seed as evenly as possible over the surface of the lawn. Sow **annual rye** at 10 to 20 pounds per 1,000 square feet, **perennial rye** at 10 to 15 pounds per 1,000 square feet. Rake lightly to be sure that the seed has contact with the soil. Cover with a light layer ($\frac{1}{4}$ inch) of organic mulch, compost, forest mulch, or similar organic matter. You can also use the clippings from the previous mowing.

In cool areas, plant **fescue** from seed. Use the same bed preparation techniques found on page 134. Use between 7 to 10 pounds of seed for every 1,000 square feet. Water once or twice daily until seed germinates; thereafter, water to maintain soil moisture 4 to 6 inches deep.

Two weeks before planting, reduce watering on the lawn by half. Stop mowing one week before seeding.

Fescue lawn

CARE

Bermudagrass lawns begin to turn brown and quit growing this month. This is the signal that the grass is going dormant. Extend the time between waterings by another two or three days, but continue to water deeply. Do not fertilize the lawn at all once if it begins to show signs of going dormant.

WATERING

Water a newly planted lawn two to four times a day, just enough to wet the soil until the seedlings emerge. Then reduce the watering to once a day, but be sure the seedlings do not entirely dry out between waterings. Continue to water often until the grass is over 2 inches high and has been mowed. At that time, adjust watering to the schedule it will follow all winter. The frequency will depend on the weather—it can be as often as every three to five days, or as long as every ten days, but water to a depth of 4 to 6 inches.

In Zones 9 and 10, water established but dormant lawns that are not overseeded once a week to a depth of 6 inches. Water established lawns in Zone 8 every two weeks.

Shift the time of day you water the lawn to later in the morning, ideally two or three hours after sunrise. This will help prevent cool-temperature fungal disease in your lawn.

FERTILIZING

Two weeks after overseeding, feed the lawn with a lawn-starter formula or a blend that is about 16-20-0 to stimulate the roots and get growth going. After this, fertilize monthly with a product that has a 3-1-2 NPK ratio or a product specifically rated for winter lawns. Apply at a rate of 3 or 4 pounds for each 1,000 square feet of lawn.

Fertilize **St. Augustine** and **zoysia** for the last time this year.

MOWING

Mow a newly planted lawn when the grass blades are 2 inches tall, trimming them back to $1\frac{1}{2}$ inches. Continue to mow **annual rye** to a height of 1 to $2\frac{1}{2}$ inches, and **perennial rye** to a height of $\frac{3}{4}$ to $2\frac{1}{2}$ inches.

When the flowering stalks of ornamental grasses become floppy or irregular, or the stalks are spent, prune them by cutting them as far back as you can reach. Many gardeners use them in dried arrangements, or you may leave them on the plant for birds.

PESTS

Keeping birds away from overseeded lawns can be a chore. They are strongly attracted to the seed and can become a pest while the seed is germinating. Nothing works perfectly, but "shoo-aways" made of strips of shiny silver paper attached to stakes so they blow in the breeze, scarecrows, or a hunting cat are all mildly effective.

NOVEMBER

GRASSES

 PLANNING

Dormant lawns do not have to be an eyesore in the garden. Consider incorporating the tan or brownish shade into the entire scheme of the garden. Look for plants that will complement or be complemented by those shades. Strong-colored perennials and heavy-leaved succulents like **aloes** or **agaves** set off the light tones of a dormant lawn. Consider overplanting with wildflowers, especially natives that do not need excessive watering, or other annuals that would thrive on the same watering schedule as the lawn. Mix in winter-flowering bulbs to help provide interest and splendid color.

 PLANTING

Continue to overseed through mid-month, especially in the warmest parts of the state.

 CARE

Because water does not evaporate from the soil as quickly during cooler months, take care not to run heavy equipment or furniture over wet lawn areas. It takes much longer to repair such damage on a lawn when it is cold.

 WATERING

Water dormant **bermudagrass** every other week in Zones 9 and 10. Water lawns once a month in Zone 8. Water to a depth of 6 inches.

Water overseeded lawns every seven to ten days to a depth of 4 to 6 inches. Soil moisture is affected by the type of soil, the temperatures, and the type of plants that are growing. Test how deeply the water is penetrating with a rod or probe directly after watering at two-day intervals to determine the correct frequency for your lawn.

 FERTILIZING

Apply fertilizer to an overseeded lawn this month with a product that has a 3-1-2 NPK ratio or a product specifically rated for winter lawns. Be sure the lawn has been growing for at least two weeks before beginning regular fertilization. Most growers recommend that the first fertilization after germination be a high-nitrogen/phosphate blend (16-20-0 or similar), then all remaining fertilizations be done with a complete balanced blend used at a rate of 3 to 4 pounds per 1,000 square feet of lawn.

 MOWING

Begin mowing an overseeded lawn when it is 2 inches high, and mow it to a height of 1 1/2 inches. After that, mow according to the recommendations on page 138.

Spent flowering stalks on ornamental grasses may be removed any time. Do not cut back ornamental grasses this month, as most are still actively growing.

 PESTS

Weeds can flourish in the lawn even in winter. While the use of preemergent chemical controls is common, these chemicals should be used with strict attention to the label directions for application. Many interact with the dry, alkaline soils of the region in ways that are destructive, and many are considerably more persistent than previously thought. Before beginning any chemical weed-spraying program, check with the Extension Service in your area for recommendations on appropriate chemical controls.

Weeds can also be eliminated with careful use of full-strength vinegar or a vinegar solution. Make a collar from an old plastic jug so that you can direct the spray only to the weed.

December

GRASSES

PLANNING

Give the lawn a hard look and decide how much of it you use and need. Lawns can be attractive in setting off certain styles of plantings, but they are exorbitant users of water and require intensive cultivation and maintenance to look really good.

Bermudagrass lawns use the equivalent of 42 inches of rain in one growing season, and that is a lawn that is allowed to go dormant. Overseeded lawns may use as much as the equivalent of 60 inches of rain a year. In a region that receives between 3 and 12 inches of rain a year, large expanses of lawn require a huge infusion of water to stay healthy.

Look at how you use the lawn, and maintain only as much as you need and use. Spread out the effect of a lawn by adding decorative pavings or walkways to minimize the amount of grass. The size of the lawn should be in keeping with the size and character of the entire garden.

Switch to low-water-use groundcovers in areas that do not have heavy foot traffic. Plan to expand perennial or bulb beds to take up more of the garden. Keep on the lookout for ever-improving varieties that are being bred and developed that use less water but

hold up to the rigorous growing conditions of the region.

Above all, monitor the water use of your lawn carefully year-round, giving it only what it needs, not what a water schedule dictates.

PLANTING

Do not plant either lawns or ornamental grasses this month.

CARE

Cut back ornamental grasses that have stopped growing. Save any flowering heads for use in dried arrangements or holiday wreaths.

WATERING

Water dormant **bermudagrass** once a month to a depth of 6 inches throughout the region. Water overseeded lawns every other week to a depth of 4 to 6 inches. The weather is variable this time of year, so keep an eye on the soil moisture.

Cut back watering of ornamental grasses to every other week. Most ornamental grasses are either dormant or barely growing in the coldest months of the year.

FERTILIZING

Fertilize an overseeded lawn with a complete balanced fertilizer. Apply 3 or 4 pounds for every 1,000 square feet of lawn.

Do not fertilize **bermudagrass** lawns that are not overseeded.

Do not fertilize ornamental grasses.

MOWING

Late in the month, ornamental grasses can be cut back to within 6 to 8 inches of the ground. Be sure the grasses have gone dormant before cutting severely. This annual shearing helps revitalize bunch grasses and cuts down on competition for the new shoots that will emerge next year.

PESTS

Fungal disease in winter grass usually results from too much water. If conditions have encouraged fungal disease to get started, the increasing temperatures of late winter will cause it to flourish. Prevent these problems by watering in the morning while the weather is cold, two or three hours after dawn.

PERENNIALS

Perennial is one of those terms that has a specific botanical meaning but has taken on a significance to gardeners far beyond its original use. Botanically, any plant is a perennial that lives out its life over more than two seasons.

That means that agaves, cacti, succulents of all types, shrubs, trees, and most bulbs share this trait. But in the world of gardening, perennial has come to mean a special group of plants that are not large, that have multiple semiwoody or soft stems, and that bloom over many seasons. They are smaller than a shrub and generally not woody . . . but there is a lot of room for confusion at the margins.

In the Desert Southwest, the confusion worsens when plants that are perennial, in both the botanical and the gardening sense, are used as annuals in the winter because they cannot tolerate the des-

ert summer. Many of these species are listed on the chart on pages 153-155. In Zone 8, however, most of these species can be used as the spring- and summer-flowering garden perennials they are.

Perennials are popular because once they are well situated in the garden, they will grow and bloom over many seasons. They create a more stable and permanent style for a garden than do annuals or bulbs and are the basis of some long-standing styles in gardens throughout the world.

The perennial border is a traditional way of using a wide array of perennials in a blended, naturalistic planting. Originally named because it bordered a lawn, this style of planting is dramatic in a location that allows for long lines and deep beds, or along a walk or drive. It isn't necessary for a perennial planting to border a lawn, however, it can just as

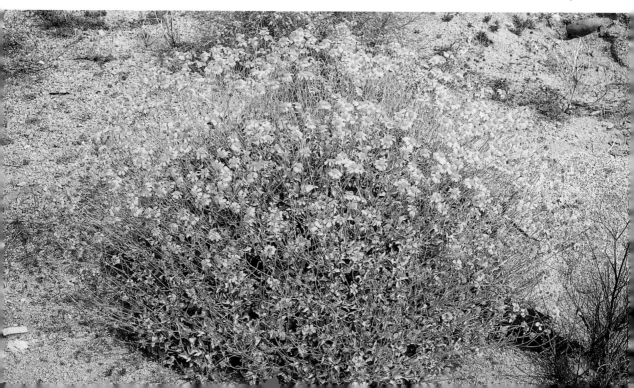

easily border a dirt walk, the pavement of a patio, or the decking of a pool. In most perennial border designs, many perennial species are used. Plants are chosen with an eye to size and texture, color combinations, and time of blooming.

There are countless ways to blend plants, but because borders are generally 8 to 12 feet deep, large plants, sometimes even shrubs, are used to form a background or anchor for the bed. This is followed by an organized jumble of perennials to fill in the space toward the edge. In the most elaborate variation of this planting style, plants that bloom at one end of the seasonal color spectrum are gradually replaced as you move down the bed until the border finishes with a flourish at the opposite end of the spectrum.

Repeating plants at various intervals keeps large perennial plantings from looking chaotic. While much of the charm and appeal of perennial beds is the great variety of plants, too much variety is unsettling, as your eye does not know where to stop. Repetition acts like a signpost to keep you moving in the intended direction.

Think in threes when using perennials, and try to repeat at least some of the perennials three times.

Fill in spaces in perennial beds with annuals or bulbs. These plants generally bring strong color or interest to the bed in a particular season. In the Southwest, where everything seems to bloom in the spring, a strong dose of winter- or summer-flowering annuals or bulbs helps keep the bed interesting throughout the year.

Perennial plantings should have textural contrast to keep the full, billowing shape of most perennials from becoming boring. Arizona gardeners are overwhelmed with plants that provide the bold, sharp edges that light up a perennial planting. Dasylirion, manfreda, yuccas, and a wide array of agaves and other succulents blend beautifully with perennials. The strong lines and bold textures of these kinds of plants mark a perennial garden in the Southwest as a new twist on an old garden idea.

But most of us do not have the room that a true perennial border demands. It doesn't matter—the principles of planting a perennial bed are the same even if it is only 6 feet long and 3 feet deep. Choose plants that bloom in different seasons so that the bed does not explode into bloom for a few months and then look destitute for the remainder of the year. If you use a lot of deep-green-leaved plants, look for white, mottled, or variegated leaves to shift your eye. If too many plants have small or finely cut leaves, add a few with large dramatic leaves. And if a plant doesn't seem to work or if it clashes hideously with what surrounds it, do not be afraid to move or replace it.

Perennials also make a dramatic statement when used singly in mass plantings. This is a highly effective way to treat a strip of ground that is narrow, or that has too much sun or too much shade. Using all one species is a dramatic flourish for what could be a dull area. Choose species that bloom a long time or have outstanding foliage as well as flowers for these kinds of perennial beds.

GROUNDCOVERS

Groundcover is another of those odd horticultural terms that actually defines a use for a plant but has come to be used to describe particular species. Groundcovers are plants that have long, extended stems that sprawl over the soil. This style of growth offers a lot of advantages for the gardener, and these plants are a particularly beneficial part of a desert garden.

Covering the soil cools the surface of the soil, both directly under the stems as well as in surrounding areas. Because the plant is absorbing most of the radiation and heat of the sun, the strong reflective heat is prevented from bouncing up onto patios, walkways, or buildings.

Keeping the soil covered, and therefore cooler, also cuts down on soil evaporation, working precisely as a living mulch. The retention of even a small amount of soil moisture helps cut down on

watering frequency and keeps plants from wild swings of being too dry, then too wet.

Beneath a groundcover is a minute compost pile of dead leaves, spent flowers, and seed. As this detritus decays, it enriches the soil and over time changes the soil's texture and quality.

Because some groundcovers root along the ground as the stems grow, they have become common as stabilizers for erosion-prone areas. The expanding network of roots keeps soil in place along steep banks, on open slopes, or in newly disturbed areas.

Many short perennials form a small mound or spread in a limited pattern, and when they are planted close together form a dense mat of cover. Although not usually described as groundcovers, plants like Angelita daisy and bush morning glory grow this way and are highly valued in our region.

VINES

Vines, too, can be a groundcover in the right situation. The annual vine buffalo gourd covers a lot of ground quickly and is particularly useful for newly disturbed or hot, dry areas. Unlike many groundcovers, buffalo gourd does not require the entire area to have good growing conditions, it only needs its roots to be in a bed that receives regular watering. Perennial vines like Arizona grape ivy or pink trumpet vine are excellent groundcovers that root anywhere they touch the ground when grown without a trellis or arbor.

But we usually have something different in mind for vines. Because vines reach and stretch for the sun, they are useful for covering ugly walls or buildings, providing highly visible color, crowning an arbor, or making a colorful roof for a seating area.

Because perennial vines will be seen all the time, it is important to choose them with care. Vines that are deciduous are wonderful as a covering for a patio roof or seating area. They grow through the summer, providing shade and cover from intense sun, then open up in the winter when sun is welcome. But deciduous vines are less effective as a covering for an entry arbor or other focal spot where lack of leaves would look dreary and dull during the winter.

Vines can be planted on a wide range of supports. On a trellis, they can be trained to cover a wall or a fence. Sturdy poles or arbors allow vines to grow nearly upright and become a feature in any planting. When trained over an arbor or beam, they are a beacon to another area of the garden. And when grown at the base of a tree they will climb its limbs, blooming amidst the branches for an unexpected delight.

Use vines where they will be seen from a distance so they draw your eye far into the garden. Blooms can be spectacular as they appear to rise up behind a wall or spill down an embankment.

NATIVE PERENNIALS

Native perennials are prized for their beauty and durability in the face of harsh desert growing conditions. As more species and selections become available, desert gardeners have a wide array from which to choose. Perennials that are native to the Mohave and Sonoran deserts tend to be spring- or early summer–flowering, while those from the Chihuahuan deserts often bloom through the summer and into the fall.

If you intend to attract butterflies into the garden, natives are important. These are the plants that provide food and shelter not only to the lovely adults, but also to the larvae and pupae as they develop.

Hummingbirds and other birds will come to a garden that has what they crave—food, shelter, and nest sites. Some of the most colorful and long-blooming natives, like justicias, penstemon, and salvias, are preferred by hummingbirds for food. Generous numbers in the garden assure that you will have these visitors throughout the year.

CHAPTER SIX

Perennials

Common Name	Botanical Name	Mature Height	Native
Angelita daisy	Tetraneuris scaposa	1–2 ft.	Yes
Asparagus fern	Asparagus densiflorus 'Sprengeri'	1–2 ft.	No
Aster	Aster novae-angliae	2–4 ft.	No
Autumn sage	Salvia greggii	2–4 ft.	Yes
Beebalm	Monarda didyma	2–4 ft.	No
Blackfoot daisy	Melampodium leucanthum	2–4 ft.	Yes
Blanket flower	Gaillardia x grandiflora	1–2 ft.	No
Blood flower	Asclepias curavassica	2–4 ft.	No
Blue mist	Ageratum corymbosum	1–3 ft.	Yes
Blue sage	Salvia azurea	1–2 ft.	No
Brittlebush	Encelia farinosa	2–4 ft.	Yes
Butterfly weed	Asclepias tuberosa	2–4 ft.	Yes
California fuschia	Epilobium cawm	1–2 ft.	Yes
Candelilla	Euphorbia antisyphilitica	2–4 ft.	Yes
Canyon penstemon	Penstemon pseudospectabilis	1–2 ft.	Yes
Chocolate flower	Berlandiera lyrata	1–2 ft.	Yes
Chrysanthemum	Chrysanthemum x hybrids	1–2 ft.	No
Chuparosa	Justicia californica	2–4 ft.	Yes
Cigar plant	Cuphea ignea	1–3 ft.	No
Coneflower	Ratibida columnifera	2–4 ft.	No
Coral penstemon	Penstemon superbus	1–2 ft.	Yes
Coreopsis	Coreopsis verticillata/lanceolata	2–4 ft.	No
Cup flower	Nierembergia caerulea	1–2 ft.	No
Damianita	Chrysactinia mexicana	2–4 ft.	Yes
Daylily	Hemerocallis spp.	1–2 ft.	No
Desert marigold	Baileya multiradiata	1–2 ft.	Yes
Desert milkweed	Asclepias subulata	2–4 ft.	Yes
Dicliptera	Dicliptera resupinata	1–2 ft.	Yes
Dusty miller	Centaurea cineraria	1–2 ft.	No
Firecracker penstemon	Penstemon eatonii	1–2 ft.	Yes
Firewheel	Gaillardia aristata	1–2 ft.	Yes
Four o'clock	Mirabilis jalapa	2–4 ft.	No
Foxglove penstemon	Penstemon cobaea	1–2 ft.	No
Gaura	Gaura lindheimeri	1–2 ft.	Yes
Geranium	Pelargonium spp.	2–4 ft.	No
Globe mallow	Sphaeralcea ambigua	2–4 ft.	Yes
Golden columbine	Aquilegia chrysantha	1–2 ft.	Yes
Goodding's verbena	Glandularia gooddingii	1–2 ft.	Yes

CHAPTER SIX

Common Name	Botanical Name	Mature Height	Nativ
Gopher plant	*Euphorbia rigida*	1–2 ft.	No
Hill Country penstemon	*Penstemon triflorus*	1–2 ft.	Yes
Hollyhock	*Alcea rosea*	2–4 ft.	No
Jerusalem sage	*Phlomis fruticosa*	2–4 ft.	No
Lantana	*Lantana camara* and hybrids	2–4 ft.	No
Malabar nut	*Justicia adhatoda*	2–4 ft.	No
Marguerite	*Chrysanthemum frutescens*	2–4 ft.	No
Maximilian sunflower	*Helianthus maximilianii*	2–4 ft.	No
Mexican honeysuckle	*Justicia spicigera*	1–2 ft.	No
Mexican oregano	*Poliomintha maderensis*	2–4 ft.	No
Mt. Lemmon marigold	*Tagetes palmeri*	2–4 ft.	Yes
Paperflower	*Psilostrophe cooperi/tagetina*	2–4 ft.	Yes
Parry's penstemon	*Penstemon parryi*	1–2 ft.	Yes
Pincushion flower	*Scabiosa caucasica*	1–2 ft.	No
Pine leaf milkweed	*Asclepias linaria*	2–4 ft.	Yes
Pine leaf penstemon	*Penstemon pinifolius*	2–4 ft.	Yes
Prairie penstemon	*Penstemon ambiguus*	2–4 ft.	Yes
Purple coneflower	*Echinacea purpurea*	2–4 ft.	No
Red hot poker	*Kniphofia uvaria*	2–4 ft.	No
Red justicia	*Justicia candicans*	2–4 ft.	Yes
Red lobelia	*Lobelia laxiflora*	2–4 ft.	Yes
Red salvia	*Salvia coccinea*	1–2 ft.	No
Rock penstemon	*Penstemon baccharifolius*	1–2 ft.	Yes
Rocky Mountain penstemon	*Penstemon strictus*	1–2 ft.	Yes
Rudbeckia	*Rudbeckia fulgida*	2–4 ft.	No
Ruellia	*Ruellia brittoniana*	2–4 ft.	No
Ruellia 'Katy'	*Ruellia brittoniana*	1–2 ft.	No
Russian sage	*Perovskia atriplicifolia*	2–4 ft.	No
Sacred datura	*Datura wrightii*	2–4 ft.	Yes
Salvia	*Salvia x jamesii*	2–4 ft.	No
Scarlet penstemon	*Penstemon barbatus*	1–2 ft.	Yes
Shasta daisy	*Chrysanthemum maximum*	1–2 ft.	No
Shrimp plant	*Justicia brandegeeana*	2–4 ft.	No
Sonoran water-willow	*Justicia sonorae*	1–2 ft.	Yes
Tufted morning glory	*Oenothera caespitosa*	1–2 ft.	Yes
Valerian	*Centhranthus ruber*	1–2 ft.	No
Western mugwort	*Artemesia ludoviciana*	2–4 ft.	Yes
Wormwood	*Artemisia absinthium*	2–4 ft.	No
Yarrow	*Achillea millefolium*	2–4 ft.	No

CHAPTER SIX

Groundcovers

Common Name	Botanical Name	Native
Desert zinnia	Zinnia acerosa	Yes
Lippia	Phyla nodiflora	No
Mexican evening primrose	Oenothera berlandieri	Yes
Missouri evening primrose	Oenothera macrocarpa	No
Moses in the cradle	Tradescantia spathacea	No
Moss verbena	Glandularia pulchella	No
Prairie zinnia	Zinnia grandiflora	No
Saltillo evening primrose	Oenothera stubbei	Yes
Sundrops	Calylophus hartwegii	Yes
Trailing lantana	Lantana montevidensis	No
Trailing smokebush	Dalea greggii	Yes
Vinca	Vinca major/minor	No
Wandering Jew	Tradescantia fluminensis	No
Winecup	Callirhoe involucrata	Yes

Vines

Common Name	Botanical Name	Native
Arizona grape ivy	Cissus trifoliata	Yes
Blue crown passion flower	Passiflora caerulea	No
Bougainvillea	Bougainvillea hybrids	No
Bush morning glory	Convolvulus cneorum	No
Cat's claw	Macfadyena unguis-cati	No
Clematis	Clematis hybrids	No
Lilac vine	Hardenbergia violacea	No
Mile-a-minute vine	Merremia dissecta	Yes
Old man's beard	Clematis drummondii	Yes
Passion flower	Passiflora foetida	Yes
Pink trumpet vine	Podranea ricasoliana	No
Purple butterfly vine	Mascagnia lilacina	Yes
Queen's wreath	Antigonon leptopus	No
Snapdragon vine	Maurandya antirrhiniflora	Yes
Trumpet vine	Campsis radicans	No
Yellow butterfly vine	Mascagnia macroptera	Yes
Yuca vine	Merremia aurea	Yes

JANUARY
PERENNIALS

PLANNING

Perennials like **Angelita daisy, chuparosa,** and **red justicia** are blooming vigorously. If you are keeping a journal or record of your garden, it is always helpful to take note of when various plants come into bloom. It can also help you plan for what to plant next fall. **Justicia** is a large genus of showy plants that are excellent perennials for mild-winter areas. Some are native to the region, and most do well in all parts of Zones 9 and 10. All **justicias** make plenty of nectar and are a favorite of hummingbirds.

• **Chuparosa** is a rambling perennial with widely spaced leaves, giving the plant a twiggy, branched look. The red tubular flowers bloom throughout the winter.

• **Mexican honeysuckle** is a low-growing plant with bright-orange flowers and pale-green leaves. This **justicia** grows best in light shade and blooms spring through late fall.

• **Red justicia** has numerous 3- to 4-foot stems crowded with light-green leaves. The red-orange flowers cluster in the leaf axils and are most abundant from late fall through spring.

• **Shrimp plant** is a fast-growing low plant that gets its name from its orange flowers surrounded by showy pink-brown to deep-copper-red bracts in a congested, often curled, stalk. **Shrimp plants** bloom from late spring through summer.

• **Malabar nut** (*Justicia adhatoda*) is a large plant, over 5 feet tall, with clusters of large white flowers at the ends of its stems.

• **Sonoran water-willow** (*Justicia sonorae*) is a low, sprawling perennial with few leaves widely spaced on its fine stems. The vivid blue flowers bloom through fall and winter.

PLANTING

Many native perennials, like **brittlebush, desert marigold, globe mallow,** and **penstemons,** reseed freely. Seedlings that arise where they aren't wanted, or in difficult spots, can be moved this month. It is often best to do this right after a rain, or soak the soil well before you start.

Take a shovel or trowel, and lift up the entire plant with as much soil as possible. Have the new hole ready, and place the plant into the hole, covering it immediately with any leftover soil. It is not necessary to amend the soil or to add anything to the backfill. Water well after planting, and water daily until the plant begins to grow again.

Angelita daisy

CARE

Be prepared to cover frost-tender perennials if freezing temperatures threaten. Use a deep layer of straw, pine straw, lightweight blankets or sheets, or frost cloth to protect perennials.

WATERING

Established perennials that are actively growing should be watered to a depth of 2 feet. Check the depth the water is penetrating by using a probe or metal rod. In some years, winter rains can be abundant this month. If rains are regular, adjust the watering schedule accordingly.

Perennials that are not actively growing need to be watered only half as often as when they are actively growing. Although they may look dormant, the roots are still active and need moisture.

Water newly planted plants weekly to help them establish good root systems before the summer heat.

FERTILIZING

Do not fertilize this month.

GROOMING

At the end of the month, cut back leggy growth from perennials that are not subject to frost damage like native **autumn sage, plumbago,** and **red justicia.** Wait to prune frost-tender perennials until all danger of frost is past.

Pink trumpet vine begins to come out of the winter doldrums toward the end of the month. Cut it back just as the new growth emerges. Cut out all the stems that are near the ground, for they will root on the surface if you leave them. **Pink trumpet vine** can be severely pruned this month to reduce the size of the plant.

PESTS

In the warmest parts of the region, watch for early aphids feeding on tender new growth. Remove by hand, with strong sprays of water, or with a soapy water solution. Treat aphids early before they become large infestations, which are much more difficult to control.

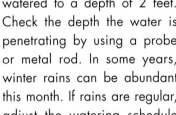
NOTES

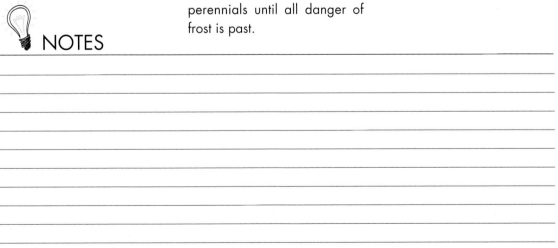

FEBRUARY

PERENNIALS

 PLANNING

Many gardeners find that hummingbirds are one of their greatest delights in the garden. It is not necessary to hang feeders or provide artificial food to attract hummingbirds; instead, choose plants that provide food throughout the year. Here are some suggestions.

- Try a selection of **justicias,** including the winter-flowering **chuparosa** and *J. sonorae,* and the year-round flowers of **red justicia.**
- Try **autumn sage,** which blooms in spring and again in fall in the hottest areas, and throughout the summer in cooler areas; and its relative, **red sage,** which blooms year-round in the warmest areas and from spring to first frost in colder areas.
- **Mexican oregano** (*Poliomintha maderensis*) blooms in late spring through early summer; although the flowers are lavender, hummingbirds feed regularly on this plant.

- **Penstemons** of any type are great favorites of hummingbirds. In the warmest areas, look for **firecracker penstemon, Parry's penstemon** for spring bloom, and **rock penstemon** for the summer. Cooler-zone gardeners can use **pine leaf penstemon** (*Penstemon pinifolius*) and **scarlet penstemon** (*P. barbatus*) as well, and many others for spring through summer flowering.

 PLANTING

As the weather warms in Zones 9 and 10, begin planting spring- and summer-flowering perennials.

To plant perennials, dig a hole that is two to three times as wide as the container and just as deep. Add compost mixed with a small amount of mulch, slow-release fertilizer, or well-composted manure to the backfill. Set the plant in the hole so that it is slightly higher than the soil line. Fill in the hole, firming it gently as you go, and add a 1-inch layer of mulch at the root zone.

Firewheel, golden columbine, and **valerian** can be planted in Zone 8. Many of the perennials that are used as winter annuals in the hottest areas bloom in spring and summer in this region. Consult the Annuals Chart on pages 153-155, and begin planting these perennials from now until May.

 CARE

Continue to provide frost protection to tender plants if there are late freezes.

 WATERING

Water established perennials to a depth of 2 feet; in the warmest zones, this may mean a watering frequency of every seven to ten days. If it rains more than $1/2$ inch, skip a watering.

 FERTILIZING

Do not fertilize this month.

 GROOMING

Once all danger of frost is past, cut back perennials that have extensive frost damage or are leggy and overgrown—cut back to 6 inches or less from the ground. Water well after pruning, but do not fertilize severely pruned plants until they are actively growing again.

Summer-flowering species and winter-growing perennials that are nearing the end of the blooming cycle respond to pruning this month in the warm regions. Wait a month to prune in the cooler areas of Zone 9, and up to two months in Zone 8.

Plants like **blanket flower, California fuchsia, chuparosa, red justicia,** and **ruellia** respond to a hard prune at this time.

Do not prune any spring-flowering perennials.

Prune **western mugwort** low this month in the warmest zones. Prune **wormwood** and other **artemesias** this month in the warmest areas of the region. Many of these plants have irregular, often fanciful growth patterns, and it is best to prune them one branch at a time, evaluating the effect as you go.

HELPFUL HINTS

The success of pruning depends not only on your skill but on the quality of your tools. Keep all pruning tools sharp and rust-free by cleaning them thoroughly after each use. Dry out the tool, then apply motor oil, machine oil, or another oily product that will keep the metal parts from rusting.

One handy method for oiling tools is to prepare a bucket of sand mixed with oil. Plunge the metal parts of the tool into the bucket after each use. The sand will scour off particles of dirt and grime, and the oil will protect it from rust.

When chuparosa nears the end of the blooming cycle, it responds well to a hard prune.

PESTS

Watch for aphids on the growing tips and flower buds of winter-growing perennials. These tiny sucking insects can become numerous quickly; control by hand removal or washing them off a stem with a strong jet of water. Insecticidal soaps and soapy water solutions are effective if used frequently.

MARCH

PERENNIALS

PLANNING

This is high spring and everything seems to be in bloom at once. In the cooler parts of the region, bloom is just beginning, and in the coldest areas, this is the month to start watching for new growth after the winter freezes.

Take out your journal and make notes of especially good combinations or effective placements, and resolve to expand or encourage them in your fall planting.

Look to the future and the summer-flowering season. If you can see that you will have holes or weak spots in the garden, start planning for summer-flowering perennials. In all but the hottest areas it is early to plant summer-flowering perennials, but it helps to plan ahead.

Groundcovers are widely used to mitigate heat, retain soil moisture, and stabilize banks or slopes. Use groundcovers like **vinca** or **Arizona grape ivy** for shady areas. In areas with more sun, groundcover choices include **Mexican evening primrose** and **trailing smokebush** its better-behaved relatives **Missouri primrose** and **Saltillo primrose. Sundrops** are beautiful plants with cheery yellow flowers, and they make excellent groundcovers throughout the region.

Angelita daisy, moss verbena, and succulent groundcovers like **carpobrotus** and **malephora** are very drought-tolerant choices. Although **pink trumpet vine** is usually grown as a vine, it is an excellent groundcover for a large area, like an embankment, because of its habit of rooting where its stems touch the ground. In the mild-winter areas, **lippia,** which has tiny green fragrant leaves and white flowers, is a charming sturdy groundcover where there is no foot traffic.

PLANTING

Sow seeds of **four o'clock** late in the month. In all but the coldest areas, four o'clocks are perennials that die away in winter to return in late spring from their large swollen root. They grow quickly from seed and should be planted where you want them. They can be difficult to transplant because the root does not like to completely dry out.

Begin to plant **chrysanthemum, Shasta daisy, statice,** and **Maximilian sunflowers** in the cooler zones, as well as **penstemons** and summer-flowering **salvias.**

Continue to plant spring- and summer-flowering perennials in the warmest areas, including **blackfoot daisy, lantana, penstemons,** and **salvias.** In Zone 8, continue to plant these as well as **delphinium, blanket flower, beebalm,** and **penstemons.**

CARE

Many clump-forming perennials should be divided every three or four years to keep them healthy and tidy. Plants like **chrysanthemum, daylily,** and **Shasta daisy** often require dividing.

Use a shovel or turning fork to dig out the entire clump when dividing a plant.

1. To begin, water the entire plant and the surrounding soil well. Dig out the entire clump with a turning fork or shovel, laying it on the ground or moving it to a work bench. Clumps are heavy, and if you want to keep the area where you are working tidy, cover the ground or lawn with a large cloth or tarp.

2. Using a sharp-bladed shovel or long knife, cut the clump in half. Do not be too concerned about the foliage and any flowers—they will all regrow in a few months. If the pieces are too large, cut each one in half again until you have a clump that is about the size that would fill a 1-gallon container.

3. To replant, set back a portion of the plant in the original hole into which you have worked some slow-release fertilizer or good compost, making sure the plant sits at the same soil level as before. Water well, then water every day or two for two weeks. Continue with weekly watering until the plant is well established, or through the entire summer.

4. Take the leftover clumps and put them in containers to give to friends, or replant them in other areas of the garden. If there is just too much of the plant, do not hesitate to contribute it to your compost pile.

HELPFUL HINTS

Four o'clocks come in a wide array of colors and will cross-pollinate freely. If you find a color you particularly like or want to maintain, be sure to remove all plants that are not that color. You may have to do this over two or three years, but eventually you will have a single color stand.

WATERING

In Zone 10 and the warmest parts of Zone 9, the weather can shift to hot late in the month. As temperatures climb to 90 degrees Fahrenheit or more, monitor the watering schedule for perennials carefully. Be sure they are being watered to a soil depth of 2 feet.

FERTILIZING

In the warmest areas, apply a 2- to 3-inch layer of compost or mulch to all perennial beds. Not only will this help retain soil moisture as the weather heats up, but it will provide a long, slow release of nutrients to your plants.

GROOMING

Prune winter-damaged branches from **bougainvillea, lantana,** and other frost-tender plants once all danger of frost is past. Do not be impatient—if you prune too early, late freezes and cold, drying winds can be devastating to tender new growth.

Bougainvillea and **lantana** can be pruned as hard as is necessary to keep them the size and shape you want.

Prune **pink trumpet vine** as soon as the new leaves emerge and throughout the summer to keep it shapely and under control. This fall-flowering vine grows quickly through the summer, and it is advisable to prune out unruly branches, or those growing along the ground, once a month through the growing season.

PESTS

Spider mites become active as the temperatures warm up. These tiny insects are drawn to hot, dusty conditions. The best control is to spray leaves regularly to keep down the dust and raise the humidity around the plant.

APRIL
PERENNIALS

 PLANNING

Butterflies are such delicate visitors in the garden that we forget what important work they do. These nectar feeders are important pollinators for a host of plants, and gardens can be an important feeding ground for them during all stages of their life. To encourage butterflies in your garden, think of the three parts of their life-cycle: larva, pupa, and adult. The larvae need food, lots of it, and many are particular about what is a food plant. Pupae need a place to form in peace and hide as they develop. Adults need food plants and suitable areas to lay eggs for the next generation.

To create a good butterfly garden in your yard, start by growing perennials that are in bloom and full of nectar when most butterflies are active: in summer. Plants in the **verbena** family are renowned butterfly attracters. Use a generous number of verbenas of any type, but **moss verbena** and **Goodding's verbena** are a good start. Look also to add a number of different-colored **lantana** to attract butterflies. The colors do not matter, so pick varieties that go with whatever else you have. If you have a small garden or grow plants only in contain-

ers, **lantana** make excellent pot plants, even in full sun, and **trailing lantana** is lovely in hanging baskets. But there are many others plants that attract butterflies, including **blue mist** and **mistflower** (both with delicate blue flowers in late summer), the orange-flowered, cold-hardy **butterfly weed,** creamy white **pine leaf milkweed** and **desert milkweed,** and the orange-and-yellow-flowered **blood flower.**

 PLANTING

Continue to plant summer-flowering perennials in the warmest parts of the region. Mix them among the spring-flowering shrubs for continuous color in the beds through summer. Good summer bloomers for the hottest zones include **blue mist, lantana, red justicia, red salvia,** and **Russian sage.**

In the cooler areas of Zone 9 and throughout Zone 8, continue to plant late spring-flowering perennials like **gerbera daisy, golden columbine,** and the biennial **hollyhock,** as well as natives like **damianita, globe mallow,** and **penstemon.** Once all danger of frost is past, sow the seed of **four o'clocks.**

 CARE

Once **globe mallow** have finished the first flush of bloom, cut back the plants to encourage a second bloom. Water well after this pruning. Continue to remove the spent flowers of spring-flowering perennials (called deadheading), as this will encourage a second bloom cycle. Unless you are saving seed, cut off **penstemon's** blooming stalks once they are finished blooming. This will help direct more energy to the plant and away from making seed.

 WATERING

Even in the hottest parts of the region, water native perennials like **brittlebush, damianita, fairyduster, globe mallow,** and **penstemons** deeply but infrequently to prevent these plants from becoming overgrown, floppy, and subject to rotting. If your plants are too large, cut them back and reduce the frequency of watering.

Continue to water other perennials to a depth of 1 foot; in the warmest areas, this may be as often as once a week. Check the watering depth to establish a watering schedule.

FERTILIZING

As the spring-flowering perennials in the warmest areas begin to fade and the summer flowering starts, it is an ideal time to renew the fertility of the beds. Spread a layer of 2 to 3 inches of compost or mulch mixed with a small amount of well-composted manure over the entire area around perennials. Water it in well. Alternately, apply fertilizer at the rate of about 1 pound per 100 square feet. Use a well-balanced complete formula like 10-10-10. Be sure to water the day before you spread the fertilizer, and immediately afterward. Providing added nutrients at this time helps spring-flowering plants prepare for summer and encourages summer-flowering perennials to grow rapidly this month.

GROOMING

Cut back spring-flowering perennials after the flowers have faded. Many members of the **mint** family, like **Jerusalem sage** and **salvias,** send up a long, leafy growing shoot that ends in a blooming stalk. Once the flowering stalk has bloomed out completely, it will quickly die off. Cutting out these old stalks to the ground as soon as they are spent allows the small emerging shoots from the base of the plant, known as basal growth, to thrive. This growth will be the next round of flowering stalks.

PESTS

Not all the insects you see are harmful. The large, heavy-bodied black bees, often called Carpenter bees, will become active this month. These are excellent pollinators and should be left to their work. A white frothy foam that often shows up on new growth of perennials is the protection for the nymph of spittlebugs. The bugs are generally harmless, but if you like, you can rinse them off with the garden hose.

TWO PRUNING TECHNIQUES

Deadheading is cutting off only the flowers of a perennial. To deadhead a plant, cut the flowering stalk back to the first leaves. This will encourage another set of flower buds to form, giving a longer blooming season. In some perennials, especially **salvias**, there may be a group of flowering stalks at the end of the branches. Deadheading these plants is the removal of only the stalk that has finished flowering, leaving the rest to complete their bloom.

Pruning back a perennial is reducing the size of the plant by cutting a stem back to a leaf node to encourage the plant to grow more stems. To prune back a perennial, cut back a stem by at least a third of its length, more if you want the plant to be smaller. Be sure to cut just above a leaf node (where leaves join the main stem). This type of pruning will encourage the growth of more shoots, which makes a plant look fuller while reducing its height.

NOTES

_____
_____
_____
_____
_____
_____
_____
_____
_____
_____
_____
_____
_____
_____

MAY
PERENNIALS

PLANNING

Shade offers so many advantages to desert gardens that it is often hard to think of the problems it can cause. High filtered shade like that provided by **mesquites, palms, palo verdes,** and other desert trees allows almost any kind of plant to thrive under it. But the shade of deciduous trees, tall fences and buildings, or north-facing areas can be a bigger problem. For areas that have this kind of shade, look for plants that either bloom well in the shade or have colorful leaf patterns. Some good perennials for the shade include the following.

- **Asparagus fern**

- **Coleus** (an annual except in frost-free areas where it is a perennial).
- The perennial **impatiens** (*Impatiens balsamina*), especially the so-called **New Guinea impatiens** with their sensational colors. Although perennial, these plants are more commonly used as long-season annuals.
- **Red lobelia**
- **Transvaal daisy,** also known as **gerbera daisy** (a perennial, but usually grown as an annual).
- **Wandering Jew** or **Moses in the cradle** (vivid purple)

In the warm areas, look also for **cigar plant, four o'clocks,** and the unusual shrublike *Jatropha integerrima.*

Chocolate flower

PLANTING

Set out transplants of **blue mist, gaillardia, gloriosa daisy, lantana,** and **salvia** in the warmest zones. In addition to these, look for transplants of **coleus** to lighten up shady spots in the cooler areas.

CARE

Continue to cut back flowering stalks from spring-flowering perennials as they fade. If you have not done so already, lay down a 2- to 3-inch layer of mulch on your perennials to get them prepared for the summer.

Geraniums can be difficult to bring through the summer in the hottest zones. As the heat increases the leaves will begin to yellow, dry, and fall off. Many gardeners simply contribute them to the compost pile and use the **geraniums** as seasonal annuals. If you want to bring them through the summer, however, try the following tips.

1. As **geraniums** lose leaves, cut back on watering and allow the plant to go dormant.

2. If they are in containers, move them into the shade. If they are in the ground, be sure they are shaded from the afternoon sun.

Four o'clocks

3. Water only enough to prevent the tips from wilting, and if you are uncertain, do not water.

4. When the weather begins to cool in September, cut back all dead or damaged stems. At the first sign of leaves, begin to water regularly. Once the plant is fully leafed out, fertilize it lightly.

 WATERING

Water perennials, other than natives, every five to seven days throughout the region. Check the soil with a probe or metal rod to be sure water is penetrating to a depth of 2 feet every time. When the soil is moist 6 inches or less from the surface, it is time to water.

 FERTILIZING

If you did not do so in April, apply a 3- to 4-inch layer of compost or mulch. If you prefer, apply a slow-release, well-balanced fertilizer to summer-growing perennials. Water well before application, scratch it into the soil lightly, and then water when complete.

 GROOMING

Pinch back summer-flowering plants like **lantana** to encourage them to grow more densely. This will also encourage more blooms on these plants. Continue to deadhead **coreopsis, gaillardia, rock penstemon,** and **salvias** regularly to keep them reblooming.

 PESTS

Monitor watering carefully as the weather heats up to prevent soils from becoming soggy. Warm, continuously moist soils encourage root rots that cause the plant to become weakened and yellowed, lose vigor, and eventually die.

 NOTES

_____
_____
_____
_____
_____
_____
_____
_____
_____
_____
_____
_____

JUNE
PERENNIALS

PLANNING

Vines are one of the best ways to increase shade in a small garden. Planted on a trellis, arbor, or open roof, they provide welcome shade to seating areas, porches, and patios without taking up the room necessary for a tree. Perennial vines are particularly effective because they tend to grow larger over the years and can be shaped and pruned to fit whatever space is available. Some vines for the region include the following.

- **Arizona grape ivy**—stems hardy to 30 degrees Fahrenheit, roots hardy to 25 degrees. Deciduous. Flowers unremarkable, deep-green foliage. Fast-growing, with tendrils.
- **Bougainvillea**—stems hardy to 28 degrees, roots hardy to 20 degrees. Evergreen, but deciduous in hard frosts. Colorful bracts from late summer to late spring. Moderate growth rate, woody without tendrils.
- **Cat's claw**—hardy to 25 degrees. Evergreen or deciduous with hard frost. Yellow flowers briefly in spring. Fast-growing, with tendrils.
- **Clematis**—variable in both cold and heat tolerance, most hardy to well below freezing. Most heat-tolerant are the varieties of *C. viticella*. The Texas native *C. texensis*, with bell-shaped red flowers, is hardy throughout the region. Deciduous. Moderate growth rate, most with tendrils.
- **Lilac vine**—hardy to 25 degrees. Evergreen. Deep-purple flowers in summer. Moderate growth rate, no tendrils.
- **Mile-a-minute vine**—stems and leaves hardy to 30 degrees, roots hardy to 15 degrees. Deciduous. White morning glory-like flowers in summer. Fast-growing, with tendrils.
- **Passion flower**—hardy to 20 degrees, perhaps more. Native *P. foetida* has small lavender flowers. Deciduous. Moderate growth rate, with tendrils.
- **Pink trumpet vine**—hardy to 22 degrees. Evergreen or semideciduous. Large pink flowers in fall. Fast-growing, without tendrils.
- **Purple butterfly vine**—hardy to 15 degrees. Evergreen in frost-free areas and otherwise deciduous. Lavender to purple flowers in spring. Moderate growth rate, without tendrils.
- **Queen's wreath**—stems hardy to 28 degrees, roots hardy to 20 degrees. Deciduous to evergreen in warmest areas. Small, clustered, pink to red flowers in summer. Fast-growing, with tendrils.
- **Snapdragon vine**—hardy to 20 degrees. Deciduous. Small lavender flowers in late spring to summer. Fast-growing, with tendrils.
- **Trumpet vine**—hardy to 0 degrees. Deciduous. Large orange to red flowers in summer. Vigorous, moderate at first, fast-growing after two or three years, and woody.
- **Yellow butterfly vine**—hardy to 15 degrees. Evergreen in frost-free areas, otherwise deciduous. Yellow flowers briefly in spring, attractive pods all summer. Moderate growth rate, without tendrils.
- **Yuca vine**—stems hardy to 30 degrees, roots hardy to 20 degrees. Deciduous. Bright-yellow flowers in summer. Fast-growing, with tendrils.

PLANTING

Continue planting summer-flowering perennials in cooler zones. Plant in a well-prepared hole that is the depth of the pot and three to five times wider than the pot's diameter. Water after planting, and continue to water two or three times a week for the first two weeks. Mulch heavily around the roots to maintain even soil moisture. Plant **chrysanthemums** in Zone 8.

CARE

Many perennials make wonderful pot plants. When growing perennials in pots, it is important to water regularly, especially in the hottest zones. Water when the surface of the soil feels dry. If the plant is drying out too frequently or is wilting, move it to a shadier location for the summer.

WATERING

Perennials in the hottest areas may need their watering increased to every three to four days to maintain a watering depth of 1 foot. Water early in the morning, as plants take up water most quickly in the hours right before dawn. Mulch heavily to conserve soil moisture.

FERTILIZING

Plants in containers need to be fertilized more frequently than those growing in the ground. The continuous watering leaches out nutrients quickly. Add a slow-release granular fertilizer to the soil, and water well both before and after applying.

If you use a liquid fertilizer on container-grown perennials, fertilize twice a month while they are actively growing. Dissolve the fertilizer in water in a bucket or watering can, or make use of a water siphon if you have numerous pots.

GROOMING

Flowers of **chrysanthemums** occur on the tips of new stems. Pinch back the plants to encourage vigorous tip growth and flowering. Deadhead summer-flowering plants regularly to promote continuous bloom.

Pinch back **lantana** to keep it tidy and promote continuous flowering through the summer.

In cooler areas, cut back spring-flowering perennials when they are finished blooming. Water well after pruning, but wait until the plants show new growth before fertilizing them.

PESTS

Spray plants early in the day when it is hot, dry, and dusty to keep the foliage clean and discourage spider mites.

Blanket flower

JULY
PERENNIALS

PLANNING

Many perennials are grown for their interesting foliage rather than as flowering plants. They add rich texture and vivid contrast to a garden. Many have pale, nearly white foliage, which offers a spot of contrast in a dark spot or highlights other colors in the bed. Perennials that offer interest other than flowers include the following.

• **Bush morning glory** has both interesting foliage and pretty flowers. The white flowers are numerous on the plant in spring, and the dusky gray-green foliage is evergreen. These plants are heat-tolerant and maintain a tight, almost round form without pruning.

• **Candelilla** is a semi-succulent perennial native to the western part of the region. The numerous thin, light-green, drought-hardy stems form a tidy plant.

• **Desert milkweed** is a tall, wispy plant with numerous gray-green stems topped with creamy heads of flowers through the spring and summer. Up to 4 feet tall, it is effective in corners or smaller areas, especially where it is hot or dry.

Bougainvillea

• **Gopher plant** is a low-growing perennial with pale grayish-green leaves. The bracts of the flowers are chartreuse in spring.

• **Western mugwort** is native to parts of the region and forms a spreading multistemmed plant with grayish-white foliage. Cut back in late winter or spring to maintain form.

• **Wormwood** is a finely cut, white, semiwoody plant that has a full, rounded shape. The hybrid 'Powis Castle' is especially vigorous and drought-hardy.

PLANTING

This is a difficult month to plant perennials in Zones 9 and 10. In Zone 8, continue to plant summer-flowering perennials.

CARE

Pinch back **chrysanthemums** once again to encourage new shoot growth. In the hottest areas, many spring-flowering perennials look weak, yellowed,

HELPFUL HINTS

Many perennials are easy to grow from cuttings. This is a good way to increase the number of plants of a rare or hard-to-find variety, or to root extras to give to friends. Begin by examining the stems. The oldest wood on the stem will be hard, brown, and hard to bend. The next oldest, known as semihardwood, will be firm but a little pliable and is usually green. The newest part of the stem is soft—usually it will bend around your finger—and is closest to the tip. This is called softwood. You will want to make a cutting that is at least half semihardwood.

1. Cut a piece 3 to 4 inches long that has at least four leaf nodes. Strip off all the leaves that will be beneath the soil, and cut out any flowers or flower buds. Dip the cut end in a rooting agent like Hormodin or Dip 'n' Gro™, making sure it coats at least two leaf nodes.

2. Stick the cutting in a pot that is filled with a 50:50 mixture of perlite and vermiculite, or with sterile potting soil. Water thoroughly. Cover the pot with plastic film or a plastic jug from which the bottom has been removed, and put it where it will receive bright indirect light and won't get too hot. Watch the covering so you will know when you need to water. If there are water droplets on the covering, the cuttings are fine; if there are no droplets, water gently. It is important to keep the cuttings evenly moist without rotting the stems.

3. Once new leaves have emerged, fertilize with a weak solution of water-soluble fertilizer. Plants can be gradually brought out to more light and transplanted to larger pots two to three weeks after the leaves begin to grow.

and dreary owing to heat stress. To help them through the summer, provide temporary shade and keep them well watered but not saturated.

WATERING

Avoid overwatering desert-adapted spring-flowering perennials like **brittlebush, desert milkweed,** and **penstemon,** regardless of their looks; they are highly susceptible to root rots in warm, moist soils. Water every other week, just enough to maintain them.

Continue to water actively growing perennials regularly, and apply a 3- to 4-inch layer of mulch if necessary.

FERTILIZING

Except for plants growing in pots, do not fertilize this month.

GROOMING

In the hottest areas, prune back summer-flowering **blue mist, justicias,** and **salvias** to keep them tidy. Keep deadheading all flowering perennials to pro-

long the bloom. In cooler areas, continue to deadhead; in these areas, perennials may be lightly pruned through the summer to maintain a tidy appearance.

PESTS

Grasshoppers may appear anytime in the summer. If there are just a few, handpick them to prevent minor damage, but if they appear to be getting out of control, try one of the formulations specifically designed for grasshoppers. Follow package directions for both timing and rates of application.

AUGUST

PERENNIALS

 PLANNING

This is a good month to evaluate the performance of many of your perennials. Spring-flowering plants may look a little pale in the heat but they should still be fairly vigorous, with healthy green leaves. Summer-flowering perennials are often in need of a bit of pruning or fertilizer at the end of the summer, but likewise should look generally healthy and vigorous. Plants that look unhealthy or stressed may be growing without enough water, receiving too much sun or shade, or unable to withstand the long, hot summer. This can be especially true in the hottest parts of the region. Look at their performance carefully and decide now whether they just need a boost or if they need to be replaced.

 PLANTING

It is a difficult time to plant in the warmest parts of Zone 9 and all of Zone 10. Late summer- or fall-flowering perennials can be planted in Zone 8, but get them in early so they have a good root set before the first frost.

 CARE

Cease pinching **chrysanthemums** in August, as plants begin to set flower buds. In Zone 8, plant new **daylilies**, and divide any established clumps that have become overgrown.

Lantana grown in pots may begin to look peaked this month. To rejuvenate them, move the container to a shady spot, cut the plant back by 1/4, and feed it with a well-balanced water-soluble fertilizer. It will begin to grow vigorously again within a month and can be put back in the full sun to bloom until frost.

 WATERING

In areas of the region that receive summer rain, the rain is unpredictable but can occur in drenching downpours. Adjust watering schedules after a heavy rain, but be prepared to shift schedules quickly if the weather becomes extremely hot or dry during the month. Perennials perform best when watered to a depth of 1 foot, and that is generally every three to four days in the hottest areas.

Continue to maintain a 3- to 4-inch layer of mulch around all perennials.

 FERTILIZING

Do not fertilize perennials this month. The exceptions are plants growing in containers.

 GROOMING

Cut back overgrown perennials by about a third this month. There is still plenty of time in the warmest zones for them to recover before cold weather sets in. In cooler zones, prune more carefully, removing only overgrown limbs, weak or crossing branches, and all old flowering stems that are no longer blooming.

 PESTS

Continue to hose off plants frequently, once or twice a week, to control spider mites. As humidity rises, powdery mildew may show up on **plumbago** and other soft-leaved perennials. Although it rarely causes more than cosmetic damage to healthy perennials, rampant infestations can be prevented by spraying at the first eruption of the distinctive white mottling on the leaves.

HELPFUL HINTS

Many beneficial insects show up in the garden throughout the year. It is important to recognize these "good guys" and give them a home in your garden. Some are voracious predators of much more destructive insects, while others are entirely benign with no impact on any of your garden plants. Some of the most common beneficial insects, and a few other beneficial "critters" include the following.

• **Praying mantis** are odd-shaped insects with large splayed legs and disproportionately large heads. They generally remain still, waiting for insect prey to move within range, and it takes a sharp eye to find them on a stalk.

• **Ladybugs** are renowned for eating aphids. Releasing purchased ladybugs is extremely difficult and if not done at precisely the right time, they simply fly away. It is best to have a healthy place for them to live and wait for them to come around in their own time.

• **Lacewings** are small, delicate creatures with finely webbed wings that give them their name. They are, however, terrific predators of aphids, spider mites, and other hungry critters in the garden.

• **Earthworms** are not really an insect, but they are so helpful. Earthworms plow through soil, eating it, and their tunnels create necessary air spaces while their excretions help increase soil nutrients. They do not live in soils that are too hot or too dry, or those that are without organic matter. Purchased earthworms, also called red crawlers, are sensitive to heat and rarely live over the summer in the hottest areas.

• Almost any kind of **spider** is a helpful partner in the garden. Because the poisonous black widow spider lives in much of the area, many people think all spiders are a problem. It is just the opposite. Most spiders are fierce predators of other insects and can be a boon. Give them plenty of room, and leave them undisturbed to spin those webs to trap marauding pests.

• **Bees** are the single most useful insect in any garden. Bees are mighty pollinators, and most of the fruit and vegetables we eat are pollinated by these wonderful insects. Although so-called killer or Africanized bees can be a problem in some areas, most bees are merely out for the nectar and pollen of the flowers in your yard. Bees are extremely sensitive to most chemical sprays; if you use such sprays, do it in the early morning before bees are active.

• **Ants** are such admirable insects it is hard to think ill of them until they sting you. Many are the garbage collectors of the area, taking in old leaves, dead bugs, and other detritus and turning it into food for their young. It is sometimes tempting to think that ants are the problem with a plant because they are what you see, when most of the time the plant has begun to rot and die and the ants are attracted by the various other bugs and bacteria that are part of the decay. But ants often find themselves living right where you want to stand, sit, or work in the flower bed. When ants become a problem, there are more benign ways to get rid of them than using the dangerous chemicals sold for this purpose. Cut up one or two oranges into a blender. Add enough water to make a thick slurry when you blend. Take this concoction immediately to the ant hole and pour it over the top. Volatile oils from the rind swirl through the tunnels and chambers, killing the ants. Once the slurry has dried you can remove it and put it on the compost pile, its work is done.

SEPTEMBER

PERENNIALS

 PLANNING

If you have healthy **poinsettias** and you want to encourage them to bloom for the holidays, begin this month. First lightly prune the plant to stimulate the growth of new stems—that is where blooms will arise. Water well, and feed lightly after pruning. Do not fertilize again.

Put the plant in a place that is cool and where it will be dark for a full twelve to fourteen hours each night. These plants are extremely light-sensitive, so be sure there are no streetlights or other light sources. It is helpful to put a cardboard box or other covering over the plant if you are unsure of the light. Keep **poinsettias** well watered by drenching the pot only when the surface of the soil is dry to the touch.

Leave it in dark conditions for three to four weeks. Check to be sure that flower buds are forming. It is the large bracts around the flowers that are so colorful, and they form in response to flowering.

 PLANTING

In Zones 9 and 10, begin to plant spring-flowering perennials late in the month. Many of these plants are cold-hardy enough, or the area has a warm-enough winter that they will grow through the entire winter.

Plant in well-prepared beds, and water well after planting. Apply a 2- to 3-inch layer of mulch to keep up the soil fertility and shelter the tender roots.

If you want to grow perennials from seed, begin planting seed of **asters, columbine, hollyhock, statice,** and **yarrow** this month. They will be ready to transplant into the garden in about eight weeks.

 CARE

Divide perennials like **daylily** and **Shasta daisy** every three or four years as the clumps become overgrown. In Zone 8, continue to divide these perennials this month. In warmer areas, wait until October when temperatures are lower. There are two ways to divide perennials.

1. One is to remove the entire clump from the ground with a turning fork or spade. With the whole mass on the ground, take a sharp shovel or long knife and cut it into as many sections as you like. Replant one to maintain the plant. The rest can be planted in other locations, put in pots, or discarded.

2. The other way is to take a sharp shovel and cut into the plant without removing it from the ground. Using the shovel as a pry, pull and cut out as much of the plant as it takes to reduce it as much as you want. What you dig out can be replanted elsewhere, potted up, or discarded.

 WATERING

It will begin to cool off in Zone 8, and by the end of the month temperatures will be below 90 degrees Fahrenheit. In the warmer areas, temperatures should be below 100 degrees by the end of the month. Once temperatures have cooled down, adjust watering schedules to maintain a watering depth of 1 foot. This will usually mean expanding the time between waterings to five to seven days.

 FERTILIZING

To encourage good fall growth and renew summer-flowering perennials, lay down a 4- to 6-inch layer of compost, or mulch mixed with a small amount of well-composted manure or other organic amendments on the perennial beds.

Alternately, apply a well-balanced slow-release granular fertilizer to the bed. Water well both before and after applying fertilizer.

GROOMING

In cooler areas, do not prune frost-sensitive plants now; wait until warm weather returns next spring. Pruning encourages new growth, and the tender shoots can be severely damaged by an early frost.

PESTS

Whiteflies can appear in small or large numbers this month. Perennials like **justicias, lantana, salvias,** and other soft-leaved plants are particularly susceptible. There is little that can deter whiteflies, but washing off plants with a soapy water solution, using an insecticidal soap, or even covering them with a light row cloth can help keep infestations under control.

NOTES

_____
_____
_____
_____
_____
_____
_____
_____
_____
_____
_____
_____

California Fuschia

OCTOBER

PERENNIALS

PLANNING

Penstemons have become one of the mainstays of the perennial garden in Arizona. There are dozens of species that do well in the region, many of which are native. **Penstemons** bloom in a wide array of colors, and there are good choices for all areas of the region. Some of the most popular include the following.

• **Canyon penstemon** is full of long spikes of bright pink flowers and unusual serrated leaves that surround the stem. It does especially well in the cooler parts of Zone 9.

• **Firecracker penstemon** sends up spikes of intensely red flowers in spring, and in the cooler parts of Zone 9 will bloom into the summer.

• **Foxglove penstemon** sends out large bulbous flowers in pale white, pink, or lavender. It is hardy throughout the zone, blooming in spring where winters are mild and through the summer in cold-winter areas.

• **Hill country penstemon** blooms on sturdy, upright spikes with pink to lavender flowers. It flowers in late spring to early summer in the warmest areas, and through the summer in cooler areas. Like **foxglove penstemon**, it grows and blooms in the shade in the hottest areas.

• **Parry's penstemon** has tall spikes of pink flowers in spring or early summer.

• *Penstemon superbus* has tall stalks of coral flowers. There are many hybrids between this and *P. parryi* on the market that are exquisite but unnamed. It is spring-blooming and, like *P. parryi*, it is one of the earliest to bloom in the hottest areas.

• **Pine leaf penstemon** has long-lasting red to red-orange flowers throughout the summer in the cooler parts of the region. This plant can be difficult in the hottest areas.

• **Rock penstemon** is a shorter, red-flowered plant with deeply serrated leaves. This is the only **penstemon** that reliably blooms in the summer in Zone 10 and the hottest parts of Zone 9. It blooms throughout the summer elsewhere. Removing spent flowering stalks encourages it to bloom repeatedly through the summer.

• **Scarlet penstemon** blooms with thin red flowers, in the spring in warm areas and through the summer in the cooler areas of the region.

• **Scented penstemon** grows tall (up to 6 feet) flowering stalks of large, rounded, fragrant pink flowers. It blooms from late spring (in mild-winter areas) though summer (cooler areas). It is one of the few **penstemons** whose flowers make good cut flowers.

Firecracker penstemon
(*Penstemon eatonii*)

Colorful blooming perennials to add to your garden also include **autumn sage, blackfoot daisy, bush morning glory, gaura, globe mallow, Mexican honeysuckle, moss verbena,** and **salvias.**

PLANTING

In Zones 9 and 10, this is the ideal month to plant perennials that are not frost-tender. There is a wide range of native and desert-adapted perennials in nurseries this month. Once established, these plants need minimal care and thrive on modest amounts of supplemental water.

Plant perennials in a hole that is three to five times as wide as the container but just as deep. Hot-region natives like **brittlebush, desert marigold,** and **globe mallow** do not need to be grown in well-amended or overly rich soils. **Penstemons** need excellent drainage, as does **blackfoot daisy. Salvias, justicias, ruellia,** and most members of the **sunflower** family do best in well-amended soils with good drainage.

In Zone 8, plant cold-hardy, or native, perennials by the middle of the month. Continue to plant **delphinium, golden columbine, marguerite, pincushion flower, sweet William, valerian,** and **wallflower** through the end of the month.

CARE

In the warmer areas of the region, continue to dig and divide perennials like **beebalm, daylily,** and **Shasta daisy** every three to four years or if the plants are crowded and overgrown. One indication that a perennial needs to be divided is when both the number and the size of blooms begins to decrease.

WATERING

Water perennials weekly to a depth of 1 foot. Water newly planted perennials every two to three days for the first two weeks. Then expand the watering to once a week, and finally to watering every eight to ten days.

FERTILIZING

In the warmest parts of the region, fertilize the perennial bed with either a layer of organic matter or a well-balanced slow-release granular fertilizer if you did not do so in September. Do not fertilize in the colder parts of the region.

GROOMING

Cut back spring-flowering perennials like **brittlebush, globe mallow, ruellia,** and groundcovers like **sundrops** and **trailing smokebush** hard this month. Prune to remove at least 1/3 of the plant and more if it is especially leggy or unruly. Water well after pruning.

PESTS

Penstemon and other desert perennials are highly susceptible to root rots when grown in the shade. Prevention is the best weapon against these soil borne fungi. Provide good drainage and mulch **penstemons** minimally to discourage an outbreak.

NOTES

175

November

PERENNIALS

 PLANNING

In the mild-winter areas, this is an excellent month to consider moving established perennials to a new location. Begin by determining where you want the plant to be relocated. Dig the new hole wider than the rootball of the plant but just as deep. Amend the backfill with compost or mulch, and mix them together well.

Dig out the plant with a turning fork or shovel that is large enough to get under the entire plant. If the plant is hard to remove, soak the ground before digging. Take out the plant with as much soil as you can, and set it in the new hole immediately. Take care that it is planted at the same depth as it was in the previous hole. Backfill by working soil around the rootball, pressing it gently as you go to remove air pockets and voids. Water well when finished, and lay down a 2- to 3-inch layer of mulch.

Pick a cloudy day to move a plant; it cuts down on evaporative loss. Water the new hole, letting it drain completely before you plant. This helps cut down on transplant shock to the roots. The following tips will help ensure transplanting success.

• Do not cut back the plant or do more than incidental pruning when you move a plant. Wait until it is actively growing again before you prune.
• Water deeply and often for the first two weeks or until you see new growth.
• Apply fertilizer the following spring.

 PLANTING

Zone 8 gardeners can still plant **cup flower, dusty miller,** and **violets** this month, as well those recommended for last month. When planting perennials in this zone, be sure to plant only natives or cold-hardy species this month. Otherwise, plants will be lost in an early freeze before they have time to establish their roots. Do not fertilize newly planted perennials in this zone; they are only growing roots until late in the spring, and you do not want to encourage a flush of tender new growth.

 CARE

Protect tender plants or newly planted perennials from freezing temperatures with frost cloth, blankets, boxes, or other light-weight materials. For plants that are known to be frost-sensitive, pile up a 6-inch layer of mulch, straw, or pine needles around the base of the plant.

 WATERING

Established perennials should be watered every eight to ten days in the warm areas of the region. Newly planted perennials need to be watered weekly. Water perennials that are dormant every three to four weeks over the winter.

 FERTILIZING

Do not fertilize this month.

 GROOMING

If there is frost damage on perennials, it is usually best to wait until all danger of frost is past in the spring before pruning it off.

 PESTS

You can expect few pest problems this month and through the winter.

DECEMBER

PERENNIALS

 PLANNING

One of the most traditional of all Christmas plants is the **poinsettia.** Not so many years ago, **poinsettias** were either large, woody shrubs that thrived in mild-winter gardens, or they were dwarf, long-blooming potted plants. But now the range and color choices are amazing. In addition to the standard bright-red varieties, there are varieties that are pink, white, cream with red edges, mottled or speckled leaves, and even a creamy yellow form. To keep a **poinsettia** healthy and colorful through the holidays, remember the following.

1. The colorful part is made of enlarged bracts that turn into vivid hues in response to blooming. The longer the bloom, the longer the color lasts, so buy plants with tight, unopened buds rather than ones in full bloom.

2. Place plants where they receive bright but indirect light. Avoid placing them near a west- or southwest-facing window, or near fireplaces and heaters. Keep plants out of the air flow from heater vents, and do not place them on heat-generating appliances like televisions or refrigerators.

3. Water thoroughly when the surface of the soil is dry. Remove any decorative wrapping or foil to water, and let the water drain away completely before you put them back in these coverings.

4. Do not fertilize the plants through the holiday season.

5. Hose off your **poinsettia** once a week to keep off dust and insects. This also helps raise humidity for the plant.

Once the holidays are over, **poinsettias** can continue to live outside in their pots on a shaded porch or patio. Many gardeners like to try to keep them over the year in the ground. The old-fashioned red varieties usually work best, but even they can be tricky in this region. Plant **poinsettias** after frost danger is past in rich, well-amended soil with bright indirect or only-morning light. If they make it through the summer, they will bloom again if they are able to kept dark and cool enough in the fall.

 PLANTING

Even in the mild-winter areas, this is a difficult month to plant perennials. The cold soils, light freezes, and long nights make it hard for a plant to establish well.

 CARE

Protect tender plants from freezing temperatures. Keep a close watch on perennials that are in pots, as they are more vulnerable to freezes than plants in the ground.

 WATERING

Check soil moisture before watering perennials. If winter rains are abundant, plants may not need to be watered as frequently to maintain soil moisture of 6 inches. Most established perennials need watering every other week when the weather is cold. Continue to water dormant perennials in cold areas of the zone every three to four weeks.

 FERTILIZING

Do not fertilize this month.

 GROOMING

Do not prune this month.

 PESTS

Hose off indoor plants like **Christmas cactus, poinsettias,** and other holiday plants at least once a week. This will help raise the humidity around the plants and keep down the dust, which harbors spider mites.

ROSES

Roses are arguably the oldest garden plants in the world. Cultivated in China and parts of Europe for centuries, these extraordinary plants hold a special place in the hearts of gardeners everywhere.

There are countless varieties of roses in a bewildering array of styles and forms. Old varieties that go by the names antique roses, heirloom roses, or old garden roses are generally big, shrubby plants. Some make excellent climbers when trained to an arbor or a wall. Many of the varieties in this group bloom once in the spring, but over the years the ones that repeat their bloom through the year have gained more favor. Many of these varieties are among the most fragrant of roses, with rich and full smells that no artificial rose aroma can match.

The so-called modern roses fall into five general categories:

1. Hybrid teas are upright bushes with a single rose at the end of a long stem. This class accounts for most modern roses, in almost any color or color combination.

2. Floribunda are medium-sized bushes with flowers that are clustered at the end of the branch. Flowers are usually larger and fuller than those of hybrid teas.

3. Grandiflora are similar to floribunda but are generally larger, shrubby plants with much larger flowers.

4. Climbers are roses that can grow canes over 20 feet, and are used to cover a wall, trellis, or arbor. These long canes are the support of the plant; it is on the numerous secondary canes that climbers bloom.

5. Miniatures, as the name suggests, are varieties that are much smaller than the average rose. Most are less than 2 feet tall, and the leaves and flowers are smaller as well. Flowers may be solitary as in hybrid teas, or multiple as in floribunda.

Roses bloom in a vast array of colors regardless of class or variety, although a true blue has yet to be found. Blends are flowers that begin as one color and fade to another as the flowers mature. Rose growers also describe flowers that are rimmed, speckled, or flecked with another color as a blend. Flowers may be single, meaning there is only one row of petals that are wide open at maturity, or have dozens of petals tightly wound around a single axis, similar to the flower of a camellia.

CARE OF ROSES

Desert conditions, especially in Phoenix, Tucson, and cities along the Colorado River, can be difficult for many rose varieties. Many require dedicated care to look their best in these areas. Roses like steady, deep watering and grow best where the soil is not permitted to dry out completely. Poor drainage or swampy conditions are also to be avoided, however, so be sure that the drainage is good in the beds where you grow your roses.

The blazing heat of summer can dry out roses severely, and the limb and leaf loss at the end of the summer in many varieties is the result of this struggle with the heat. Afternoon shade in the summer mitigates this problem for most varieties and can mean the difference between struggling bushes and vigorous, full-blooming ones.

Because roses grow best in rich soils, many gardeners maintain a regular fertilization program. A healthy bush blooms well and lives longest. But the real key to healthy, vigorous plants is the soil. Plant all roses in soil that has been heavily amended with organic material, and keep replenishing it steadily over the years. Adding compost or mulch or both deeply three or four times a year ensures that the roses are kept in soil that is rich enough to meet their needs.

Fertilizers, especially inorganic fast-acting ones, provide a quick dose of nutrients that results in faster shoot development and therefore bloom. This strenuous fast growth and heavy blooming shortens the life of a plant, and the varieties that depend on this cycle (most modern hybrids) live only about ten years in the garden. Heirloom, native shrub roses, and shrubs, live much longer, sometimes for many decades.

The dry air of the desert region discourages the most serious diseases and pests of roses. A little powdery mildew when conditions are just right, a few aphids and cane borers from time to time are about all the pests most rose growers will ever encounter in this region.

Although hybrid teas are tender in some parts of Zone 8, piling up mulch or soil around the base of the plant will keep them from serious freeze damage.

Pruning roses accomplishes two things. In hybrids, it reduces the amount of old wood and stimulates the plant to put on a flush of new growth that will bloom that season. In all roses, pruning removes dead, diseased, or damaged wood from the plant where it harbors insects and disease. Pruning is also helpful from time to time to keep large roses in bounds.

Styles and timing of pruning is covered in the text, but remember the following general guidelines.

• Keep tools sharp and clean so they make a smooth cut and do not spread disease from one plant to another.

• Cut at a 45-degree angle just above a bud.

• Make the cut in the direction in which you prefer the stem to grow. If you cut and leave the bud to the outside of the stem, the stem will grow away from bush. A cut that leaves the bud facing into the bush will encourage a stem that grows upright in the center of the bush.

• Deadhead often to sustain a longer bloom, keep the plant tidy and to reduce stress on the plants in summer. Always cut back to the first set of five leaves when deadheading.

• Prune at the correct time of year for your area and for the type of rose.

USING ROSES IN THE GARDEN

It seems a shame that roses are so often grown only in a rose bed. These are beautiful garden plants that can be used in a wide variety of ways throughout the garden.

Blending roses with other perennials in a perennial bed is a splendid way to get some height, contrast, and extended bloom out of the bed. The tall, rigid form of many hybrid roses blends nicely with the softer lines of smaller perennials like chrysanthemums, daylily, scabiosa, and other flowering plants. Choose rose varieties that bloom over a long period and have colors that complement and blend with the colors in the perennial bed.

Shorter varieties, either miniatures or smaller shrubs, make delightful, colorful borders around larger plants or along narrow walks or drives.

Pruning roses

Shrub roses and many of the heirloom varieties are large, full shrubs that fill up sunny corners, add interest to a dull wall, or hide an unfortunate view. It is an added pleasure when you have a variety that blooms repeatedly over the summer or is especially fragrant.

One of the most traditional uses of roses, growing them over an arbor to frame an entry, is still one of the best. These evergreen plants look good throughout the year, and if the variety has a color or style of bloom that is especially striking, it gives the entry extra interest and drama. Highly fragrant roses make passing through such an entry a memorable time in the garden.

CHAPTER SEVEN

Cultivar Name	Color
CLIMBERS	
Altissima	red
Berries and Cream	red blend
Blaze Improved	dark red
Don Juan	dark red
Fourth of July	red blend
Zephrine Drouhine	pink
FLORIBUNDAS	
Amber Queen	apricot
Angel Face	mauve
Betty Boop	red blend
Brass Band	apricot
Bridal Pink	mauve
Cherish	orange/pink
Dicky	orange/pink
Escapade	mauve
Europeana	dark red
Fragrant Apricot	apricot
French Lace	white
Gene Boerner	medium pink
Iceberg	white
Intrigue	purple
Ivory Fashion	white
Kanagem	orange red
Koricole	white
Lavaglut	dark red
Oregold	dark yellow
Playboy	red blend
Playgirl	medium pink
Poulsen's Pearl	pink
Sarabande	orange red
Scentimental	red blend
Sexy Rexy	medium pink
Showbiz	medium red
Summer Fashion	yellow blend
Sunsprite	deep yellow
Traumerei	orange
Trumpeter	orange

Cultivar Name	Color
GRANDIFLORAS	
Arizona	orange blend
Gold Medal	medium yellow
Love	red blend
Queen Elizabeth	medium pink
Tournament of Roses	medium pink
HYBRID TEAS	
Ain't She Sweet	orange red
Bride's Dream	light pink
Chrysler Imperial	dark red
Color Magic	pink blend
Dainty Bess	light pink
Double Delight	red blend
Elizabeth Taylor	dark pink
First Prize	pink blend
Fountain Square	orange red
Fragrant Cloud	orange red
Honor	white
Kardinal	red
Lanvin	light yellow
Mikado	red blend
Mister Lincoln	dark red
Mrs. Oakley Fisher	yellow
Olympiad	medium red
Peace	yellow blend
Pristine	white
Royal Highness	light pink
Secret	pink blend
Sheer Elegance	orange pink
Silverado	mauve
Touch of Class	orange pink
Tropicana	orange red

Cultivar Name	Color
MINIATURES	
Arizona Sunset	yellow blend
Dazzler	red
Fairhope	light yellow
Gourmet Popcorn	white
Hot Tamale	yellow blend
Irresistible	white
Jean Kenneally	apricot blend
Just For You	dark pink
Kristin	red blend
Little Artist	red blend
Little Jackie	red blend
Lipstick'N Lace	red blend
Magic Carousel	red blend
Minnie Pearl	pink blend
My Sunshine	medium yellow
Over The Rainbow	red blend
Pacesetter	white
Pierrine	orange pink
Pinstripe	red blend
Popcorn	white
Pucker Up	orange red
Red Beauty	dark red
Roller Coaster	red blend
Rainbow's End	yellow
Snowbride	white

Cultivar Name	Type	Color
SHRUBS		
Ballerina	Small shrub	medium pink
Belle de Crecy	Shrub	mauve
Cecile Bruner	Polyantha	light pink
Dortmund	Shrub	medium red mc
Delicata	Hybrid rugosa	mauve
First Light	Shrub	peach/pink
Frau Dagmar Hartopp	Hybrid rugosa	pink/mc
Heritage	Shrub	pink

Cultivar Name	Type	Color
SHRUBS		
Lady Banks' Rose	Large shrub/climber	yellow/white
Margo Koster	Polyantha	orange blend
Martha Gonzales	Small shrub	medium red mc
Paul Neyron	Shrub	pink
Reine des Violettes	Polyantha	mauve
Sally Holmes	Shrub/climber	white
The Fairy	Polyantha	light pink

JANUARY
ROSES

 PLANNING

It's time to roam through the nurseries and decide which plants you are going to put in your garden. This is the ideal month to plant bare-root roses in Zones 9 and 10. Look for plants that are rated #1 grade. The plants should have three or four large canes above the bud union and several good anchor roots. At least a few of the roots should be branched and have secondary roots with small root hairs attached.

Bare-root roses must never dry out, from the time you buy them until you put them in the ground. If possible, wet the root zone and wrap it in a plastic bag at the nursery to take it home. Once home, immerse roots in a bucket of either plain water or water with a weak solution of water-soluble fertilizer. Set the bucket in the shade and let the plants soak for at least a day, although they can be left for up to a week before planting.

Container-grown plants will also become available this month. Look for plants with at least three or four vigorous, healthy canes. The bud union should be visible well above the soil line, and there should be no soft spots, scale, or other discolorations on the canes. Container-grown plants can be kept in the pot for weeks or even months before planting if well cared for.

 PLANTING

Begin to plant either a bare-root or container-grown rose by digging a hole that is much larger than the root mass of the plant. Generally, a hole should be as deep as the roots but four or five times wider than the rootball. Add a generous layer of compost, fine mulch, and a slow-release fertilizer. Many gardeners in Zones 9 and 10 recommend an extra handful of soil sulphur as a soil conditioner. If drainage is poor, add sharp sand to the soil. Mix all the amendments well and fill the hole with about half the mixture, forming it into a slight mound in the hole. Place the rose on the top of the mound so that the roots fall away from the plant and go down the sides of the mound. Backfill with the rest of the mix, gently pressing the soil around the roots to minimize air pockets and to keep the soil from subsiding too much when it is watered. Be careful that the bud union (swollen area where the grafted plant and rootstock meet) stays well above the surface of the soil. Create a shallow basin around the plant and water deeply, but slowly, to settle all the dirt.

 CARE

If you can't plant your container-grown roses right away, place them in a spot with full sun, and water thoroughly when the surface of the soil is dry to the touch.

In Zone 8 and other cold areas, mound leaves, straw, or even soil around the base of the plant to prevent freeze damage. Plants can also be completely covered with frost cloth, blankets, or a cardboard box on freezing nights.

 WATERING

Water established roses deeply every two weeks. Water newly planted roses every two to five days (depending on the temperatures and how quickly the soil dries out for the first two weeks), then spread out the watering to once a week.

 FERTILIZING

Unless you have been fertilizing on a six-week schedule during the winter, do not fertilize roses this month. Do not fertilize any plants that have just been pruned. Do not fertilize newly planted roses until the new leaves emerge.

GROOMING

If the canes of bare-root roses are longer than 10 to 12 inches above the bud union, prune to that length. Some growers suggest pruning even more, to 6 to 8 inches. It is better to have new growth start low on the plant.

Prune established bushes hard this month in Zones 9 and 10. Take out all canes that are weak, crossing, diseased, or dead. Prune with attention to the position of the buds on the branch and make the cut at a 45-degree angle so that the bud closest to the cut is facing outward from the plant. This will ensure that the new cane grows in an upright, shrubby form. Prune back the entire plant by 1/3. Strip all the leaves from **climbers, floribundas, grandifloras**, and **hybrid teas**.

Climbers are pruned differently. **Climbers** have large, long primary canes, which set the direction of growth for the plant. This type of cane should not be pruned until the rose is the size that you desire. The other type of canes, secondary canes, grow from the primary canes, and it is from these canes that blooms are formed. They are usually smaller in diameter than primary canes and should be pruned annually to maintain both form and good bloom. Prune out all but five to seven secondary canes. Be sure that the canes you leave are growing in the desired direction.

Clean up all debris, including old leaves, from around the plant to discourage the spread of insects or disease.

PESTS

Cane borer larvae eat the interior of a cane; when it is cut, a hole in the middle of the stem is seen. If you find cane borer damage, cut back until there is no sign of the borer, and seal the cut with white carpenter's glue to prevent further infestation.

If you use horticultural oil on your roses to deter insect infestations later in the year, apply it while temperatures are cool. Horticultural oils all have a limited temperature range in which they are effective. Check the label carefully and be sure to follow the recommended temperature and dosage.

HELPFUL HINTS

• If you are new to pruning roses, look for workshops offered by public rose gardens or rose societies this month. Attending a workshop is an outstanding way to learn correct pruning techniques for roses, and you will be helping maintain a public planting.

• Things change constantly in a garden, and a good location for a rose years ago may have changed over the years, becoming too shady or too hot, or you may have just changed your mind about where they would look good. Roses transplant easily in the cool days of January. Choose a cool, cloudy day. Lift the plant and inspect the roots carefully. Remove any diseased or dead roots, but do not prune more than absolutely necessary. Dust the roots with sulphur to help heal small lesions and prevent rotting problems. Plant as directed for new bare-root roses.

NOTES

_____
_____
_____
_____
_____
_____
_____
_____
_____
_____
_____

FEBRUARY
ROSES

PLANNING

The classes of roses are confusing and often difficult to distinguish. The most common designations are the following.

- **Hybrid Teas.** These are tall plants that are fairly compact with an upright, shrubby habit. **Hybrid teas** grow one flower for each shoot and they may bloom many times over the season. Flowers usually have many petals that are closely held with tight, attractive buds.

- **Floribunda.** These are tall plants, often with many branches and rounded, full form. **Floribundas** grow multiple flowers on each shoot, and most bloom throughout the season. They make excellent cut flowers because of their abundant blooms.

- **Grandiflora.** This is a hard group to recognize. Like **floribunda,** these are large, rounded, many-branched plants with multiple flowers per shoot, but generally the flowers are larger than those of **floribunda.**

- **Climbers.** These are large roses with stems up to 20 feet long. Like many vines, they are not clinging and require the support of trellis or arbor to make them act like a vine. Otherwise they are large, loose, cascading plants. Flowers are variable; some varieties have small flowers that bloom once a year, others are exuberant bloomers with multiple blooms per stem over a long season. Many **heirloom roses** are **climbers** or can be trained to be **climbers.**

- **Miniatures.** These roses are rarely over 2 feet tall, with dense, complicated branching that gives them a compact appearance. These are some of the most reliable roses for long-season bloom.

- **Shrub Roses.** This is an indefinite class of roses that includes **species roses** as well as **damask, moss,** and **rugosa roses,** among others. Plants are large, loosely branched, and freely flowering. These roses are very hardy and usually have excellent disease resistance. The most popular types in modern times are a complicated hybrid group from the old-fashioned **shrubs** and modern **floribundas** developed by David Austin that carry his name. Many **shrub roses** are fragrant.

PLANTING

In the hottest parts of the region, continue to plant bare-root roses through mid-month. In Zone 8, plant bare-root roses from now through early March. Protect from late freezes by stripping any leaves from the plant and mounding mulch around the base to protect the bud union.

Container-grown roses can be planted in the warmest parts of the region through May, and through the rest of the year in cooler areas.

CARE

Establish a basin around both new and existing plants to maximize watering. Scrape up dirt to create a dike approximately 4 inches tall around the entire perimeter of the plant. Large plants may need a taller dike, smaller ones may need a shorter one. Extend the dike about 3 feet from the base of large bushes, less for smaller ones. Large bushes will need a dike at least to the drip line, but it is even better if it is a foot or two wider than the drip line. Add 3 to 4 inches of mulch to prevent the soil from drying out too quickly.

WATERING

Water established roses weekly to a depth of 16 to 18 inches in the warm areas. Newly planted roses may need more-frequent watering for the first two weeks, but it is more important to water deeply than to water often.

FERTILIZING

Renew a regular fertilization schedule for established roses in mid-month. There is a wide range of schedules and methods for fertilizing roses. Here are a few that are used by growers in the region.

• In Zone 8, feed roses in March, April, May, September, and October.

• In Tucson, many growers recommend using a liquid fertilizer only while roses are flowering heavily in the spring and switching to a slow-release granular fertilizer for the summer.

• In Phoenix and other hot areas, most growers fertilize from February to May with regular or slow-release formulas. No fertilizer is applied during the summer. Fertilization resumes from September to November and ceases altogether in December and January.

• Organic rose growers apply a 3- to 4-inch layer of compost or mulch monthly with additional alfalfa meal, bloodmeal, or organic blends when the roses are actively growing. If you apply manure to roses, be sure it is well composted and that you mix it with compost or mulch before spreading it around the roses.

HELPFUL HINTS

When pruning roses, look for two types of new growth around the graft. New basal canes arise at or just above the graft (rather than as an offshoot of another large cane). These shoots will develop into strong main canes and should not be pruned out. Shoots that arise from below the graft, or from underground, are canes off the rootstock. These canes should be pruned out as soon as they appear.

GROOMING

In cooler parts of the region, this is the month for the hard-prune described in January. In Zone 8 gardens, wait until after mid-month to hard-prune roses.

PESTS

Watch for aphids around new growth or on emerging buds. Spray with a strong jet of water or use a soapy water spray (1 teaspoon Dawn® dishwashing liquid to 1 gallon of water) to remove. Ladybugs and green lacewings appear later in the month; these natural predators of aphids are voracious and help keep them under control.

Thrips appear on the flower buds of roses. These insects may mar the flower, or its outer petals, but they require no control unless you are planning to enter roses in a show where perfect petals are required. Otherwise,

the damage is only cosmetic and won't affect the plant.

Watch for powdery mildew, which appears as small blisters on the leaf followed by white, weblike patches that will rub off. It is especially abundant when nights are cool and days are warm and if left untreated will spread over the entire leaf. Unchecked, it can defoliate a plant, which may not kill the plant but will severely affect its vigor. Always remove infected leaves from the plant and spread out plants for good air flow. Wash down leaves often, as the fungus cannot establish well on wet leaves. Treatments include sulphur powder, but it must be used in temperatures below 90 degrees Fahrenheit. A spray made of 1 teaspoon baking soda, 1 teaspoon dishwashing liquid, and a gallon of water is highly effective. Commercial fungicides with an active ingredient of copperoleate work best to prevent infection rather than cure already-infested plants, and it should be used before there is any sign of powdery mildew.

MARCH

ROSES

PLANNING

There are so many ways to use roses that almost any style of garden can accommodate them. Short, compact **miniatures** make a reliable, colorful border around a shrubby perennial bed or even the vegetable garden. Look for long-limbed **climbers** to cover a porch, define a walkway, or crawl over an arbor. If the plant selected is fragrant, put it where traffic is heavy or near seating areas to take full advantage of the delectable rose scent. Roses mix well with other perennials, especially those that need the highly amended soil and intensive watering that roses demand. Blend them with perennials, both to cover their summer doldrums and to give architecture and structure to the bed.

Roses are wonderful in containers, and this is a great way to grow them, either where space is limited or where their cultural demands cannot be met in the ground. Use a rich mix of soil, compost, composted manure, and mulch with some sand for drainage. Roses in containers need to be fertilized monthly, except during the hottest part of the summer, and given shade from the afternoon sun in the summer.

PLANTING

Continue to plant container-grown roses throughout the region. **Heirloom** types are less particular about the time of year they are planted and can be planted year-round even in the hottest areas.

To protect roses from severe heat stress, plant them on the north or east side of the yard. In areas with hot, drying winds, plant near a windbreak or other protection. In all areas, look for a location that has plenty of sun in the winter, but provides afternoon shade in the summer.

CARE

To encourage larger flowers, remove any side buds that arise around the flower of a **hybrid tea**. On **floribunda**, **grandiflora**, or **shrub** roses, remove the center bud of the cluster to increase flower size.

WATERING

Continue to water every five to seven days, and spread mulch around the plants if you have not already done so.

Floribunda rose

FERTILIZING

Rose growers differ on fertilization schedules for roses. Many fertilize once a month, but discontinue fertilizing in the hottest part of the summer. Others fertilize every two weeks through the growing season, and monthly during the summer. Others fertilize every six weeks throughout the year. Experiment with your own roses to find the schedule that suits both you and your roses. Here are a few tips.

• Roses are heavy feeders, and those grown in containers, or in soils that were not heavily amended when the roses were planted, may need the most frequent fertilization.

• Organic fertilizers, like alfalfa meal, compost, or formulations for roses than blend many ingredients, work more slowly and can be applied more frequently.

• Fertilizers made from inorganic sources are often potent, and plants respond more quickly to their application. These should be used less frequently. They are the ones that are most often recommended to be discontinued when the weather is hot and roses are actively growing.

A rosebud infested with aphids.

GROOMING

In Zone 8 and other colder areas, finish pruning roses by the end of the month. Remove all leaves and weak, crossing, diseased, or damaged canes, cutting back the entire plant to 24 inches tall. Leave three to five healthy canes.

PESTS

Continue to monitor for aphids and powdery mildew on the plants. Powdery mildew is often spread by leaving infected leaves around the plants, or by splashing from overhead watering. Keep the area around your roses free of debris, and mulch heavily to prevent splashing.

NOTES

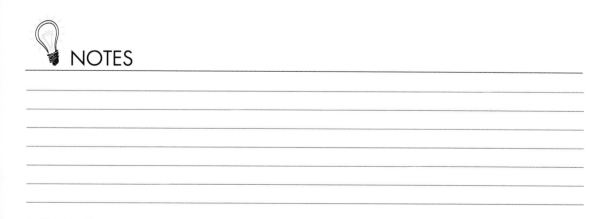

APRIL

ROSES

PLANNING

Roses known as **antique, heirloom** or **old garden roses** do remarkably well in the hot desert region. The old rose varieties, especially, are either of European origin and bloom once during the year and are cold-hardy, or are of Asian (usually Chinese) origin and bloom repeatedly with more variable hardiness. All of these types have been crossed countless times over during the course of the development of the roses we see today.

There are numerous classes of these roses, and these are a few of the most common.

- **Alba** are upright roses that grow to 6 feet or more. Once blooming, the whitish to pink flowers are clustered and semi-double.
- **Bourbons** are low bushes or large climbers, depending on the variety. These are lushly petaled flowers that are fragrant and repeat through the season.
- **Centifolia** are also tall, with large, rounded leaves. The flowers are likewise large and floppy, with numerous petals making them generous doubles. They bloom once.
- **China roses** are about 5 feet tall but grow larger in other climates. This class blooms almost year-round in the deserts with small, thin-petaled flowers that are lightly fragrant.
- **Damask** are larger than **Gallica** but also spreading. The clustered flowers occur once in spring among the thorny branches and grayish leaves. These are extremely fragrant and a source of perfume oil.
- **Gallica** are short, spreading plants with rough foliage. Flowers occur once in spring, with the small flowers clustered on sturdy stems. This ancient class was grown in the Middle Ages.
- **Hybrid Perpetual bush roses** are tall, thin, and vigorous. They most resemble modern **hybrid teas** and are repeat bloomers as well.
- **Noisette** is a highly variable class that can be small or large, tight or sprawling. The thin-petaled flowers occur in clusters on the stem, are fragrant, and usually repeat.
- **Teas** are similar to modern **hybrid teas** but have much weaker stems, and the flowers tend therefore to nod. They are repeat bloomers.

PLANTING

Continue planting container-grown roses throughout the region.

CARE

Remove spent flowers regularly in a process known as deadheading. Cut back to the first set of leaves with five leaflets when you cut off a flower or flower cluster. For miniatures, this continuous pruning maintains a long blooming season.

WATERING

Watch the weather—it can get hot this month in Zones 9 and 10. In the warm zones, water deeply to a depth of 16 to 18 inches. This is usually achieved by watering once a week, but check the watering depth to be certain. In Zone 8, water every eight to ten days.

FERTILIZING

Many rose growers like to use soluble fertilizer this month because the roses are in heavy bloom and this type of fertilizer is more quickly available to the plant. If using a soluble fertilizer, use it every two weeks during the blooming period, then switch to dry formulas for the rest of the year.

 GROOMING

 PESTS

 NOTES

Deadhead roses regularly as they bloom to maintain a continuous bloom. Deadhead by cutting the stem back to the first set of five leaves. Make a clean cut at a slight angle.

Wash off plants regularly to control powdery mildew and spider mites. If aphids are still a problem, remove them daily by hand or with either strong jets of water or a soapy water spray.

Thrips may still be active this month.

HELPFUL HINTS

Soaker hoses can be a useful way to water roses. These hoses, usually made from recycled tires, allow water to ooze out of minute perforations in the wall of the hose. They can be buried so that water loss to evaporation and problems from water splash are eliminated, and they provide water only to the root system of the plant. In addition, soaker hoses are pliable and can be set in a circle around the plant to ensure even watering around the root zone.

Not all roses have thorns. Although renowned for their thorns, a few roses have no thorns. The large, rambling **climber** 'Lady Banks' rose is thornless, as is the **old garden** variety **climber** with the delicious rose fragrance 'Zephirine Drouhin'. Many **shrub roses** have minimal to no thorns, including 'Belle de Crecy', 'Heritage', 'Paul Neyron', and 'Reine de Violettes'.

'Lady Banks' rose

MAY

ROSES

 PLANNING

Roses make good potted plants in all areas of the region. There are many advantages to growing roses in containers. If you live in an area that is either very hot or very cold for roses, raising them in pots offers a lot of flexibility. Container-grown roses can be moved into the shade for the summer in the hottest areas, or moved into a shed or other shelter during the winter in colder areas. They offer gardeners with small gardens or limited planting space the opportunity to grow and enjoy roses.

In all areas it is best to grow roses in plastic pots rather than clay ones. Because clay allows evaporation on all sides of the pot, roses may dry out too often in the summer and decline as a result of water stress. If you have a decorative clay pot you would like to use, plant the rose in a plastic pot and drop it in the clay one. The extra insulation will also help keep the rose roots cooler in the hottest areas.

 PLANTING

Continue to plant container-grown roses. Choose a pot that is large enough to hold the root system of the rose and pro-

vide plenty of soil for the roots. Roses do not like to grow with a crowded or restricted root system. In addition, soil insulates the roots from both the heat and cold extremes, so choose a pot that is generously proportioned for the plant.

Mix up a rich soil mix of good-quality potting soil and compost or mulch or a mixture, adding sand for drainage. You can also add a well-balanced, slow-release granular fertilizer to the mix. Fill the container about 2/3 full, leaving a small mound in the center. Place the rose at the top of the mound, spreading the roots evenly around the stem. Backfill with the remaining soil mix. Be sure that the bud union is well above the soil line. It is also helpful to leave about an inch between the top of the soil and the top of the pot. This allows the pot to be watered thoroughly without overflowing.

Water well after planting. Roses in containers need full sun during active growth. In the warmest areas, potted roses should be moved into afternoon shade in the hottest part of the summer.

 CARE

In the warmest zones, many **hybrid** roses begin to slow down as the weather heats up. Taking

care of roses in these areas can be difficult in the summer, but the following tips may help.

• If roses are planted in areas that receive over six hours of afternoon sun or are in areas of reflected heat, as when they are planted against a wall, provide artificial shade during the summer. This can be a crude tepee of bamboo poles covered with shade cloth, or a frame like a box or arbor covered with cloth.

• Move potted roses to a location that receives afternoon shade.

• Double check your watering schedule to be sure roses are kept well watered.

• Slow down fertilization beginning this month. If you have been using liquid fertilizer, switch to granular or slow-release, or quit fertilizing altogether until September.

• Apply a heavy mulch, up to 6 inches thick, to all roses. Keep the mulch away from the main stem to avoid too much moisture on the stem.

 WATERING

Roses like abundant water but will decline quickly if kept continuously wet. It is important to check the depth to which water is penetrating with either a probe or metal rod. Water frequently, but let the soil dry out slightly between watering. Once the soil is dry 6 inches below the surface in the ground, or 1 inch in a pot, it is time to water again. This usually means watering every three to four days in the hottest zones, every five to seven days in cooler ones. Roses in pots may need water daily in high temperatures. In the coolest areas, water newly planted roses twice a week for the first year, then once a week in the winter.

FERTILIZING

Although growers differ widely in their recommendations for summer fertilization, in the hottest parts of the region it is generally accepted that fertilization should cease during the summer. You can provide one application of a slow-release fertilizer now to carry plants through the summer if you like.

In cooler areas of Zone 9, many growers prefer to fertilize with either standard rose food or a water-soluble formula at six-week intervals through the summer.

Plants growing in containers should be fertilized regularly through the summer regardless of the zone. If you used a slow-release fertilizer in the mix, renew it every two months through the

HELPFUL HINTS

• If you decide to fertilize during the summer months, use only half the recommended dose. Organic fertilizers work much more slowly than traditional chemical fertilizers and can be used throughout the summer to maintain soil fertility without causing the plants to grow too quickly.

• Shade cloth is a woven material that blocks a given amount of sunlight. The amount of protection is expressed as the percentage of available light that is deflected. Therefore, 30% shade cloth reflects back 30% of the available sunlight, 50% cloth allows in half the available sunlight, and 80% deflects all but 20% of the available light. Shade cloth is sold in most nurseries, but a wider selection of protection and special sizes are available from nursery supply catalogs. In the hottest areas, a minimum of 30% shade and a maximum of 60% is recommended.

• How can you tell how old rose canes are? One-year-old wood is green and often pliable; two-year-old wood is brownish green, sometimes even reddish; and three-year-old wood is brown and sometimes plated with wood. Canes older than three or four years are woody, gray, and furrowed.

hot weather. If you use a water-soluble fertilizer, apply it monthly during the summer.

GROOMING

Do not prune this month in the hottest areas of the region other than to remove spent flowers. It is best not to allow plants to bloom when it is extremely hot, so remove buds as soon as they form.

In cooler areas of the region, continue to deadhead plants regularly. **Shrub roses** can be lightly pruned throughout the summer in these areas. Prune these

roses as you remove the blooms, cutting back the branches to reduce a plant to the size you want.

PESTS

Spider mites thrive in the dusty conditions of the Desert Southwest. Spray the foliage regularly early in the morning to prevent infestations of these tiny insects. The slight rise in humidity also helps the roses withstand hot, dry days. Be careful not to water during the hot part of the day when the leaves can be burned.

JUNE
ROSES

PLANNING

Modern hybrid roses are not long-lived plants. Although many of the older varieties and **heirlooms** live for decades, most of the **modern hybrids** last about ten years. If you have roses that have been in the garden for over ten years and are beginning to lose vigor, bloom less, or are looking poor, plan for their replacements this fall and winter.

PLANTING

Plant container-grown roses only in the coolest areas of the region.

CARE

Watch for symptoms of heat stress. Plants with leaves that turn brown and fall off, or that have flowers that are small or misshapen and with bleached-out colors, or that have dying limb tips or canes that are cracked or split are suffering from too much sun and heat. Provide afternoon shade immediately, and consider relocating the rose the following winter.

A spectacular grandiflora rose

WATERING

Keep roses deeply watered, mulch heavily, and provide afternoon shade. Many will lose leaves, but maintain a steady watering schedule and they will recover when temperatures moderate.

It can sometimes be difficult to know if plants are getting enough water. Symptoms of too little water include:

- plants that are small for their age (roses generally grow fast and should reach their mature height in one or at most two seasons)
- plants with small or sparse blooms
- plants with sudden leaf loss and tip burn

FERTILIZING

Follow summer fertilizing guidelines on page 191.

GROOMING

In Zone 8 only, cut roses back by about a third in a hard prune. Follow pruning guidelines on page 185.

PESTS

Continue to wash off plants regularly to keep the dust down and control spider mites. Spray early in the morning.

If you notice round or semi-circular cutouts on the leaves, it is the work of **leaf cutter bees**. These tiny native bees use the leaf pieces to form their nests. The damage is cosmetic and causes no harm to the plant. There is no viable control, but you can cover the plants with light row covers if you want to discourage the foraging. But a word of caution: these bees are great pollinators and are a highly beneficial insect in the garden, well worth a few cutout leaves. Other insects that might be encountered around your roses are the following.

• **Aphids** are small sucking insects that can be black, white, gray, gold, or nearly clear. The adults are not as big a problem as the immature forms, which are eating steadily. Aphids arrive at different times of the year, depending on the species, and can reach staggering numbers in certain years. Early detection is key. As soon as you notice them, begin to remove them by hand, or spray them off with strong jets of water, a soapy water solution, or insecticidal spray. Aphids restrict themselves to new growth, so concentrate spraying there.

• **Thrips** are small, dark, rod-like insects that feed on leaves and flower buds. Leaves and flowers become deformed by their feeding. Use the same controls as for aphids. Thrips cause only cosmetic damage to the plant and are usually around for only a short time. Unless you plan to enter a rose show, control is not necessary.

• **Spider mites** look like dust grains, but you know they are present by their white webs on the undersides of the leaves. They thrive in dry, dusty conditions, so keeping plants sprayed off and clean is the best remedy.

• **Whiteflies** are small, white flying insects that may erupt in vast flocks in the late summer and fall. Because the flies you see are on the move, controlling the adults is generally futile. Look on the underside of the leaves for the tiny, almost clear immature forms that are feeding on the plant. Control with daily sprays of water, insecticidal soap, or soapy water. Most chemical controls are ineffective. Row covers can help prevent adults from landing on the plants.

• **Spittle bug** is seldom seen, but the frothy egg case is a sure sign of its presence. These cases occur on the stems of a wide variety of plants, including roses, and are harmless.

• **Cane borers** are nearly impossible to prevent, but good culture helps mitigate the problem. The adults lay eggs in soft cane tissue, but you notice the damage when you prune a stem and it is hollow for at least part of its length. Remove any infected stem at least an inch or two beyond the hollowed-out area. Seal the cut with white carpenter's glue. It is also a good practice to seal all other pruning cuts with glue to help prevent these borers, but do not seal cuts made when deadheading or cutting flowers.

• **Grasshoppers** are fond of the new growth of roses and many other ornamentals. In small numbers they cause only cosmetic damage and are easily controlled by hand removal. Large numbers are difficult to control, although a formula produced specifically for grasshoppers can help.

JULY
ROSES

 PLANNING

In most of the state, it is hot and uncomfortable outdoors, and your roses are not at their prime. It is time to update your journal about which varieties have done the best for you, which bloomed the longest or the best. And it is time to study the catalogs and prepare for which varieties might be at home in your garden.

Take time to visit a good public rose garden in your area and see how the roses are doing. If you see a variety you grow, but they look better in the public garden, ask about how they are cared for to learn what you might do differently. Look for varieties that are doing well during the summer heat—they might be good roses for your garden as well.

Take time to catch up on your reading about roses, their care and their history. A good book to help you along through the summer is *In Search of Lost Roses* by Thomas Christopher. It was originally published in 1989 by Summit, then reissued in 1996 by Bloomsbury Press. This is a delightful book on the history and reemergence of so-called **old roses**. It is a fine way to spend an afternoon.

 PLANTING

In Zone 8, continue to plant most roses through the end of the month. Take special care to maintain a steady watering regimen, shade the plants if necessary, and protect them from hot winds if planting this late in the season. Container-grown roses are the best choice for planting this late. In the hotter parts of the region, this is not a good month to plant roses.

 CARE

Trim off spent blooms from roses that keep trying to flower. Add extra mulch, and if you use basins to water, be sure they are in good shape.

It is common for plants in the hottest areas to have saltburn during the mid- to late summer. Saltburn shows up as brown, dry edges on the leaves of the plant and is caused by a buildup of salt in the leaf. The best way to prevent saltburn is to water plants even more deeply than your regular depth about once a month to leach the salts out of the root zone. Many fertilizer formulations can exacerbate saltburn, so if you are using fertilizer in the summer, be doubly sure you are following the recommended doses or quit summer fertilization. Watering thoroughly before and after fertilizing also mitigates salt damage.

 WATERING

Continue to water every three to five days or when the soil is dry 6 to 9 inches below the surface. Be sure you water slowly and long enough to let water penetrate 16 to 18 inches.

 FERTILIZING

Do not fertilize this month, even if you are generally providing fertilizer through the summer.

 GROOMING

Do not prune this month except to remove spent flowers.

 PESTS

Continue to hose off plants every day or two to add extra humidity and control spider mites.

HELPFUL HINTS

- Always water roses from below rather than with overhead sprinklers. While a light spraying helps reduce pest problems and raises humidity, the drenching of overhead watering encourages many fungal disease like blackspot and powdery mildew.

- One way to evaluate how much water a rose is getting is to use a water meter. Place the probe in the soil just after watering; it should indicate that the soil is completely saturated. After two days, run the probe in at approximately the same spot, and see how much water the plant has used. Do it again in two days. For roses, you want the soil to be no less than 50% saturated between waterings.

- Another way to evaluate how much water a rose is getting is to use a stick, or long metal rod, and stick it in the soil. Mark off 12 and 18 inches on the stick. Run the stick in the ground a day after watering. It will move easily through wet soil and be harder or stop altogether in dry soil. Do it again in two days, and see where the moisture line is. Continue until you find that the moisture line is halfway up the marked portion of the stick (6 or 9 inches). That is when you need to water again.

- Spider mites hatch in the soil beneath a plant and then crawl up the leaves to feed on the rose. Keeping roses leafless 8 to 10 inches above the soil line helps control these insects.

- For good cultural advice, look to the chapter on rose growing in *Desert Landscaping for Beginners* edited by Cathy Cromell and published by Arizona Master Gardener Press in 2001, and the book *Roses in a Desert Garden* by Hallie Beck, published by *Phoenix Home & Garden Magazine* in 1996.

NOTES

AUGUST
ROSES

PLANNING

Start evaluating how your plants are taking the summer heat as well as the effectiveness of your watering schedule. All roses lose a lot of leaves toward the end of the summer in the hottest parts of the zone, and many suffer some tip dieback. But if the symptoms seem severe or the plant is nearly defoliated, consider moving it to a shadier location.

PLANTING

In the hottest parts of the region, this is not a good month to plant roses. In cooler parts of Zone 8, roses that will be grown in containers can still be planted. If you plant this late, be careful to keep the plants well watered and protected from harsh winds and afternoon sun.

CARE

During the summer, especially in the hottest areas, roses can suffer not only overall heat stress, but be subject to some nutrient deficiencies. Potted roses, with the continual leaching of frequent watering, are particularly susceptible.

If you suspect a nutrient deficiency, do not try to correct it by adding a jolt of the needed nutrient (the only exception is the addition of chelated iron for iron chlorosis). It is much better to adjust the type of fertilizer you are using and continue to apply it in your regular schedule. Nutrients other than nitrogen, phosphorus, and potassium are called micronutrients and are often part of well-balanced (often called complete) fertilizers. It is important to recognize the difference between a nutrient deficiency and general heat stress. Here are some guidelines.

1. **Nitrogen deficiency** often cause older leaves to turn pale green or completely yellow. Plants may also show reduced growth, smaller than normal leaves, and weak or spindly stems. Do not provide a huge dose of nitrogen all at once to the plant, but adjust your fertilizer, and increase the overall fertility of the soil.

2. **Iron deficiency**, known as iron chlorosis, is common in the dry, alkaline soils of the Southwest. Symptoms include young leaves that are pale or yellow, sometimes white, with green veins. An application of chelated iron corrects this problem. Follow label directions carefully.

3. **Magnesium deficiency** is indicated when older leaves turn yellow, are smaller than normal, and show white areas on both sides of the leaf. The edge of old leaves may curl downward, and some roses develop dark brown to purple spots randomly on the leaf. To correct this condition, apply $1/4$ cup of magnesium sulfate (Epsom salts) to the plant two or three times a year. Many growers follow this recommendation routinely as a preventive measure.

4. **Phosphorus deficiency** shows up as stunted leaves that turn a dusky or grayish green color, and they drop without turning yellow.

5. **Potassium deficiency** symptoms include flowers that are deformed or stunted with no evidence of insect damage. Often flowering stems are shorter than normal. Leaves may turn yellow and drop as well.

6. **Zinc deficiency** and the rare **copper deficiency** show much the same symptoms. Leaves turn pale green and form a central crease as if they are trying to fold up. Leaves may tend to cluster rather than open wide and spread normally.

7. **Boron deficiency** is uncommon, but shows up as a short, flattened bud, especially when buds are expected to be pointed. Know your plants to identify this problem, however, because many **heirloom roses** naturally have flattened buds. Boron deficiency may also result in an increased number of abnormally short petals in the flower. This is especially noticeable in **hybrid teas** which have uniformly long petals.

If you have a doubt, take a soil sample in for testing to be sure that a mineral deficiency is the problem.

Heirloom rose

 WATERING

Continue to water deeply, soaking to 16 inches or more.

 FERTILIZING

Fertilize only according to the guidelines on page 191

.

 GROOMING

Deadhead roses as soon as the flowers are spent. Roses that are showing signs of heat stress should have blooms removed as soon as they form, as the added energy drain of blooming further stresses the plants.

In the cooler areas, once temperatures are below 90 degrees Fahrenheit, prune plants lightly to remove dead, damaged, or crossing branches.

 PESTS

Dry, dusty weather often results in an outbreak of spider mites on roses and other perennials. Symptoms of these minute, reddish insects are mottled leaves with fine white webs on the underside of the leaf. Hose off plants daily, early in the morning, to keep plants clean.

SEPTEMBER

ROSES

PLANNING

This is a good month to evaluate the roses you have for how well they endured the summer. Plants that lost over half their canes or that have numerous yellowed or dying leaves need a shadier or cooler location. Be honest about how the watering schedules went, and consider whether they need to be adjusted for your plants next summer. If all the cultural conditions seem appropriate and in good order, but the plant had a hard time in the summer, perhaps it is just a variety that does not do well in the region.

This is a good time to plan where new bushes will be planted over the winter. Look through catalogs for the options for your area. **Shrub roses** live a long time, often decades or more, and do well in the cooler areas of the region. Many of the **modern hybrids** begin to decline in about ten years regardless of how well cared for; if you have aging plants, begin to plan for replacements.

Look for plants that are rated for good heat tolerance or that are recommended by local rosarians. Check the plants at local public rose displays to see which ones are looking best during the final days of the summer. These are the best places to find out which are the varieties that you might want in your garden.

PLANTING

In the hottest parts of the region, you can begin to plant container-grown roses. Days are still hot, so be prepared to water deeply and often to establish the plants. Plants that will be grown in containers may also be planted this month, but the same cautions apply. In the cooler areas of Zone 8, **shrub** and **heirloom** types may be planted early to give them enough time to root in before cool weather. But wait until spring to plant **hybrids** or bare-root plants.

CARE

Roses in the hottest zones are often stressed from the long summer. Continue with their regular

'Carefree Delight' shrub rose

watering schedule, and most will recover quickly when the temperatures cool down.

WATERING

It is still hot enough in September to continue to water every three to five days in the hottest areas, and weekly in the cooler areas.

FERTILIZING

If you discontinued fertilizing in the summer, resume a regular fertilization schedule this month. If you were fertilizing through the summer at low rates, switch to full-strength doses of fertilizer this month.

When using a granular fertilizer on roses, water the plant thoroughly before it is applied, then scatter it evenly around the plant. Scratch it in the soil carefully so as not to disturb the roots. Water the plant deeply when finished.

GROOMING

In the warmest areas, prune roses lightly. Wait until the temperatures stay below 100 degrees Fahrenheit to begin pruning. If you did not prune lightly in the cooler zones, do so by mid-month. Take out all dead canes. Remove canes that are diseased or

---

HELPFUL HINTS

Water plants early in the morning, ideally before dawn. Plants take up moisture most rapidly in the hour or two before dawn.

deformed, or those with severe tip damage. Take off any yellowed or diseased leaves, and pick all fallen leaves around the plant. Discard the leaves. Take out any canes that arise from below the bud union, but leave any that begin just above it.

Do not prune healthy or growing canes at this time; they will begin to grow later in the month and put on a strong fall bloom.

NOTES

PESTS

As you prune, watch for signs of cane borers. A stem that was infested with this insect or its larvae will be hollow. Cut the cane until there is no further sign of borers, then coat the cut with white carpenter's glue to prevent reentry.

OCTOBER

ROSES

PLANNING

With good care, roses will provide a vigorous fall bloom. This bloom is usually shorter in duration and has fewer flowers than the spring bloom, but is welcome nonetheless.

PLANTING

In the warm areas, container-grown roses may be planted this month. This is a particularly good time to plant **heirloom** or **old garden roses**. When planting **old garden roses**, dig and prepare the hole as you would for any rose, but try to keep as much of the soil from the container around the plant's roots as you can. Even when growing on their own roots, roses should be planted at or slightly above the soil line of the container. Water thoroughly, to a depth of 12 to 16 inches, and apply a 2- to 3-inch layer of mulch.

CARE

Allow roses in cooler areas to adjust to the dropping temperatures and prepare for cold weather by reducing the frequency of watering and discontinuing all fertilizer. This encourages the plants to slow their growth and will help reduce the risk of severe cold damage. Mulch the root zone heavily with 6 to 8 inches of light mulch like straw, leaves, or pine needles, and let some of the mulch pile around the base of the plant to protect the bud union.

WATERING

In the warmest areas, continue to water regularly to 16 inches. This is usually weekly. While roses like to dry out somewhat between watering, do not allow plants to become completely dry.

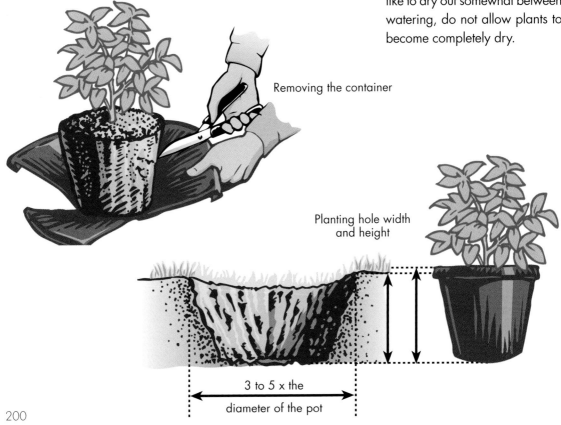

Removing the container

Planting hole width and height

3 to 5 x the diameter of the pot

FERTILIZING

In the warmest areas, fertilize with balanced dry formulations once this month. Some growers recommended using the faster-acting water-soluble fertilizer twice this month to encourage even more fall bloom. If you are entering a show, this might be advisable. Whichever method you choose, water well, fertilize, then water again. If you are using organic fertilizers like alfalfa meal or a balanced formula, apply once this month.

In cooler areas, do not fertilize this month, and discontinue fertilization until spring.

HELPFUL HINTS

Diagnosing what is wrong with roses can be difficult. (See page 196 for information on nutrient deficiencies.) But not all yellowing leaves are caused by nutrient problems.

• If the yellowed leaves occur only on the lower part of the plant, this is the natural die-off of old leaves.

• If the yellowed leaves occur first on the lower part of the plant, then appear to spread upward and there are green veins in the leaves, it most likely caused by overwatering or poor drainage. Plants need oxygen in the soil just as they need water, and if there is too much water or it stays around the roots too long, plants suffocate.

• If yellowed leaves occur suddenly and are all over the plant, check for herbicide damage. Herbicides are potent chemicals, and even a tiny amount that drifts onto a plant can cause severe damage.

• If the leaves are yellowing, the edges turn brown and dry and fall off, and such leaves are found anywhere on the plant rather than in one part of the plant, it usually means heat or salt damage or both in the summer. Continue to water deeply and regularly, and shade the plant if possible. It will recover when the weather cools.

GROOMING

Deadhead blooming roses regularly. There is still time to lightly prune plants in the warmest areas of the region. Remove only dead or diseased canes.

PESTS

Occasional aphids or spider mites may be found on plants this month. Grasshoppers may arise in certain years. Pick off the insects and destroy them when there are just a few, or use a specially formulated insecticide for grasshoppers if there are numerous individuals. Be sure to keep the area around the plants clean of debris and fallen leaves, particularly if powdery mildew has been a problem.

NOVEMBER

ROSES

PLANNING

In most areas, the fall bloom of roses begins to dwindle this month. As the days get shorter and the nights cooler, roses will enter their short winter dormancy.

Continue looking at catalogs, placing orders for new roses for the garden or roses to replace those that gave out over the year.

The designation AARS Winner means that the rose has been sent out to trial gardens under the auspices of All-America Rose Selections. These gardens are all over the country, and roses are rated for their cold or heat tolerance, disease resistance, ease of culture, style and quantity of bloom, and overall vigor. They are generally grown for two or three years in the garden before evaluation. Each fall, members of the evaluation committee meet to determine who are the winners.

There is an AARS trial garden in Mesa, Arizona, on the grounds of Mesa Community College. If you are in the area, visit the AARS garden and see what roses are coming up in the near future.

PLANTING

Plant container-grown roses, **heirloom**, or **old garden roses** in the warm zones.

CARE

In areas with regular freezes, prepare for freezing nights by having covers like blankets, frost cloth, or cardboard boxes on hand to protect sensitive plants. **Hybrid teas** are generally the most sensitive of all roses, with **shrub roses** and many **heirloom** or **old garden rose** varieties the most cold-tolerant. Put coverings on the plant in the afternoon so that it will collect heat. Remove the covering, especially any that does not permit light to penetrate, as soon as temperatures rise above freezing the next day. Some frost cloth products allow a lot of light on the plants and can be left on for a day or two.

WATERING

In the mild-winter cities, extend watering to every ten days, depending on the weather. In the colder areas, continue to water deeply every two to three weeks, less if the soil stays moist.

FERTILIZING

In the warmest parts of the state, apply the final fertilization of the year. Organic gardeners can apply a layer of compost or mulch mixed with a small amount of organic amendments (well-composted manure, bloodmeal, or alfalfa meal) this month. Be sure to water well after fertilizing.

GROOMING

Do not prune roses this month.

PESTS

Crown gall is a bacterial infection that can be a difficult problem once it is established in your yard. The best prevention is to buy from reputable dealers who aggressively treat to prevent the disease in their growing yards. Roses that are too cheap compared with others in the area are at great risk of spreading this disease. It is known by a crusty, black gall at ground level and eventually kills the plant. Dig up and destroy infected plants immediately.

Rose mosaic virus appears as yellow zigzag lines on all or part of leaf. It is spread by budding plants onto affected rootstock, and infected plants must be destroyed. Again, the best prevention is buying from well-known, reputable dealers and growers who aggressively manage and eliminate this disease in their operations.

December

ROSES

 PLANNING

Roses make a wonderful gift, but pick the variety with the recipient in mind. If your friend or relative does not have the room or the ability to take care of plants in the ground, look for roses that do well in containers. Although almost any rose will grow in a container, **miniatures** and smaller **heirloom** varieties are good choices. These types of roses tend to bloom over a long season and require basic care. For a more memorable gift, pick a fragrant variety.

 PLANTING

Begin planting bare-root roses as soon as they appear in nurseries. Because you have a month or more to plant them, take some time to look around for the best-quality plants in the varieties that you want. Bargain prices often mean inferior plants, so take a careful look at the discount-priced plants. A plant should have large, healthy canes with no leaves but visible buds, and strong anchor roots with at least some secondary and feeder roots. Pull the wrapping gently away to look at the roots—this is the most important part of the plant you are buying. Never buy roses that have been dipped in wax.

Keep plants cool, moist, and in the shade until you are ready to

plant. Be prepared to plant within a week of purchasing your new bare-root roses.

  CARE

If freezes are expected, be prepared to protect plants in the ground. Move container-grown roses to a sheltered location, shed, or garage during freezing nights.

 WATERING

Water deeply every seven to ten days. If winter rains are abundant, adjust your watering schedule.

 FERTILIZING

Do not fertilize this month.

 GROOMING

Prune only to remove spent flowers and any dead canes that are still on the plant. Do not prune any roses you planted this fall. Give them time to establish a root system, and prune them lightly just to remove dead stems in January. Resume a normal pruning schedule after your roses have been in the ground a year.

 PESTS

It is too cool for most pests and diseases, but aphids might show up toward the end of the month. Remove by hand or use strong jets of plain or soapy water.

SHRUBS

The deserts of the American Southwest are full of shrubs; they are the most common type of plant in the Mohave, the Sonoran, and the Chihuahuan deserts. These are plants that have devised a wide range of strategies to cope with the heat, aridity, and soils of the region.

Many are legumes, that huge family familiar to most gardeners as the botanical home of beans, lupines, mesquites, and peas. Legumes have small compound leaves, a form that dramatically reduces the surface area of the leaves, which in turn cuts down on evaporation. Desert shrubs often have hard, even waxy leaves, again an adaptation to cut down on water loss and forestall heat stress. Some are deciduous, losing leaves not when it is cold, but when it is dry. When rain returns and the soil moisture increases, the plants flush out with leaves. All have wide, spreading root systems that take up water quickly and can glean water from nearly parched soils. Creosote are so efficient at taking up water from soils that are on the brink of complete desiccation that they have been known to live for three years without rain.

USING SHRUBS

Shrubs that are native or well adapted to the region are both beautiful and easy to care for in the garden. Woody shrubs can be used in a variety of ways, but some of the most common are the following.

Hedges. This is perhaps the oldest use of woody plants by humans. Originally planted in Europe, they were made famous in England as long lines of limbs and twigs that eventually became living boundaries as birds and other animals spread seed around underneath them. The use of living lines of evergreen shrubs to mark a boundary is still with us. Hedges can be any size, and while most are uniform, made up of one species, beautiful hedges can be made by blending species. When choosing a shrub for a hedge, give strong consideration to its ultimate size to be sure it conforms to the scale of the garden it surrounds, and determine whether the character and form of the shrub will blend with the surroundings.

Screening. Shrubs can act in the same way vines do to hide an unfortunate view or protect the privacy of the garden. Evergreen shrubs are especially valued for this use because they grow so thickly and stay the same throughout the year.

Background. Shrubs can form a graceful backdrop for more colorful perennial or annual plantings. Here, too, scale and character are important so that the background does not clash with the plantings in front of it.

Filler. Shrubs can be useful to fill up the space in a difficult corner or an odd spot between beds or buildings, or to focus your eye on a particular spot in the garden. Shrubs used like this are often chosen for their colorful flowers because they lend another bit of interest to the garden.

Tough Spots. The outer edges of a desert garden can be a rough place for plants. If the area does not have regular irrigation or is beyond the area that is intensively cultivated, shrubs, especially those that are native or desert-adapted, can fill the need perfectly. Choose shrubs with minimal care requirements for such places. Be prepared to water then generously, even if temporarily, to get them off to a good start and again during long, dry spells. If well chosen, they will live a long time with minimal care.

CARING FOR SHRUBS

Woody shrubs are perhaps the easiest plants to care for in any garden. Most are best planted during the cooler times of the year, from fall to early spring. While they may not appear to grow during this time, the moderate temperatures allow the formation of strong root systems.

Water newly planted shrubs deeply and often during their first year or two in the ground. This will encourage a deep and vigorous root system, which is what will sustain them for the years ahead. Water established shrubs to a depth of 3 feet. As is true for most woody plants, it is much better to water deeply at a slow rate than to provide shallow, frequent waterings. Resist pruning any newly planted shrubs until they have been in the ground at least a year, if not longer.

Most shrubs do not need annual pruning. Pruning to reduce their size or to thin is necessary only every few years. A shrub that needs regular or routine pruning is the wrong shrub for the site and you could consider moving it in the winter, or replacing it with more suitable species.

It is easy to control the size of a shrub with both watering and fertilization. After a shrub has reached a size that you find desirable, reduce the watering to the minimum necessary to keep it healthy, but not enough to encourage rampant growth. The same principle holds for fertilization. While fertilizer helps a young plant grow steadily, it only encourages new growth that needs to be pruned in a plant that is already the size you need.

Shrubs do not have many pests or diseases that routinely attack them. Young plants can be susceptible to aphids, thrips, and other insects that feed on tender new growth, but early detection and quick response are usually enough to keep the plant from suffering a serious decline.

Texas mountain laurel is especially susceptible to webworms in the spring. These tiny larvae are enclosed within a gossamer tent that surrounds the tips of the stems. The larvae feed on the ten-

CHAPTER EIGHT

der new shoots. In small shrubs they are easily removed by pruning the stem, but in larger plants, or if there are too many of them, the problem can be serious. Destroy the web as best you can and apply an insecticide like *Bacillus thuringiensis* (Bt) to kill the larvae.

Shrubs

Common Name	Botanical Name	Form	Height x Width	Water Use	Cold Tolerance
Algerita	*Berberis trifoliolata*	Evergreen	6–8 × 6–8	Moderate	Hardy
Apache plume	*Fallugia paradoxa*	Evergreen	6 × 4	Low	Hardy
Argentine tecoma	*Tecoma garrocha*	Semi-deciduous	5 × 5	Moderate	Moderate
Arizona mescal bean	*Sophora arizonica*	Evergreen	3–10 × 3–10	Moderate	Hardy
Arizona rosewood	*Vauquelinia californica*	Evergreen	10–25 × 5–15	Moderate	Hardy
Baja senna	*Senna purpusii*	Evergreen	4–6 × 4–6	Low	Frost tender
Barbados cherry	*Malpighia glabra*	Evergreen	4–10 × 3–10	Moderate	Moderate
Barberry	*Berberis fremontii*	Evergreen	6–8 × 6–10	Moderate	Hardy
Beach vitex	*Vitex rotundifolia*	Deciduous	4–8 × 4–8	Moderate	Moderater
Bee bush	*Aloysia wrightii*	Semi-deciduous	6–9 × 6–9	Moderate	Moderate
Bitter condalia	*Condalia globosa*	Semi-deciduous	20 × 15	Low	Moderate
Black dalea	*Dalea frutescens*	Evergreen	3–4 × 3–4	Moderate	Hardy
Blue rain sage	*Leucophyllum zygophyllum*	Evergreen	3–6 × 3–6	Low	Hardy
Brazilwood	*Haematoxylon brasilleto*	Semi-deciduous	7–20 × 5–20	Moderate	Frost tender
Bush dalea	*Dalea pulchra*	Evergreen	4–6 × 3–5	Moderate	Hardy
Butterfly bush	*Buddleja davidii*	Deciduous	4–10 × 4–10	Moderate	Hardy
Cape honeysuckle	*Tecoma capensis*	Evergreen	6 × 6	Moderate	Frost tender
Cape plumbago	*Plumbago auriculata*	Evergreen	6–10 × 6–10	High	Frost tender
Cat claw acacia	*Acacia greggii*	Semi-deciduous	4–5 × 6–20	Low	Hardy
Chihuahuan rain sage	*Leucophyllum laevigatum*	Evergreen	5 × 5	Low	Moderate
Chihuahuan leather-leaf sumac	*Rhus choriophylla*	Evergreen	12–18 × 12–18	Moderate	Hardy
Chinese hibiscus	*Hibiscus rosa-sinensis*	Evergreen	6–25 × 6–15	Moderate	Frost tender
Chisos rosewood	*Vauquelinia corymbosa*	Evergreen	10–25 × 5–15	Moderate	Hardy
Cinnamon sage	*Leucophyllum langmaniae*	Evergreen	5 × 5	Low	Moderate
Cliff rose	*Purshia mexicana*	Evergreen	6–8 × 3–6	Moderate	Hardy

CHAPTER EIGHT

Common Name	Botanical Name	Form	Height x Width	Water Use	Cold Tolerance
Copper leaf caesalpinia	Caesalpinia pumila	Evergreen	6–10 × 8–15	Low	Frost tender
Crape myrtle	Lagerstroemia indica	Deciduous	5–20 × 5–20	Moderate	Hardy
Creosote	Larrea tridentata	Evergreen	4–12 × 4–12	Low	Hardy
Damianita	Chrysactinia mexicana	Evergreen	1–2 × 3	Low	Hardy
Desert barberry	Berberis haematocarpa	Evergreen	6–8 × 6–10	Moderate	Hardy
Desert broom	Baccharis sarothroides	Evergreen	3–9 × 3–9	Low	Hardy
Desert honeysuckle	Anisacanthus thurberi	Semi-deciduous	3–5 × 4	Moderate	Moderate
Desert lavender	Hyptis emoryi	Semi-deciduous	4–8 × 4–8	Low	Frost tender
Desert ruellia	Ruellia peninsularis	Evergreen	2–5 × 2–5	Low	Moderate
Desert senna	Senna artemesioides v. filifolia	Evergreen	6 × 6	Low	Moderate
Emu bush	Eremophila glabra	Evergreen	5 × 10	Low	Moderate
Euonymus	Euonymus japonicus	Evergreen	8–10 × 6–10	High	Hardy
Evergreen chaste tree	Vitex trifolia	Semi-deciduous	10–20 × 15–25	Moderate	Frost tender
Fairyduster	Calliandra eriophylla	Semi-deciduous	1–3 × 3–4	Low	Hardy
Feathery cassia	Senna artemisioides	Evergreen	3–5 × 3–5	Low	Frost tender
Firebush	Hamelia patens	Semi-deciduous	5–20 × 5–20	Moderate	Frost tender
Firethorn	Pyracantha coccinea/hybrids	Evergreen	8–10 × 8–10	High	Hardy
Flame anisacanthus	Anisacanthus quadrifidus	Deciduous	3–4 × 3–4	Moderate	Hardy
Four-wing salt bush	Atriplex canescens	Evergreen	8 × 8	Moderate	Hardy
Greythorn	Zizyphus obtusifolia	Evergreen	8–10 × 6–10	Low	Moderate
Guajillo	Acacia berlandieri	Semi-deciduous	10–15 × 10–15	Moderate	Moderate
Guayacan	Guaiacum coulteri	Evergreen	6–15 × 6–15	Moderate	Frost tender
Heavenly bamboo	Nandina domestica	Semi-deciduous	6–8 × 3–4	Winter	Hardy
Holly leaf salt bush	Atriplex hymenelytra	Evergreen	3–4 × 3–4	Low	Frost tender
Hopbush	Dodonaea viscosa	Evergreen	12–15 × 12	Moderate	Moderate
Huachuca sumac	Rhus virens	Evergreen	8–12 × 6–10	Moderate	Hardy
Jojoba	Simmondsia chinensis	Evergreen	6–8 × 6–8	Low	Moderate
Knife leaf acacia	Acacia cultriformis	Evergreen	10–15 × 10–15	Low	Moderate
Lemonade bush	Rhus trilobata	Evergreen	3–5 × 3–5	Moderate	Hardy

CHAPTER EIGHT

Common Name	Botanical Name	Form	Height x Width	Water Use	Cold Tolerance
Little leaf cordia	*Cordia parvifolia*	Evergreen	6–10 × 6–10	Low	Moderate
Little leaf desert sumac	*Rhus microphylla*	Deciduous	8–15 × 12	Moderate	Hardy
Lucky nut	*Thevetia peruviana*	Evergreen	8–25 × 8–20	Moderate	Frost tender
Mexican buckeye	*Ungnadia speciosa*	Deciduous	8–12 × 8–12	Moderate	Hardy
Mexican jumping bean	*Sapium biloculare*	Deciduous	6–8 × 6–8	Low	Moderate
Natal plum	*Carissa macrocarpa*	Evergreen	5–7 × 5–7	High	Frost tender
Notable acacia	*Acacia notabilis*	Evergreen	6–8 × 6–10	Low	Moderate
Oleander	*Nerium oleander*	Evergreen	3–20 × 3–20	Low	Frost tender
'Orange Jubilee'	*Tecoma* hybrid	Semi-deciduous	8–10 × 4–5	Moderate	Frost tender
Oregon grape holly	*Mahonia aquifolium*	Evergreen	6 × 5	High	Hardy
'Pink Beauty'	*Eremophila laanii*	Evergreen	6–10 × 5–8	Low	Moderate
Pink bush morning glory	*Ipomoea carnea*	Deciduous	6–8 × 6–8	Summer	Frost tender
Popcorn cassia	*Cassia didymobotya*	Semi-deciduous	8 × 8	High	Frost tender
Quail bush	*Atriplex lentiformis*	Evergreen	6–10 × 8–15	Low	Hardy
Red bird of paradise	*Caesalpinia pulcherrima*	Deciduous	4–10 × 4–6	Moderate	Frost tender
Red fairyduster	*Calliandra californica*	Evergreen	2–5 × 2–5	Low	Frost tender
Rose of Sharon	*Hibiscus syriacus*	Evergreen	10–12 × 6	Moderate	Hardy
Rosemary	*Rosmarinus officinalis*	Evergreen	3–6 × 3–6	Low	Hardy
San Carlos hibiscus	*Gossypium harknessii*	Evergreen	4–6 × 5–8	Low	Frost tender
Shrubby alfalfa	*Medicago arborea*	Deciduous	4–6 × 4–6	Low	Moderate
Shrubby senna	*Senna wislizenii*	Deciduous	5–8 × 5–10	Moderate	Moderate
Shrubby xylosma	*Xylosma congestum*	Evergreen	4–6 × 4–6	Moderate	Hardy
Silver dalea	*Dalea bicolor*	Evergreen	3–4 × 3–4	Moderate	Moderate
Silver senna	*Senna artemesioides v. petiolaris*	Evergreen	4–6 × 4–6	Low	Moderate
Sky flower	*Duranta erecta*	Evergreen	10–25 × 6–10	Moderate	Frost tender
Spotted emu bush	*Eremophila maculata*	Evergreen	3–4 × 4–5	Low	Moderate
Sturt's senna	*Senna artemisioides v. sturtii*	Evergreen	3–6 × 3–4	Low	Moderate
Sugar bush	*Rhus ovata*	Evergreen	15 × 15	Moderate	Hardy
Texas mountain laurel	*Sophora secundiflora*	Evergreen	15–25 × 5–15	Moderate	Hardy

CHAPTER EIGHT

Common Name	Botanical Name	Form	Height x Width	Water Use	Cold Tolerance
Texas olive	*Cordia boissieri*	Evergreen	10–25 × 10–25	Moderate	Moderate
Texas persimmon	*Diospyros texana*	Evergreen	15 × 15	Moderate	Moderate
Texas ranger	*Leucophyllum frutescens*	Evergreen	4–8 × 4–8	Low	Hardy
Texas ranger	*Leucophyllum pruinosum*	Evergreen	6 × 6	Low	Moderate
Texas sage	*Leucophyllum revolutum*	Evergreen	4 × 4	Low	Hardy
Turpentine bush	*Ericameria laricifolia*	Evergreen	3 × 3	Moderate	Hardy
Twisted myrtle	*Myrtis communis*	Evergreen	9–12 × 9–12	Moderate	Hardy
Violet silverleaf	*Leucophyllum candidum*	Evergreen	6–10 × 5–8	Low	Moderate
Wax-leaf privet	*Ligustrum japonicum*	Evergreen	10–12 × 8	High	Hardy
White bursage	*Ambrosia dumosa*	Evergreen	2–3 × 2–3	Low	Moderate
White thorn acacia	*Acacia constricta*	Semi-deciduous	6–20 × 6–20	Low	Hardy
Wolfberry	*Lycium brevipes*	Semi-deciduous	6–12 × 6–12	Low	Moderate
Woolly butterfly bush	*Buddleja marrubiifolia*	Evergreen	4–5 × 4–5	Low	Hardy
Yellow bird of paradise	*Caesalpinia gilliesii*	Semi-deciduous	5–10 × 4–6	Low	Moderate
Yellowbells	*Tecoma stans*	Semi-deciduous	10–25 × 5–15	Moderate	Moderate

Evergreen = retain leaves all year, losing them gradually
Semi-deciduous = may lose all or most leaves in severe cold or in high heat
Deciduous = lose all leaves seasonally

Low Water Use = plants that are either native to the region, or well adapted, require only minimal supplemental irrigation
Moderate Water Use = may be native or not, require supplemental irrigation in summer, or when grown in warmer areas than those to which they are native
High Water Use = generally not desert adapted, require intensive supplemental irrigation especially in warmest areas

Frost tender = plants that are sensitive to temperatures at or near freezing; many are more root hardy
Moderate = tolerate cold to the high 20s, may lose leaves but are hardy in the region, may need some protection in coldest areas
Hardy = tolerate cold in all areas, in hottest areas may need sun protection

JANUARY
SHRUBS

PLANNING

This is a good month to take out your journal and see how things stand in the garden. If you are in a new house or planning a new area, think about the shrubs you have or might want for it. Shrubs are reasonably permanent parts of a garden, the largest plants after trees that you will put in. Like trees, they set the tone and style in the space they are planted. Before you decide which shrubs you want, consider the following questions.

1. Do you want the shrubs to hide anything? If so, be sure you get shrubs that are large enough

Jojoba

to screen whatever it is that needs to be hidden. To judge how large a shrub needs to be to hide something outside the yard, like a neighbor's window, or a terrible view, take a long stick or bamboo pole and hold it up in the area where you intend to plant the shrub. It should give you an idea of how tall your plant needs to be to accomplish its job.

2. Do you want it to bloom at a particular time of the year? Many shrubs are wonderful flowering plants, and their blooms are excellent parts of a garden. If a shrub is especially colorful, consider putting it where it will be seen, either up close or as part of a view. Have a large shrub rise up over a shed, or wall, or other structure so that it appears to peek at you and invite you to go see it.

3. Do you want to use shrubs to define space in the garden? One of the ways to make a small space look larger is to create visual barriers that prevent you from seeing it all at once. These are sometimes called garden rooms, but it can be just a matter of making you walk around a shrub to get to the side yard, or putting a dense layer of shrubs behind the patio so that you have to walk around to see what is behind them.

4. Are the choices you made compatible with all the rest of your garden or your area? Nothing looks more ridiculous than immense towering shrubs hovering over a small house and yard; or the converse, tiny neat shrubs lining the driveway of a naturalistic yard. Give some thought to the style of plants in the rest of the area.

Finally, choose plants that do not require excessive amounts of water when they are mature and that have sufficient heat or cold tolerance for your area.

PLANTING

Continue planting cold-hardy shrubs in all areas of the region. Plant cold-hardy deciduous shrubs before they begin to leaf out, which in the warmest parts of the region means planting them by the end of the month.

CARE

Even in the warmest areas of the region, be prepared to protect tender shrubs like **red bird of paradise** or **yellowbells** on cold nights. Throw a sheet, blanket, or frost cloth over the plant to provide temporary protection. In the colder zones, where freezes are more common, be sure to maintain regular watering around shrubs, and mulch the root zone heavily.

 WATERING

In Zone 8, water shrubs every three to four weeks through winter.

In the warmer parts of the region, water shrubs every two to three weeks, depending on the temperatures.

Water cold-sensitive shrubs or dormant shrubs in the warmer regions every three weeks to a month while it is cold.

 FERTILIZING

Do not fertilize this month.

 PRUNING

Do not prune shrubs this month. Wait to clear out any frost damage on shrubs until all danger of frost is past. Wait another month to prune deciduous shrubs in the colder parts of the region.

 PESTS

Many gardeners use dormant oil, also called horticultural oil, to prevent insect infestations. Use these products this month in the warmest parts of the region. Horticultural oils must be applied in a narrow range of cool temperatures, so follow label directions for temperature and application rates carefully.

 NOTES

Cold Protection

Sheets, blankets
or frost cloth

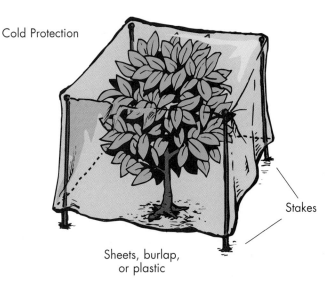

Stakes

Sheets, burlap,
or plastic

FEBRUARY

SHRUBS

PLANNING

Here is a list of winter-flowering shrubs for the warm areas of the region.

• **Baja senna**—uncommon shrub with dusky evergreen foliage with a purple blush and open bright-yellow flowers in the winter. Extremely heat- and drought-tolerant.

• **Desert senna**—attractive light-green foliage, dark-yellow flowers on a tidy bush. Not as aggressive about reseeding as the closely related **feathery cassia.**

• **Emu bush**—most members of this large group bloom in winter or early spring. The selections 'Valentine' and 'Rosea' bloom particularly early. The red to pink (occasionally yellow) flowers of all species and varieties are crowded along the stem.

• **Knife leaf acacia**—an Australian plant with interesting wavy, gray-green foliage and yellow puffball flowers along the stem.

• **Notable acacia**—a large, loosely branched Australian shrub with reddish stem, dark-green phyllodes, and golden flowers along the stem. Handsome choice for accent or specimen plant.

• **Red fairyduster**—brilliant red puffballs coat this desert legume. Extremely heat- and drought-tolerant. Very attractive to hummingbirds.

• **Shrubby alfalfa**—brilliant green foliage and bright yellow flowers all winter from this Mediterranean relative of the forage crop **alfalfa.** Extremely heat- and drought-tolerant, deciduous.

• **Silver leaf senna**—long, flat, gray to whitish phyllodes (leaf-like structures) frame the creamy yellow flowers of this Australian shrub.

• **Wolfberry**—native shrub with complex branching that has a profuse bloom of lavender, purple, or white flowers, depending on the species, in the winter. Excellent hummingbird plant.

PLANTING

After mid-month, begin to plant cold-tender shrubs in the warmest areas of the region. Plant shrubs as you do trees by digging a hole three to five times the diameter of the container and only as deep. Do not add soil amendments or other additives to the backfill. In rocky or hard soils, scratch the inside and bottom of the hole to break it up before planting.

Set the plant in the hole, backfill, and gently press the soil to remove air pockets and firm the plant in place. For large shrubs, water with a basin as for trees, and provide a 1- to 2-inch layer of mulch after planting. Water well.

In Zone 8, continue to plant cold-hardy, evergreen, or deciduous shrubs. Winters are generally

Emu bush

mild enough to allow plants to continue to grow a good root system in preparation for the spring growing season, but hard freezes or severe weather can occur suddenly in some years. If severe weather is predicted, delay any planting until it moderates.

CARE

Continue to provide protection to cold-tender shrubs in your area until all danger of frost is past.

WATERING

In the colder areas, continue to water shrubs every three weeks.

In warmer areas, water shrubs every two to three weeks depending on the temperatures. Soak a shrub to a depth of at least 2 feet, and to a depth of 3 feet if the plant is over 8 feet tall.

Water newly planted shrubs two or three times a week, soaking deeply each time. Continue this schedule for two weeks. Gradually extend the watering frequency until they are being watered every eight to ten days. Continue that schedule through the first year.

FERTILIZING

Do not fertilize this month.

PRUNING

Wait to prune frost-damaged plants until the first of next month at the earliest, or until they begin to show signs of spring growth.

NOTES

PESTS

Weeds can be a serious problem in a year with abundant winter rainfall. It is worth the time to get rid of as many as you can, even around shrubs. Not only are they unsightly, but they are serious competition for water and nutrients to all your plants. Remove weeds before they bloom, or if they get away from you, pull the ones in flower first and work on the others later.

MARCH

SHRUBS

PLANNING

If you are considering the addition of shrubs this spring, be sure you understand how large they will grow when mature. Use a bamboo stake or other long pole, and mark the ultimate height of the shrub. Then have a friend stand where the shrub will be planted. Do the same for its width. This will help you visualize how big it will actually be and whether the shrub will fit the space, preventing crowding and shading problems in the future.

PLANTING

Plant summer-flowering or cold-tender shrubs as early as possible after all danger of frost is past. In the warmest areas, plant cold-tender shrubs like **desert ruellia, red bird of paradise, red fairyduster,** and **yellowbells.**

CARE

Strong drying winds can cause problems for newly planted or weak-stemmed shrubs. Where wind is a particular problem, plant shrubs against a windbreak of trees or more durable shrubs. Shrubs in high-wind areas will need water more often as well because of the drying effect of the wind.

WATERING

In all areas, including the colder ones, water shrubs every two weeks. Water to a minimum of 2 feet, more if the plants are large.

Established native shrubs may not need to be watered as frequently.

FERTILIZING

Apply a 2- to 3-inch layer of compost or mulch around the root zone of all shrubs. A feeding once in the spring and once in the early fall is all the fertilization most shrubs will need for the year.

Alternately, apply a well-balanced granular fertilizer evenly around the base of the shrub. Follow label directions, and water well both before and after fertilizing shrubs.

Do not fertilize newly planted shrubs until next fall.

PRUNING

Prune out all stems that were killed or damaged by frost, cutting back the stem to just above the new growth. Prune shrubs that are not frost-damaged lightly, either pinching back new growth to encourage more branching or removing selected stems.

Few shrubs respond well to a severe shearing. The exceptions are fast- growing summer-flowering shrubs like **yellowbells** and **red bird of paradise.** It is usually best not to remove more than $1/3$ of even these shrubs in any given year.

Water shrubs well after pruning, and wait about two weeks to fertilize a heavily pruned shrub.

This will be the only time you heavily prune summer-flowering shrubs. Most bloom on new wood, and pruning encourages a flush of new growth.

If a shrub has become too large, prune to reduce its size in one of the following two ways.

1. **Heading back.** Prune back each stem to the same length over the entire shrub. Be sure to make the cut at a junction of branches. This type of pruning maintains the shape of the plant but reduces the overall size.

2. Cutting out selected branches that are too long. Begin by looking at the overall shape and size of the plant and mentally decide how big you want it. If you will have to take more than $1/3$ of the plant, reduce the size of the plant over more than one growing season. Cut the longest branch as far back as necessary to leave it the size you want the entire plant. If other branches need to be cut far back to match the size, cut them. After you have the main branches the size of the plant, head it back as described above to encourage the plant to fill out with smaller branches.

Shrubs sometimes need to be thinned. This type of pruning is to reduce the size of the plant, remove unwanted stems, and clear out the middle of the plant. Begin by deciding how much you want to remove. Prune stems to be removed by cutting them as far into the plant as you can, or at a junction with a main stem. Be sure to make a clean cut just above the junction. Take a hard look at the plant after each cut. It is generally a good idea to take two branches at a time, on opposite sides of the plant, to keep the plant symmetrical.

HELPFUL HINTS

• It is not necessary to add rooting hormones and vitamins when planting any plant.

• Avoid fertilizing a shrub when you plant it and for at least six months afterward.

• Wait to prune a newly planted shrub until it is actively growing. Better yet, do not prune until it has been in the ground a year.

• Do not prune a shrub in the container before you plant it. It needs all the leaves it can get to settle in after transplant and get off to a good start. There is plenty of time to correct unruly growth or bad form in the future.

 PESTS

Watch for aphids on tender stems of spring-growing shrubs. Remove quickly. In the warmest zones, leaf cutters and chewing insects may emerge if the weather turns hot quickly. These small bees are not harmful to the plant and will cause only cosmetic damage.

Heading back

Thinning or rejuvenating an older plant

APRIL

SHRUBS

PLANNING

The decision about whether to use evergreen or deciduous shrubs can be difficult. Evergreens are often the first thing that comes to mind when planning for shrubs, but there are excellent choices in either group. Generally if you are looking to hide a view, mask an ugly building or wall, or provide a uniform background for other plantings, evergreen shrubs are good choices. Deciduous shrubs often blend well in mixed plantings, provide showy seasonal color, or make excellent accent or focal plants. Consider where a shrub will be growing and what its use in the garden will be before making your choice.

PLANTING

Plant frost-tender and summer-flowering shrubs in all zones. Evergreen and cold-hardy shrubs have a more difficult time becoming established when they are planted late in the spring. If you plant these shrubs in the hot weather, be prepared to provide extra shade protection and extra watering to get them through the first summer.

Texas mountain laurel

CARE

Many of us remember the graceful flowering of **azaleas,** the stunning beauty of **camelias,** and the delightful fragrance of **gardenias.** But these are difficult plants to grow in the Desert Southwest. All of these plants grow best in acidic soils, and all the soils in the region are slightly to extremely basic (alkaline). All of these plants thrive in high humidity and with ample rainfall both in winter and summer. Here, there may or may not be rainfall, and it is rarely humid enough to suit them. Drying winds exaggerate the effects of saltburn and heat stress in these plants.

Even in areas where they are well adapted, they grow best in filtered shade. The intense light of the region combined with the dry air and low rainfall results in severe heat stress. To provide acceptable conditions for them is a labor of love and is best achieved in containers. If you have a deep, dark corner where you can entirely change out and redo the soil and you are prepared to water extravagantly, then these charming spring-flowering plants might make it for a few years.

It is probably wiser to accept where you live, and look to the host of beautiful spring- and summer-flowering shrubs that thrive in our region.

WATERING

Begin to water shrubs every two weeks in Zone 8, and continue this schedule through the summer.

In the warmer areas, check watering schedules to be sure that shrubs are being watered to a depth of at least 2 feet. Depending on the temperatures and your soil, this may be as infrequently as every other week or as frequently as once a week.

Established shrubs that are either drought-tolerant or native need to be watered every three to four weeks during the hottest part of the year.

FERTILIZING

Almost everything in the garden can use a dose of fertilizer this time of the year. Apply 1 pound of 10-10-10 fertilizer per 100 square feet, or spread a generous 2 to 3 inches of compost. Water the day before you spread the fertilizer and immediately afterward.

PRUNING

Prune spring-flowering shrubs after they bloom. Water well after pruning, and try not to remove more than 25% of the plant in any one season. Prune fall-flowering shrubs lightly, and wait until after they have bloomed for any heavy pruning

PESTS

The young, new tips of **Texas mountain laurel** are often covered with a fine web that surrounds small caterpillars feeding on the shoots. The webbing prevents effective use of most chemical treatments; pruning out the webbing and destroying the caterpillars is usually the best option.

HELPFUL HINTS

You can control how large a shrub becomes by how much water you give it and how much you fertilize it. Once a shrub has become as large as you need it, reduce the amount you fertilize it significantly. Fertilizer is, after all, added to promote growth, and if you no longer need a plant to grow quickly, slow it down.

The same is true of water. One of the advantages of well-adapted plants in any region is that when mature, they need little supplemental irrigation beyond what is provided naturally. Take advantage of this trait, and water shrubs only enough to keep them healthy once they are full-size.

NOTES

_____
_____
_____
_____
_____
_____
_____
_____
_____
_____
_____
_____
_____
_____
_____
_____
_____
_____
_____
_____
_____

MAY
SHRUBS

PLANNING

Many newcomers to Arizona find themselves with unusual local native shrubs like **creosote.** Mature specimens of these slow-growing plants are treasures, both for your yard and the wildlife that depend on them. If you have mature **creosote,** incorporate them into your garden plans, taking advantage of their open growth habit and astounding drought tolerance. **Creosote** provide excellent shade for smaller succulents or low perennials and attract a host of birds to feed on their flowers and fruit. Water around **creosote** carefully; plants that receive abundant water quickly grow very large, often overwhelming the plants around them. If you have the room and plenty of **creosote,** use groups of the shrubs to create a border or boundary within the garden, or to mark a shift from highly maintained areas to more natural-looking areas.

PLANTING

In Zones 9 and 10, plant summer-growing, heat-loving shrubs like **black dalea, firebush,** or **red bird of paradise.**

Creosote bush

CARE

Add 2 to 3 inches of mulch around the root zone of shrubs in all areas of the region. This will help protect the root zone from excessive evaporation, hold down heat buildup around the roots, and gently increase the fertility of the soil.

WATERING

Continue to water shrubs every two to three weeks. Established native or desert-adapted shrubs may be watered less frequently. Shrubs that are actively growing and blooming may be watered every week in the hottest areas.

FERTILIZING

Fertilize all shrubs in the cooler areas by the end of the month, if you did not do so in April.

PRUNING

Prune fall-flowering shrubs like **leucophyllums** lightly this month for shape. It is important not to prune **leucophyllums** in the summer, for that will reduce or eliminate the bloom. All the **leucophyllums** have excellent natural form and need only modest tip pruning to maintain a pleasing form.

If you have an evergreen hedge or other formal planting of shrubs, prune lightly this month to encourage further branching to help them fill out. It is much better to prune just a bit from the tips on a hedge while it is actively growing than to reduce it severely all at once.

PESTS

Hose off evergreen shrubs weekly to reduce dust and help prevent spider mite infestations.

HELPFUL HINTS

Choosing among the various types of fertilizer can be confusing and frustrating for many gardeners. Fertilizers basically are offered in two forms: dry or liquid. Whether dry or liquid, they are derived from either inorganic or organic sources.

Dry fertilizers are most commonly sold as a granular formulation, although there are powdered forms available. Some dry formulas are pressed into stakes that can be driven into the ground or in the pot. The nutrients of most inorganic dry formulas will dissolve in the water in the soil and are then absorbed by the plant. This means that the nutrients are not available to the plant over a long time but rather as a jolt of nutrients. Formulas that are labeled slow-release are made to release nutrients over a longer period of time and generally last from one to two months.

Compost is the most widely known and distributed dry organic fertilizer. You can make it yourself or purchase it in bags. Both compost and mulch continue to decompose and help nourish the entire army of soil organism that make healthy, fertile soil. There is also a wide range of either individual organic fertilizer products (bloodmeal, cottonseed meal, alfalfa meal, and so forth) or blends of many ingredients to make a well-balanced fertilizer. Organic fertilizers act more slowly by releasing nutrients over a long period of time. The effect of all these products is cumulative, and soils improve over time with their continued use.

Liquid fertilizers are already dissolved and in solution. These are the fastest-acting of all fertilizers and provide the quickest "pop" of nutrients to plants. They disappear just as quickly and must be reapplied often.

NOTES

JUNE
SHRUBS

Yellowbells

PLANNING

Hedges are a long gardening tradition and have many uses in the garden. They provide visual screens, mark property or other boundaries, and can be a living backdrop for colorful mixed plantings.

There are many shrubs that make good hedges, including some unexpected choices. Most gardeners prefer evergreen shrubs for hedges because they provide the dense, consistent appearance that is the hallmark of a hedge.

But it can be just as interesting to consider another type of hedge, known as a tapestry hedge. Here, plants are mixed up, and a wide array of different textures and colors are used together to form the hedge. Some deciduous shrubs may even be mixed in the planting.

Some well-adapted, low-water choices for an evergreen hedge include **hopbush, jojoba, leucophyllums,** and **rosewoods.** For a tapestry hedge, a blend of low-water-use shrubs like any of the previous shrubs with **barberry, eremophilas, guajillo, little leaf sumac, salt bush, Texas mountain laurel,** or **yellowbells** would provide interesting contrasting blooms throughout the year.

PLANTING

In cooler areas, continue to plant summer-flowering shrubs. In all other areas, especially the hottest areas, resist planting woody shrubs until the fall.

CARE

Apply a 4- to 6-inch layer of mulch around all shrubs to cut down on evaporation and water loss. Do not pile up mulch around the bark of shrubs but spread it over the root zone.

WATERING

Continue to water shrubs regularly. Check the watering schedules often to be sure that you are watering to a depth of at least 2 feet. If not, increase the amount of water at each watering rather than changing the frequency.

FERTILIZING

Do not fertilize this month.

PRUNING

Yellow bird of paradise presents an interesting pruning challenge. This is a gangly shrub that is part

SUMMER-FLOWERING SHRUBS

- **Argentine tecoma**—clustered heads of narrow light-orange tubular flowers.
- **Butterfly bush** (*Buddleja davidii*)—dense heads of small flowers in deep purple and shades of lavender and white. Very attractive to butterflies.
- **Crape myrtle**—large clusters of flowers in a wide array of pinks, reds, lavender, and white.
- **Firebush**—clusters of orange to red tubular flowers. Highly attractive to hummingbirds.
- **Flame anisacanthus**—numerous brilliant orange-red, narrowly tubular flowers with flared ends. Highly attractive to hummingbirds.
- **Red bird of paradise**—large heads of red, orange, yellow, or mixes of all these colors.
- *Tecoma* **hybrid 'Orange Jubilee'**—large clusters of bright-orange flowers.
- **Yellowbells** in shrubby variety *angustata*—small clusters of narrow bell-shaped yellow flowers. In the treelike variety *stans*, the bloom is large congested clusters of 2-inch bright-yellow flowers
- **Yellow bird of paradise**—loose heads of large yellow flowers with 6-inch-long red stamens.

tree and part shrub. If you want it to resemble a small tree rather than a shrub, select a single trunk that is growing more or less straight and remove all suckers or other low-growing branches. If you maintain a rigorous schedule of pruning out lower branches, this main stem will strengthen and become wider, and the tree-form will be easier to maintain.

To retain the loose-flowering look, prune gently throughout the year to keep spent flowering heads cut and remove any damaged or dead limbs. Take out low-growing suckers. Cut when it is hot; the plant will recover quickly if watered well after pruning.

Deadhead **red bird of paradise** regularly. This will favor new heads that are constantly

forming and keep the plant looking tidy. Prune low-growing or crossing limbs in the summer.

Yellowbells can be lightly pruned throughout the summer. If yellow bells or their relatives need a hard prune, do it early in the year, just after they begin to bloom. But it is generally best to prune lightly through the summer to maintain a pleasing form and keep them the size you need.

'Orange Jubilee' is a large *Tecoma* hybrid that is popular in the hottest zones. This plant can be pruned almost any amount during the summer. The long stems grow quickly; to reduce its size, prune the longest one to the base of the plant annually. Be sure to water well after pruning.

Some people are allergic to the pollen of **desert broom.**

Because these plants produce only one sex of flower on a plant, grow only female plants if you are allergic to the pollen. To keep **desert broom** from taking over the yard, tip-prune just after the flowers have opened. **Desert broom** has a habit of germinating in difficult places, inside a clump of **cactus** or behind a thorny shrub, so removing flowers promptly makes them easier to control.

PESTS

Continue to monitor shrubs, especially evergreens, for spider mites. The best control is prevention, so spray plants frequently to keep down dust, which harbors spider mites.

JULY
SHRUBS

PLANNING

Shrubs are important for birds. They provide a regular source of food, abundant cover, and good nesting sites. Shrubs that strongly attract birds include the following.

• **Barberry** and **desert barberry**—fleshy seeds enjoyed by numerous birds. The dense foliage makes a good nesting site for mockingbirds, cardinals, towhees, and others.

• **Bee bush**—tiny seeds are a favorite of lesser goldfinch.

Hibiscus

• **Creosote**—nuts of **creosote** are preferred by verdin over all other food. Quail and towhees feed through the litter and gather the flowers and fruit from beneath the shrub.

• **Firebush**—nectar is a feast for hummingbirds and verdin.

• **Greythorn**—the tiny black berries are eaten by thrashers, mockingbirds, doves, and others. The thorny branches make good nesting sites for cactus wrens and thrashers.

• **Quail bush**—appropriately named. Quail eat the fruit and find the low-hanging branches perfect cover for their nests and young.

• **Red fairyduster**—a red-flowering shrub that strongly attracts hummingbirds.

PLANTING

In the coolest areas, continue to plant summer-flowering, heat-loving shrubs. This is a difficult time to plant shrubs in the warmer areas. Newly planted shrubs are even more susceptible to rapid moisture loss, heat stress, and drying winds. For better results, wait until fall to plant shrubs.

CARE

Many shrubs that are not desert-adapted begin to show signs of heat stress and saltburn. Symptoms include yellowing leaves that fall off, leaves that are paler than normal, or in the case of saltburn, brown, dry edges on the leaves. If the symptoms are severe or the shrub is new, provide artificial shade for the summer. If this is an ongoing problem, consider moving the shrub next winter to a shadier location.

Saltburn is the result of dissolved salts in the soil collecting in the root zone of the plant as moisture is rapidly evaporated. The best remedy is to water deeply every time, and water twice as long as usual every three or four waterings. This will have the effect of moving the dissolved salts further down the soil column and out of the root zone. Mulching the root zone heavily during the summer slows down the evaporation rate and helps ameliorate the problem.

WATERING

In the hottest areas, continue to water to a depth of 2 feet. This usually means watering weekly.

FERTILIZING

Make a light application of fertilizer to summer-flowering shrubs like **crape myrtle, hibiscus,** and **red bird of paradise.** Use half the recommended amount, or apply a 1- to 2-inch layer of compost around the roots of the shrub. Do not feed any **dalea** or any of the **leucophyllums.** For shrubs in containers, apply a water-soluble fertilizer once a month in the summer.

PRUNING

Resist the urge to prune any shrubs this month in Zones 9 and 10. Pruning exposes the plant to possible sunburn injury. In addition, plants can become severely stressed due to the loss of too many leaves during hot, dry weather, resulting in less overall vigor.

PESTS

Cotton root rot (also called Texas root rot) is a root fungus (*Phymatotrichum omnivorum*) that is common in the dry soils of the warm parts of the region. The hairlike hyphal structures spread through the soil looking for appropriate host plants. When they come into contact with the roots of a host, they penetrate the root system and ultimately cause the decline and death of the plant. Occasionally you see a white cottony or spongy spore mat at the surface after a rain, but generally it is an invisible disease. Symptoms of Texas root rot are clear. A formerly healthy plant will have a limb or branch that suddenly wilts, turns brown, dries, and dies, but the dead leaves will remain on the plant. There is no cure, and the best strategy is to use plants that are resistant to the fungus.

Although any woody plant could get the disease, the most susceptible are **bottlebrush** and trees that are not from desert areas like **pepper trees,** or riparian species like **ash** and **sycamore.** Native shrubs and those from other desert regions are generally not susceptible.

Oleander gall shows up in the summer as a knob on the limbs of **oleander.** This is not a serious problem and can be removed by pruning the limb and discarding it. Be sure to disinfect the pruning shears with a solution of 1 part bleach to 9 parts water before you use them again.

HELPFUL HINTS

Desert broom is an aggressive reseeder, usually in a difficult location. Prune back lightly to remove as much bloom as you can to reduce this problem.

NOTES

223

AUGUST

SHRUBS

PLANNING

Texas rangers are outstanding evergreen flowering shrubs for the entire region. Most are native to western Texas and Mexico but have proven that they can tolerate the heat, aridity, and varying soils of the entire region. All prefer extremely well-drained soils and should not be overwatered, even in summer in the hottest areas. This preference for dry soils and tolerance of any amount of heat and good cold-hardiness make them unrivaled as shrubs for the region. There are currently seven species and nearly twice that many selections and cultivars available. They include the following.

• **Blue rain sage** (*L. zygophyllum*) is a smaller shrub (4 feet x 3 feet), with wide tan-to-white cup-shaped leaves and dark purple flowers.

• **Chihuahuan rain sage** (*L. laevigatum*) has small, deep green leaves, spreading more open branching, and dark lavender flowers.

• **Cinnamon sage** (*Leucophyllum langmaniae*) is characterized by thick dark green foliage and blue-to-violet flowers. This vigorous shrub and *L. pruinosum* bloom repeatedly through the summer. 'Lynn's Legacy', also sold as 'Lynn's Ever Blooming', is an upright form with an especially long season of bloom.

• *Leucophyllum pruinosum* has pale gray-green leaves and powerfully fragrant lavender flowers.

• *Leucophyllum revolutum* looks nothing like the others, with an upright vase-shaped form and narrow light green leaves. The flowers are lavender to purple.

• **Texas ranger,** also known as **Texas sage** (*Leucophyllum frutescens*), is a large shrub (6 to 8 feet x 4 to 6 feet) with hairy gray-green foliage. Selections include 'Green Cloud', with green foliage and dark rosy-pink flowers; 'White Cloud', with grayish foliage and white flowers; and 'Compacta', a smaller version of 'Green Cloud', with green leaves and light purple flowers. Two hybrids are also offered: 'Heavenly Cloud', a vigorous shrub with dark green leaves and purple flowers thought to be a hybrid of 'Green Cloud' and *Leucophyllum laevigatum*; and 'Rain Cloud', a hybrid between this species and *L. minus*—it has nearly white foliage and deep, royal purple flowers.

• **Violet silverleaf** (*L. candidum*) is an equally large shrub that has pale gray to nearly white, rounded leaves and deep-purple to violet flowers. This species requires dry soil conditions. The selection 'Silver Cloud' has nearly white foliage and dark-

purple flowers; 'Thunder Cloud' is smaller (4 feet x 3 feet), with a compact form and dark purple flowers tightly congested on the stem.

PLANTING

This is a difficult month to plant shrubs. Almost all shrubs will have a better chance of success if you wait to plant in the fall. Subtropical shrubs like **yellowbells** and **red birds of paradise** may be planted in the warmest areas if they can be provided with adequate shade and generous watering after planting.

CARE

Summer heat and increasingly dry soils can build up salt levels in the soil. In addition, in most of the region, local water supplies become saltier as the summer progresses. To minimize salt damage, water plants twice as deep as normal at least once a month.

WATERING

Continue to water shrubs every two to three weeks in the cooler zones. Water regularly in warmer zones, often up to every other week, depending on the species and the soils.

Even rugged native shrubs like **creosote** should be watered monthly during the summer. Although they can survive on less, providing minimal watering during the summer keeps the plant healthy and slows down limb loss that is an adaptation to severe drought.

FERTILIZING

Other than plants in containers, do not fertilize this month.

PRUNING

Prune **oleander, red bird of paradise,** and **yellow bird of paradise** lightly to keep tidy. Deadhead summer-flowering shrubs regularly. **Oleander, red bird of paradise, sky flower,** and **yellow bird of paradise** especially respond to deadheading with increased bloom.

PESTS

Grasshoppers may show up in the late summer and feed on tender new growth. Handpick or use a product specifically formulated to control grasshoppers when infestations are large.

HELPFUL HINTS

Shrubs make excellent pot plants as long as the container is large enough to provide an adequate root system. Frost-sensitive shrubs like **hibiscus, red bird of paradise, sky flower,** and **tecoma** can be used in pots for summer color in areas where it is too cold for them in the ground. Pots can be moved into sheltered locations for the winter.

NOTES

September

SHRUBS

PLANNING

Not all shrubs have to be large. There are a number of shrubs for the region that are under 5 feet tall that would be particularly effective in smaller gardens or spaces. These choices include **beach vitex, black dalea, dwarf oleander, flame anisacanthus, rosemary, turpentine bush,** and **woolly butterfly bush.**

PLANTING

In the warm regions and after mid-month in the cooler areas, begin to plant shrubs that are not cold-sensitive. Woody shrubs are best planted through the fall so they can establish a vigorous root system through the mild winters of the region.

Planting holes that are filled with too much organic matter or other amendments create a "sweet zone" for the roots, which will be reluctant to grow beyond it. It is much better to use mulch on the surface than to put it in the hole.

CARE

As the weather cools and days begin to lengthen, most shrubs begin another flush of growth before the weather gets cold. This growth is important in advance of winter to be assured that the shrubs are vigorous and healthy through the cool season. Maintain steady watering during this time, and follow fertilization recommendations on this page.

WATERING

In the cooler areas, begin to extend watering to every three weeks by the end of the month. Continue to water established shrubs twice a month in the warmer parts of the region.

Newly planted shrubs should be watered every two or three days for the first two weeks. Be sure to water deeply, and check to be sure that water is penetrating at least 2 feet with each watering. Reduce frequency gradually until the shrubs are being watered every other week through the winter.

FERTILIZING

Apply a 4- to 6-inch layer of compost—or a mixture of compost, mulch, and a small amount of well-composted manure or other organic amendment—to the root zone of all shrubs. Alternately, apply a slow-release balanced fertilizer to the root zone of all cold-hardy shrubs. Do not fertilize frost-tender shrubs with fast-acting inorganic fertilizers, as that would encourage new growth that can be killed in an early freeze. The slower-acting, organic amendments may be successfully used this month even on frost-tender shrubs.

PRUNING

Prune cold-hardy summer-flowering shrubs like **daleas, rosewoods,** and **Texas ranger** and its relatives to maintain natural form, thin them out, or reduce their size. To reduce the size of these shrubs, pinch back the tips or remove selected branches back to a junction. Never shear these plants as routine pruning—it not only ruins their form but can severely reduce flowering.

Continue to deadhead summer-flowering, frost-sensitive shrubs, but be careful not to prune back too much, which would encourage new growth.

Knowing when to prune is just as important as knowing how to prune.

• Prune flowering shrubs after their bloom. For most evergreen shrubs this is in late spring, but many evergreen flowering shrubs in the Southwest also bloom in the summer. These shrubs should be pruned in late summer or early fall.

• Summer-flowering, frost-sensitive shrubs should be pruned in spring after all danger of frost is past or just after they begin to vigorously grow. Pruning too early risks losing new buds to late freezes. Prune lightly and deadhead throughout the summer, but do not prune severely after mid-September.

• Prune evergreen and coniferous shrubs that are cold-hardy in the late winter or early spring. Most evergreen, cold-hardy shrubs grow vigorously as it warms in the spring, and you want to prune just before this growth spurt.

• Prune deciduous shrubs just before they leaf out.

HELPFUL HINTS

Consider the mature size of shrubs when you plant. While it is always best to plant as small (therefore young) as you can, space them out as if they were mature. They may look sparse right now, but shrubs fill out quickly. Shrubs that are too crowded create competition, ruin their form, and shade each other inappropriately.

PESTS

One of the most effective means of transmitting disease in shrubs is through pruning tools. Good maintenance and sanitation practices help reduce the incidence of most infectious disease of shrubs.

NOTES

To prevent the spread of plant diseases, take these precautions.

• Clean tools after each use.

• Disinfect after each cut with rubbing alcohol, Lysol®, or a bleach solution— 1 part water to 9 parts bleach (although this can damage some tools over time).

• Never add diseased prunings to a compost pile or leave them around the base of a plant. Bag and discard such prunings immediately.

OCTOBER

SHRUBS

PLANNING

Native plants have numerous advantages in any region. They are completely at home in the soils of the area. They usually require much-less-frequent fertilization to look their best. Many are considerably more cold- or heat-tolerant than shrubs from other regions, and they exhibit a wider tolerance of local pests. All mature native shrubs will survive on natural rainfall, and only minimal irrigation keeps them looking their best throughout the year. But their most sterling quality is their beautiful fit into the look and feel of the region. Nothing marks a garden to its location like the large, woody plants that form its outline. Using native shrubs also encourages and sustains a healthy blend of wildlife, including beneficial insects, in your garden. Here is a list of native shrubs for the Desert Southwest.

• **Apache plume**—hardy throughout the zone, white to pink flowers following by clouds of pinkish plumes.

• **Black dalea**—silver to blue-gray foliage with indigo flowers in spring and fall.

• **Creosote**—the most common desert shrub throughout the region, deep-green leaves against gray to black branches, bright-yellow flowers, and fuzzy white seedpods.

• **Desert senna**—deciduous shrub with deep-green foliage and brilliant yellow flowers in summer.

• **Flame anisacanthus**—orange flowers throughout the summer.

• **Hopbush**—insignificant white flowers, but striking tan to red seedpods.

PLANTING

Fall planting begins in earnest this month. Throughout the entire region, plant all but frost-tender woody shrubs this month.

Plant shrubs in a hole that is three to five times as wide as the container and just as deep. Most soil amendments, including mulch, are unnecessary. If you choose to use mulch or compost in the hole, scratch it in well and roughen the sides of the hole to encourage plant roots to move out of the hole.

CARE

Renew mulch that has reduced or worn down around the root zone of all shrubs. In cooler areas this will hold in moisture, reducing the frequency of watering, and protect the roots from the cold. In the warmest areas, mulch is the best strategy for reducing watering frequency and maintaining soil moisture for your plants.

WATERING

In the cooler areas, water established shrubs every three weeks. In the warmer areas, extend watering to every three weeks by the end of the month. Be sure to continue to water deeply.

FERTILIZING

If you did not fertilize established cold-hardy shrubs last month, do so early in the month. This is the final fertilization of the year.

PRUNING

It is tempting to prune shrubs in containers that are overgrown or unruly or have lost their form. But pruning as you plant can severely reduce the vigor of the plant and increase the time it takes to overcome transplant shock and start to grow a good root system. It is best not to prune anything other than dead wood from a plant as you plant it, or directly after planting. There will be plenty of time next year to correct any deficiencies in the form of the plant.

 PESTS

Many species of caterpillars begin to move around at this time. In some years there appear to be vast waves of them moving through the area. Generally, they are harmless. They are done eating and growing and are looking for a safe spot to pupate. Leaving them alone will assure a bounty of lovely butterflies in the garden next summer.

HELPFUL HINTS

Fall color is uncommon in most of the region, but a few plants rise to the challenge.

• **Beach vitex**—before this deciduous shrub loses its leaves, they turn a dusky purple-red.

• **Copper-leaved caesalpinia**—the small leaves turn from a deep burnished red to a bright golden red through the winter.

• **Crape myrtle**—coloring is variable, but most plants turn a reddish hue before they lose their leaves.

• **Firebush**—as the weather cools, leaves begin to turn a dark, coppery red. They remain this color through the winter.

• **Heavenly bamboo**—this Asian plant turns bright-red to red-orange in the fall.

• **Mexican jumping bean**—this hot-region native's leaves turn a fiery red in late winter.

NOTES

November

SHRUBS

PLANNING

Senna, formerly known as *Cassia*, is a huge genus of flowering shrubs in the legume family. Flowers are open, with five petals, and most are bright yellow. There are some excellent species for the region, including the following.

- **Baja senna**—gorgeous thick deep-green leaves with purple accents, and yellow flowers in the winter. Evergreen and extremely drought-tolerant.
- **Feathery cassia** and its varieties—evergreen Australian natives with variable leaves, most of which are gray-green, and prolific yellow flowers in winter.
- **Little leaf desert sumac**—deciduous shrub native to the region, bright-yellow flowers in summer.
- **Shrubby senna**—deciduous shrub with bright-yellow flowers against deep-green foliage in summer.

PLANTING

Continue to plant frost-hardy and native woody shrubs like **Apache plume, jojoba, Texas mountain laurel,** and **Texas ranger.**

If you have shrubs that need to be relocated, transplant them from now through January. In the cooler areas, schedule transplanting to avoid severe weather.

1. Begin by digging the new hole for the shrub. Make the hole wider than the rootball but just as deep. Do not add amendments or mulch, but scratch the sides and bottom of the hole to rough it up. Fill the hole with water and let it drain completely before planting.

2. Remove the shrub, taking it out with as much soil as you can. If conditions are dry or the soil is light and subject to fall away from the rootball, water the shrub deeply before lifting it. This will help keep as much soil as possible around the root zone.

3. Place in the new hole and check to be sure the shrub is no deeper than it was in the original hole. Fill in with the backfill, firming it gently to remove air pockets and secure the shrub. Build a basin around the shrub and mulch heavily. Water well, and keep well watered for the first two weeks after transplanting.

4. Water transplanted shrubs every week for a month, then every eight to ten days until they begin to grow in the spring. Do not prune any part of the transplanted shrub until it has begun to grow in the spring.

CARE

Protect frost-tender plants with blankets, frost cloth, sheets, or a frame covered with plastic or burlap.

Frost cloth is a commercial product that resembles floating row covers and usually keeps the temperature about 5 degrees Fahrenheit above the outside temperature. It lets in air and light (usually about 85% of available light) and can be left on for days or even weeks in the winter.

Any covering other than frost cloth or plastic should be removed as soon as temperatures are above freezing.

WATERING

In cold areas of the region, water established shrubs once a month. In warmer parts, water shrubs every three weeks during the winter.

FERTILIZING

Do not fertilize this month.

PRUNING

Do not prune this month.

PESTS

Most insect pests and diseases are inactive during the coldest part of the winter. Keep the area around shrubs free of any diseased prunings or fruit to prevent future problems.

HELPFUL HINTS

Feathery cassia is a plant that is commonly used in the hottest areas, but it is grown at a price. This is an aggressive reseeder, and in areas near a park, preserve, or natural area, it can escape and become an invasive problem. To minimize this possibility:

• Never plant this species if your garden adjoins a park, preserve, or natural area.

• Once the plant has finished blooming, prune it to remove all the flowers, or green seedpods. Be sure to prune before the pods turn brown.

• Pull any seedlings as soon as you find them.

NOTES

DECEMBER

SHRUBS

PLANNING

Holly is a traditional Christmas plant, but it grows only in the coldest areas of the region. Gardeners in the warmer areas can substitute **barberry** for holiday decorations. This evergreen desert shrub has dark green to gray-green leaves with small teeth along the tips. There are two closely related species, the **desert barberry** (*Berberis haematocarpa*) and the **barberry** (*B. fremontii*), which are cold-hardy enough to use throughout the state. Both offer the look and feel of **holly** but thrive in the hot, dry conditions of summer and require only modest supplemental irrigation.

Both of these **barberry** species are rugged natives with dusky three-lobed leaves that end in sharp points much like **holly**. Flowers are bright yellow in the spring, and the bright red fruit is devoured by birds.

PLANTING

Cold-hardy shrubs can be planted.

CARE

Provide protection for cold-tender shrubs, like **hibiscus** and **red bird**

of paradise, on cold nights. A quick covering for shrubs is to throw frost cloth or a sheet over the plant and secure it with clothes pins to prevent it from blowing off.

Shrubs that are not entirely cold-hardy will need to be protected on freezing nights. If you are trying to grow something a little marginal for your area, consider making a frame of wood or plastic pipe that fits over the shrub. The frame can be left in place all winter and covered with plastic (as long as it does not touch the plant), blankets, burlap, frost cloth, or sheets on freezing nights. Only commercially available frost cloth and plastic allow in enough light to leave on for extended periods.

WATERING

Even though the weather is cool and many shrubs are dormant, continue to water every four weeks in the coldest zones, and every three weeks in the warmer areas. Mulch heavily around sensitive shrubs, and mound up the mulch around the base of the plant. Use a light mulch like straw or pine needles so moisture does not build up around the stems.

FERTILIZING

Do not fertilize this month.

PRUNING

Do not prune this month. Even if there is some cold damage on your shrubs, wait until all danger of frost is past before you prune it off.

Many evergreen, cold-hardy shrubs can be pruned lightly this month. Take only what is necessary to maintain good form or to reduce the size of the plant. Gradual light pruning throughout the year is a good way to prune evergreen shrubs and helps prevent that sheared look that can take a long time to outgrow.

Do not prune cold-tender shrubs, even if they have cold damage, until all danger of frost is past.

Do not prune newly planted shrubs until they have been in the ground for a year.

PESTS

Although most insect pests and diseases are inactive during the coldest part of the winter, take some preventive steps to reduce future problems. Remove litter, fallen fruit, or diseased prunings quickly from around shrubs. Many diseases overwinter in fallen fruit or old limbs. Keep mulch away from the bark, but around the root system. Water only as needed so that the soil does not become soggy.

TREES

Trees are such an important part of a garden's style and character that it is no wonder they are some of the most popular ornamental plants we have. Trees appear to preside over a garden rather than just blend in, so it is important that you pick just the right tree for whatever spot you have.

While trees have a number of uses in the garden, none is more important than their ability to provide shade.

SHADE TREES

Any tree casts shade as sunlight is broken up and scattered through its branches and countless leaves. But the type and style of shade varies greatly from species to species.

Trees that are tall with either intermittent branching or small leaves cast light or high, filtered shade. Almost any plant grows well in the desert regions under shade like this, including cactus, native shrubs and perennials, and succulents of all types. The trees that best provide this type of shade are date palms; mesquites, both natives and the South American hybrids; and palo verdes.

Trees that are evergreen, have intricate branching structure, or have large, dense leaves cast deep or full shade. Trees like Indian laurel fig,

sisoo, and Texas ebony fit this category. The crowns may be high or short, but the shade pattern is darker than that of many other trees. Even so, because of the intensity of the light in the desert regions, most plants still grow well beneath the canopy of these evergreen trees. Aloes and other succulents, many perennials, and some bulbs need the thicker shade that this kind of tree provides.

Many trees that do well in the deserts are grown not just for their shade but for their spectacular blooms. Cascalote, royal poinciana, and other subtropical trees fall into this category. Most of these trees are better suited to the mild-winter areas of the region, but the summer-flowering desert willow and the hybrid chitalpa can be grown throughout the region for their extravagant blooms.

CHOOSING A TREE

When you are buying a tree, it can be hard to make a selection from numerous species available. But consider a few key criteria before you decide.

1. How big do you want or need it to be? Trees that look small now may grow to over fifty feet tall in just a decade or so. If you do not have that much vertical room or if it would be too large a tree for your garden, look for smaller alternatives. Do not make the mistake of thinking that you can just keep cutting it back to keep it the size you want. This type of pruning only ruins the form of the tree.

2. Is it meant to be a shade tree, and what will it shade? If it is meant to shade a patio or seating area, choose a tree with a wide, spreading crown, and be sure to plant it on the sunniest side of the area. If the tree is to be in the middle of a seating area, choose one with interesting bark or dramatic branching patterns to add further interest to the area.

3. Will it grow near or over a pool? Frankly, no tree should be planted so that it overhangs a pool because all trees lose their leaves, their flowers, and their seed annually. But if you decide you must have a tree near a pool, consider a palm that has the least litter possible, or a tree that has larger leaves or seed that won't clog a pool filter. To provide shade for a pool, it is often wiser to site the tree away from the pool on the west and southwestern sides of the yard to block the afternoon sun.

WATERING TREES

Trees need a lot of water, even if they are desert trees or local natives. But most of them thrive on ample water provided at long intervals, rather than small amounts doled out weekly.

To provide a healthy root system for a newly planted or young tree, water deeply and at long intervals in an ever-widening circle from the base of the tree. Tree roots, like the roots of all plants, grow in response to water and this ever-increasing moist root zone encourages the roots to spread out, sink deeply, and form the anchor that is vital to the long-term health of the tree. Young trees that are growing too fast or have abundant top-growth are almost always being watered too much, too often, and too shallowly, and they will be the first trees to heave out of the ground when high winds occur.

The most important time to water a tree, particularly a desert tree, is in the winter. This is the time of year when trees grow their root system, and that in turn provides the basis for growth in the spring and summer. Water young trees every three weeks in the winter, established trees monthly. It takes an inch of rain to replace an irrigation cycle for a tree, so monitor rain levels before you water.

CHAPTER NINE

HOW TO WATER

Drip irrigation is an excellent method for watering young, newly planted trees. It is important to provide enough emitters to give the tree enough water to soak the entire area around the drip line to a depth of 3 feet. Use a metal rod or probe to determine the depth of each watering.

But drip irrigation rarely provides enough water for trees after they are over five years old, or are over 10 feet tall. By that time the root system is too large and the feeder roots too far away for the system to be effective. Lay down a hose near the edge of the tree and let it soak the tree at slow, steady drip to provide a deep soak of the root system.

Basins built around the drip line are also an effective way to water trees. Basins are filled with water that is then allowed to slowly percolate into the soil. Basins continue to be a good watering method as long as they are expanded to match the size of the growing tree.

Ultimately, large shade trees outgrow your ability to water them unless you are able to flood the entire yard. This is when well-adapted and low-water-use trees earn their place as the trees of choice. These are trees that at maturity need only intermittent deep irrigations, often provided by natural rainfall, in order to stay healthy.

PRUNING

Pruning is an art that should be performed only when actually necessary for a tree. Mature trees do not need to be pruned annually except to remove dead wood. Young trees, however, can be gently pruned to encourage a particular form or direction of growth.

To train young trees, go at it slowly. Do not do any pruning for the first year the tree is in the ground. Every year after that, lightly prune, taking no more than $1/4$ of the mass of the tree, to get rid of branches that are growing toward the ground, those that are growing toward the center, and any that are crossing or lying on each other. Do not try to get the final form of the tree all at one time, but shape the tree over many growing seasons.

Prune mature trees only when there is a problem like dead wood, crossing branches, wind- or freeze-damaged limbs, or limbs that have become diseased. Be sure to prune all trees at the appropriate time of year for the species, and make sharp, clean cuts that do not cut into the branch collar.

PRUNING PALMS

While it is fashionable to prune palms annually, it is entirely unnecessary. A living leaf should never be pruned from a palm unless it poses a direct hazard to people walking by the leaf.

Palms are not woody plants, and their leaves serve different purposes than leaves do in most woody plants. The entire head of leaves in a palm is balanced to provide a steady supply of nutrients to the plant. As new leaves emerge, energy from the older leaves is directly transferred to the younger leaves. This is why palms only have a set number of leaves; once spent, the old leaves simply die off. Older leaves also serve as props for new leaves until they are fully formed. And the entire head is aerodynamic to prevent wind throw of these tall plants.

While you never want to prune living leaves if you can help it, you can prune dead leaves any time during the warm weather. Blooming stalks also can be pruned at any stage without harming the tree.

CHAPTER NINE

Trees

Common Name	Botanical Name	Type	Height	Cold Hardiness
Afghan pine	*Pinus eldarica*	Evergreen	to 50 ft.	Frost tender
Aleppo pine	*Pinus halapensis*	Evergreen	to 60 ft.	Moderate
Arizona cypress	*Cupressus arizonica*	Evergreen	to 50 ft.	Hardy
Blue hesper palm/ Mexican blue palm	*Brahea armata*	Palm	to 30 ft.	Moderate
Blue palo verde	*Parkinsonia floridum*	Semi-deciduous	to 30 ft.	Moderate
Calabrian pine	*Pinus brutia*	Evergreen	to 50 ft.	Frost tender
California fan palm	*Washingtonia filifera*	Palm	to 45 ft.	Hardy
Canary Island date palm	*Phoenix canariensis*	Palm	to 40 ft.	Moderate
Canary Island pine	*Pinus canariensis*	Evergreen	to 40 ft.	Moderate
Cascalote	*Caesalpinia cacalaco*	Evergreen	to 30 ft.	Frost tender
Chaste tree	*Vitex agnus-castus*	Deciduous	to 25 ft.	Moderate
Chihuahuan orchid tree	*Bauhinia macranthera*	Semi-deciduous	to 20 ft.	Moderate
Chinese elm	*Ulmus parvifolia*	Deciduous	to 30 ft.	Hardy
Chinese pistachio	*Pistacia chinensis*	Deciduous	to 30 ft.	Hardy
Chitalpa	× *Chitalpa taskentensis*	Deciduous	to 30 ft.	Hardy
Coolibah	*Eucalyptus microtheca*	Evergreen	to 40 ft.	Hardy
Cork oak	*Quercus suber*	Evergreen	to 40 ft.	Moderate
Date palm	*Phoenix dactylifera*	Palm	to 50 ft.	Moderate
Desert fern	*Lysiloma watsonii*	Deciduous	to 30 ft.	Frost tender
Desert hackberry	*Celtis pallida*	Evergreen	to 15 ft.	Hardy
Desert willow	*Chilopsis linearis*	Deciduous	to 30 ft.	Hardy
Emory oak	*Quercus emoryi*	Evergreen	to 50 ft.	Hardy
Forman's eucalyptus	*Eucalyptus formanii*	Evergreen	to 30 ft.	Frost tender
Golden lead ball	*Leucaena retusa*	Deciduous	to 25 ft.	Hardy
Guayacan	*Guaiacum coulteri*	Semi-deciduous	to 20 ft.	Frost tender
Escarpment oak	*Quercus fusiformis*	Evergreen	to 30 ft.	Hardy
Honey mesquite	*Prosopis glandulosa*	Deciduous	to 30 ft.	Hardy
Indian laurel fig	*Ficus microcarpa*	Evergreen	to 35 ft.	Frost tender
Ironwood	*Olneya tesota*	Evergreen	to 30 ft.	Frost tender
Italian stone pine	*Pinus pinea*	Evergreen	to 40 ft.	Moderate
Jacaranda	*Jacaranda mimosifolia*	Semi-deciduous	to 50 ft.	Frost tender
Jelly palm	*Butia capitata*	Palm	to 15 ft.	Moderate
Kidneywood	*Eysenhardtia orthocarpa*	Semi-deciduous	to 15 ft.	Moderate
Little leaf palo verde	*Parkinsonia microphyllum*	Semi-deciduous	to 25 ft.	Moderate
Mediterranean fan palm	*Chaemerops humilis*	Palm	to 15 ft.	Moderate
Mexican ebony	*Havardia mexicanum*	Deciduous	to 45 ft.	Hardy

CHAPTER NINE

Common Name	Botanical Name	Type	Height	Cold Hardiness
Mexican bird of paradise	Caesalpinia mexicana	Semi-deciduous	to 15 ft.	Frost tender
Mexican fan palm	Washingtonia robusta	Palm	to 80 ft.	Moderate
Mexican redbud	Cercis mexicana	Deciduous	to 25 ft.	Hardy
Mt. Atlas pistachio	Pistacia atlantica	Deciduous	to 45 ft.	Hardy
Narrow-leafed gimlet	Eucalyptus spathulata	Evergreen	to 20 ft.	Moderate
Netleaf hackberry	Celtis reticulata	Deciduous	to 30 ft.	Hardy
Orchid tree	Bauhinia variegata	Semi-deciduous	to 25 ft.	Frost tender
Palo blanco	Acacia willardiana	Evergreen	to 30 ft.	Frost tender
Palo brea	Cercidium praecox	Semi-deciduous	to 25 ft.	Moderate
Palo colorado	Caesalpinia platyloba	Evergreen	to 30 ft.	Frost tender
Pinyon pine	Pinus edulis	Evergreen	to 20 ft.	Hardy
Pistache	Pistacia lentiscus	Deciduous	to 25 ft.	Moderate
Pygmy date palm	Phoenix roebelenii	Palm	to 10 ft.	Frost tender
Queen palm	Syagrus romanzoffianum	Palm	to 40 ft.	Frost tender
Red gum	Eucalyptus camaldulensis	Evergreen	to 80 ft.	Frost tender
Redbud	Cercis occidentalis	Deciduous	to 20 ft.	Hardy
Royal poinciana	Delonix regla	Semi-deciduous	to 40 ft.	Frost tender
Screwbean mesquite	Prosopis pubescens	Deciduous	to 25 ft.	Hardy
Scrub oak	Quercus turbinella	Evergreen	to 10 ft.	Hardy
Senegal date palm	Phoenix reclinata	Palm	to 30 ft.	Frost tender
Shoestring acacia	Acacia stenophylla	Evergreen	to 30 ft.	Frost tender
Sissoo	Dalbergia sissoo	Evergreen	to 50 ft.	Frost tender
Sonoran palmetto	Sabal uresana	Palm	to 30 ft.	Moderate
South American mesquite	Prosopis chilensis/ alba hybrids	Semi-deciduous	to 40 ft.	Moderate
Sweet acacia	Acacia farnesiana	Evergreen	to 25 ft.	Moderate
Tenaza	Havardia pallens	Evergreen	to 30 ft.	Moderate
Texas ebony	Ebenopsis ebano	Evergreen	to 25 ft.	Moderate
Texas palmetto	Sabal mexicana	Palm	to 30 ft.	Frost tender
Texas red oak	Quercus texana	Deciduous	to 30 ft.	Hardy
Velvet ash	Fraxinus velutina	Deciduous	to 45 ft.	Hardy
Velvet mesquite	Prosopis velutina	Semi-deciduous	to 30 ft.	Hardy
Willow acacia	Acacia salicina	Evergreen	to 25 ft.	Moderate
Windmill palm	Trachycarpus fortunei	Palm	to 20 ft.	Hardy

JANUARY
TREES

PLANNING

While almost all trees provide shade in the garden, some trees have other design uses as well. In the hottest parts of the region some trees flower in the winter, providing highlights to the garden. Here are some winter-flowering trees to consider.

• **Brasilwood** (*Haematoxylon brasilleto*)—is a small tree that provides winter color not with its flowers, but with its fruit. The small hanging pods are a deep rose color through the winter and so abundant they appear to change the color of the tree.

• **Cascalote**—a 25- to 30-foot tree with dark green leaflets and tall pyramids of flowers at the tips of the branches. The bright yellow flowers show a small dot of orange when looked at closely and are profuse on the tree.

• **Sweet acacia**—a 20- to 25-foot tree with dark brown limbs and a dense crown of deep green leaves. The round puffball flowers are deep gold and have a luscious perfume. This species has long been valued in Europe as a component of perfumes, and the scent will linger over the garden throughout the winter.

PLANTING

If you had a living Christmas tree that was a **pine** species, plant it this month. Begin with a hole that is three to five times wider than the container and just as deep. Take special care with the roots of the **pine** tree—they are sensitive to root damage and resent being overly disturbed. One way to help prevent this is to have the hole and the pot wet before you plant. Then cut away the container with a pair of heavy-duty scissors or pruners. Keep as much of the soil as you can with the plant, and do

not pull it away from the roots as you would with other trees. Set it in the hole, firm the soil around the roots to remove air pockets, and water well after planting.

CARE

Young trees are much more susceptible to frost damage than older ones. Protect young trees like **jacaranda** and **cascalote,** and other subtropical species, with blankets, sheets, or frost blankets on nights that might freeze. While these species are too tender for the cool areas of

Eucalyptus (Gum Tree)

the region, they do fine in the warmer regions if protected when they are young.

Mesquites begin to lose their leaves this month. Leaves fade to yellow or brown and begin to fall off. This is normal leaf loss in these plants. While **screwbean mesquite** is completely deciduous each year, **velvet mesquite** usually loses its leaves in response to cold temperatures, and the **South American mesquites** lose their leaves gradually, often as the new leaves emerge.

WATERING

If winter rains are abundant, established desert-adapted trees do not need supplemental watering this month. Otherwise, water deeply once during the month.

Water non-desert trees deeply once this month. Continue to water newly planted trees every two to three weeks, depending on the temperatures.

Watering mature trees now— even native trees—helps keep them vigorous through the long warm season ahead. It is considered by many horticulturists to be the most important watering that trees will receive. Long, slow soaks in the region around the tree are best. Be sure you water to a depth of at least 3 feet when watering a tree.

FERTILIZING

Do not fertilize this month.

PRUNING

This is an excellent time to prune deciduous trees like **Arizona ash, Chinese elm,** and **pistache.** Remove diseased or damaged limbs, limbs that are crossing through the center of the tree or rubbing on another limb, and limbs that are growing toward the ground. If you are raising or lowering the crown, do that pruning this month, or before the tree begins to show buds and leaf out. To raise the crown, remove two to four of the lowest limbs of the tree. (See page 244 for directions on lowering the crown.) In the warmest areas, this is the most reliable month to prune deciduous trees,

but you may have up to two months left for such pruning in cooler regions. Do not prune any frost-sensitive trees, evergreens, or leguminous trees like **acacias, ironwood, mesquite,** and **palo verdes** this month.

PESTS

If you have had problems with insect damage on deciduous trees, apply horticultural oil this month. This will kill overwintering insects, eggs, and larvae and may help reduce infestations next year. Horticultural oils are temperature-sensitive and can damage plants when applied at higher temperatures than recommended. Follow label directions. In the warmest zones, the optimal temperatures for using horticultural oils last only a short time, so application this month is best. In cooler zones, there is a month or two left to apply safely.

NOTES

_____
_____
_____
_____
_____
_____
_____
_____

FEBRUARY

TREES

PLANNING

While we tend to think of **pines** as mountain plants, there are a number of **pines** that are from desert regions. These species are some of the best choices for gardens throughout the region.

• **Afghan pine** is closely related to **Aleppo pine** but has a different form. It is a denser tree with a strongly symmetrical shape. This is a fast-growing species well suited to gardens in Zone 9 and 10, as well as the warmest parts of Zone 8.

• **Aleppo pine** is a tall tree with low, often very large branches. While there are only a few branches, as they age they may turn and twist in remarkable ways, giving old trees a fanciful look and an enormous spreading form. **Aleppo pine** is excellent in a place large enough to contain it and is an extremely drought-tolerant species. It is hardy in Zones 9 and 10. Mature trees do well in the warmest parts of Zone 8, but young trees are more frost-sensitive and need protection during the winter.

• **Calabrian pine** is similar to both **Aleppo** and **Afghan pines,** and is usually mistakenly identified as **Aleppo pine. Calabrian pine** is a denser, more erect plant and does not exhibit the erratic low branching so remarkable in **Aleppo pine.** It has the same tolerance to heat, alkaline soils, and drought had by both the other species.

• **Canary Island pine** grows rapidly to 50 to 80 feet tall, although the height is somewhat less in the hottest region of the Desert Southwest. It begins as a narrow pyramid of a plant, and as it matures, the space between the short branches extends, giving it the tiered look that is the hallmark of the species. Hardy to below 20 degrees Fahrenheit, it is both drought- and heat-tolerant.

• **Italian stone pine** is a distinctive plant with a mature height of 40 to 60 feet and an unbranched trunk topped by a broad, dense, rounded crown like an immense mushroom. Because it is slow growing, it is more common to see the loose, bushy pyramid shape of its juvenile form. The seeds are edible and known as *pignolia* throughout southern Europe.

PLANTING

Continue to plant **pines** and deciduous trees. Most desert-adapted trees can be planted toward the end of the month, but do not plant any species that are frost-tender until all danger of frost is past.

CARE

Freezing temperatures are still possible in all but the warmest parts of the region. Be prepared to protect young or newly planted trees when freezing temperatures threaten.

WATERING

In all parts of the region, water established trees once during the month unless winter rains have been abundant. Even deciduous trees need to have soil moisture maintained during the winter.

In all parts of the region, water newly planted or young trees every three weeks during the winter. Provide enough water to soak to a depth of 3 feet.

FERTILIZING

Do not fertilize trees this month.

PRUNING

Continue to prune deciduous trees as long as the tree is still dormant and there are no buds or growth on the plant.

Mesquites may ooze a black, sticky sap in the late winter. This normal and there is rarely cause for alarm.

PESTS

Apply horticultural oils as long as the temperatures are well within the range indicated on the label directions of the product.

HELPFUL HINTS

Many people are confused by the indefinite terms used by gardeners and horticulturists to describe the age of a tree. While conditions of soil, care, and watering can affect the growth rate and size of a tree, the following is generally true.

• A newly planted tree is one that has been in the ground less than one year.

• A young tree is one that has been in the ground less than three years and is much less than half the expected height and width of a mature tree.

• An established tree has been in the ground at least five years and is about half the height and width of a mature tree,

• A mature tree has been in the ground ten years or more and is at least $3/4$ the expected height and width of the species

Prune branches that cross through the center of your tree.

MARCH
TREES

PLANNING

Bark is one of the most visible parts of a tree, and it is also vital to its health and growth. Bark is a combination of both living and dead tissue. The outermost layer is thin and is made up of the remains of the vascular system of the tree that has lignified (turned to wood) from age. This sturdy layer of dead tissue protects the two parts of the vascular system that are vital to the life of the tree: xylem and phloem.

• The tissue just below the surface of the bark is made up of long pipelike structures that move water and nutrients up through the tree called xylem.

• Directly adjacent to xylem is the similarly constructed system that moves water and nutrients toward the roots; it is known as the phloem.

The largest layer and the one that is the interior of the trunk is called heartwood. This is the lignified remains of vascular tissue and bark that has accumulated as the tree has grown. In most trees it is a roughly circular series of easily seen bands that mark the tree's pattern and rate of the growth.

Because the most important part of the living tree is closest to the surface, it is wise to take special care of the bark of the tree. It

Jacandra

is a delicate organ and can provide entry to bacteria, fungus, and virus. Prune carefully and at the appropriate time. Always protect the bark from excessive water standing around it and from cuts and damage from lawn mowers, string cutters, tools, and equipment, including cars. The reward will be a long-lived, healthy tree for your garden.

PLANTING

Plant any desert legumes or other desert-adapted trees this month. Wait to plant species like **jacaranda,** or others that are frost-sensitive until after the last frost date for your area.

CARE

If you use mulch around a tree, be sure that it remains well away from the bark. This prevents excess moisture from building up on the trunk, which can cause disease or damage to the bark.

WATERING

As the weather warms, it may be necessary to increase the frequency of watering on young and newly planted trees to maintain a watering depth of 3 feet. Use a soil probe or rod to test water penetration this month, and adjust the schedule accordingly.

Check the basin on growing trees, and expand it if the tree has outgrown it. A basin should extend at least to the drip line of the tree, but a foot or two beyond is even better if there is room. Water rarely goes into the soil in a straight line.

FERTILIZING

Fertilize young trees once this month with a complete balanced fertilizer. This will help ensure a strong spring growth cycle before summer. Wait to fertilize newly planted trees until they have been in the ground at least three weeks and are beginning to show new growth.

Brown needles and the death of selected limbs may affect **pine** trees. This is a physiological condition called pine blight that is common in the hottest areas. Even well-adapted **pines** like **Aleppo pine** may show these symptoms. This is not a disease but a response to inadequate watering the previous year and high heat in the previous summer. Prevention is key—keep **pines** watered deeply during the winter as well as the summer.

PRUNING

Prune frost-sensitive plants once all danger of frost is past. Clear out any winter-damaged limbs, remove suckers coming up from the base of the plant or along the trunk, and remove limbs that are crossing through the middle of the plant or are growing downward.

PESTS

Small sucking insects called psyllids may show up on some legumes this month. *Caesalpinia* species are particularly susceptible. Spray with strong jets of water or soapy water as soon as they are detected. These insects multiply rapidly in the warm spring and can defoliate a tree if left unattended. Happily, these kinds of legumes are accustomed to a periodic dry season and will regrow their leaves quickly once the insects have moved on in the hot weather.

NOTES

_____
_____
_____
_____
_____
_____
_____
_____
_____
_____
_____
_____
_____
_____
_____
_____
_____
_____
_____
_____
_____
_____
_____

APRIL

TREES

PLANNING

It is a beautiful month for trees, as deciduous trees leaf out and **mesquites** take on their chartreuse color. This is a good time to take out your journal and note how large the trees are and how much and where they are casting shade. Shade will change over the course of the year and over the course of the life of the tree. Make note of the plants growing under the trees. Do they appear to be stretching out, which would indicate too much shade? For these species, it is time to look for a new spot or move them to outer edges of the trees. Others may be looking better than they ever have, indicating that the amount of shade has become just right for them.

When shade overtakes an area, think of it as an opportunity rather than a difficulty. The high, filtered shade of leguminous trees is ideal for growing almost anything in the intense sun of the region. Plants that do well in such filtered shade include succulents like **agaves, aloes, bulbines, furcraea,** and **gasterias,** as well as perennials like **salvia, justicia, butterfly weed,** and most summer-flowering bulbs. The possibilities are endless once the trees have begun

to form a filtered canopy over the yard.

Look at the way in which the tree is growing. Are limbs starting to move toward the roof of the house? Are low-growing branches starting to be in the way of a drive or walkway? Removing limbs that are inclining in the wrong direction before they become large supporting branches is good for the tree and saves a lot of trouble and work later. Walk all the way around a tree when trying to determine how it is looking and how the shade and form are affecting the yard.

If a tree is becoming too large for the location where it is growing, you can lower the crown. This is a hard-prune, so be sure to find out the right time of year for this type of pruning based on the species of the tree. To reduce the crown, take out the leader; this is the main trunk of the tree or the part of the tree that is growing straight up rather that out. Reduce it by about $1/4$ to $1/3$ the height of the tree, and be careful to cut it back to a joining branch. If it is heavy or especially large, cut the limb in sections so that the final cut can be made by hand. Cut just above the branch collar of an adjoining limb, being careful not to cut into it.

Never reduce the crown of a tree by cutting the tree off evenly across the top like a hedge. This type of pruning is ruinous to both the health and the looks of the tree.

PLANTING

Continue to plant desert-adapted trees and any that are frost-tender. It is still a little early to consider planting **palms.**

CARE

Small trees rarely need to be staked when they are planted. Strength is built up by having the main stem move and bend in the wind. If you must stake, put two poles or stakes in the ground in a line even with the tree. Set them 2 to 4 feet from the trunk, depending on the size of the trunk. Wrap tree wrap, cotton rope, or other material that won't cut the bark of the tree around one stake, and tie it off. Take the untied end and wrap it around the trunk of the tree gently, then end it at the other stake. This figure-8 effect is easy to do, and it gives the tree plenty of room to move without falling over. Another method is to loop the rope around the tree and tie it off on one stake. Do the same thing with another piece just above the first loop, and tie it off to the second stake. Whichever method you use, be sure the tree can move somewhat inside the rope and that nothing is so tight it will cut the bark. Remove any staking within three to four months after planting.

WATERING

As the weather warms throughout the region, increase watering frequency on newly planted and young trees. Water to a depth of at least 3 feet—by this time of the year that may be every seven to ten days. Increase the watering frequency of **palms** to every other week. Give **palms** a deep soak to a depth of 3 feet each time you water, and be sure the water extends 2 to 3 feet beyond the trunk.

FERTILIZING

If you did not fertilize in March, or if it was still cold in March and trees were not beginning to grow, fertilize established trees this month. Use a balanced complete fertilizer like 10-10-10 at a rate of 1 pound per 100 square feet of coverage. Measure the area of the drip line of the tree, adding a foot or two, to calculate the square footage.

Do not fertilize **palms** this month.

PRUNING

It is late to prune deciduous trees except for removal of dead limbs. Wait to hard-prune any leguminous desert trees until it is hotter. Do not prune **palms** this month, even though many will begin to lose a leaf or two after the winter.

PESTS

In the hottest areas, watch for aphids and their look-alikes, psyllids, on leguminous trees. Wash off with strong jets of water as soon as you see them—large infestations can be difficult to treat on a tree.

NOTES

_____
_____
_____
_____
_____
_____
_____
_____
_____
_____
_____
_____
_____
_____

MAY

TREES

PLANNING

Palms give a special effect to any garden and have many design uses. Not all **palms** look like tall poles, and there are many native and desert-adapted **palms** from which to choose.

• **Date palms,** especially the fruiting **dates,** are large trees with long featherlike leaves. Where there is space for them, they offer excellent high shade when planted in groups. Look for the gray-green desert native **date palm,** the heftier **Canary Island date palm,** and the diminutive **pygmy date palm,** as well as the less-common **Senegal date palm.**

• *Brahea* is the genus of a small group of moderate-sized **palms.** The **blue hesper palm** has large fan-shaped, gray-blue leaves that are stunning even when it is young; this is one of the most beautiful of all **palms.**

All other members of the genus have deep green leaves and are well suited for the hottest parts of the region.

• *Sabal* is a genus of **palms,** many of which are native to the deserts of northern Mexico into southern Texas. These are fan-leaved **palms** with deep-green leaves that resemble the **California** and **Mexican fan palms** but do not grow anywhere near as large. Look for the **Sonoran palmetto** and the **Texas palmetto** as especially good choices for our region.

PLANTING

Begin to plant **palms** as the weather turns hot.

Plant **palms** by digging a hole that is the same depth as the rootball and twice as wide. Mix compost or mulch with the soil at a 50:50 ratio. Set the **palm** in the hole, taking care that only the roots will be below the soil line when it is planted. **Palms** that are planted too deeply rot easily if there is too much water or the drainage is poor.

Backfill, pressing the soil down with your foot or a tool to remove air pockets. If the plant is large, it may need to be staked for a month or two until the roots set. Use a staking sys-

Date palm

tem that is similar to the one for trees described on page 244, and never use carpet, boards, or unwrapped wire along the trunk. If the fronds were tied up during planting, cut the twine after planting to release them.

Plant desert-adapted or native trees through the month. **Palo verdes** trees have thin bark and when they are planted in the spring or summer, they should be protected from the sun during the first summer. **Texas ebony** and its relatives are also highly susceptible to sunburn and should have the bark protected when newly planted.

To protect young trees, use shade cloth or tree wrap, or set up a frame on the southwest side of the tree with shade cloth draped over it. Make sure that the protection does not hold water against the bark. Never paint the bark of a tree with any kind of product.

CARE

If you added stakes to trees that you planted in the fall, it is time to remove them. When you take away the stakes, expect the tree to lean at first, especially if it is small. It will correct itself quickly as it gains strength.

WATERING

Increase the watering of newly planted or young trees to maintain a watering depth of 3 feet. This may mean watering once a week if the temperatures are hot already, or the soil drains quickly.

Water newly planted **palms** every two days for two weeks, then reduce frequency to every two weeks throughout the first summer.

FERTILIZING

Apply a balanced complete fertilizer to established **palms.** Some species of **palms** are sensitive to micronutrient deficiencies, and fertilizers specifically formulated for **palms** are helpful in keeping the right nutrient balance for these plants. Apply fertilizer that is available in spikes now. These spikes need to be replaced annually. Use the number of spikes recommended on label directions.

If using a dry formula, water well around the plant, sprinkle the fertilizer evenly around the base using the amount recommended on the label, and water well after fertilizing. Fertilize desert species every other month during the summer; fertilize other species once a month.

PRUNING

Prune desert legumes like **palo verde** or **mesquite** lightly to remove dead limbs and small crossing branches this month. Delay hard-pruning these plants until later in the summer, as early-summer pruning in these species encourages a heavy regrowth.

PESTS

There are few pest problems on trees as the weather heats up.

JUNE
TREES

 PLANNING

Good tools take a lot of work and worry out of pruning. Look for tools that are durable and will keep a sharp edge. Pruning edges of hard steel can be kept sharper than those made of stainless or other softer steel.

To cut small limbs and for light pruning, choose bypass pruners. These will cut a branch up to 1/2 inch in diameter with ease and allow a lot of flexibility in getting to small or hard-to-reach branches. Bypass pruners work like scissors and make a clean, sure cut. Anvil pruners are not recommended because they tend to smash the limb and leave a ragged cut.

For larger limbs, up to 1 1/2 inches in diameter, using long-handled bypass loppers. Try them out before you buy them, as the action is different on all of them. The cutting head should be made of hard steel that can be kept sharp and is set as a bypass rather than an anvil cutter.

Prune limbs over 1 1/2 inches with a saw. The easiest saw for home use is a handsaw with a narrow, curved blade that has razor teeth. The size makes it easy to work the saw in tight places and get it in position for a good cut. The razor teeth cut on the pull stroke and leave a smooth, even cut. Most have removable blades so that you can keep a clean, sharp blade in place at all times.

Clean pruners after each use with soapy water. Dry thoroughly and apply oil or other anti-rust products to keep them in good shape for years to come.

 PLANTING

Continue to plant **palms. Palms** are sensitive to the soil temperature and establish best when the weather is hot.

June is hot throughout the region, and planting can be a considerable shock to trees, even desert trees, at this time. If you decide to plant this month, be prepared to keep the tree shaded, especially on its south and western sides, and maintain a generous watering schedule.

 CARE

Add 2 to 4 inches of mulch over the root zones of trees. Never allow mulch to touch the bark or pile up around the main trunk of the plant.

 WATERING

Unless your lawn is watered by a deep flood-style irrigation, lawn watering is never enough to support a tree. Trees that are growing in a lawn need to be watered independently of the turf. Lay down a hose on a slow drip around the drip line of the tree to water it slowly and deeply. An overnight soak is required for larger trees.

Water established desert trees monthly, although many native species like **ironwood, palo verde,** and **velvet mesquite** can live on natural rainfall once they are fully mature. Water deciduous trees deeply twice this month.

Water established **palms** every other week through the summer.

Water newly planted or young trees weekly during the summer.

FERTILIZING

Fertilize **palms** once this month. Apply a dry or granular palm formula to moist soil, then water it in well. If you are using stakes, there is no need to add more fertilizer. When choosing a palm fertilizer, look for one that has added micronutrients in the formula for best results.

PRUNING

Prune blooming stalks from **palms** if you do not want the fruit. Cutting off blooming stalks can be done anytime and has no effect on the plant.

Prune only dead leaves from actively growing **palms. Palms** derive energy from the combination of old leaves and newly emerging leaves in the crown of the plant. Upsetting this balance by pruning too many mature, living leaves reduces the vigor and health of the plant.

Many infections are transferred from **palm** to **palm** by pruning tools and the shoes of those pruning who climb the trunk. If you climb a **palm** to prune it, do not penetrate the stem. Clean shoes and all pruning equipment before moving on to the next tree. If you hire services to prune your **palms** and they are unwilling to take such precautions, look for another service. It is easier and cheaper than replacing diseased plants.

Prune desert legumes lightly to remove crossing branches or those that are threatening to lie on the roof.

PESTS

Watch **palo verde** and other thin-barked desert trees for symptoms of sunburn. These symptoms include cracking, yellowing, and splitting of the bark, particularly if it is only on the south or west side. This is a serious problem that can lead to infections. If the tree is small, young, or doesn't have a large number of limbs, protect it with shade cloth. For larger trees, prevent sunscald by delaying any pruning until late in the summer so that the branches will shade the bark.

NOTES

JULY
TREES

PLANNING

Mesquites are perhaps the most commonly used shade tree in the region, and for good reason. They have outstanding drought tolerance, many species are native to the region, and they quickly grow into graceful specimen trees with nearly perfect shade. There are a number of species available, so choose the one that suits your situation.

• **Honey mesquite** is more cold-tolerant than **velvet mesquite** and is native in a wide band from northwest Mexico through western Texas. This is one of the few **mesquites** that is completely deciduous in winter. Leaflets are larger and deep green; old, multitrunked specimens are spectacular.

• **Screwbean mesquite** is more of a shrub than a tree and is completely deciduous. Smaller than all others, it is 12 to 15 feet tall in this region and has outstanding heat, salt, and drought tolerance. The twisted pods are very attractive and often used as ornaments.

• **South American mesquites** are the largest of those commercially offered, often growing 40 feet tall. The trees in this group generally have strong single trunks and make tall, spreading shade trees. Like almost all **mesquites,** they have thorns on young limbs that fall off as they age. Thornless selections of all of the species are frequently offered.

• **Velvet mesquite** is native to the hottest parts of the region and is a black-barked, multi-trunked tree with gray-green foliage. Mature plants thrive on natural rainfall, even in the Phoenix area. Most plants hold their leaves until the new leaves push them out, but they will drop them all in a sudden cold spell. Trees are generally 30 feet tall when mature.

PLANTING

Plant only **palms** and tropical species like **jacaranda** or **royal poinciana.**

CARE

Summer thunderstorms are common in the region. These storms produce gusty, often destructive winds, and wind throw of trees and limb damage are common. The best strategy to protect trees is to thin the crown of overgrown trees, water newly planted and young trees deeply to promote a good root system, and never stake a tree with a single pole attached to the trunk.

Many **palms** lose the old leaf bases, called boots, during these storms. This self-cleaning is particularly pronounced in **California fan palm** and **Mexican fan palm**.

Continue to monitor young, newly planted, or thin-barked species for sunburn. The first

Honey mesquite

symptoms are cracking or mottling of the bark. Protect with shade cloth or other coverings as soon as you see any symptoms.

WATERING

Water established desert-adapted plants deeply, to a depth of 3 feet, once during the month; a rainfall of between $1/2$ and 1 inch can replace this watering. Water non-desert-adapted plants deeply twice during the month; for these trees, it takes a rainfall of about 1 inch to replace a watering.

Water newly planted trees and young trees every two to three weeks to a depth of 2 to 3 feet. Be sure to provide water to all trees in a wide radius around the tree, at least to the drip line and a few feet beyond if possible.

Water newly planted **palms** weekly for the first three weeks, then expand the time between waterings until they are being watered every other week for the remainder of the summer.

FERTILIZING

Fertilize **palms** once this month with a dry or granular palm formula. Water well both before and after applying fertilizer.

HELPFUL HINTS

If you need to find a professional to prune your trees, look in the Yellow Pages under Tree Care or Landscape Services. Ask for a certified arborist that is familiar with the types of trees you have. Ask to see trees that the arborist has pruned before you decide whether this is the right arborist for you.

PRUNING

Trees like **acacia** and **mesquite** are particularly prone to have a thick, congested crown. Thinning will help protect them from blowing over or heaving out of the ground during strong winds.

Sweet acacia and many other types of **acacia** can develop extremely dense crowns during their flush of late-spring growth. It is helpful to open the crown of such trees before the high winds of the monsoon season to prevent wind throw.

To thin a tree, begin by taking two or three fairly large branches that are at regular intervals up the main trunk of the tree. Look for branches that have a lot of side branches. After you take them out, look at the tree. It should always looks symmetrical, but you should be able to stand under it and see sky through the tree canopy. Thinning is best done a little at a time, looking at the tree after each cut, from all angles, to see how it is going.

PESTS

Palo verde beetle adults emerge this month from their long life underground. These huge beetles fly around looking for a mate for only a week or two in the late summer. Their larvae develop underground, living on plant roots, at the base of a wide range of trees and large woody shrubs. If you remove a large tree or it falls in storm, you often see many of these huge larvae around the rootball. The beetle larvae rarely cause any noticeable problems for a vigorous, healthy tree. But once a tree becomes deeply stressed, is old, or has severe damage, the larvae are often the final blow. Treatment is difficult and unsuccessful because the larvae live deep in the soil and are in the larval stage for up to five years. Plants that are overwatered or pushed to grow too fast appear to be more susceptible to larvae damage than those that grow with more modest care.

AUGUST
TREES

 PLANNING

In many parts of the state, caliche is present near the surface of the soil. This rock layer of calcium carbonate is impermeable to water and can stunt a tree permanently if not recognized before planting.

In some areas it is a deep layer that is visible on the surface and acts like an impermeable cloak on the ground. In other areas it is cracked and broken and can be penetrated with a pick or similar tool. If you find you have caliche in the area and want to plant a tree, dig the planting hole and fill it with water. Leave it overnight. If the water is gone the next morning, go ahead and plant the tree. If water can penetrate caliche, roots can also.

If water remains in the hole, however, the caliche is too near the surface, too extensive, or too thick to allow the growth of a root system. While the area may accommodate the smaller root system of a perennial or a succulent, it will never support a tree. There is no option but to find another spot for the tree.

 PLANTING

In the cooler parts of the region, this is the best time of year to plant hardy desert trees. Even in the hottest parts of the region, this can be a good planting month. Use the guidelines for planting on page 212 and maintain a generous watering schedule to get the trees off to a good start. As the weather cools, they will be establishing a good root system. As these trees grow through the fall and winter they will be in a much better position to handle next summer's heat than spring-planted nursery stock.

 CARE

Summer storm damage can occur throughout the region. Limbs often shear or break, leaving a ragged cut. Prune the limb as soon as you can to make a clean cut that will heal better. Do not use seals or other products on the cut; it will heal best naturally.

If the plant splits in two, which is common in plants that branch too low, check to see if one half is in good condition. Prune the other side away, favoring the best side, and see if the tree will recover. Otherwise, remove it.

If a small plant is heaved out of the ground, it can be yanked back into place with a rope or sling around it and then pulled back into the hole. Begin by soaking the hole and the area around the roots that remain in the ground. Create a "splint" by wrapping the trunk with layers of cloth to protect it and a strong board (like a 2x6) fastened around the tree. Pull it gently into place a bit at a time. It may take a day or two to get it completely back in the ground. A rachet, also called a come-along, can be helpful if the tree is larger. This technique works well with small to medium-sized young trees. Unless a mature tree has special value, if one comes out of the ground it is better to consider it lost. Large, old trees do not recover from such trauma well. They are best used as firewood.

To help reduce storm damage, keep the crown of a tree open to air flow and remove any stakes that are adjacent to the trunk.

WATERING

Rain can be plentiful in some areas this month. Adjust watering schedules around rains that are ¹/₂ inch or better. Keep trees well watered, and give a good long soak this month.

FERTILIZING

Other than **palms**, do not fertilize this month.

PRUNING

Eriphyid mites cause a clustered bunch of twisted needles on **pines,** and have a similar effect on **palo verdes.** Use a miticide if you can find one. Apply carefully. You can also just prune out the branch, but remove it so the mites do not have a chance to jump back on the tree.

PESTS

Symptoms of cotton root rot (also known as Texas root rot), a fungal disease of the roots of woody plants, show up this time of year. Symptoms include a sudden wilt of the leaves on all or a portion of the plant followed by death of the leaves. Leaves dry but stay on the plant. Susceptible plants include **Arizona ash, bottle tree** (*Brachychiton populneus*), **cottonwood** (*Populus fremontii*) **elms, sycamore** (*Platanus wrightii*), and **silk oak** (*Grevillea robusta*)**.** Plant resistant species, as there is no method of control. Resistant species include **acacias, Aleppo pine, desert fern, desert willow, hackberry, mesquite,** and **palo verde.**

Desert willow

SEPTEMBER

TREES

PLANNING

One of the most important decisions you will make in a garden is where you plant the trees. Trees are large and important parts of any design, and they are difficult, and often expensive, to remove once they are fully grown. They will determine the pattern and style of shade and sun for the entire garden, and they visually dominate the scene.

In addition, trees make a great impact on your water use. Deciduous trees like **ash, sycamore, mulberry,** and **Chinese elm** need enormous amounts of water to thrive and be healthy, long-lived trees. These trees need to have water available on a more or less continuous basis and do not withstand long periods of dry soils or drought well. Desert native or desert-adapted trees like **mesquites, palo verdes, Texas ebony, ironwood, acacias,** and numerous other species are loaded with adaptations that make them able to thrive and remain vigorous in the alkaline soils, dry conditions, and heat of the desert regions.

Ask yourself some important questions before you buy a tree.

1. Why do you want it? If it is for shade, look for a tall, spreading species. If you want light shade in a small area, look

Sycamore

for a tree that is less than 20 feet tall or has widely spaced limbs making for an open form. If it is to help provide privacy or block a view, look for a tree with a dense crown that branches freely almost to the ground. If it is to shade a hot west-facing wall or window, a deciduous tree might be best.

2. Do you care if it has showy flowers? The most gorgeous flowering trees are the subtropical and tropical species like **jacaranda, cascalote, orchid trees,** or the tree form of **yellowbells.** If you use a tree with showy flowers or especially colorful foliage, put it where it can be seen clearly when in its best color.

3. How will you water it? If it will be on an automated irrigation system, put it with all your trees on one valve (station), and be prepared to add emitters regularly as the tree grows. If it will be watered by hand, be sure there is room for a basin that can be expanded to accommodate the growing tree.

4. Are there special considerations? If the tree will be near a pool, avoid types that have tiny leaves, small flowers, or small seedpods, as they can gum up filters. Will it be directly adjacent to a walkway or other heavily used area? If so, avoid trees with lots of thorns or wide expansive growth that will need constant pruning.

Answering all these questions before you pick out a particular species helps narrow down the choices to those that will fit the space and your needs.

PLANTING

Plant any tree that is not frost-tender this month. Most desert species establish best when planted in the fall, and although it may still be hot in some areas, temperature will moderate soon and trees will have ample time to begin setting a solid root system.

Most deciduous trees are best planted while they are dormant. In most of the region, planting deciduous trees this month does not allow enough time for the tree to set a root system before the leaves drop. Wait a couple of months to plant deciduous trees or until they are available as bare-root trees in the nurseries.

CARE

Trees are sensitive to damage to their bark. Protect trees that are in the path of mowers and other equipment with plastic tree guards. Do not use string trimmers near trees; it is much safer for the tree to trim by hand near the bark.

WATERING

Provide a deep soak to mature trees, even desert species, once this month. Water all other trees to a depth of 3 feet once or twice during the month.

Continue to water newly planted trees every other week, and young trees every two to three weeks during this month.

FERTILIZING

Fertilize all trees that have been in the ground a year or more with a complete balanced fertilizer or an application of ammonium sulphate at 1 pound per 100 square feet.

Some **palms** may be chlorotic this time of the year; continue to apply chelated iron according to the label directions through this month. This will be the final fertilization of the year for **palms**.

Avoid fertilizing any trees that are frost-tender.

PRUNING

Prune only to correct storm damage or to remove dead leaves from **palms.**

Desert legumes like **mesquite, kidneywood,** or **palo verde** may need minor pruning this month if they have grown too much in response to summer rains. This is a good time to clean up unwanted suckers, shape a young tree, or clear out the crown. Do not give trees a hard-prune this month.

PESTS

In the hottest parts of the region, termite mud tunnels may become more visible along the trunks of **palms**, **cactus**, and other trees. These insects are harmless to your plants, as they feed only on dead wood. Most of these insects prefer to live underground, and these are temporary tunnels.

NOTES

OCTOBER

TREES

PLANNING

Many of us have gardens that are small, perhaps only a patio or courtyard. Small places demand trees that will provide shade, contrast, and perhaps color but will not overwhelm the space. Small trees that can have a big impact include the following.

• **Desert fern**—may be a large tree with ample water, or a modest-sized tree when grow on a leaner water diet. This is a splendid shade tree for a smaller space, and its lacy compound leaves provide a tropical touch for the garden.

• **Kidneywood**—rarely over 15 feet tall, this tree with light-gray leaves is perfect for a small space. Tiny, fragrant, white flowers in miniature pyramids through the summer are a bonus.

• **Mexican bird of paradise**— related to the other showy **birds of paradise,** this one grows to a tree less than 20 feet tall with dark green leaves. It has bright yellow flowers intermittently through the summer. It is evergreen in most of the region.

• **Palo blanco**—while tall, up to 30 feet, this is a thin wisp of a tree. Long stems hang gracefully from the few branches cascading down the white trunk. These delicate stems float in the breeze, making this one of the most fascinating of all trees for a small or columnar space.

• **Pygmy date palm**—not all **palms** are large. This diminutive relative of all **date palms** grows only to 6 to 8 feet tall with soft, graceful, feather-shaped fronds. Able to withstand full sun if its roots are in rich, well-watered soil, this is a particularly good choice near pools or around small patios.

PLANTING

Continue to plant all trees that are not deciduous or frost-tender in your area. In the mild winters of the region, trees have ample time to establish a sturdy root system before the rigors of their first summer. The heat is gone and they are not subjected to severe drying heat or winds and dry soils while they are recovering from transplant.

Jelly palm

Do not plant **palms** from now until May. **Palms** deeply resent being planted in cool or cold soils and often fail to establish, languish for months, or die outright.

CARE

If you buy a bare-root tree, plunge the entire rootball into water as soon as you receive it from the nursery. Keep the entire rootball submerged for at least a day before you plant it. Plant as soon as possible after this.

WATERING

Extend watering times for all established trees to no more than once a month. Mature trees and desert trees can be gradually adjusted to watering every four to six weeks through the winter.

Water newly planted trees weekly for the first three weeks, then extend watering gradually so they are being watered twice a month during the cool weather.

HELPFUL HINTS

When buying a tree, think small. Look for plants in 5- or 15-gallon containers. Young trees transplant better, recover and grow quickly after transplant, and have larger, more vigorous root systems, which is the most important part of your tree.

In addition, look for trees that are proportional to the size of the pot. Plants that are extremely tall for the pot are often plants that have spent too much time in the pot. Always look at the roots before you buy. Take the plant gently out of the pot, or have the nursery personnel do so. The rootball should come out in one piece if it is well rooted, and you should see a fine network of weblike roots along the edge of the pot. If the roots are large or woody, or are wound around each other, look for another tree.

Water young trees every three to four weeks during the cool season.

Water **palms** once a month during the winter.

FERTILIZING

Do not fertilize trees this month.

PRUNING

Avoid any pruning this month unless it is to correct wind damage or remove dead leaves from a **palm.**

PESTS

Rabbits can be a terrible pest of young trees. They appreciate the tender stems and new shoots that arise this time of the year. Nothing stops a rabbit but a fence, so cage young trees with a wire fence up to 3 feet tall until there is enough bark to deter these voracious plant predators.

NOVEMBER
TREES

PLANNING

There are only a few trees that provide good fall color in the warmest regions.

• **Chinese pistachio** is one of the few trees that is reliably red in the low zones. Mature trees are stunning with their flame-red leaves in late fall. These large trees grow best in deep soils with deep irrigation.

• **Cottonwoods** are common along the waterways of the state and in the early fall turn a warm, glowing yellow before the leaves fall. **Cottonwoods** are difficult in yards; they need permanent running water to do their best. But if you are fortunate enough to live near a creek or river, they make spectacular specimen trees.

• **Peach** trees have leaves that sometimes fade yellow, then brown, but often the leaves become a deep, burnished red before they fall. Check with a nursery about varieties that are especially colorful.

• **Velvet ash** has leaves that turn a brilliant yellow late in the fall. This is a large tree that performs best in deep soils where deep flood-style irrigation can be provided.

Chinese pistachio

PLANTING

In all zones, plant only cold-hardy trees this late in the fall. Evergreen and deciduous trees both establish best in the cool temperatures of the fall and winter. Keep newly planted trees watered regularly through the winter. Water established trees monthly.

CARE

Protect cold-sensitive trees from freezing nights, especially if they are small or were planted this year. Throw a blanket, sheet, or frost cloth over the tree in the afternoon before a freeze is predicted. Remove the covering as soon as temperatures are above freezing the next day.

WATERING

Water newly planted trees every two to three weeks through the winter. Water established trees monthly in all zones through the cold months. Water **palms** and frost-sensitive trees carefully; once a month is usually plenty during the cold months.

FERTILIZING

Do not fertilize this month.

PRUNING

Do not prune this month. Although deciduous trees have lost their leaves, they are still not fully dormant this early in the season. Wait until later in the winter to prune deciduous trees.

HELPFUL HINTS

Leaves are priceless mulch and compost material. If you have too many for the size of your compost pile, gather them in plastic bags, close the bags, and leave them to decay in the bag. In the spring, open the bags and pour the partially composted leaves on the garden beds.

Invest in a minimum/maximum thermometer to keep track of cold in your yard. Hang it at about eye level, in the shade under a porch or tree. In all parts of the region, microclimates are plentiful, even within a yard. In a yard with significant slope, there can be as much as 6 to 10 degrees difference in temperature. This makes a big difference to your plants and is easy to track with your own thermometer. It also allows you to adjust your expectations of the overnight temperature reported by news broadcasters.

PESTS

Clean up all debris and prunings that might be left around your trees. Borers, especially those that invade **mesquite,** winter over in the refuse and dead limbs of the tree.

NOTES

DECEMBER

TREES

PLANNING

If you are considering buying a living Christmas tree this year and want to plant it in your yard, be sure to check out its ultimate size and shape. These are some that are commonly sold in the area.

- **Afghan pine** is well suited to the warmest areas and grows quickly to over 40 feet tall.
- **Aleppo pine** is hardy only in the warmest parts of the region and is extremely drought- and heat-tolerant. It grows to be over 50 feet tall with a wide spreading crown.
- **Arizona cypress** grows throughout the region, growing moderately fast to become a spectacular evergreen tree over 40 feet tall.
- **Italian stone pine** does well in the warmest areas and grows slowly to over 40 feet tall.
- **Palo verdes** of all types have enough branches and space between the branches to hold ornaments, lights, and other decorations well, even though it is traditional to consider evergreens like **firs, pines,** and **spruce** as Christmas trees. While not strictly evergreen (it loses its leaves to conserve moisture for most of the year), a **palo verde's** green bark makes a beautiful foil for bright Christmas decorations.

- **Pinyon pine** is particularly well suited to Zone 8 and cooler areas of the region. This tidy native **pine** grows about 25 feet tall.

PLANTING

Continue to plant bare-root or deciduous trees. Do not plant cold-sensitive trees or **palms** while it is cold.

CARE

Keep a living Christmas tree away from fireplaces and heater vents to prevent it from drying out too quickly. Water whenever the surface of the soil is dry.

After the holidays, take any living Christmas tree out of the house and wash it thoroughly with a hose. This will remove dust from the leaves, reducing the chance of spider mite problems later. Water well and keep it well watered until it is planted.

If you have a cut tree, when you get it home make a new cut as soon as you purchase it and immediately plunge it into a bucket of water. Let it stand in the water overnight. Use a stand that will hold water, and never let it dry out while the tree is in

Sweet acacia

the house. Keep cut trees out of hot drafts, away from fireplaces, and away from western windows to keep them from drying out too quickly.

WATERING

Rain this time of the year is vital for the success of your trees. If rains are abundant or occur regularly, established desert trees will not need supplemental irrigation. But even mature desert species will need a deep irrigation if there has been no rain for 60 days.

Water established non-desert species once this month to a depth of 3 feet.

Water newly planted and young trees every three to four weeks depending on the frequency and amount of winter rains.

HELPFUL HINTS

Once the holidays are over, the limbs of cut evergreen trees make great mulch. Cut off all the limbs and spread them over vegetable, herb, bulb, or other beds just as they are. Or if you have a shredder, turn them into excellent fine mulch for any area of the garden. The branches or the entire bare tree can also be placed in the ground and used as a perch for birds coming and going in the garden.

FERTILIZING

Do not fertilize this month.

PRUNING

Do not prune this month.

PESTS

The mesquite twig girdler is a beetle that feeds on the bark of a branch, girdling and finally killing the branch. To prevent future problems, clean up fallen twigs where adults and eggs will overwinter, and remove hanging deadwood on **mesquite** trees. In addition, do not prune **mesquite** trees in winter.

NOTES

VEGETABLES & HERBS

It is a great shock to many newcomers to the area that vegetable and herb gardens are so productive in the state, especially the deserts. But with a long growing season—virtually year-round in the warmest areas—gardeners can be eating out of the garden most of the year.

Conditions are different in the deserts, however, and both the varieties that work and the times they need to be planted are foreign to many newcomers. Planting tomatoes in May is certain death in most of the state, and some newcomers are shocked to find gardens that are at their most productive in the winter!

SELECTING THE RIGHT VARIETIES

Winter gardens in all but Zone 8 are full of root crops, cole crops, and any kind of green, leafy vegetable. In the summer, heat-seeking vegetables like black-eyed peas, corn, eggplant, melons, okra, and squash take over gardens throughout the region.

The most difficult crops are the ones that need a warm, not hot, season to mature, like most cucumbers, some beans, and that queen of the vegetable garden: tomato. But again, it is not only a matter of using the varieties that will contribute to a successful tomato harvest, but of learning new timing. In the warmest zones, tomatoes should be planted as early as February so they will flower, fruit, and ripen before the deadly heat of summer.

Ironically, some of the best varieties of tomatoes for the hot deserts are the short-season varieties developed in high-latitude cold areas like New England and Russia. Cherry tomatoes, paste, and

roma also grow well throughout the region but are especially successful in home gardens in Zones 9 and 10.

Peppers have a reputation for growing in the heat, but the heat of the summer in the hottest parts of the region is too much for many varieties. Sweet peppers and many European varieties like bells and pimento, and high-elevation varieties like ancho and guajilla, thrive in the warm spring and fall, but can have a difficult time in the hottest part of the summer. Varieties from the deserts of Mexico like chiltepines and those from the hot tropics like 'Thai Hot', however, continue to produce through the heat. The long, warm summer in Zone 8 is ideal for peppers and most of these warm-season crops.

RAISED VEGETABLE BEDS

One of the most productive ways to grow vegetables is in a raised bed. Raised beds can be made of almost anything, water-resistant wood like redwood or cedar; stacked concrete blocks are inexpensive and easy to use, and can be rearranged whenever the need arises. For a more permanent raised bed, some gardeners make the walls of concrete.

Raised beds allow you to make the soil you need to grow vegetables. All vegetables like to grow quickly without water stress to finish out their productive life in one season. Fill raised beds with a rich combination of mulch, compost, high-quality topsoil or potting soil, sand, and either organic or slow-release fertilizer. As you grow vegetables, add a 4- to 6-inch layer of compost or mulch twice a year to reinvigorate the soil. Mulch is also important to maintain even soil moisture for your plants.

Raised beds can be made any height that is useful for you. They need to be a minimum of 8 to 10 inches tall to accommodate the root systems of most vegetables, but they can also be built to sitting

height (24 to 27 inches) or standing height, which is usually 3 feet.

Build beds that are no wider than 4 feet so that you can work all sides of the bed without walking on the soil. One of the advantages of raised beds is that the soil is lightly worked and never walked on, which cuts down on compaction. If you can't reach 4 feet, build the bed to match your reach.

Raised beds also permit vegetables to be grown intensively. There are many ways to grow vegetables intensively, but all rely on a rich, well-amended soil that is continuously renewed and on keeping the beds planted most of the time.

You can design the bed into a grid pattern of 12-inch squares and plant within each square. With this system, a large plant like corn would take up most of a square, and up to sixteen small plants like radishes would fill another square.

You can also just plant crowded for the most interesting intensive method of all. In this style, there is no regard for rows or keeping similar plants or varieties together. Plants are simply planted where there is room for them, wherever that might be. It is, however, important to make sure that small plants are not shaded out by larger plants.

Vining vegetables like cucumbers and melons can be grown in raised beds, even intensively planted ones, with a trellis or cage to keep them clear of the ground. This not only saves space in the garden but helps keep fruit clean and free of rot.

INTERPLANTING

The last of the winter garden is going strong, spinach and Swiss chard are at their peak, garlic is growing, and tomatoes are blooming . . . but where will you find room for the melons, cukes, and beans? Try interplanting. The spinach will be gone in a month, so plant some melons beside them; lettuce will be worn out about the time squash is big enough to bloom.

CHAPTER TEN

Companion planting is the practice of choosing plants that are not only compatible but may help each other out during the growing season. Typically, one plant either repels harmful insects or so strongly attracts them that the other plant is protected from overwhelming infestations. Onions and leeks are renowned for repelling a wide array of insects. Marigold and dill are valued as 'trap' plants for insects. But companion planting must be lush, so plant as many or more of the helpful companions as you plant of the desired vegetables. Many gardeners plant in alternating rows, or line the beds or perimeter of the garden with the helpful companions.

Some companion plantings are destructive. Do not plant beans and onions in close proximity, or they will stunt the growth of each other. Sweet and hot peppers planted side by side will cross-pollinate and the dominating genes for hotness usually prevail, turning all fruit at least somewhat hot. Good companions include the following.

• Beans with cauliflower, cucumber, corn, potatoes, strawberries
  • Beets with leeks, lettuce, cabbage, onions
  • Broccoli with onions
  • Cantaloupe with chives, lettuce
  • Carrots with peas, radish
  • Corn with peas, beans, cucumber, melons, squash
  • Cucumber with bush beans, corn, cabbage
  • Lettuce with red cabbage, radish, broccoli, beets
  • Melon with radish, corn
  • Onion with cabbage
  • Potato with horseradish
  • Pumpkin with corn, radish
  • Radish with peas
  • Spinach with strawberries
  • Squash with marigold, nasturtium
  • Swiss chard with marigold, nasturtium
  • Watermelon with marigold, nasturtium

HAND-POLLINATION

If your cucumbers, melons, or squash are blooming but not setting fruit, you might want to hand-pollinate them. Remove the entire male flower, which is identified by its long, thin stalk, open flowers, and cone-shaped set of anthers with bright-yellow pollen. The female flower is identified by the tiny fruit at the base (the ovary), somewhat more closed flowers, and a three-part club-shaped stigma. Rub pollen on the stigma. You can use a brush if you prefer, and you can pollinate more than one flower with a single male flower. If you want to prevent any other pollination, gently tie the female flower closed with twine. Fruit that begins growing but then suddenly dies, turns yellow, or aborts is a sign of poor pollination.

WATERING

Vegetables should never be allowed to dry out completely, so it is important to have a watering system that helps you provide water frequently and in appropriate quantities. It is difficult to water sufficiently by hand, especially if the beds are large or extensive.

Modified drip irrigation is a wonderful way to water vegetables. Lines can be run down rows or through beds in any configuration. If you use emitters, space them at 10- to 12-inch intervals so they soak the entire bed. Underground soaker hoses are also useful for watering vegetable beds; because they are underground, they do not wear out in the sun as fast. Attach either type of watering system to a battery-powered timer at the faucet to make it easier and more reliable.

Avoid overhead watering of vegetables. Not only is it extremely inefficient, but it can damage tender seedlings and newly planted transplants.

Mulch vegetables and herbs continuously to keep the soil from drying out. Any sort of organic mulch is effective, but do not put fresh grass clippings directly on the beds, since they break down

quickly, and the decomposition will rob the soil of nitrogen temporarily.

FERTILIZATION

Vegetables like it rich, and a soil that is continually replenished with compost, mulch, and other organic additives is perfect. Fertilizing is helpful to increase fruit production or to make fruit larger, but it does little to improve the soil. Over the years, a vegetable bed becomes a haven for the delicate balance of microorganisms, insects, and other creatures that thrive in a healthy soil. It cannot be said enough—good soil grows good plants, and it is worth all the time and trouble to culture your soil just as much as you culture your plants.

HERBS

Most herbs used for cooking grow without difficulty or special culture in the region. Mediterranean herbs like rosemary, sage, and thyme thrive in the well-drained, alkaline soils of the deserts. Our long, dry summers suit these herbs, as they are highly susceptible to root rots in warm, continuously moist soils. Some of the easiest herbs to grow include the following.

• Basil is grown as a summer annual throughout the region, although African basil can live for many years in the warmest parts of Zone 9 and in Zone 10.

• Chives, both garlic and Chinese varieties, are reliable perennial herbs in the region.

• Cilantro/coriander has delicate leaves that are called cilantro and are important in Oriental and Mexican cooking. This is an annual herb that grows quickly in cool weather but cannot withstand the summers in the hottest areas. Coriander is the name given the seed, which is used in both savory cooking and baking.

• Dill grows as an annual through the winter in the warmest areas and the summer in cooler areas of the region.

• Epazote is an annual herb that is prized in Mexican cooking. It grows any time but the coldest part of the winter.

• Fennel is closely related to dill. It grows as a cool-season annual whose leaves taste of anise.

• Lemon grass is a perennial grass that is widely used in Asian cooking. The roots provide the flavoring, and this cold-tender herb thrives in the heat of the desert summer.

• Marjoram is perennial in the region and has a flavor similar to oregano but somewhat milder.

• Mints offer numerous varieties, and all do well in the shade with ample moisture in the region. Most are perennial, but some can die out in the summer where it is extremely hot.

• Oregano, both European and Mexican varieties, thrives in the region and grows as a perennial. Mexican oregano becomes a short bush and is one of the most heat-tolerant of all herbs. The flavor of each of these oreganos is entirely different—the European oregano is a milder herb, and the Mexican provides a sharper flavor.

• Parsley is an annual herb that grows throughout the cool season and late spring in the region.

• Rosemary is a perennial shrub that is one of the most drought- and heat-tolerant plants in the garden. It is often used as an ornamental evergreen shrub because of its tolerance of desert conditions.

• Sage is a perennial in most areas but can die out in the late summer in some areas. It grows quickly during the long, cool fall and spring.

• Sorrel grows as an annual in the herb garden over the winter and spring.

• Sweet bay is a small tree or shrub that needs light shade in the deserts.

• Thyme offers numerous varieties and selections. Most do well in the region. The culinary English thyme and a Middle Eastern variety called conehead are the most tolerant of conditions in the warmest regions.

JANUARY
VEGETABLES & HERBS

PLANNING

Although plants like **peppers** and **tomatoes** are truly perennial, we grow them as annuals in our vegetable gardens. But some perennial vegetables like **asparagus** must be allowed to grow for many seasons to get the full benefit of the tasty stems.

Asparagus is planted from dormant roots and increases in both number and size over the years. In the desert regions, **asparagus** is particularly well suited to growing in raised beds because, like most vegetables, it needs an extremely rich, well-amended soil. A bed of any size will do, depending on space and your interest, but one that is 5 feet by 5 feet will give you all the **asparagus** spears you can eat over the years.

Begin a new **asparagus** bed by adding in copious amounts of compost, composted manure, and other amendments like forest mulch and sand to create a rich soil. Dig out a trench that is 6 inches deep, and set in the dormant roots about 12 inches apart. Cover lightly. Over the next month, as the spears begin to grow, continue to cover them lightly until you have filled the trench. Water well during this time, soaking the bed to at least 6 inches, although up to 12 is even better.

Allow the plants to grow without cutting or disturbance for an entire year. They will go dormant in the fall, usually by November, and should be left entirely dry during that time. As spears begin to emerge in late January or February of the next year, cut any you like as long as they are more than $1/4$ inch in diameter. Leave smaller ones to grow through the summer and sustain the plant. Continue the same culture every year, dry dormancy in the late winter, cutting in the late winter and spring, but leaving all stems less than $1/4$ inch to grow in the summer.

Every winter and again in the late spring, lay a 6-inch layer of compost or mulch on the plants. **Asparagus** continues to produce well for ten to twelve years, after which time the plants are spent and should be replaced.

Look for the old standby 'Martha Washington', or newer varieties like 'New Jersey' and 'UC 157'.

PLANTING

Early in the month in the hottest regions and throughout the month elsewhere, continue to set out transplants of **broccoli, green onions, Jerusalem artichoke,** and **kohlrabi.** There is still ample time to sow seed of **beets, bok choy, cabbage, carrots, Chinese cabbage, collards, lettuce, mustard greens, peas** (short-season varieties), **radishes, spinach, Swiss chard,** and **turnips.** Many of these vegetables can be planted from transplants if you prefer.

When planting **potatoes,** choose tubers that are firm and have well-formed and prominent buds, called "eyes." Be sure a tuber is free of any soft spots. If the tubers are small, plant the entire **potato** with the eyes up. If they are large, cut into 2-inch pieces and dust with sulphur to encourage the cut sides to dry out and prevent disease.

Begin the year by sowing seed of the herbs **basil** and **chives** and of the vegetables **eggplant, melon,**

Asparagus

pepper, and **tomato** indoors. Keep seedlings in a warm location with bright, indirect light and even moisture. Plants should be ready to transplant in six to eight weeks. Direct-sow seed or set out transplants of the herbs **borage, calendula, chamomile, chervil, cilantro, dill, garlic chives,** and **thyme.**

CARE

Divide **garlic chives** if the clumps have become overgrown. Be prepared to protect sensitive plants from overnight freeze. Plants in pots are much more susceptible to freeze damage, so be prepared to move them to a warmer location where they can receive overhead protection, or cover them with frost blankets or sheets.

WATERING

Established herbs need to be watered every week to ten days during the cool days of January. Water vegetables every three days or often enough to be certain they do not dry out between waterings. If winter rains are plentiful, adjust watering so that plants do not become waterlogged.

HELPFUL HINTS

Succession plantings are a great way to provide a steady harvest, instead of having a windfall of a crop. Planting at intervals can also extend the length of harvest. Fast-growing plants and those whose leaves are eaten work especially well for succession plantings at two-week intervals. Good succession choices are: **arugula, bok choy, Chinese greens, cilantro, dill, lettuce, mache, parsley,** and **radish.** Crops like **beets, carrots,** and **Swiss chard** that tolerate late-spring heat can be planted at three-week intervals.

Instead of planting in rows, take all your greens and mix the seeds together. Then broadcast the seed lightly over a prepared bed. Pull out thinnings and eat them young, creating your own mixed salad.

Potatoes can be grown in all kinds of odd spots. Many gardeners find success in growing them directly in bags of compost or mulch. Just slit the bag, set in the tuber, and keep it well watered. Others find they spring up easily in the compost pile and let them say there until the tubers are fully formed.

FERTILIZING

Do not fertilize this month.

GROOMING

No pruning is necessary this month.

PESTS

Watch for gray aphids, and spray them off with strong jets of water. They are particularly fond of **broccoli** and its relatives and can congregate in large numbers on these plants. If the water treatment is not successful, use an insecticidal soap, a soapy water spray made of 2 tablespoons soap (Dawn® works particularly well) to 1 gallon of water. A 50:50 ratio blend of alcohol and water is also useful against aphids.

FEBRUARY
VEGETABLES & HERBS

 PLANNING

This is **tomato** month in the warmest parts of Zone 9 and all of Zone 10. In the rest of Zone 9, wait a month to set out **tomatoes**, and in Zone 8, plant in late March and through mid-April.

Set out transplants as early as possible. Early-maturing varieties are highly recommended because the optimal growing time for **tomatoes** is short in this area. Varieties with less than 75 days to maturity, those with small to medium fruit, paste varieties, and cherry types perform best in the heat of late spring. One of the most prolific **tomatoes** for the hot regions is the heirloom 'Punta Banda' found and offered by Native Seeds/SEARCH. The fruit is small, firm-fleshed, and delicious, and this **tomato** stands up to the heat with ease. Small to medium-sized slicers like 'Celebrity', 'Pearson', or the heirloom 'Cherokee' are also recommended.

Plant **tomatoes** in rich, well-irrigated soil. Plunge the transplant into the soil so that only the top leaves are above the ground. The plant will root along the stem, and this will give it both extra vigor and good wind resistance. Keep plants evenly watered, and put a cardboard box, cutout milk jug, or other protection on them if cold nights occur.

Tomatoes put in early in the season often appear to do nothing at first, but they are growing roots. Cool temperatures, especially night temperatures, hold back growth on **tomatoes**. If the spring is particularly cool, try heating up the plants by covering them with a cage covered with plastic, setting a plastic jug over them, or using water-wall planters.

Established **asparagus** beds are sending up shoots and are ready to cut. Cut below the soil at a 45-degree angle with a sharp knife.

 PLANTING

Continue to sow seed of **beets, bok choy, carrots, collards, mustard greens, peas, radishes, spinach,** and **turnips.** Set out transplants of **bunching onions** and **potato** slips through mid-month. Get a jump on the spring vegetables by sowing seed of **cucumbers, muskmelon, peppers, summer squash,** and **watermelon** late in the month indoors.

In cooler areas of Zone 9 as well as most of Zone 8, set out transplants of **artichoke, asparagus, broccoli, Brussels sprouts, bunching (green) onions, cabbage, cauliflower, chives, horseradish,** and **leek.** Direct-sow seed of **beet, carrot, chard, Chinese cabbage, endive, kale, kohlrabi, lettuce, mustard greens, parsnips, radish, rhubarb, rutabaga, salsify, spinach,** and **turnips.** Wait until late in the month to sow seed of **collards** and **peas.**

Growing herbs from seed is often the only way to get unusual varieties for your garden. Start seed of **basil, lavender** (after first soaking the seed overnight in warm water), **marjoram, oregano, sage, summer savory,** and **winter savory** indoors. Direct-sow **borage, calendula, German chamomile, cilantro, cumin, dill, parsley, summer** and **winter savory,** and **sesame** in the herb garden.

 CARE

Protect young plants or newly transplanted vegetables and herbs from overnight frost with blankets, frost cloth, or cardboard boxes.

Divide overgrown plantings of **chives, garlic chives, lemon balm, lemon grass, oregano, peppermint,** and **spearmint.** Use the same guidelines as for dividing perennials on page 160.

To multiply your herbs either for yourself or for friends, root cuttings this month of **catnip, lavender, Mexican oregano, peppermint, rosemary, spearmint,** and **sweet bay** (it takes up to six months to set).

WATERING

Maintain a regular watering schedule for vegetables. In most areas they can be watered every three days, but test to be certain water is penetrating 6 to 8 inches and that the plants never dry out.

FERTILIZING

Fertilize established **asparagus** beds with a thick layer of compost.

GROOMING

No pruning is necessary this month.

TIPS FOR GROWING GOOD TOMATOES

1. Time planting so the **tomatoes** will grow in optimal temperatures. They grow best in temps of 70 to 90 degrees Fahrenheit but can tolerate both lower and higher temperatures for short periods of time.

2. Time **tomato** growth so that flowering occurs before it is too hot. Flowers begin to suffer in extended temperatures over 90 degrees Fahrenheit, and pollen begins to die at temperatures over 95 degrees. Temperatures over 104 degrees for more than four hours cause flower formation to abort. In addition, night temperatures over 75 degrees reduce flowering and fruit set.

3. Spray often. Another important factor affecting fruit set is humidity. Spraying plants with water often helps raise humidity around the plants when air temperatures are 90 to 100 degrees and night temperatures are less than 75 degrees. Spraying also discourages many insects, but the benefits are lost when the daytime temperatures are much more than 100 degrees and the nighttime temperatures are greater than 75 degrees.

4. Fertilize appropriately. Many gardeners feed **tomatoes** heavily, especially with nitrogen-rich fertilizers. But an overabundance of nitrogen can be harmful to **tomatoes** and affect fruit set. To judge whether your plants have adequate nitrogen or not, look at the part of the stem that is about 6 inches from the end of the major branches. The stem should be about $1/2$ inch in diameter. If it is much smaller, additional nitrogen is called for, but if it much larger there is already an oversupply. Nitrogen encourages leaf and top growth, often at the expense of fruit.

PESTS

Irregular holes on the leaves of **cabbage, broccoli,** and other cole crops indicate cabbage loopers. Handpicking is the best control for these caterpillars, but *Bacillus thuringiensis* (Bt) may also be used. Be sure to spray it on the underside of the leaf where the caterpillars are more likely to be found.

MARCH
VEGETABLES & HERBS

 PLANNING

Plants we know as the vegetables **pumpkin, squash,** and **zucchini** are all closely related and are found in the genus *Cucurbita*. If you save your own seed, it is important to know which species you are growing. Most species of *Cucurbita* will not cross with each other, but within a species hybrids are to be expected.

• *Cucurbita argyrosperma* includes the heirloom varieties of **cushaws** as well as the 'Veracruz Pepita', which is grown for its delicious seeds.

• *Cucurbita maxima* includes **winter squash** and **pumpkins.** These varieties have kidney-shaped leaves that are not as rough as those of other species. Common varieties include 'Hubbard', 'Turban', the heirloom 'Mayo Blusher', 'Buttercup', and 'Blue Hubbard'. These **squash** take from 80 to 120 days to mature and need to be planted early in the warmest parts of Zone 9 and Zone 10 to assure they will have plenty of time to set fruit before it is hot.

• *Cucurbita moschata* includes **butternut** and big cheese varieties. These are also good keepers with delicious, non-stringy fruit. Varieties for the deserts include

Make cuttings of thyme and other herbs growing in your garden.

'Butternut', 'Long Island Cheese', and the heirloom 'Magdalena Big Cheese'. These varieties generally need from 70 to 100 days to mature.

• *Cucurbita pepo* includes a wide array of varieties of **acorn squash, patty pan squash, pumpkin,** and **zucchini.** Plants may be vines or bushes with deeply lobed leaves and rough, irritating hairs. Varieties for the desert include 'Early Bush Scallop', all **zucchini** types, 'Early Prolific Straight Neck', 'Table King', 'Fordhook Acorn', and 'Clarimore'. These varieties need from 45 to 60 days to mature.

• **Chayote** (*Sechium edule*) is a closely related plant whose delicately flavored, pale green–

ribbed fruit grows well in warm climates. This **squash** grows as a perennial from a tuberous root in mild-winter areas of Zone 10 and 9.

Squash names are sometimes misleading. What we call **winter squash** are really just mature fruit whose outer skin has hardened and whose flesh will keep under the protective shell. They are usually large, have firm, sweet flesh, and grow on large vines. **Summer squash** is immature fruit that is eaten before the skin has time to harden, whose flesh is generally pale green to white, and which grows on either large vines or bushes.

PLANTING

In Zone 10 and the warmest parts of Zone 9, sow seed of **amaranth, asparagus, beans, black-eyed peas, bush beans, carrots, cucumber, gourds, jicama, lima beans, melon, okra, peanuts** (late in the month), **pumpkin, summer squash, sweet corn,** and **watermelons.**

In the cooler areas of Zone 9, wait until the middle of the month to plant **artichoke, asparagus, bulb** and **bunching onions, chives, eggplant, horseradish, kale, kohlrabi, leeks, peppers, potatoes,** and **tomato.** Continue until mid-month to sow seed of **beet, carrot, chard, collards, endive, mustard greens, parsley, peas, radish, rutabaga, spinach,** and **turnips.** Near the end of the month, sow **bush and pole beans, cantaloupe, celery, corn, cucumber, muskmelon, peanuts, pumpkin, summer squash, watermelon,** and **winter squash.**

Artichoke and **Jerusalem artichoke** transplants may be set out throughout both zones.

Plant **tomatoes, peppers,** and other summer vegetables late in the month in Zone 8.

Warm-season herbs like **basil, bay, calendula, chives, Cuban oregano, lemon grass, lemon verbena, marjoram, Mexican mint marigold, Mexican oregano,** and **peppermint** may be planted now through May in the warmest areas and through the summer in Zone 8. Sow seeds of **epazote, parsley,** and **sesame** in all zones.

CARE

Make cuttings of **bay, lavender, lemon balm, lemon verbena, marjoram, oregano, Cuban oregano, Mexican oregano, peppermint, pineapple sage, rosemary, sage, spearmint,** and **thyme.** Continue to divide herbs like **lemon grass, oregano,** and **peppermint** if they are overgrown.

WATERING

Increase watering frequency for herbs to every five to seven days. Watch vegetables, and be prepared to increase watering if temperatures rise quickly. By the end of the month, they will probably need to be watered every other day in the hottest areas.

FERTILIZING

Add a layer of compost to all herb and vegetable beds. If using inorganic fertilizer, apply monthly to **peppers** and **tomatoes.**

GROOMING

Cut out winter damage on perennial herbs. Most perennial herbs benefit from a hard prune, cutting back by a third, this month. This is especially effective for soft-leaved herbs like **basils, lemon grass, marjoram, mint, oregano,** and **sage. Mints** often die back from the center. To reinvigorate the plant, cut straight down through the roots several times in a cross-hatch pattern.

PESTS

Check for hornworms on **tomato** plants. These large green caterpillars leave a distinctive trail of pruned leaves. Cut off damaged leaves and remove them, then turn over remaining leaves or inspect the stems to find the hornworm and remove it. Hornworms can strip an entire plant in a matter of days. Sprays are not effective against this caterpillar.

APRIL
VEGETABLES & HERBS

PLANNING

Melons and **cucumbers** are some of the easiest vegetables to grow for the summer. In the Desert Southwest, the earlier they start, the better the crop. The hottest parts of the summer, especially June, are usually not good. Plant early enough so that they are ripe long before the hottest days of summer.

There are a number of forms of **cucumber,** including long, green-ribbed fruit usually called 'Armenian'. This species is exceptionally good in hot desert areas and will produce in the summer. The long dark-green varieties with a tougher skin do best when they ripen before it is extremely hot. Recommended varieties include 'Bravo', 'Frontier', 'Gemini 7', 'Lemon', 'Marketmore 70', 'Meridian', 'Poinsett', 'Triple Cross', and 'Triumph', all of which mature in 50 to 80 days. **Gherkins** are a related species of **cucumber,** and the small, tasty fruit yields well in hot, humid areas.

Like **cucumbers, melons** are so refreshing in hot weather because they are mainly water.

- **Cantaloupes,** the commercial variety, have a warty, scaly skin with netting and tasty, pale orange flesh.

- **Crenshaws** are large, sometimes ribbed, often yellowish when ripe, with flesh from white to orange.

- **Muskmelons** have netted skin with highly aromatic green to orange flesh.

- **'Ogen'** is an Israeli variety with smooth round **melons** that love the heat.

- **Watermelon** is a different species than other **melons,** with large fruit; smooth, green, hard shells; and red and occasionally yellow, fragrant, tasty flesh. **Watermelon** varieties include 'Dixie', 'Klondike', 'Peacock Improved', 'Sugar Baby', 'Yellow Baby', and the heirloom 'Tohono O'odham Yellow'. Look for varieties that mature in less than 80 days for best results.

- Green-fleshed, smooth-skinned varieties are often called **winter melons,** or **honeydews.** Fruit ranges from white to pale green. When planted in the summer and allowed to ripen in the fall, they can be stored through the winter, thus their name.

PLANTING

Plant **black-eyed peas, carrots, cucumber, Jerusalem artichoke, jicama, lima beans, melons, okra, peanuts, snap beans, summer squash,** and **watermelons** in all zones.

In cooler areas and in Zone 8, plant **asparagus, bulb onions, cantaloupe, cucumber, eggplant, lima beans, muskmelon, okra, peanut, pepper, radish, snap beans, sweet corn, sweet potato, pumpkin, squash, tomato,** and **watermelon.** In Zone 8, plant **bush** and **pole beans** before the middle of the month.

Herbs like **basil, bay, Cuban oregano, garlic chives, lemon grass, marjoram, Mexican mint marigold, oregano, Mexican oregano, spearmint,** and **thyme** may be planted in all zones.

CARE

Mulch vegetables and herbs before the weather gets too hot. Use a 3- to 4-inch layer of any organic material like clippings, prunings, straw, or leaf litter. Do not use grass clippings unless they are well composted; they break down quickly and rob nitrogen from the soil as they do so. In addition, **bermudagrass** will sprout from seed or small pieces of root that did not completely decay.

Make the mulch layer only 1 to 2 inches on herbs like **rosemary, lavender, sage,** and **thyme,** because these herbs do not like to have moisture around their roots.

Continue to make cuttings of herbs like **bay, Cuban oregano, lemon verbena, marjoram,** and **mints.**

Blossom end rot may appear on **tomatoes** as a blackened, flat spot on the tip of the fruit. This condition has long been described as a calcium deficiency, and while that may be part of the problem, light, infrequent irrigation or erratic irrigation where plants dry out and then are overwatered is the principal contributing factor to this condition. Water **tomatoes** deeply and less frequently, and mulch heavily to conserve moisture. In low-desert areas, provide shade for **tomatoes** after daytime temperatures are regularly over 100 degrees Fahrenheit. Use a 30% to 50% shade cloth on a frame for best results.

HELPFUL HINTS

• Remove flowers from **garlic** to increase bulb size, and then eat the flowers or use in arrangements.

• You can build a shade structure for **tomatoes.** The simple way is to take either masonry wire or PVC pipe and create a quonset-type frame over the entire bed. Be sure that the **tomatoes** will not touch the shade cloth and that you can reach in and harvest the fruit. Lay shade cloth directly over the frame and secure it with wire or string to prevent it from blowing away.

• Know your plants before you fertilize. Leafy greens and other fast-growing plants whose flowers or leaves are eaten can be fertilized frequently with low concentrations of fertilizer. Use fish emulsion or liquid organic fertilizer like sea kelp blend every two weeks during the growing season. Root vegetables like **beets, carrots, radish, turnips,** and **onion** do not respond well to frequent fertilization. These plants are better fertilized at the beginning of their growing cycle, and once about halfway through the season. If your root vegetables have great tops but no roots, overfertilization is usually the reason.

WATERING

Check all irrigation for vegetables and herbs and be sure they are being watered deeply. Increase watering of plants in containers to twice a week.

FERTILIZING

Be careful not to overfertilize **peppers** and **tomatoes,** par-ticularly with nitrogen. Do not fertilize winter-growing herbs like **lavender, marjoram, rosemary, sage,** and **thyme** from now until the fall.

GROOMING

Prune back any overgrown herbs that are summer-growing, like **basils, lemon grass, Mexican mint marigold,** and **mints.** Do not prune woody herbs like **lavender, rosemary, sage,** and **thyme** from now until fall.

PESTS

Spittlebugs are relatively harmless insects that feed on plant sap and create a "foam" to hide them from predators. The foam is often seen on woody herbs like **rosemary** and **sage.** Use a strong jet of water to rinse off the bugs.

MAY
VEGETABLES & HERBS

PLANNING

Most of us are familiar with vegetables like **beans, corn, peppers, squash,** and **tomatoes,** but there are numerous less-common vegetables that can be grown in the desert garden that are delicious and productive.

• **Amaranth** is a delectable pot herb whose young seeds are excellent steamed or sautéed. The small seeds are used like **poppy** seeds or ground into a nutritious flour, and are excellent when dried and popped like **corn.** These attractive plants like the heat and grow through the summer.

• **Chayote** is in the **squash** family, growing as a perennial vine from a tuberous root. Use as you would **squash.**

• **Fava beans** are one of the most beautiful of all vegetables. These European **beans** grow as a tall multistemmed plant over the winter. **Beans** are held in large pods that arise at leaf nodes up the stalk. They are eaten raw, green or dried.

• **Fennel** is available in two types, but the bulbing varieties are the ones to grow as a vegetable. Young bulbs are delicious raw or cooked, and grow easily through the winter or early spring.

• **Jerusalem artichoke** is a member of the **sunflower** family and grows from a tuberous root. It requires about 120 days from planting to harvest.

• **Jicama** is a perennial vine that grows from a tuberous root. The crisp flesh of the root is delicious and refreshing and is used in lots of tropical cooking. It can be eaten raw or cooked and is harvested about 120 days after planting.

• **Tomatillo** is a fruit similar to **gooseberry** that makes delicious sauces and salsa. Fruit is held in a husk, and this fruit is highly productive in warm weather.

PLANTING

Jerusalem artichoke is a long-season crop that requires over six months to form the tuber we eat. Sow as early as possible for best results.

In the hottest areas, continue to sow seed of **black-eyed peas, cucumber, melons,** and **okra,** and set out slips of **sweet potatoes** and **Jerusalem artichokes.** Direct-sow seed of **amaranth** and **basil.**

In the cooler areas, continue to plant **cantaloupe, cucumber, muskmelon, okra, pumpkin, squash, sweet potato,** and **watermelon** either from seed or transplants. If you have not planted **peppers** and **eggplant,** do so before mid-month.

CARE

Check to be sure that vegetables and herbs are well mulched as the heat continues to rise. **Multiplying** or **green onions** may go to flower this month. Let them flower, then harvest the remaining bulbs, dry them out in the shade, and store in a dry location for replanting in the late summer and fall. Harvest **garlic** late in the month. **Garlic** is ready to harvest when the top of the plant is almost all dry. Pull the plants and let them lie in the bed for a day. Gather them up and store in a dry, shady spot so that they do not touch each other for a week or two. Then store in a cool, dry location and use throughout the year, saving at least one head to replant next fall.

WATERING

Water herbs deeply every three to five days, and water vegetables daily. Check to be sure they are being watered to a depth of at least 6 inches, but up to 12 inches is even better.

FERTILIZING

Fertilize summer-growing herbs like **basil, Mexican oregano,** and **mint** with an organic formula that is low in nitrogen. Cover beds generously with mulch or compost or both. Sidedress **okra** with a balanced slow-release fertilizer, or apply a thick layer of compost.

GROOMING

Snap off side shoots from **tomatoes** to direct growth and increase production. Cut back **basil** regularly to prevent it going to bloom and to increase the amount of leaf production.

PESTS

Shading not only protects **tomatoes** from sunburn but discourages leaf hoppers, which are vectors of curlytop virus. If you suspect this virus, have a sample analyzed, because **tomato** leaves can curl because of nutrient deficiencies, high heat, and insufficient water as well. If plants are infected with the virus, remove and destroy them. Do not compost them, and look for resistant varieties or adjust culture next year.

HELPFUL HINTS

Watering by hand can become onerous if you have a large vegetable garden. It can often result in insufficient or erratic watering. Here are two different methods for helping vegetables stay evenly watered through the summer.

1. Grow vegetables in small depressions, often called waffle beds. This can be one large area or many small ones. The small ones are much easier to manage. Begin by scraping the soil to the sides to create a berm that is about 6 inches tall. Make sure the soil is well amended and prepared for vegetables. Plant in the depression. Water by placing a slow-running hose in the bed and letting it slowly fill the area. A depth of 1 or 2 inches is plenty for seeds, but as the plants grow, increase the level of the water. These beds work especially well in combination or on slopes where water can be channeled from one bed to the next by an opening in the adjoining berms.

2. Use a version of drip irrigation for the beds with a timer. Set out drip lines along the growing area, or use weeping hoses through the area. Plant where the water lines are. Use a battery-operated timer on the hose, and be sure to have in-line valves where there are multiple beds so you can open or close the bed depending on whether you are growing in it or not. Adjust the watering times so that the beds are thoroughly watered.

To reduce corn borer damage, many gardeners recommend applying a drop of mineral oil on the tip of the ear of **corn** just as the tassels begin to brown.

Watch for sudden death of a **squash** leaf or a section of the vine. This could be the work of squash vine borers. Cut off the affected part—the insect is usually burrowed inside the stem. Destroy the cutting and the insect.

Snap off side shoots from tomatoes to direct growth and increase production.

JUNE
VEGETABLES & HERBS

PLANNING

The fun of growing vegetables is eating them, but it is sometimes difficult to tell when they are ready. Use some of the following tips to determine when your vegetables are ready to eat.

• Pick **cantaloupe** when the skin is well netted and the fruit slips from the vine with little pressure.

• **Corn** is ready to eat when the tassels turn brown, milk comes out of the kernels if they are gently cut with a fingernail, and all the kernels are full-size.

• Use **eggplant** once the skin is firm, dark, and shiny and the fruit has quit growing. **Oriental-**type **eggplants** can be harvested anytime after they are 3 inches long, and they keep longer on the plant without becoming bitter than do other varieties.

• Most **peppers** are sweeter after they turn color, but pick them when they are full-size and the skin is firm and shiny.

• New **potatoes** should be pulled just after plants flower. If you want full-size tubers, wait to harvest until the tops start to die.

• **Watermelon** is ready when the fruit has quit becoming larger, it feels heavy for its size, and the tendrils closest to the fruit begin to turn brown. Ripe **watermelons** often have yellow spots on the underside.

• Harvest **broccoli** and **cauliflower** while the buds are tight and before they show color.

• **Cucumbers** and **summer squash** are best when they are small. Pick while the flower is still attached or when fruit is less than 4 inches long.

• Harvest **bunching onions** anytime. Pull up all but one of the clump, and leave one to continue to multiply. Pull out **bulb-forming onions** in the early summer once the tops have turned brown. Pick flowers as they develop.

Eggplant ready for harvest.

• **Radishes** are sweet and delicious when small, hot and bitter when too old. Eat **radishes** as soon as the top of the root is visible. **Daikon-style radishes** grow much larger and stay sweet regardless of their size.

PLANTING

In the warmest areas, sow **Armenian cucumber, basil, black-eyed peas, cantaloupe,** and **okra** now. Set out transplants of **sweet potatoes** early in the month.

In the cooler areas of Zone 9, sow **tomato** seeds indoors for transplanting into the garden in late July for a second crop

Pick peppers when they are full-size and the skin is firm and shiny.

that takes advantage of the monsoon season. Recommended varieties include 'Champion', 'Early Girl', 'Heatwave', 'Solarset', 'Sunmaster', and 'Sure Fire'. Continue to plant from seed or transplant **cantaloupe, cucumber, eggplant, muskmelon, pumpkin, squash,** and **watermelon.** At the end of the month, begin planting **sweet corn** from now through July.

CARE

Tomatoes that are shaded will continue to ripen fruit, but most do not set new fruit because of the high temperatures.

This is a good time to make cuttings of warm-season herbs like **basil, Cuban oregano,** and **pineapple sage.** Cut a length of stem that is 3 to 4 inches long and remove the lowest leaves and flowers. Coat with a rooting agent like Hormodin, and place in a soilless mix. Cover the pot loosely with plastic wrap or a milk jug to retain moisture, and set in a warm, brightly lit location but not in full sun. Cuttings should be ready to transplant in four to six weeks.

HELPFUL HINTS

Place clean straw under vining fruits like **tomato, squash, cucumbers,** and **melon** to keep fruit off the ground. For large fruits like **squash, pumpkin,** and **watermelon,** set the young fruit on a brick or piece of wood to keep it off the ground while it ripens.

 WATERING

Water herbs twice a week to maintain moisture 10 to 12 inches deep. Water vegetables daily, and if they are wilting at the end of the day, provide shade or lengthen the watering time.

 FERTILIZING

Do not fertilize this month in the warmest areas.

 GROOMING

Other than pinching back **basils** to keep them from flowering, do not prune this month.

 PESTS

Watch for squash borers, insects that bore into the stems of **squash.** Symptoms are a sudden wilting of a leaf. Cut out the leaf to remove the bug.

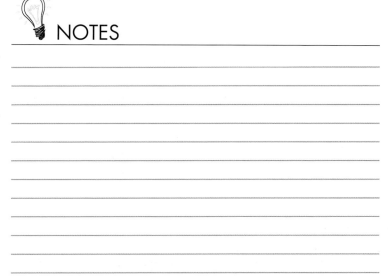 NOTES

JULY
VEGETABLES & HERBS

PLANNING

Corn is a two-season crop in the warmest parts of the region. **Corn** planted in April is just finishing up, and a second crop can be planted in midsummer that will be ready in the early fall. This is an old style of planting in the Southwest, with crops planted in advance of widely anticipated summer rains.

Like **tomatoes,** most **corn** varieties in seed catalogs are designed for long seasons of relative warmth, but not the high dry heat of the desert. Look for short-season varieties, or better yet, heirlooms and local varieties that are known to do well.

Historically, the agricultural use of most **corn** was to save it, as either flour or dried kernels. This dried crop was made into a wide array of staples like tortillas, masa, posole, and tamales, or toasted as elote or popcorn. Some was invariably eaten when it was young, but **sweet corn** as we know it is a relatively recent phenomenon.

When looking through the vast array of **corn** varieties, keep the following designations in mind. **Corns** labeled dent, flint, or flour are types of **corn** whose ears are generally unsuitable for eating fresh and are meant to be dried. **Corns** that are called sweet corn are generally those that have been developed specifically to eat fresh. Varieties like 'Golden Cross Bantam', 'Bonanza', 'Jubilee', and 'Seneca Chief' ripen in 70 to 100 days, and heirloom sweet corns like 'Cocopah' and 'Yuman Yellow' are especially well suited to planting this time of the year. If you want to grow flour corns, start with varieties like 'Hopi Blue', 'Tarahumara', 'Tohono O'odham 60-day', and 'Blando de Sonora'.

Late summer is also the time to plant decorative corns. These varieties are usually flints or flour corns and are dried for decorations and ornaments in the fall and through the holidays. Good decorative varieties include 'Inca Queen' and 'Painted Mountain'.

PLANTING

In Zones 9 and 10, continue to plant **Armenian cucumber, black-eyed peas, bush beans, corn, melon, pinto beans, pumpkin,** and **winter squash** after mid-month. For a fall crop in the cooler parts of Zone 9, set out transplants of **peppers** and **tomatoes** late in the month.

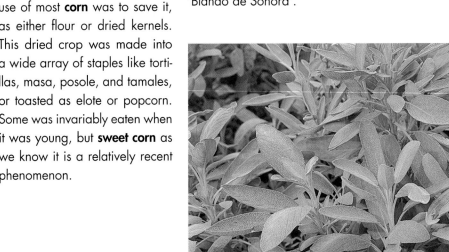

Double-check that your herbs have excellent drainage during exceptionally hot tmperatures. They rot easily in hot, wet soil.

In the hottest parts of the region, **pepper** and **tomato** seed may be planted indoors and set out in late August or September for a fall crop.

CARE

During the summer monsoon season that occurs in most of the region, monitor the watering of Mediterranean herbs like **lavender, rosemary, sages,** and **thyme** carefully. These herbs enjoy a dry summer, but if there have been exceptionally hot temperatures or no rain, water deeply to keep healthy. Double-check that they have excellent drainage during monsoon rainy season—they rot easily in hot, wet soils.

Tomato plants are often done in by this time. Many gardeners prune them back and keep them for a fall crop, but it is usually more productive to root cuttings or start anew from seed for a fall crop.

WATERING

Water vegetables daily and deeply enough to prevent them from wilting in the high heat. In addition, water herbs twice a week to a depth of 10 to 12 inches.

FERTILIZING

Do not fertilize this month in the warmest parts of the region. In cooler areas, fertilize actively growing vegetables once during the month with a sidedressing of compost or balanced complete fertilizer.

GROOMING

Do not prune this month.

PESTS

Grasshoppers sometimes come through this time of year. Hand-pick if there are small numbers, or spray with a formula specifically designed for grasshoppers.

NOTES

AUGUST

VEGETABLES & HERBS

PLANNING

If you haven't been gardening through the summer, or if you are ready to begin your first vegetable garden, it's a good time to prepare beds for the flurry of planting in the next two months.

Begin by selecting a site that receives six or more hours of sunlight a day even in winter. If you are going to have beds directly in the ground, spread a 6-inch layer of compost, mulch, sand, and good-quality topsoil or potting soil on the ground. Mix it all in thoroughly. Wet it completely, and be sure the water soaks down at least 10 to 12 inches. Leave it for a week, then add some more organic matter and, if you prefer, a balanced fertilizer, and mix it again thoroughly. Water it well, then keep watering the bed weekly until you are ready to plant.

If you are using raised beds, build a bed that is no more than 3 feet wide and as long as you wish out of any material you like. Unmortared concrete block, redwood or cedar planks, used lumber, or poured concrete all work equally well. Be careful not to use treated wood, as most treatment chemicals leach slowly into the soil. Beds may be as short as 10 inches or tall enough so you can sit while you garden (about 27 inches) or stand, up to 3 feet. It is not necessary to fill all of a tall bed with soil. Fill the bottom half to a third with scraps, prunings, or rubble. It not only saves precious soil but helps prevent heaving of the sides from the weight of the soil. Make a soil mix as described above, and incorporate some native soil into the mix to provide micronutrients and soil microorganisms. Blend well, and fill the beds with it. Water once or twice to let the soil settle before planting for the first time.

PLANTING

In Zones 9 and 10, plant fast-maturing varieties of **corn** and **summer squash** early in the month. Later in the month, start early plantings of **beets, bok choy, broccoli, Brussels sprouts, cabbage, Chinese cabbage, carrots, cauliflower, collards, cucumber, kale, kohlrabi, lettuce, leeks, mustard greens, snap beans,** and **Swiss chard.** Set out transplants of **bunching onions.**

In cool areas of Zone 9, start early plantings of **parsnips, peas, radish, rutabaga, spinach,** and **turnips** in addition to those listed above.

In Zone 8, sow seed of **bok choy, broccoli, Brussels sprouts, cabbage, Chinese cabbage, carrots, cauliflower, collards,**

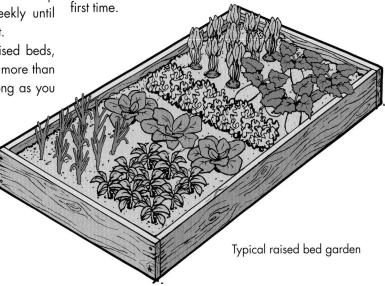

Typical raised bed garden

cucumber, kale, kohlrabi, lettuce, and **leeks.** Continue to plant these vegetables through mid-September.

In the warmest parts of Zone 9 and Zone 10, if you have **pepper** or **tomato** transplants, set them out this month.

In all zones, the cool-season vegetables listed above can also be started indoors this month and planted out in late September and October.

Sow seed of the herbs **calendula, chamomile, chives,** and **Roman chamomile** late in the month.

CARE

Divide **garlic chives, lemon grass,** and **mints.** See page 172 for guidelines on dividing perennial plants.

WATERING

Water vegetables daily, and watch emerging cool-season crops carefully if they were planted this month. Whether early plantings are successful or not greatly depends on the weather, but keep them well watered and well mulched to improve their chances. Water perennial herbs every two to five days, depending on the temperatures. Container-grown herbs or vegetables still need to be watered daily.

FERTILIZING

Do not fertilize now, and do not fertilize any newly planted vegetables or herbs until the weather cools in September or October.

GROOMING

If you kept **eggplant** and **pepper plants** through the summer, cut them back to the newest leaves. This will rejuvenate the plants and they will bear a good fall crop.

NOTES

PESTS

Translucent skeletonized patches appearing on **corn** leaves are usually the work of corn borer larvae. Spray the plants, especially where leaves join the stalk, with *Bacillus thuringiensis* (Bt). A drop of mineral oil on the top of the tassel may also help prevent infestations.

In some areas, whiteflies can be a significant problem this month. These tiny white flying insects are not harmful in small numbers, but infestations can become large quickly, and then they can devastate vegetable plants. Adults land briefly, and washing off plants daily or using an insecticidal soap regularly will discourage large infestations. Cover susceptible plants with row covers if the numbers begin to increase dramatically.

SEPTEMBER
VEGETABLES & HERBS

 PLANNING

Desert areas are blessed with a long, benign winter-growing season. This is a wonderful time to grow many cole crops, greens, and root vegetables.

Cole crops are a group of vegetables and their varieties that come from one species, *Brassica oleracea*. Cole crops include **broccoli, Brussels sprouts, cabbage, cauliflower, collards, kale, kohlrabi,** and **rapini** (also known as **broccoli raab**).

Broccoli has many varieties, and the heads can be purple, deep green, or almost chartreuse. Most are either so-called sprouting like 'Purple Cape' (also sold as 'Early Purple Sprouting') which has many small heads formed along the sides of the shoot, or they grow a dominant single head at the end of the stem. Some dominant-head varieties make side shoots after the large head is removed. **Broccoli** grows quickly in the cool season, and if you grow it from seed, plant at two- to three-week intervals to extend the harvest. Space **broccoli** plants about a foot apart.

Brussels sprouts are trickier to grow in the desert regions. Although two varieties do well, 'Jade Cross' and 'Long Island Improved', they are sensitive to heat and need to be planted so

they form during the coolest part of the year.

Cabbage is a term for a high-variable group of varieties.

• **Head cabbages** may be green or red, and the leaves turn in on each other in a tight, rounded head. **Savoy** and **head cabbage** form slowly; most will take from 80 to 100 days to form. Look for early varieties like 'Golden Acre', 'Copenhagen Market', and 'Early Jersey Wakefield' that take only 60 to 75 days. Longer-maturing varieties include 'Emerald Cross', 'Red Acre', 'King Cold', 'Danish Ballhead', and 'Flat Dutch'.

• **Oriental cabbages** show even more variation of form than do the **savoy** and **head cabbages.** Some are formed like **savoys** and often called **Chinese cabbage** or **Pe-tsai;** other form a distinct rosette of leaves but not a head and usually go by the name **pak-choi** or **tatsoi;** and those that have prominent ribs ending in large, firm leaves are generally known as **bok choy.** These are only the common names—there are dozens of different varieties of **Oriental cabbage,** and all do well in the long cool growing season of mild-winter areas.

• **Savoy cabbages** have loose heads of crinkled leaves, and the leaves are usually much longer than they are wide.

Cauliflower, like **broccoli,** forms a dominant head of flowers at

the end of the stem but is much less likely to have small side shoots. **Cauliflower** heads are dense, and the characteristic white color is the result of covering the head by tying the large leaves over the bud as it develops. Varieties include 'Snowball', 'Snow Queen', and 'Snow King'. Italian varieties of **cauliflower** like 'Violetta Italia' have purple heads.

Collards and **kale** are non-heading forms of cole crops. The young shoots are delicately flavored and highly nutritious; older leaves may be bitter. These leafy **cabbages** are good candidates for succession planting.

Ornamental kale is used frequently in winter garden displays, and although edible, is not particularly tasty.

Kohlrabi is a fast-growing member of the group. The swollen leaf bases that look like roots grow above the ground and may be white, green, or purple, depending on the variety. They are delicious raw or cooked and do well in succession plantings, taking only 55 to 70 days to mature. Varieties include 'Purple Vienna' and 'White Vienna'.

Cole crops need a rich soil with steady moisture to do their best. While they tolerate some heat, depending on the variety, they really take off when the temperatures fall. Gardeners who plant them early may see them "stand still" until the temperatures cool down, but then they are ready to take off. Sow seed at two- to three-week intervals to have some ready through the entire season.

PLANTING

In Zones 9 and 10, sow seeds of **snap beans, beets, bok choy, Brussels sprouts, cabbage, carrots, Chinese cabbage, celery, collards, cucumber, endive, fennel, kohlrabi, leek, lettuce, mustard greens, peas, radish, spinach, Swiss chard,** and **turnips.**

Set out transplants of **broccoli, Brussels sprouts,** and **cauliflower,** and plant **potatoes.** Late in the month, plant **garlic** and both **bulb** and **bunching onions.**

In Zone 8, set out transplants of **bok choy, broccoli, Brussels sprouts, cabbage, Chinese cabbage, carrots, cauliflower, collards, kale, kohlrabi, lettuce,** and **leeks.**

Once the temperatures in Zones 9 and 10 have dropped below 100 degrees Fahrenheit, plant seeds of the herbs **anise,** **borage, salad burnet, calendula, German** and **Roman chamomile, chervil, cilantro, cumin, dill, fennel, parsley,** and **French sorrel.**

Plant perennial herbs like **bay, Chinese** and **garlic chives, lavender, marjoram, rosemary, sage,** and **thyme.**

CARE

Divide **garlic chives, oregano, marjoram,** and **mint** if you haven't already done so.

WATERING

Provide a long, deep watering of vegetable or herb beds once during the month to leach out salts and restore deep soil moisture. This is especially critical if the late-summer rains have been inadequate. As the temperatures decline, adjust watering schedules for perennial herbs to every four to five days. Continue to water vegetables daily.

FERTILIZING

A sidedressing of compost can be added to the vegetable and herb beds this month. If you use inorganic fertilizer, make one application this month.

GROOMING

Prune back summer-damaged stems of **scented geranium, rosemary, lavender, sage,** and **thyme.** If the plants are bedraggled, give them a hard prune, removing up to $1/3$ of the plant late in the month to invigorate and reshape.

PESTS

Damping off is a soilborne fungal disease that causes sudden death in young seedlings. To prevent, be sure the soil is light and well drained, that seeds are not planted deeply, and that there is time to dry out slightly between waterings.

HELPFUL HINTS

Use the following tips to harvest and store **winter squash.**

1. Pick before frost. Test the rind before picking with a fingernail or gentle pressure. The rind should be tough but yield to gentle pressure.

2. Cut the **squash** from the plant, leaving about an inch of stem attached. Some gardeners leave the fruit lying in the bed for a week to encourage further hardening of the shell; others recommend moving the fruit to a cool, dry location as soon as it is cut and leaving to dry.

3. Once the rind is dry and hard, store fruit so that they do not touch each other. If they need to be stacked, put straw or newspaper between the layers to keep them apart. Be sure the fruit is not exposed to sunlight or moisture while it is stored.

OCTOBER

VEGETABLES & HERBS

PLANNING

One of the greatest delights of vegetable gardening in the desert areas is the availability of fresh greens throughout the winter. Most **Chinese greens, collards, lettuces, mustard greens, radicchio,** and **spinach** are cool-season growers and find the long, mild winter of the desert ideal.

Greens grow best when they can grow quickly and without either heat or water stress. Plant in rich soil that is fairly loose and drains well. Water frequently, and never allow the soil to dry out entirely around the plants.

Because **greens** grow fast and are eaten quickly, succession planting is a successful way to continue the harvest as long as you can. Plant at two- to three-week intervals, beginning in the fall and continuing through the spring.

If you found that you planted **greens** too thickly, thin them at least twice during the growing season. Thin first when the plants are about 1 inch tall. Use scissors to cut the tiny plants, as pulling can remove plants that you need to remain. Thin again when the plants are 3 inches tall, and leave them at least 3 inches apart, more if they will be large. **Greens** will grow crowded for a time, however, and you can wait

to thin until they are 3 or more inches tall and use the thinnings as your own **mesclun** or **baby greens** mix.

Although most of us grow vegetables in separate rows or beds, **greens** are excellent plants for filling in some of the blanks. Plant among larger, longer-lived plants like **broccoli, cauliflower, cucumbers, fennel,** and **squash**.

Most **leaf lettuce, rapini, spinach,** and **Swiss chard** can be harvested more than once. Continue to cut the outermost leaves whenever you harvest. Or cut the plant straight off the first time, and use it again when it has regrown. This second method is especially successful early in the season.

Head lettuces are difficult to grow in the desert—the long cool season it takes to form the heads is rarely realized in the region. Varieties of **butterhead, loose-leaf,** and **romaine** are extremely successful, however. Good varieties include 'Rouge d'Hiver', 'Romaine', 'Oak Leaf' green or red, and 'Sucrine', among many others.

Radicchio and the similar **endive** are related to **chicory** and are great favorites in Italian cooking. Both grow well in the winter garden.

Spinach is one of the longest-lasting **greens** and even in the warmest areas of Zone 9 will extend well into May. Look for 'Italian Summer' and 'Italian Summer Savoy', which are especially heat-tolerant varieties.

PLANTING

In Zones 9 and 10, continue to plant **beets, bok choy, broccoli, Brussels sprouts, cabbage, carrots, cauliflower, Chinese cabbage, collards, endive, fava beans, fennel, garbanzo beans, kale, kohlrabi, lettuce, mustard greens, bulb** and **bunching onions, parsnips, peas, radishes, rapini, rutabaga, spinach, Swiss chard,** and **turnips.**

In these same areas, plant bulbs of **garlic** and **shallots. Garlic** takes a long time to mature and needs to be planted by the end of the month to assure that the bulbs will be well formed by next summer. Continue to set out slips of **potatoes.**

In the cooler parts of Zone 9, set out transplants of **asparagus** and **horseradish** in addition to all the vegetables listed above. **Horseradish** does not do well in the warmest areas of the zone, and **asparagus** should be planted in December and January in the warmer areas.

In Zones 9 and 10, continue to plant herbs like **arugula, borage, calendula, caraway, chamomile** (both **German** and **Roman** varieties), **chervil, chives, cilantro, dill, fennel, garlic chives, lavender, marjoram, mint, oregano, parsley, rosemary, sage, salad burnet, sorrel, thyme,** and **winter savory.**

 CARE

Monitor seed germination, and once seed is up and has three or four true leaves, adjust watering frequency.

 WATERING

Water herbs every four to seven days depending on the weather. As temperatures cool, reduce watering frequency.

 FERTILIZING

Fertilize established perennial herbs like **lavender, marjoram, mints, oreganos, rosemary, sage,** and **thyme** early in the month. Use a slow-release fertilizer or apply organic amendments to get perennials off to a good start during their growing season.

HELPFUL HINTS

For most woody perennial herbs, layering is a good technique for making a cutting. Take a low-lying branch that has new growth toward the tip. Place the stem on the ground, and secure it with a hairpin stake or something similar. Cover with a light layer of soil and leave it undisturbed for at least a month. Pull gently on the stem to see if there is enough resistance to suggest the formation of roots, and pull the soil away gently to check. Once roots are formed, cut the stem away from the plant, lift it gently while making sure you keep the soil around the roots, and pot it up. It will be ready to replant again in a month.

Thinning vegetables, especially root crops, is vital to get steady growth, reduce competition, and have the roots form fully. The first thinning should be made about two weeks after the plants germinate. Take out any plants that touch each other. To prevent disruption of the roots of the plants that remain, use scissors to cut off the plants to be thinned rather than pulling them out. The second thinning is in two weeks. Space the plants at least an inch apart; more is fine. For **radishes,** this will be all the thinning they need.

Other root vegetables need to be thinned gradually until they are growing 3 to 4 inches apart, or separated enough so that the roots do not touch. After the second thinning, the small greens and tiny roots are a delicious addition to salads.

 GROOMING

Prune Mediterranean herbs like **bay, Greek oregano, lavender, marjoram, rosemary, sage,** and **thyme.** These herbs are cool-season growers, especially in the hottest parts of the region, and can be pruned now at the beginning of their growing season to shape the plants, remove dead or unproductive stems, and reinvigorate old plantings.

 PESTS

If birds become a problem, use floating row covers or bird netting to protect seed and seedlings.

NOVEMBER

VEGETABLES & HERBS

PLANNING

Root vegetables like **beets, carrots, daikon radish,** and **turnips** do well in winter gardens. **Beets** and **carrots** grow through the winter season and will continue to produce until late spring.

Radishes like 'Cherry Belle' and 'French Breakfast' are fast-growing and can quickly overwhelm the garden. Plant in weekly successions to keep these tasty roots available through the entire season, and harvest them when they are less than 1 inch in diameter. **Daikon** are long, white **radishes** much favored in Oriental cooking. These delicious root vegetables also grow quickly, but they stay sweet even when they are large. Again, succession planting is useful, and pick them only when you are ready to use them.

Parsnips, rutabagas (often called **Swedes**), and **turnips** are excellent root vegetables in the desert. Varieties of **turnip** like 'Shogun', 'Tokyo Cross', and 'Purple Top' have both delicious **greens** and sweet roots. Pick **turnips** when they are less than 3 inches in diameter to eat raw or cooked. All of these root crops are best when young. **Parsnips** need a sharp chill or a few freezes to sweeten the roots before harvesting. They grow best in the coolest parts of Zone 9 and throughout Zone 8.

Carrots grow more slowly than the rest of the root crops and will last through most of the summer if kept well watered. It is easy to crowd **carrots,** and their tiny seed can be hard to plant well. Old-time gardeners advise you to plant **radishes** among the **carrots** to assist in germination. Whether it helps or not, I am not sure, but they both seem to grow well together. Thinning is essential to get well-sized and well-formed **carrots.** The tiny **carrots** from your thinnings are delicious when pickled or served in salads or stir-fries. While almost any **carrot** variety grows well in the region, short varieties often perform better in raised beds and home gardens.

Beet seed is actually a husk that contains more than one seed. This means that thinning will be required for good root formation once they germinate. **Beets** also grow through the warm weather if planted early. 'Chioggia', 'Detroit Dark Red', and 'Early Wonder' all make good crops in the region.

PLANTING

In Zones 9 and 10, continue to either plant from seed or transplant **beets, carrots, endive, kale, kohlrabi, leeks, lettuce, mustard greens, peas, radish, spinach, Swiss chard,** and **turnips. Peas** need to germinate in cool temperatures, which are assured this month throughout the region. Plant **asparagus** late in the month throughout both zones.

In the cooler areas of Zone 9, continue to set out transplants only of **asparagus, broccoli, Brussels sprouts, cauliflower, long-season cabbages, garlic, horseradish,** and **potatoes** (early in the month).

In Zone 8, plant **garlic** before the end of the month.

CARE

Watch for frosty nights, and be prepared to cover tender crops. Most cool-season vegetables are unaffected by light frost.

As established **asparagus** plants go into dormancy, discontinue watering, letting the plants dry out. Once all the stems are entirely dry, cut back the foliage to the ground. Mulch heavily, 4 to 6 inches, to protect the crowns from cold weather, and water infrequently until shoots begin to regrow.

WATERING

Water established herbs once a week or less, depending on the temperatures. Vegetables should be watered every three days.

FERTILIZING

Fertilize all leafy vegetables with a sidedressing of compost or slow-release fertilizer.

GROOMING

If you did not prune Mediterranean herbs last month, do so this month.

PESTS

Set out traps with sweet liquid (orange juice, sugar water, beer) in a shallow dish to attract and drown slugs, put out bait (but be careful there are no children or pets in the area), or search with a light at night and handpick all you find.

HELPFUL HINTS

• Soaking seeds overnight in warm water helps speed germination in many species. This is especially helpful for hard-coated seeds like **beans, beets, chervil, cilantro, dill, lavender, peas,** and **spinach.**

• **Peppermint** is a hybrid between **spearmint** (*Mentha spicata*) and **watermint** (*M. aquatica*). Therefore, do not buy seed of this plant, but rely on cuttings to be sure you get what you want. Most **peppermint** is sterile and does not set seed, or any seed that is set may not come true.

NOTES

_____
_____
_____
_____
_____
_____
_____
_____
_____
_____
_____
_____
_____
_____
_____
_____
_____
_____
_____
_____
_____

DECEMBER
VEGETABLES & HERBS

PLANNING

Many vegetables and herbs grow well in containers. This is a space-saving way to have fresh produce in a small space like a patio or apartment if you are unable to garden outdoors. Plant up a small garden of vegetables and complementary herbs as a holiday gift for friends or relatives who are unable to garden.

Good choices for such a garden are **lettuce, spinach,** and **Swiss chard** as **greens,** and some **dill, parsley,** and **sorrel** as tasty herbs. For a more Italian feel, add **arugula, basil, fennel,** and **radicchio.** For a Mexican feel, add **epazote, Mexican oregano,** a **patio tomato** variety, and a small **pepper** plant.

PLANTING

In the warmest parts of Zone 9 and Zone 10, plant transplants of **asparagus, broccoli, cabbage, cauliflower,** and **Chinese cabbage** early in the month. Continue to plant seed of **beets, bok choy, carrots, fennel, lettuce, peas, radish, rapini, spinach,** and **turnips.**

In these same zones, sow seed of **borage, caraway, chervil, cilantro, dill, fennel, parsley,** and **French sorrel.** Plant transplants of **Chinese** and **garlic chives** and **mints.**

HELPFUL HINTS

Be prepared to harvest both leaves and seed of **cilantro** (known as **coriander** when it is seed) and **dill.**

In the warm parts of the region, an early start for **tomatoes** is crucial to have a successful crop. For an early February planting, start **tomatoes** and **peppers** indoors at the end of the month. Plant seed in soilless mix or good potting soil, and keep evenly moist and in strong, indirect light. Cold temperatures stunt the seedlings, so keep them warm. They should be ready to set out in eight weeks.

CARE

Most cool-season vegetables are unaffected by light frost, but be prepared to cover tender crops with light cloth, newspaper, or frost blankets on cold nights. If you have vegetables or herbs in pots, cover them or move them to a warmer location on cold nights.

WATERING

From mid-December through January is the coldest time of the year in the region. Watch watering frequency and test the soil around vegetables and herbs to determine how often to water. Vegetables should be watered to a depth of 8 to 12 inches and perennial herbs to a depth of 2 feet. Reduce watering frequency when temperatures are near freezing.

FERTILIZING

Do not fertilize this month.

GROOMING

Do not prune this month.

PESTS

Aphids show up on vegetables and herbs in cool weather. Small infestations can be controlled with strong jets of water or hand removal. Try a blend of **garlic** or **hot pepper** to help control aphids. To make this spray, add four or five cloves of **garlic** and a quart of water to the blender and process until it is a fine slurry. Store in a labeled spray bottle. For **hot pepper** spray, process a handful of dried **hot peppers** in the blender with a quart of water until pulverized. The hotter the **peppers,** the more effective they are; do not inhale fumes. Store in a labeled spray bottle.

GLOSSARY

Alkaline soil: soil with a pH greater than 7.5. It lacks acidity, often because it has limestone in it.

All-purpose fertilizer: powdered, liquid, or granular fertilizer with a balanced proportion of the three key nutrients—nitrogen (N), phosphorus (P), and potassium (K). It is suitable for maintenance nutrition for most plants.

Annual: a plant that lives its entire life in one season. It is genetically determined to germinate, grow, flower, set seed, and die the same year.

Bare root: describes plants that have been packaged without any soil around their roots. Bulbs are often sold this way. (Often young shrubs and trees purchased through the mail arrive with their exposed roots covered with moist peat or sphagnum moss, sawdust, or similar material, and wrapped in plastic.)

Barrier plant: a plant that has intimidating thorns or spines and is sited purposely to block foot traffic or other access to the home or yard.

Basal leaves: leaves that are congested near the ground to form a rosette or as a small mound. Typically, a large blooming stalk or other leafy stems arise out of these leaves.

Beneficial insects: insects or their larvae that prey on pest organisms and their eggs. They may be flying insects, such as ladybugs, parasitic wasps, praying mantis, and soldier bugs, or soil dwellers such as predatory nematodes, spiders, and ants.

Berm: a narrow raised ring of soil around a tree used to hold water so it will be directed to the root zone.

Bract: a modified leaf structure on a plant stem near its flower that resembles a petal. Often it is more colorful and visible than the actual flower, as in bougainvillea.

Bud union: the place where the top of a plant was grafted to the rootstock; usually refers to roses and citrus.

Canopy: the overhead branching area of a tree, usually referring to its extent including foliage.

Chlorosis: a mineral deficiency. The typical symptom is a yellowing of the leaf between the veins; in extreme cases the entire leaf turns yellow.

Cold hardiness: the ability of a perennial plant to survive the winter cold in a particular area.

Composite: a flower that is actually composed of many tiny flowers, as are sunflowers. Typically, they are flat clusters of tiny, tight florets, sometimes surrounded by wider-petaled florets. Composite flowers are highly attractive to bees and beneficial insects.

Compost: organic matter that has undergone progressive decomposition by microbial and macrobial activity until it is reduced to a spongy, fluffy texture. Added to soil, it improves the soil's ability to hold air and water and to drain well.

Corm: the swollen, energy-storing structure analogous to a bulb under the soil at the base of the stem of plants such as crocus and gladiolus.

Crown: the base of a plant at, or just beneath, the surface of the soil where the roots meet the stems.

Cultivar: a CULTIvated VARiety. It is a naturally occurring form of a plant that has been identified as special or superior and is purposely selected for propagation and production. A cultivar can also be created through breeding.

Deadhead: a pruning technique that removes faded flower heads from plants to improve their appearance, abort seed production, and stimulate further flowering.

Deciduous plants: unlike evergreens, these trees and shrubs lose their leaves all at once, usually in the fall.

Desiccation: drying out of foliage tissues usually due to drought or wind.

GLOSSARY

Division: the practice of splitting apart perennial plants to create several smaller-rooted segments in order to control the plant's size and for acquiring more plants; it is also essential to the health and continued flowering of certain ones.

Dormancy: the period, usually winter, when perennial plants temporarily cease active growth and rest. Dormant is the adverb form, as used in this sentence: "Some plants, like spring-blooming bulbs, go dormant in the summer."

Espalier: A pruning practice where a plant, usually a fruit tree, is pruned to force it to grow flat against a wall or fence.

Established: the point at which a newly planted tree, shrub, or flower begins to produce new growth, either foliage or stems. This is an indication that the roots have recovered from transplant shock and have begun to grow and spread. In this book, I have used "established" (particularly with woody shrubs and trees) to mean plants that have been in the ground long enough to have their watering regimen extended.

Evergreen: perennial plants that do not lose their foliage annually with the onset of winter. Needled or broadleaf foliage will persist and continue to function on a plant through one or more winters, aging and dropping unobtrusively in cycles of three or four years or more.

Foliar: of or about foliage—usually refers to the practice of spraying foliage, as in fertilizing or treating with insecticide; leaf tissues absorb liquid directly for fast results, and the soil is not affected.

Floret: a tiny flower, usually one of many forming a cluster that comprises a single blossom.

Germinate: to sprout. Germination is a fertile seed's first stage of development.

Glochid: A fine spine, often invisible, at the base of the larger spines on prickly pear and cholla cactus.

Graft union: the point on the stem of a woody plant where a stem from another plant is inserted so that it will join with it. Roses and citrus are commonly grafted.

Grubs: larvae of insects, usually beetles. They reside in the soil and feed on plant roots (especially grass) until summer when they emerge as beetles to feed on plant foliage.

Hardscape: the permanent, structural, nonplant part of a landscape, such as walls, sheds, pools, patios, arbors, and walkways.

Herbaceous: plants having fleshy or soft stems, the opposite of "woody."

Hybrid: a plant that is the result of intentional or natural cross-pollination between two or more plants of the same species or genus.

Low-water demand: describes plants that tolerate dry soil for varying periods of time.

Mulch: a layer of material over bare soil to protect it from erosion and compaction by rain, and to discourage weeds. It may be inorganic (gravel, fabric) or organic (wood chips, bark, pine needles, chopped leaves).

Naturalize: *a.* to plant seeds, bulbs, or plants in a random, informal pattern as they would appear in their natural habitat; *b.* to adapt to and spread throughout adopted habitats (a tendency of some nonnative plants).

Nectar: the sweet fluid produced by glands on flowers that attract pollinators such as hummingbirds and honeybees for whom it is a source of energy.

Organic material, organic matter: any material or debris that is derived from plants. It is carbon-based material capable of undergoing decomposition and decay.

Peat moss: organic matter from peat sedges (United States) or sphagnum mosses (Canada), used to improve soil texture. The acidity of sphagnum

peat moss makes it ideal for boosting or maintaining soil acidity while also improving its drainage.

Perennial: a flowering plant that lives over two or more seasons. Many die back with frost, but their roots survive the winter and generate new shoots in the spring.

pH: a measurement of the relative acidity (low pH) or alkalinity (high pH) of soil or water based on a scale of 1 to 14, 7 being neutral. Individual plants require soil to be within a certain range so that nutrients can dissolve in water and be available to them.

Pinch: to remove tender stems and/or leaves by pressing them between thumb and forefinger. This pruning technique encourages branching, compactness, and flowering in plants. It is also a technique to remove aphids clustered at growing tips.

Pollen: the yellow, powdery grains in the center of a flower—the plant's male sex cells. They are transferred to the female plant parts by means of wind, animal, or insect pollinators to fertilize them and create seeds.

Psillids: Tiny sucking insects that resemble aphids.

Raceme: an arrangement of single stalked flowers along an elongated, unbranched axis.

Rhizome: a swollen energy-storing stem that lies horizontally in the soil, with roots emerging from its lower surface and growth shoots from a growing point at or near its tip, as in bearded iris.

Rootbound (or potbound): the condition of a plant that has been confined in a container too long, its roots having been forced to wrap around themselves and even swell out of the container.

Root flare: the transition at the base of a tree trunk where the bark tissue begins to differentiate and roots begin to form just before entering the soil.

Root hardy: term describing plants that may lose all foliage and stems to freezing temperatures, but the root remains undamaged and will resprout stems and leaves in spring.

Self-seeding: the tendency of some plants to sow their seeds freely around the yard. It creates many seedlings the following season that may or may not be welcome.

Semievergreen: tending to be evergreen in a mild climate, but deciduous in a rigorous one.

Shearing: the pruning technique whereby plant stems and branches are cut uniformly with long-bladed pruning shears (hedge shears) or powered hedge trimmers.

Slow-acting fertilizer: fertilizer that releases its nutrients gradually as a function of soil temperature, moisture, and related microbial activity. Typically granular, it may be organic or synthetic.

Succulent: a plant that has specialized tissue in its leaves, stem, or roots for water storage, as in cactus or aloes.

Sucker: a new growing shoot. Underground plant roots produce suckers to form new stems and spread by means of these suckering roots to form large plantings or colonies. Some plants produce root suckers or branch suckers as a result of pruning or wounding.

Tuber: swollen roots in which the nutrients are stored (example: potato).

Variegated: having various colors or color patterns. The term usually refers to plant foliage that is streaked, edged, blotched, or mottled with a contrasting color, often green with yellow, cream, or white.

Wings: *a.* the corky tissue that forms edges along the twigs of some woody plants such as winged euonymus; *b.* the flat, dried extension of tissue on some seeds, such as maple, that catch the wind and help them disseminate.

TO FIND OUT MORE

Visiting public gardens is a great way to learn what grows well in the area. Many offer gardening classes to the public and have plant sales and related gardening activities.

Arizona Sonora Desert Museum

2021 N. Kinney Road
Tucson, Arizona 85743-8918
520-883-2702
http://www.Desertmuseum.org
Large demonstration garden and extensive ornamental plantings; exquisite setting.

Boyce Thompson Southwestern Arboretum

37615 U.S. Hwy 60
Superior, Arizona 85273
520-689-2723
http://www.arboretum.ag.arizona.edu
Large collection of desert plants, especially legumes and trees; home demonstration garden.

Chihuahuan Desert Garden

El Paso, Texas
On the campus of the University of Texas at El Paso; adjacent to the Centennial Museum.
http://www.museumutep.edu
Demonstration garden, Website with plant lists, and information on the Chihuahuan Desert.

Desert Botanical Garden

1201 N. Galvin Parkway
Phoenix, Arizona 85008
480-941-1225
http://www.dbg.org
Large collection of desert plants, especially agaves and cacti. Classes in gardening. Wildflower hotline during the spring.

Desert Demonstration Garden

3701 Alta Drive
Las Vegas, Nevada 89153
702-258-3205
http://www.springspreserve.org
Garden dedicated to low-water-use plants; classes and booklets on many landscaping topics.

Living Desert Museum

47-900 Portola Ave.
Palm Desert, California 92260
760-346-5694
http://www.livingdesert.org
Large collection of plants from deserts of the world; many plantings. Excellent plant shop and a wide range of gardening classes.

Tohono Chul Park

7366 N. Paseo del Norte
Tucson, Arizona 85704
520-742-6455
http://www.tohonochulpark.org
Extensive areas of natural desert. Demonstration gardens and fine plant shop.

Tucson Botanical Garden

2150 N. Alvernon Way
Tucson, Arizona 85712
520-326-9686
http://www.tucsonbotanical.org
Many small gardens with a variety of garden themes. Classes and workshops throughout the year. Demonstration area on composting and heirloom garden vegetables.

University of Arizona Extension Offices are located in the county seat of each county in the region. Some have excellent Websites with abundant information. All are available for problem-solving and answering gardening questions. Master Gardeners work through these offices—they are a rich source of local gardening information.

Cochise County Extension

450 S. Haskell Ave.
Wilcox, Arizona 85643
520-384-3594 OR
1140 N. Colombo
Sierra Vista, Arizona 85635
520-458-8278
http://www.ag.arizona.edu/cochise
Information on topics of home gardening, questions answered by phone. Other programs available.

TO FIND OUT MORE

LaPaz County Extension
2524 Mutahar
Parker, Arizona 85344
928-669-9843
http://www.ag.arizona.edu/mohave
Principal information through calls to the office. Website offers basic information and advice.

Maricopa County Extension
4341 E. Broadway Road
Phoenix, Arizona 85040
602-470-8086
http://www.ag.arizona.edu/maricopa
Extensive site with publications and links to a wide range of information on home gardening topics. Demonstration gardens: landscape plants, heirloom roses, vegetables and herbs.

Pima County Extension
4210 N. Campbell Ave.
Tucson, Arizona 85719
520-626-5161
http://www.ag.arizona.edu/pima

Yuma County Extension
2200 W. 28th Street, Suite 102
Yuma, Arizona 82264
928-726-3904
http//www.ag.arizona.edu/yuma
Principal information through calls to the office; Website offers basic information and advice.

Water Districts and cities in the region have a range of information and activities for home gardeners on water management topics and on plants suitable for the area.

Phoenix Metropolitan Area
Water Conservation Offices:
Chandler 480-786-2768
Gilbert 623-892-0800
Mesa 480-644-3334
Phoenix 602-261-8367
Scottsdale 480-391-5690
Tempe 480-350-2668

The following are mentioned in the book and you may contact them at these addresses.

Native Seeds/SEARCH
526 N. Fourth Avenue
Tucson, AZ 85705
520-622-5561
http://www.nativeseeds.org

Telos Rare Bulbs
P.O. Box 4978
Arcata, CA 95518
http://www.telosrarebulbs.com

Yucca Do Nursery
P.O. Box 907
Hempstead, TX 77445
979-826-4580
http://www.yuccado.com

BIBLIOGRAPHY

Arizona Native Plant Society. *Desert Shrubs*. Tucson, Arizona: Arizona Native Plant Society, 1989.

Arizona Native Plant Society. *Desert Trees*. Tucson, Arizona: Arizona Native Plant Society and Trees for Tucson/Global ReLeaf, 1991.

Arizona Native Plant Society. *Desert Wildflowers*. Tucson, Arizona: Arizona Native Plant Society, 1991.

Arizona Native Plant Society. *Desert Groundcovers and Vines*. Tucson, Arizona: Arizona Native Plant Society, 1991.

Arizona Native Plant Society. *Desert Butterfly Gardening*. Tucson, Arizona: Arizona Native Plant Society and Sonoran Arthropod Studies Institute, 1996.

Arizona Native Plant Society. *Desert Bird Gardening*. Tucson, Arizona: Arizona Native Plant Society and Tucson Audubon Society, 1997.

Beck, Hallie. *Roses in a Desert Garden*. Phoenix, Arizona: Phoenix Home & Garden Magazine, 1996.

Blake, J. Warner. *Don Caliche's Gardening Book: Especially for the Southwest*. El Paso, Texas: Guynes Printing Co., 1972.

Brenzel, Kathleen N., ed. *Sunset Western Garden Book*. Menlo Park, California: Sunset Publishing Corp., 2001.

Bryan, John E. *Bulbs: Revised Edition*. Portland, Oregon: Timber Press, 2002.

Cromell, Cathy, ed. *Desert Landscaping for Beginners: Tips and Techniques for Success in an Arid Climate*. Phoenix, Arizona: Arizona Master Gardener Press, 2001.

Cromell, Cathy, Linda A. Guy, and Lucy K. Bradley. *Desert Gardening for Beginners: How to Grow Vegetables, Flowers and Herbs in an Arid Climate*. Phoenix, Arizona: Arizona Master Gardener Press, 1999.

Duffield, Mary Rose and Warren Jones. *Plants for Dry Climates*. Cambridge, Massachusetts: Perseus Publishing, 2001.

Fischer, Anne. *The Low Desert Herb Gardening Handbook*. Phoenix, Arizona: Arizona Herb Association, 1997.

Groom, Dale and Dan Gill. *Month-By-Month Gardening in Texas*. Nashville, Tennessee: Cool Springs Press, 2000.

Howard, Thad M. *Bulbs for Warm Climates*. Austin, Texas: University of Austin Press: 2001.

Irish, Mary. *Gardening in the Desert*. University of Arizona Press: Tucson, Arizona, 2000.

Irish, Mary and Gary Irish. *Agaves, Yuccas, and Related Plants*. Portland, Oregon: Timber Press, 2003.

Irish, Mary. *Arizona Gardener's Guide*. Nashville, Tennessee: Cool Springs Press, 2003.

Irish, Mary. *Perennials for the Southwest*. Portland, Oregon: Timber Press, 2006.

Johnson, Eric A., David Harbison, and Dennis C. Mahr. *Lush & Efficient: Gardening in the Coachella Valley*. Coachella, California: Coachella Valley Water District, 2001.

Johnson, Eric and Scott Millard. *How to Grow the Wildflowers*. Tucson, Arizona: Ironwood Press, 1993.

Jones, Warren and Charles Sacamano. *Landscape Plants for Dry Regions*. Tucson, Arizona: Fisher Books, 2000.

Mielke, Judy. *Native Plants for Southwestern Landscapes*. Austin, Texas: University of Texas Press, 1993.

Mills, Linn and Dick Post. *Nevada Gardener's Guide*. Nashville, Tennessee: Cool Springs Press, 2001.

Morrow, Baker H. *Best Plants for New Mexico Gardens and Landscapes*. Albuquerque, New Mexico: University of New Mexico Press, 1994.

Nabhan, Gary Paul and Jane Cole, eds. *Arizona Highways Presents Desert Wildflowers*. Phoenix, Arizona: Arizona Highways, Arizona Department of Transportation, 1988.

Nelson, Kim. *A Desert Gardener's Companion*. Tucson, Arizona: Rio Nuevo Publishers, 2001.

Nyhuis, Jane. *Desert Harvest: A Guide to Vegetable Gardening in Arid Lands*. Tucson, Arizona: Growing Connections, Inc., 1982, 1985.

Ogden, Scott. *Garden Bulbs for the South*. Dallas, Texas: Taylor Publishing Company, 1994.

Phillips, Judith. *New Mexico Gardener's Guide*. Nashville, Tennessee: Cool Springs Press, 1998.

Stokes, Donald and Lillian Stokes. *The Wildflower Book from the Rockies West: An Easy Guide to Growing and Identifying Wildflowers*. Boston, Massachusetts: Little, Brown and Company, 1993.

Texas Garden Clubs, Inc. *A Calendar for Gardening*. El Paso, Texas: Mountain-Plains District IX, Texas Garden Clubs, Inc.

Wasowski, Sally with Andy Wasowski. *Native Texas Plants: Landscaping Region by Region*. Austin, Texas: Texas Monthly Press, 1988.

INDEX

INDEX

INDEX

INDEX

INDEX

INDEX

INDEX

INDEX

MEET MARY IRISH

Mary Irish has an extensive background in horticulture, having served as an author, lecturer, educator, and garden writer. She is an accomplished gardener who has lived in Arizona for more than 20 years. Irish assisted thousands of gardeners through the years as the Director of Public Horticulture at the Desert Botanical Garden in Phoenix, during which time she managed the botanical garden's Plant Introduction and Sales Program.

Irish's educational background includes a Bachelor of Arts from the University of Texas, Austin, and a Master of Science from Texas A&M University, College Station. Irish has written extensively for periodical publishing, as well as serving as the host of a call-in radio program,

Irish is the author of another book for Cool Springs Press, *Arizona Gardener's Guide*. Other books authored or co-authored by Irish include *Agaves, Yuccas, and Related Plants, Gardening in the Desert*, and *Perennials for the Southwest*.

In addition to her frequent contributions to regional and national publications, Irish regularly teaches classes on desert gardening, the use and cultivation of agaves, and the care and cultivation of succulents. Although Irish is interested in all plants, agaves and their relatives, bulbs, and desert perennials are her primary interest. Irish and her husband, Gary, live in Scottsdale, where she enjoys birding and quilting.